Military Advising and Assistance

Nations seeking to develop and improve their military forces have often sought the advice of foreigners. Before 1815, military advice from abroad generally took the form of mercenaries, slaves, and former enemy troops pressed into service. However, with the rise of the modern nation state, the advent of the industrial revolution, and the accompanying professionalization of armies and governments, nations desiring military modernization and improvement began seeking more formal, professional advice to develop their military forces.

This edited volume presents a number of historical case studies of military advisors and/or their missions in order to provide clear examples of the functioning, motives, and evolution of foreign military and naval advising in the modern era. These are intended to show the evolution of foreign military advising from ill-organized mercenary units, to professional, government-sponsored teams driven by a desire to cultivate political and economic influence, to Cold War tools for pursuing ideological aims, nation building, and modernization, to post-Cold War elements of alliance integration. Finally, this book highlights the increasing present-day role of private corporations, some of which provide complete military forces, thereby bringing the evolution of foreign military advising full circle.

This book will be of interest to students of military history, civil–military relations, peacekeeping, security studies, and political science in general.

Donald Stoker is Professor of Strategy and Policy for the US Naval War College's Monterey Program. He is the author of *Britain, France, and the Naval Arms Trade in the Baltic, 1919–1939: Grand Strategy and Failure* (2003).

D1719237

Routledge military studies

Military Advising and Assistance

From mercenaries to privatization, 1815–2007

Edited by Donald Stoker

Routledge
Taylor & Francis Group

LONDON AND NEW YORK

First published 2008
by Routledge
2 Park Square, Milton Park, Abingdon, Oxon, OX14 4RN

Simultaneously published in the USA and Canada
by Routledge
270 Madison Ave, New York NY 10016

Routledge is an imprint of the Taylor & Francis Group, an informa business

Transferred to Digital Printing 2010

© 2008 Selection and editorial matter, Donald Stoker; individual
chapters, the contributors

Typeset in Garamond by Wearset Ltd, Boldon, Tyne and Wear

British Library Cataloguing in Publication Data
A catalogue record for this book is available from the British Library

Library of Congress Cataloging in Publication Data
A catalog record for this book has been requested

ISBN10: 0-415-77015-7 (hbk)
ISBN10: 0-415-58298-9 (pbk)
ISBN10: 0-203-93871-2 (ebk)

ISBN13: 978-0-415-77015-6 (hbk)
ISBN13: 978-0-415-58298-8 (pbk)
ISBN13: 978-0-203-93871-3 (ebk)

To Colonel Theodore S. Westhusing
Soldier, Scholar

Contents

Contributors

Jonathan Byrom graduated from the United States Military Academy in 1995 and is a cavalry officer in the United States army. He has served in various military positions in Germany, Bosnia-Herzegovina, Fort Irwin, and Afghanistan. Jon received his Masters of Business Administration from the Naval Postgraduate School in Monterey, California. He is currently serving as an economics instructor and International Security Seminar Executive Officer in the Social Sciences Department at the United States Military Academy.

Donovan C. Chau is an Assistant Professor of Political Science at California State University, San Bernardino. He is also an Adjunct Professor in the Department of Defense and Strategic Studies, Missouri State University. Dr Chau has provided consulting services to the US Departments of Homeland Security and Defense, including research on terrorist threats from Africa and Chinese influence in Africa. Previously, Dr Chau worked for the US Congress as a Professional Staff Member on the Committee on Homeland Security, U.S. House of Representatives. Dr Chau earned a PhD in Politics and International Relations from the University of Reading, an MS in Defense and Strategic Studies from Missouri State University, and a BA in Literature/Government from Claremont McKenna College.

Patrick Cullen is a published author and commentator on the privatization of security and terrorism. He has taught Strategic Studies at the London School of Economics and Political Science and taught and lectured at the War Studies Department of Kings College, London. He is currently writing his doctoral dissertation on the global private security industry.

John P. Dunn holds a PhD in History from the Florida State University and is an Assistant Professor of History at Valdosta State University. He recently published *Khedive Ismail's Army* (Routledge, 2005), which examines Egyptian military affairs in the mid-nineteenth century. He has also placed articles with *Naval History*, *The Journal of Slavic Military Studies*, *War in History*, *The Journal of Military History*, *The Journal of Central Asian Studies*, and *The Bulletin of the American Society of Arms Collectors*. In addition, Dunn has produced book reviews for *American Neptune*, *Proceedings*, and *The Journal of Military History*.

Bryan R. Gibby is a serving Army officer with a PhD in History from The Ohio State University. His overseas assignments include a one-year tour in Iraq and two and half years in the Republic of Korea. Prior to deployment to Iraq, he taught military history at the United States Military Academy, West Point, specializing in history of the military art, generalship and command, and the history of Middle Eastern warfare. He is married with five children.

William H. Grube is a Marine with 14 years of enlisted and commissioned service. He has a BS in Electrical Engineering from the Pennsylvania State University and a Master of Arts in National Security Affairs from the Naval Postgraduate School in Monterey, California. Captain Grube was the Commanding Officer of Company F, Second Battalion, Sixth Marines, which he led in security operations in Kabul, Afghanistan, as well as in counterinsurgency operations in Fallujah, Iraq. His deployments also include participation in combined exercises in Egypt, Jordan, Israel, South Korea, and Thailand. He has traveled widely in Asia and is studying Vietnamese in preparation for future duty as a Foreign Area Officer.

Christopher W. Muller entered the United States Military Academy in 1990 and served as an exchange cadet to Uruguay, Chile, and Honduras before graduating in 1994 with a BS in Environmental Science and being commissioned as an Engineer Officer. He also earned a MS degree in Engineering Management from the University of Missouri and a MS degree in Defense Analysis with a focus on Latin-American National Security Affairs from the Naval Postgraduate School. His military assignments include Fort Carson, Colorado, with the 3rd Armored Cavalry Regiment where he served as an Engineer Platoon Leader and then as the Company Executive Officer from 1995 to 1998, and V Corps Headquarters in Heidelberg, Germany, where he served as the Geospatial Engineer and Engineer Plans Officer from 1999 to 2001. In 2001, Major Muller commanded in the 94th Engineer Battalion (Combat Heavy), Vilseck, Germany. He was the MacArthur Leadership Award winner for the 130th Engineer Brigade and served as the first Army's Engineer Exchange Officer with Spain. In 2003, he served as the Aide de Camp for the Commanding General of US Army South in San Antonio, Texas. Upon promotion to major in 2004, he deployed to Colombia and served as the Operations Officer for the US Army Mission. His operational deployments include Kosovo, Haiti, and Colombia and he has visited every Spanish-speaking country in Latin America.

Douglas Porch earned a PhD from Corpus Christi College, Cambridge University. He was a senior lecturer at the University College of Wales,

Aberystwyth, before being named to the Mark Clark Chair of History at The Citadel in Charleston, South Carolina. He is now Professor and Chair of the Department of National Security Affairs at the Naval Postgraduate School in Monterey, California. Professor Porch has served as Professor of Strategy at the Naval War College in Newport, Rhode Island, and has also lectured at the United States Marine Corps University at Quantico, Virginia, the US Army War College in Carlisle, Pennsylvania, and the NATO Defense College in Rome, Italy. A specialist in military history, Porch's books include *The French Secret Services: From the Dreyfus Affair to Desert Storm* (1995); *The French Foreign Legion: A Complete History of the Legendary Fighting Force* (1991) which won prizes both in the United States and in France; *The Conquest of the Sahara*; *The Conquest of Morocco*; *The March to the Marne: The French Army 1871–1914*; *The Portuguese Armed Forces and the Revolution*; and *Army and Revolution: France 1815–1844*. *Wars of Empire*, part of the Cassell History of Warfare series, appeared in October 2000 and in paperback in 2001. His latest book, *The Path to Victory: The Mediterranean Theater in World War II*, a selection of the Military History Book Club, the History Book Club, and the Book of the Month Club, was published by Farrar, Straus, Giroux in May 2004, and received the Award for Excellence in US Army Historical Writing from The Army Historical Foundation. He travels to Colombia several times a year to advise on security issues. He has also conducted specialized seminars in Monterey, Camp Lejeune, and Fort Bragg for security and intelligence personnel, both American and international.

William F. Sater is an Emeritus Professor of History at California State University, Long Beach. A graduate of Stanford University and the University of California, Los Angeles, he is the author of seven books and numerous articles dealing with various facets of Chilean history. These include *Andean Tragedy: Fighting the War of the Pacific, 1879–1884* (Nebraska, 2007) and *A History of Chile, 1802–2002* (Cambridge, 2004). He is co-author of *The Grand Illusion: The Prussianization of the Chilean Army* (Nebraska, 1999).

Alaric Searle is currently a Lecturer in Military History in the Department of Politics & Contemporary History at the University of Salford, Greater Manchester, United Kingdom. He received his doctorate from the Free University Berlin and was previously a lecturer and post-doctoral research fellow at the University of Munich. He is the author of *Wehrmacht Generals, West German Society, and the Debate on Rearmament, 1949–1959* (Praeger, 2003), as well as numerous articles in scholarly journals on various aspects of German and British military, political, and intelligence history.

Christopher Spearin holds a PhD in Political Science from the University of British Columbia. He is an Assistant Professor in the Department of Defence Studies and the Deputy Director of Research at the Canadian

Forces College. His research pertains to US and Canadian foreign and defense policy, change in militaries, and the privatization of security in its wide variety of forms. His work has been published in a variety of forums including *Canadian Foreign Policy*, *International Peacekeeping*, *Journal of Conflict Studies*, *Civil Wars*, *World Defence Systems*, *Contemporary Security Policy*, *International Journal*, and *International Politics*.

Donald Stoker is Professor of Strategy and Policy for the US Naval War College's Monterey Program in Monterey, California. He is the author of *Britain, France, and the Naval Arms Trade in the Baltic, 1919–1939: Grand Strategy and Failure* (Frank Cass, 2003) and the co-editor (with Jonathan Grant) of *Girding for Battle: The Arms Trade in a Global Perspective, 1815–1940* (Praeger, 2003). He is also co-editing (with Kenneth J. Hagan) *Strategy in the War of American Independence, 1775–1783: A Global Approach* (Routledge) and (with Harold Blanton and Frederick Sohneid) *Conscription in the Napoleonic Era* (Routledge). He has also written for publications such as *Naval History*, *Warship International*, *Military History Quarterly*, and *Foreign Policy Online*.

John D. Waghelstein, Professor Emeritus, US Naval War College, brings 30 years of operational experience in Low Intensity Conflict, Special Operations, and Security Assistance to the Naval War College where he teaches six courses each year. In addition to two tours in Vietnam, he served five tours in Latin America and commanded US Army Special Forces at every level from "A" Detachment (Captain) to Group (Colonel). Other assignments include the following: Commander of a Mobile Training Team in the Dominican Republic, Airborne-Infantry Battalion Advisor in Bolivia, Commander of the US Military Group in El Salvador, and Executive Officer to the Commander-in-Chief, US Southern Command. He holds an MA in International Relations from Cornell and a PhD in History from Temple University.

Edward B. Westermann is a Professor of Comparative Military Theory in the Department of Military Strategic Studies at the United States Air Force Academy. He is the author of *Hitler's Police Battalions: Enforcing Racial War in the East* and *Flak: German Anti-Aircraft Defenses, 1914–1945*, both published by the University Press of Kansas. He is a former Fulbright Fellow and German Academic Exchange Service Fellow and served as an exchange instructor pilot with the German Air Force.

1 The history and evolution of foreign military advising and assistance, 1815–2007

Donald Stoker

Nations seeking to develop and improve their military forces have often sought the advice of foreigners. Before 1815 military advice from abroad generally took the form of mercenaries, slaves, and former enemy troops pressed into service. General George Washington famously employed Baron Friedrich Wilhelm von Steuben to instill some traditional military discipline into the ranks of the fledgling American fighting force. But with the rise of the modern nation state, the advent of the industrial revolution, and the accompanying professionalization of armies and governments, nations desiring military modernization and improvement began seeking more formal, professional advice to develop their military forces. This has usually meant receiving a foreign mission to directly instruct or advise in the development of domestic forces. Sometimes the nations dispatching the advisors do so for magnanimous reasons, but these states usually have policy goals beyond what the receiving nation is told or expects. But the states receiving the missions also have their own agendas (sometimes hidden ones), a point often ignored.[1] For example, in the mid-1920s the Finns employed a British military mission, and it appears that their primary objective in receiving it was not to ask for British military advice, but to strengthen their political relationship with London.[2]

Over the last two centuries foreign military advising has evolved from ill-organized mercenary units to professional, government-sponsored teams oftentimes driven by a desire to cultivate political and economic influence. In the twentieth century they became tools for pursuing ideological aims (especially during the Cold War), nation building, and modernization. The post-Cold War era added alliance integration to their tasks. The post-Cold War era has seen the increasing role of private corporations in military advising. These companies function as clearinghouses for military advice and (sometimes) quasi-mercenary forces, bringing the evolution of foreign military advising full circle, but with a modern twist.

Military advisors can be single soldiers or sailors dispatched to train the personnel of a foreign army[3] or members of a large mission sent to examine and revamp the military structures of a friendly or client state. Generally, military advising falls into one of the six categories:

1   military advising as a tool of modernization;
2   military advising as a tool of nation building;
3   military advising for economic purposes or penetration;
4   military advising as an ideological tool;
5   military advising as a counterinsurgency tool;
6   military advising for fun and profit: the corporate approach.

The beginning: from mercenaries to formal missions

The era of the French Revolution and Napoleon upset the European domestic and colonial political apple carts. In the wake of Napoleon's fall from power in 1815, a number of newly independent nations began constructing domestic military forces. Egypt was one of these states seeking the institutionalization of military experience gained during the Napoleonic Wars and began by hiring French veterans. But Mehmet Ali, Egypt's new ruler, wanted to build a modern military force along western lines, so the Egyptians sought formal, official advice; the result: a French military mission. Egypt, by obtaining the mission, sought modernization of its military structures, but this also gave them an edge over their neighbors. Egypt became a regional military powerhouse that proceeded to devastate Ottoman power and conquer much of the Middle East. The importation of foreign military advice via a formal mission proved its worth.[4]

Though the Egyptians received a formal mission, this did not end their use of mercenaries. They continued this practice throughout the nineteenth century, with many former US Civil War officers finding employment in the Khedive's ranks.[5] Formal American military and naval missions arrived later.[6] John Dunn provides a study of Egypt's transition from hiring mercenaries to employing one of the first modern military missions. At least one American veteran of Egypt went on to serve in the small US mission that served in Korea from 1888 to 1889.[7]

The experience of newly independent Chile mirrored that of Egypt in many respects. Together, these countries paint a clear picture of what was happening in the military forces of many small nations in the early nineteenth century. Gaining its independence from Spain in 1818, Chile had to build its own military forces and took a number of different routes to do so. Officers from foreign nations played an enormous role in this; 10 percent of Chile's pre-1885 officer corps came from abroad. Formal French and then German military missions followed. But Chile also produced something novel: once they acquired European military know-how they re-exported this to other Latin-American nations via Chilean military advisory teams. William Sater demonstrates the continuum of foreign involvement in the development of Chile's armed forces.

China in the nineteenth century was also a fertile ground for mercenaries. One of the most famous of these was Frederick Townsend Ward, an American soldier of fortune who went to China in 1859. He fought for the

Chinese government against the rebel Taipings and created an effective native Chinese military force led by foreign officers before his death in battle in 1862.[8]

The use of mercenaries did not end with the beginning of the twentieth century. From 1927 to 1929 Chiang Kai-Shek employed a former German officer, Max Bauer, to provide advice on military and industrial modernization.[9] By the mid-1930s a significant contingent of Germans were serving the Chinese Nationalists in a generally apolitical manner, an approach that would go into decline with the onset of the Cold War.[10] The Chinese Communists also received advice from foreigners, Soviet sponsored ones, though in a more formal manner.[11]

Missions for modernization

The desire to modernize was one of the primary reasons smaller nations in the middle- and late-nineteenth century began requesting missions from the 'Great Powers' of Europe. Latin America and the Balkans became the primary fields for the exportation of military advice during this era, though there was also some important activity in Asia, particularly in China and Japan, Japan being the most famous and most successful example.[12]

Egypt, Chile, China, and Japan are important cases of states that sought foreign military advice in order to modernize their nations. Latin America in general has traditionally been a field for this. Before World War I, the Ottoman Empire famously received foreign military assistance from a number of powers. The British naval mission to the Sublime Porte has recently been the subject of detailed study.[13]

But there were other trends that arose as well, particularly after the end of World War I. First, pariah nations such as Germany dispatched military advisors and missions as a means of cheating on the armaments provisions of the Versailles Treaty. The cooperative agreement between Weimar Germany and Bolshevik Russia is well known, but the Germans also went to great extremes to cheat on the naval clauses of Versailles. They installed a 'naval advisor' in Finland, Karl Bartenbach, who guided Finland's purchase of naval hardware from German puppet companies. These deals furthered the development of technologies indispensable to the birth of Nazi Germany's submarine arm, while permitting the Germans to train the necessary cadre of a reborn U-boat force.[14] Modernization is still a role of missions, but instead of it being just the objective of the state receiving the mission it is now also often the goal of the nation dispatching it.

Military missions as tools of economic penetration

The modernization drives of less developed nations marched hand in hand with the use of missions as tools of economic penetration. The nations selling the arms, usually European, but sometimes the US, generally wanted to place missions in foreign nations because they believed that it gave them leverage for the sale of arms. To the nation supplying the mission the sale of weapons was far more important than the modernization of the military forces of the country in question.

Economic penetration as a primary role of missions became popular in the late nineteenth century and continued to be one of the major driving forces behind the dispatch of military missions between the world wars. During this period Latin America and the Balkans were key economic battlegrounds of the European powers seeking to sell arms, and the primary task of the various military missions was to insure market dominance for their respective national weapons firms. William Sater's piece gives us a glimpse of this. The Baltic was also a fertile field for this in the post-World War I era, though the missions sometimes began as tools of alliance building and deterrence.[15] Donald Stoker's examination of the French naval mission to Poland looks at the arms trade through the lens of military advising. The various European missions to the Balkans are in need of further study.

The ideological struggle: the role of military missions

The Bolshevik rise to power laid the foundation for another new role for military missions: as prophets of revolutionary ideology. This began as early as 1921 when the Soviet Union dispatched military advisors to Mongolia. This quickly became a full advisory team that exercised immense influence and then control over Mongolian military structures, a Soviet officer generally serving as Army Chief of Staff. Moreover, the dispatch of political officers helped insure ideological indoctrination.[16] China was also a fertile ground for Soviet military advisors.[17] Ideological concerns also influenced the dispatch of military advisors to both sides in the Spanish Civil War.[18] Alaric Searle looks at the impact of ideology on the British military mission to the Soviet Union during World War II.

The ideological role of military advising intensified with the formal arrival of the Cold War and became the primary purpose of such work. As the United States strode onto the world stage for the first time, it sought means to combat communist expansion without having to commit combat troops against the Soviets and their clients. Military advisors and military advisory and assistance missions became some of these tools. One of the earliest and most successful US military missions was that to Greece in 1946–7.[19] The most heavily studied of the US missions during this period is probably the Korean Military Advisory Group (KMAG). It began life helping combat a communist insurgency but quickly went on to do other things. Bryan Gibby has recently completed a dissertation on the KMAG,[20] from which his article is drawn, but it has also been the subject of other studies.[21] Much US aid and assistance went to Chiang Kai-Shek and the Nationalist Chinese.[22] These three missions had in common the fact that they were intended to strengthen indigenous forces against internal and external communist threats.

The Soviets also invested heavily in foreign advising during the Cold War. Their mission to Cuba is probably the most famous of Soviet examples.[23] The Soviet mission in Egypt was also heavily involved in some key events of the twentieth century,[24] though the Egyptians had employed some German experts prior to the arrival of the Soviets.[25] There is some readily available material on Soviet missions,[26] even reports from participants,[27] but this is a field wide open for exploitation.

Decolonization in the wake of World War II also created many opportunities for foreign military advising and assistance.[28] The new Communist Chinese regime began exporting its military advice to some of these emerging nations, including those in Africa. Donovan Chau's article gives us an interesting picture of Chinese military assistance to the Algerians fighting against the French.[29] Today, the Chinese are not only continuing their military and developmental assistance efforts in Africa, but also exporting their knowledge to Latin America.[30]

Countering insurgencies: a new role for military advisory missions

With the onset of the Cold War one of the primary tasks of US advisory missions became conducting counterinsurgency operations or training other nations to do so. Nation building often went hand in hand with this task. There is an abundance of literature on US missions during this period, and even an early, brief history of the US efforts in Greece, Iran, the Philippines, Iran, China, Korea, and a few other places.[31] Famously, the United States sent an enormous military advisory group to South Vietnam.[32] An underexamined element is the US effort to advise the South Vietnamese Air Force, but Ed Westermann's contribution fills this gap.

Less well known is the British mission to Vietnam, which advised the South Vietnamese government in the early 1960s, concurrent with the US mission. The presence of two missions, often advising on the same topic, was sometimes a problem. Their views clashed at least on one occasion, and the British team circumvented their American counterparts to get a plan for combating the North Vietnamese-backed communist insurgency into the hands of South Vietnamese leaders. These multiple missions, though sometimes helpful, also were the sources of multiple streams of advice and multiple anti-insurgency operations. Sometimes this produced operations not supportive of one another, as well as the dissipation of resources.[33]

Latin America also became an important arena for US military advising with the onset of the Cold War. Many of the members of various US teams there have left accounts of their service.[34] John Waghelstein, a former commander of the El Salvador mission, has written extensively about his experiences there, as well as the many other places he worked as a military advisor during his army career. He provides us with a summary of lessons from his experiences. Counter-narcotics operations have sometimes been tied to military advisory groups doing counterinsurgency operations. The US military mission in Columbia is the best known of such missions. Douglas Porch and Christopher Miller have provided an examination of this US effort.

The corporatization of military advice: military advising for fun and profit

Mercenaries went out of fashion after World War I, but they never disappeared. Soldiers of Fortune experienced a renaissance in demand for their skills during the Cold War, particularly in Africa.[35] But with the end of the Cold War a new form of military advising moved to the forefront: the private corporate approach. Private military companies (PMCs) began taking on the role of training the military forces of often newly independent states.[36] Croatia provides a good early example of this.[37] But the most important current example is in Iraq, where innumerable private companies have taken on security tasks, as well as the training of Iraqi troops. Christopher Spearin has done an excellent job of shining some light on their various roles as the trainers of military and police forces and showing that while sometimes private corporations are the solution, sometimes they are also the problem. The most famous work on PMCs is *Corporate Warriors* by P.W. Singer.[38] But also readily available is the book by Deborah Avant, *The Market for Force*.[39] Public Broadcasting's *Frontline* news program has also aired a one-hour program on security contractors in Iraq.[40] There is also a useful website devoted to PMCs that details some of the available literature.[41] P.J. Cullen gives us some early PMC history, as well as a look at their current patterns of growth and development.

The military advisor: the agent of change (sometimes)

Another facet of military advising ripe for study is the personnel themselves. Who are they? How does their experience affect them? What are the lessons they learn? This is a little examined field, but there is at least one anthropologist, Anna Simons, looking at military advisors and writing about them.[42] The US government has also tried to define exactly what, or who, a military advisor is.[43] There are also a number of works examining the obstacles military advisors face[44] and that offer 'lessons learned' and general advice,[45] as well as help in dealing with unfamiliar cultures.[46] Brigadier General Daniel P. Bolger has recently added to this literature, giving guidance specific to US advisors serving in Iraq.[47]

Military advising today: all of the above and a little bit more

Even though corporations have taken on some of the advising tasks, they are still not the primary movers and shakers in the military advising business.

This is the United States, which is conducting a number of military advisory missions.[48] The one most often in the news is that in Iraq, about which much has already been written[49] and much more is in preparation. The United States is being supported by a number of other nations, particularly Great Britain, which is training the new Iraqi navy.[50] Iraq is also the beneficiary of a NATO training mission, which began training Iraqi officers on 24 August 2004.[51] An update on non-US contributions to training in Iraq was published in January 2007.[52] Williams Grube provides us with an account of a US Marine Corps officer working with an army Military Transition (or Training) Team (MiTT) moving Iraqi army battalions from dependent to independent operations.

Afghanistan is undoubtedly the second most important arena for US advising. This mission also demonstrates one of the new developments in advising: the multi-national mission. For example, teams training the new Afghan armored units, though led by Americans, worked with personnel from the Romanian and German armies. Jon Byrom recounts for us his experiences helping train the new Afghan armored forces.[53]

Multi-national missions dedicated to nation building are becoming one of the standard means of providing military assistance. As military forces continue to shrink, nations capable of developmental advising have fewer assets available for this task. Multi-national missions spread the costs, risks, and burdens of advising. On 31 March 2002 the European Union embarked upon its first military advisory mission, Operation Concordia, in Macedonia. This was done by assuming command of the NATO Peacekeeping Mission there since August 2001 that had been transformed into a smaller advisory and training mission on 16 December 2002.[54] The most multi-national of all military missions must be the International Security Assistance Force (ISAF). This initially British-led group was established in January 2002 to help rebuild Afghanistan. The first plan was for it to have personnel from eighteen nations.[55]

There is also what might best be termed a quasi-military approach, meaning that advisory or assistance teams composed of civilian and military experts, all employed by or in the service of the US government, help a nation reform or modernize its military structures. In the post-Cold War environment this has been one of the means by which new nations are prepared for membership in NATO. The rebirth and development of an independent Estonian defense structure provides a good example of this.[56]

Some conclusions

Obviously, military advising is here to stay. Nations will continue to want foreign military advice to modernize their own military forces or combat an enemy. Nations will continue to offer such advice to further their own political and economic objectives. Private providers of military expertise will continue to offer their services to virtually anyone from whom they can profit. Fortunately, the field is also acquiring new students of the art who are approaching it from a broad and comparative perspective,[57] but it is a field with abundant gaps sorely in need of a coherent history and deeper analysis.

Notes

1   States importing military ideas for their own purposes is the unifying idea of Ralston, *Importing the European Army*.
2   Stoker, *Britain, France, and the Naval Arms Trade in the Baltic, 1919–1939*, 102–19.
3   Some of the more famous examples of individual advisors include T.E. Lawrence and John Paul Vann. For their stories see, respectively, Lawrence, *Seven Pillars of Wisdom*; Sheehan, *John Paul Vann and America in Vietnam*. Also useful, and famous, is Lawrence's '27 Articles.' It can be accessed on the Web at: www.lib.byu.edu/~rdh/wwi/1917/27arts.html.
4   Dunn, *Khedive Ismail's Army*.
5   Dunn, 'Americans in the Nineteenth Century Egyptian Army.'
6   Cox, 'The American Naval Mission in Egypt'; Cox, 'Colonel John Lay's Naval Mission in Egypt.'
7   Weinert, 'The Original KMAG.'
8   Carr, *The Devil Soldier*.
9   Fox, 'Max Bauer: Chiang Kai-Shek's First German Military Adviser.'
10 Walsh, 'The German Military Mission in China, 1928–38.' See also Rostek, 'Zur Rolle der Deutschen Militärberater bei der chinesischen Nationalregierung 1928 bis 1938.'
11 For information on an early advisor to the Chinese Communists see Litten, 'Otto Braun's Curriculum Vitae,' 31–62. Interestingly, both the Chinese Nationalists and Communists had German advisors.
12 Preisseisen, *Before Aggression*; Kerst, *Jacob Mieckel*.
13 Rooney, 'The International Significance of British Naval Missions to the Ottoman Empire, 1908–1914.'
14 Stoker, *Britain, France, and the Naval Arms Trade in the Baltic*, 141–64; Forsén and Forsén, 'German Secret Submarine Exports, 1919–35.' For an example of German military dabbling in Latin America in this period see Atkins and Thompson, 'German Military Influence in Argentina, 1921–1940.'
15 Champonnois, 'Colonel Emmanuel du Parquet's Mission in Latvia, 1919–1920'; Stoker, *Britain, France, and the Naval Arms Trade in the Baltic*.
16 Kuznetsov, 'The Soviet Military Advisors in Mongolia, 1921–39,' 118–37, especially 119–22, 124, 126.
17 Litten, 'Otto Braun's Curriculum Vitae,' 31–62; Cherepanov, *Notes of a Military Advisor in China*.
18 Daley, 'Soviet and German Advisors Put Doctrine to the Test.'
19 Curtin, 'American Advisory Group Aids Greece in War on Guerrillas.'
20 Gibby, 'Fighting in a Korean War.'
21 Hausrath, *The KMAG Advisor (U)*; Millett, 'Captain James H. Hausman and the Formation of the Korean Army, 1945–1950,' 503–39; Clemens, 'Captain James Hausman, US Military Advisor to Korea, 1946–48.'
22 May, *The Truman Administration and China, 1945–1949*.
23 Woff, 'The Soviet-Cuban Military Alliance.
24 Badolato, 'A Clash of Cultures.'
25 Fahrmbacher, 'Seiben Jahre Berater bei der ägyptischen Armee.'
26 Mott, *Soviet Military Assistance*; Kipp, 'Soviet Military Assistance to the Demo-

cratic Republic of Afghanistan After the Withdrawal of Soviet Forces, 1889–1991.'
27 Cherepanov, *Notes of a Military Advisor in China*.
28 For an example see Anderson, 'Patrick Blackett in India: Military Consultant and Scientific Intervenor, 1947–72. Part One' and 'Patrick Blackett in India: Military Consultant and Scientific Intervenor, 1947–72. Part Two'; Butler, 'Recollections of Patrick Blackett, 1945–70.'
29 See also Chau, 'East to East,' 271–89.
30 Gedda, 'China Increases Foreign Military Training.'
31 Hermes, *Surveys of the Development of the Role of the US Army Military Advisor*.
32 Hickey and Davison, *The American Military Advisor and His Foreign Counterpart*; Spector, *Advice and Support*; Futrell, *The Advisory Years to 1965, the United States Air Force in Southeast Asia*; Matolda and Fitzgerald, *From Military Assistance to Combat, 1959–1965*; Clarke, *Advice and Support*.
33 Busch, 'Killing the "Vietcong,"' 135–62, especially 140–1, 146–7. This excellent article makes fine use of former East German archival material. For other examples of Cold War British advising see Corum, 'Building the Malayan Army and Police – Britain's Experience During the Malayan Emergency 1948–1960'; Ladwig, 'Security Assistance and Counterinsurgency.'
34 Some examples: Hall, *My Experiences as an Advisor in El Salvador*; Mendez, 'The Role of an MI Advisor in El Salvador.'
35 See an account by one of the most famous mercenaries: Hoare, *Mercenary*. Also available at any local bookstore is *Soldier of Fortune* magazine.
36 An early piece on this: Shearer, 'Outsourcing War,' 68–81.
37 www.abc.net.au/rn/talks/bbing/stories/s10592.htm. See also www.mpri.com.
38 Singer, *Corporate Warriors*.
39 Avant, *The Market for Force*.
40 Marcela Gaviria and Martin Smith, 'Private Warriors,' *Frontline*, transcript available at www.pbs.org/wgbh/pages/frontline/shows/warriors/etc/script/ html.
41 www.privatemilitary.org.
42 Simons, 'The Military Advisor as Warrior-King and Other "Going Native" Temptations.'
43 Froehlich, 'The Military Advisor as Defined by Counterparts.'
44 Riley, 'Challenges of a Military Advisor.'
45 Becena, 'Advising Host-Nation Forces: A Critical Art,' 26–8; Marks, 'Advisers and Advising in the 21st Century'; Marks, 'Joint Publication 3–07.15 *Tactics, Techniques, and Procedures for Advising Foreign Forces* and the American Mission.' This article also has some information on Chinese advisors to North Vietnam.
46 Guthrie, 'Conflicts of Culture and the Military Advisor.'
47 Bolger, 'So You Want to Be an Adviser.'
48 Recent information on some of these can be found in Kaplan, *Imperial Grunts*. See also James Brandon, 'To Fight Al Qaeda, US Troops in Africa Build Schools Instead,' *Christian Science Monitor*, 9 January 2006, www.csmonitor.com/2006/0109/p01s04-woaf.html; Jason Motlagh, 'US Takes War on Terror into Sahara,' *The Scotsman*, 14 December 2005, www.thescotsman.scotsman.com/print.cfm?id=id2403492005.
49 Newell, 'Building Iraqi Security Forces from the Bottom Up'; Aaron and Walley, 'ODA 542: Working with the Free Iraqi Fighters,' 86–8; Gary Skubal, 'An Iraqi Answer for Terrorists: A Day with the Commandos in Tallafar,' 14 October 2005, http://realclearpolitics.com/Commentary/com-10_012_GS_pf.html; Robert H. Scales, 'The Emerging Iraqi Army,' 14 October 2005, www.washtimes.com/functions/print.php?StoryID+20051013– 084116–5500r;

Fallows, 'Why Iraq Has No Army'; Cordesman with Baetjer, *Iraqi Security Forces*.

50 Thomas L. Friedman, 'Rebuilding Iraqi Navy Means Changing Culture of Fear,' *The Houston Chronicle*, 29 September 2005, www.chron.com/cs/CDA/ssistory.mpl/editorial/outlook/3376043.

51 Lynch and Janzen, 'NATO Training Mission – Iraq.'

52 Sharp and Blanchard, 'Post-War Iraq: Foreign Contributions to Training, Peacekeeping, and Reconstruction.'

53 An interesting take on the potential use of Afghan troops is Bran, 'An Encouraging Outcome.'

54 www.europeansecurity.net/espdptimeline2000.html, 2 February 2006.

55 Ibid. The nations were Austria, Denmark, Belgium, Bulgaria, Finland, France, Germany, Great Britain, Greece, Italy, the Netherlands, New Zealand, Norway, Portugal, Romania, Spain, Sweden, and Turkey.

56 Young, 'Approaching the Need for Defense Reform.'

57 Mott, *Military Assistance*.

2 Missions or mercenaries?

European military advisors in Mehmed Ali's Egypt, 1815–1848

John P. Dunn

> I know that of fifty men who come from Europe to offer me their services, forty-nine are like false jewels, but without trying them, I cannot pick out the one genuine diamond which may perhaps be among them."

With these words, Mehmed Ali explained his hit-and-miss efforts to find European experts who could jump-start his efforts to modernize the Egyptian armed forces. Although he certainly discovered "false jewels," there were enough "diamonds" to make the effort worthwhile.[1]

An Albanian nobody, whose fortitude, character, and iron made him Egypt's *Wali* or Viceroy (1805–1847), Mehmed Ali established a dynasty and a model for military success. As power enhanced longevity in the predatory world of the nineteenth-century Middle Eastern politics, his *al-Nizam al-jedid* (hence Nizam) was a highly visible success story.[2]

Translated into English as "the New Organization," it was a product of the *Wali*'s determination, Egyptian manpower, plus the import of western technology and advisors. Between 1815 and 1839, this combination made the Nizam a formidable army that won numerous battles in Africa, the Middle East, and Europe. By the 1830s, Nizam victories had upset the balance of power, created the largest Egyptian empire in history, and initiated the "Eastern Question." While Egypt's revenues and manpower supply partially explain why the new army was so good, training and advice from foreign military experts were also important. This essay looks at the role of foreign experts: how they were hired, where they functioned, and what they accomplished.[3]

Such men were on Mehmed Ali's mind when he arrived in Egypt during the last stages of an Anglo-Ottoman campaign to drive out French invaders. He witnessed French and British regulars in action plus sepoys fighting for the British East India Company. Mehmed Ali quickly recognized the advantages of European discipline, tactics, and technology; by 1803, he was considering how to convert local forces into a western-style army.

He was not alone in such thinking. The first decade of the nineteenth century featured a multi-party struggle to dominate Egypt, with Mehmed

Ali, rival Ottoman commanders, and surviving Mamluk *Amirs* attempting to recruit the nearly 1000 *Gallo-Egyptiens* who had not evacuated with their fellow countrymen in 1801. While many were of the most dubious quality, some of these deserters, stragglers, or ex-prisoners of war could organize squads of musketeers or operate modern artillery.[4]

The retention of foreign military technicians by Egyptian warlords began during the rule of Ali Bey Balut Kapan (1760–1766, 1768–1772), when British, Italian, and Greek experts helped improve his artillery corps. Although Ali Bey was finally driven from power in 1772, his economic, political, and military programs influenced Mehmed Ali. Later Ottoman efforts to create a western-style military machine during the reign of Selim III (1789–1807) – his *nizam-i cedid* – also influenced Egyptian affairs, as a small contingent of these troops was stationed in Cairo from 1801 to 1803.[5]

Although neither model survived the fall of their sponsor, both delivered a clear message that European tactics, technology, and firepower paid big dividends on the battlefield. One of Mehmed Ali's great skills was the ability to study these past experiments, drawing out their best components, and then tweaking them to fit current needs. He began doing so by gaining the lion's share of the *Gallo-Egyptiens* and using these men to destroy Egyptian-based rivals.

By 1805, Mehmed Ali's power was enough to make him the *Wali* or governor of Egypt. By 1811, he had eliminated all significant internal opposition. From that point onward, his attentions focused on a program of fiscal, economic, educational, and military reforms. Its purpose was to cement Mehmed Ali's internal authority, extend his control to neighboring lands, like the Sudan or Arabia, and create a hereditary dynasty so his family would enjoy the wealth of Egypt for generations to come.[6]

Although the *Wali* was keenly aware of the advantages offered by a European army, finding leaders to direct such a force presented his greatest challenge. At first, he followed the traditional path and purchased Mamluks. This was no easy task in the early 1800s, as Russian conquests were eliminating Caucasian markets for these "slave soldiers," while Ottoman leaders impeded sales to limit the already too powerful Egyptian *Wali*.

With too few Mamluks for commanding the mass-conscript force envisioned by their commander in chief, Mehmed Ali next turned to fellow Ottomans, offering lucrative pay and bonuses to any who would join his army. Although more available, and in many cases completely at ease serving against the Sultan, these men were poorly prepared to direct a modern army, as most had but a superficial knowledge of modern strategy and tactics.[7]

Indeed, General Pierre Boyer, writing in the 1820s, complained that few company level officers could read or write. Another critic, Jules Planat, argued that too many captains, some only sixteen years old, were promoted, "... without examination, and without passing through the ranks of ensign and lieutenant."[8] Edmund Cohorn, writing in 1829, commented that "the principal vice of the new army" was its lack of men trained for high command. General Henryk Dembinski echoed this view in 1833, saying that a true European style general staff was "indispensable."[9]

Mehmed Ali's desire for rapid expansion made some of these deficiencies unavoidable. Conservative attitudes prejudice plus an antiquated educational system exacerbated the problem. The *Wali* tried fixing it by sending selected officers on European study tours. Starting in 1809, his men visited France, Italy, Austria, and England. By 1826, the Egyptian Military School was established in Paris. Although successful graduates could proceed to official French military academies, most did not get that far. Egypt's class system, along with overly generous allowances, distracted from study. As one inspector put it, "if they carry anything away from Paris, it is its vices and not its virtues."[10]

As Mehmed Ali's ambitions did not allow for a gradual process of education, his next strategy was to hire foreign mercenaries. Although unusual, this was not a novel idea, as Egyptian armies once were dominated by Mamluks – the famous "slave soldiers" who, by tradition, could come from anywhere *except* Egypt. Mehmed Ali had just completed a long struggle with the Mamluks, killing most of their leaders in the celebrated massacre of 1811.[11]

Although Mamluks figured in Mehmed Ali's household forces well into the 1840s, he needed a very different foreigner for his Nizam. Enter the European mercenary. Previously employed in very limited numbers, and only for specialized duties in the artillery or engineers, it had been difficult to integrate these non-Muslim outsiders into Middle Eastern armies. Even reform-minded Ottoman Sultans, like Selim III (1789–1807), were unable to utilize significant numbers of western mercenaries or push for a European-style army.

Despite previous records, Mehmed Ali not only hired hundreds of European mercenaries, but even progressed to official advisory teams. Why did he succeed? First, unlike previous military innovators, Mehmed Ali faced very different internal dynamics. Between the late 1790s and the 1810s, Egyptians suffered from plagues, famines, invasions, civil wars, and banditry. Poorly disciplined soldiers only added to the general misery, so much so that noted historian Abd al-Rahman al-Jabarti cursed them as "God's scourge on His creatures."

Thus after nearly twenty years of hell, Egypt was devastated to the point that, any leader guaranteeing peace had an instant following. In addition, conservative elites were less powerful in 1820s Egypt. Also, Mehmed Ali had crushed the Mamluks, defeated British efforts to capture Rosetta (al-Raschid) in 1807, and defied the Sultan. The new *Wali* did not simply talk about the business of power, he delivered with interest. Locals were either cowed or willing to re-consider their opposition to his new-fangled military – they had no other options.

Fortunately for Mehmed Ali, as he overcame local opposition, the 1820s were a buyer's market as regards martial talent. Demobilization, along with political changes in post-Napoleonic Europe, placed many officers out of a job. One might also note that expanding armies attract a certain type of man who simply enjoys fighting and adventure – for such, peace time garrison duty is hell.

Thus, via the offers of reemployment, good pay, or an exotic change in pace, Mehmed Ali attracted quite a few "soldiers of fortune." Represented were Frenchmen, Italians, Poles, Spaniards, Germans, Englishmen, and Americans. While obviously difficult to coordinate, this motley collection was a purposeful choice. Future events could produce war or at least bad relations with a mercenary's homeland. In such a case, it would be dangerous to have "all the eggs in one basket."[12]

Despite a desire for variety, one finds French and Italian officers predominating in the 1820s and 1830s. *Gallo-Egyptiens* partially explain the former, while the latter resulted from historic linguistic ties and contemporary politics. With extensive trade relations dating back to the Middle Ages, Italian was the most widely spoken European language of early nineteenth-century Egypt and the Levant. Also, post-1815 political settlements, combined with revolutionary turmoil, provided steady streams of Italian refugees. Although none made it to the top, numerous Italians held mid-level ranks, mainly as instructors at Mehmed Ali's military schools.[13]

Italian and French mercenaries served in all parts of expanding Egyptian empire. Unlike their British and German counterparts, they tended to mix better with local traditions and co-exist with Arab and Turkish culture. Captain James MacKenzie, Bengal Light Cavalry, explained why in his report on the Egyptian Army:

> From my experience abroad, I should say that the English do not adapt themselves to the manners and customs of a foreign country and indulge in the humors and prejudices of the people, as readily as the French and Italians – hence the preference shown, in Egypt particularly, to natives of the above countries.[14]

A perfect example of such can be seen in the Nizam's most famous western recruit, Octave Joseph-Anthelme Sève (1788–1860). A big man, "... rough of speech, and with the manners of a grenadier," he was born in Lyon, saw service as a gunner at Trafalgar, joined a hussar regiment in 1807, and was an infantryman during the invasion of Russia.[15] Captured, freed, wounded several times, he was awarded the Legion of Honor and promoted to captain during the Hundred Days. After 1815, he was placed on half-pay.[16]

With no future at home, Sève packed his sword and took off for Egypt. Arriving at the start of the *Wali*'s expansion program, he was quickly employed. A somewhat apocryphal story has Mehmet Ali asking the Frenchman to train a modern army. Sève was supposed to have answered, "Yes, on condition that his Excellency gives me three things: time, money and his backing."[17] Whatever the case, Sève was among the earliest foreign contract officers and obtained the rank of *bey*.[18] His first assignment was to train company level officers in French drill and tactics. Not taking well to instruction from a non-Muslim, several soldiers fired at him, but missed. Cursing the lot as *triple canailles, porceaux maudits, et fils de chiens*, Sève offered to fight any, or all, on the spot.[19] With no takers, he next castigated them for such poor shooting and ordered practice to continue. Impressed by his nerve, the soldiers returned to work and ended their mutiny.

Later, Sève solved the problem completely by conversion to Islam, adopting the name Sulyman. Mehmed Ali rewarded this move with promotion to the status of *basha*, command of an infantry regiment, and, according to a contemporary, three wives. From here on, Sève/Sulyman obtained one success after another. He became inspector general of all military schools in 1832 and was chief of staff to Ibrahim, the *Wali*'s son. The new *basha*'s advice helped to formulate successful campaigns in Greece and Syria.[20]

Captain Charles Scott, a keen observer of the Egyptian scene, credited Sulyman with "possession of rare military qualities."[21] This opinion was obviously shared by Mehmet Ali, for by 1847, our French convert was the sixth highest paid officer in the Nizam; his 167,000 piasters per year salary a far cry from half-pay status back home.[22]

Hard working, talented, and willing to reinvent himself, even to the point of embracing Islam, Sulyman was one of Mehmed Ali's "diamonds." Others, like ex-U.S.M.C. Lieutenant George Bethune English, could also follow this road, but they were exceptional. Westerners who became Muslims were usually dismissed by their countrymen as "renegades," men of dubious mental or moral character. The traveler Madden noting mercenaries from Naples, Spain, Piedmont, and France called them "the refuse of Christendom."[23]

Muslims, on the other hand, saw them as *muhtadi* – one who discovered the truth path. Still immersed in Ottoman culture, where one's position in society was determined by race, occupation, or religious affiliation, to discriminate in favor of such men was a given. Those mercenaries who would not embrace Islam, the vast majority, discovered varying degrees of friction as they attempted to deal with their status.[24]

With Mehmed Ali in charge, this was not an insurmountable task. The rest of his western mercenaries did not rise as high, or make as much as Sève, but their pay was good by standards of the 1820s. Although each contract was different, most received the salary of a captain or major. They also obtained rations, a uniform allowance, and unlike Egyptian officers, were supposed to be paid in Spanish "dollars," a much more stable currency than the local piaster.[25]

How did Mehmed Ali find these men? Recruitment was a mix of private applications, "head-hunting" missions, and finally via an official advisory team. First, the *Wali* employed early hires, like Florent Tourneau or Colonel

Lith (Light?), to scout Europe for specified experts. Although these ventures brought small numbers, the catch included exactly what one would expect in this approach to the business of finding mercenaries.[26]

A good example was Mari *Bey* (aka Mary *Bey*, Bekir *Agha*, or Bekir *Bey*). Also called "the Corsican Liar," he had served either as a sergeant major with the British-raised Corsican Rangers or as a drummer boy in the French army, the latter providing his second nickname, *Le Colonel Tapin*. Whatever the case, he came to Egypt with claims of being Colonel and was quickly hired as a captain to drill Nizam privates. Mari went on to help translate a French "school of the soldier" manual into Turkish, was promoted to lieutenant colonel, and served in Arabia and the Morea. He ended up highly placed within the Cairo Police.[27]

Mari's story was repeated by other "false jewels" with equally dubious resumes. Prince Puckler-Muskau, writing in the 1830s, noted Mehmed Ali's Egypt as "... an El Dorado for blockheads and idlers looking to get rich quick."[28] While characters like Mari might serve to teach rudimentary drill, the Nizam needed genuine majors, colonels, and generals to make it effective. It also required many more mercenaries than those obtained in the initial manner.[29]

Then, a French diplomat with long ties to Egypt, Bernardino Drovetti (1776–1852), pushed to establish a regular team of military instructors. Drovetti, who had first seen Egypt as an aide-de-camp to General Murat in 1798, possessed considerable influence with Mehmed Ali. He had already been instrumental in pushing the *Wali* toward individual French candidates and also convinced him to pick France over Italy as the location for Egypt's European-based military school.[30]

By 1823, Drovetti's local influence, combined with glowing reports on potential opportunities for France, convinced the government of Louis XVIII to authorize an official military mission for improving Mehmed Ali's Nizam. Fourteen officers arrived in 1824, under the command of General Pierre Boyer.[31] The general, along with most of his subordinates, were no strangers to Egypt, having previously served there under Napoleon.[32]

Boyer's mission looked to complete the transformation started by Mehmed Ali in the 1810s, with the Nizam set to be organized, equipped, and drilled *à la française*. Possibly Boyer wondered about this goal, as he tried on his very un-French uniform "covered with gold lace, with a half moon of diamonds on each breast computed to be worth twenty thousand piasters'!"[33]

Boyer's men were attached to schools and field units. Their main purpose was to improve on drill. This may seem of slight use to the modern reader, but one should remember that soldiers of this era still maneuvered and fought in large, dense formations. Every soldier had a specific place, and control was a product of continual practice on the parade grounds. Even firing was "by the numbers," with continual exercise providing the steady pattern of hits deemed necessary for victory.[34]

By 1826, European advisors were attached to each infantry regiment of the Nizam. Units sent to Greece that year had the largest number, five or six, and successfully participated in combat against the insurgents. Encouraged by such, Mehmet Ali asked Boyer for more artillery officers, while the General himself wanted fifty additional infantry experts. These plans, however, were never completed, for the French mission was about to end.[35]

Despite high hopes, and contracts which, in the words of Planat, "were carried out with munificence," friction resulted from several factors.[36] First, there was the war in Greece, where Muslim Egyptians fought for their suzerain, the Ottoman Sultan, against Christian rebels. As European public opinion was strongly "Philhellene," service in the Nizam became uncomfortable for Boyer and other "on-loan" officers.[37]

In addition, the French came expecting massive salaries or other rake-offs but obtained little beyond the agreed terms. Combine this with poorly managed government revenues, typical in the nineteenth-century Egypt, and there was great anger when pay was late, as often happened after 1826. Also significant, the animosity generated between Boyer's mission and other European officers. He considered the Spanish and Italian mercenaries to be "refugees ... men without respect for authority, without fidelity, law and honor."[38]

There were petty squabbles that had less to do with politics and more to do with personal advancement. The Nizam's mix of ethnicities and languages probably enhanced this as French, Italian, and Spanish officers jockeyed for influence. Sometimes the contest was petty, like Scott's possibly apocryphal tale of the English mechanic who heard French officers complain about his copying shorter British style bayonets, and said, "There's no pleasing them ere French foreigners, now they find our bayonets too short – at Waterloo they found 'em too long."[39]

Power plays, however, could involve much more than the length of a bayonet. A good example was the case of Antonio de Seguerra y Cavajal. The top-ranking Spanish mercenary, he had fought against Napoleon and then against his king in the failed revolution of 1820. In Egypt, he ranked as a colonel and directed the *Madrasat al-Tobjiyya* (artillery school). Seguerra maintained a poor opinion of the French, but this did not preclude scheming with a faction trying to undermine Sulyman. They failed, and Seguerra plus the French veterinary doctor Hamont soon departed. Boyer also contested Sulyman's influence, but his greatest difficulties were with the *Wali*, whose vision for his Nizam did not always mesh with Boyer's plans. This may have been the decisive failure, for as historian James Heyworth-Dunne succinctly puts it, Mehmed Ali "wanted servants, not masters."[40]

By 1826, many western advisors resigned over pay and promotion disputes. In August of that year, after twenty months of service, Boyer and nine of his senior aides followed suit. This greatly reduced the first of several French missions to help organize an Egyptian army. It did not, however, significantly reduce French influence in the Nizam. Colonel Gaudin took

over Boyer's position, and a small team of French officers, along with mercenary types, maintained important roles in Egyptian military education.
Indeed, even after Mehmed Ali's great wars ended in 1840, the French were
still connected to the Nizam and other branches of government. Charles
Murray, the British consul general, complained in 1847 that:

> Every department of the public service is more or less in the hands of
> the French, the younger members of the reigning family were all edu-
> cated, either in Paris or under French instructors; the medical, educa-
> tional, and engineering schools are entirely French; Alexandria has been
> fortified by a Frenchman [Gallice Bey]; the effective commander-in-
> chief of the army is a Frenchman by birth [Seves], and the foreign
> minister [Artin Bey] is a Frenchman by adoption.[41]

A radically different team was considered in the early 1830s. The failure of
another Polish uprising against Russia resulted in large numbers of military
émigrés. Ibrahim pressed his father to form a general staff, and provide more
regimental instructors, by hiring 400 of these men. Previously the Nizam
employed a few Poles, like Colonel August Szule ("Jussuf Aga"), an engineering expert, or Count Rzewuski, an adventurer who fought in the
Wahhaby wars. This time Egypt could attract significant talent, like
General Henryk Dembinski, who arrived in 1833 and made a detailed
analysis of the Egyptian military. Unfortunately, this attempt also failed,
partially due to Russian machinations, but also from misunderstandings
between Polish and Egyptian leaders.[42]

Despite these disconnects, mercenaries, from either the Boyer Mission or
private hires, played a significant role in Mehmet Ali's drive to establish a
complete system for military education. Mainly classified as *talimji* (instructor), they taught in training camps at or around the cities of Alexandria,
Cairo, and Aswan. MacKenzie claimed *talimji* had high ranks, but their
authority was "little more than that practiced by a drill sergeant in a British
regiment."[43]

While true for some, others were attached directly to military units and
were deployed with these to battlefields in Arabia, the Sudan, and Greece.
Individuals were also used to provide specific skills on the battlefield, like
George B. English, who commanded the artillery train for the first Egyptian
invasion of the Sudan, or "Atkins," a British officer who aimed Congreve
rockets against rebellious Assir tribesmen in 1834.[44]

Whatever their role and status, by 1831, the foreign officers were teaching Egyptian officers at infantry, cavalry, and artillery specialist schools. The
best instructors went to the General Staff Academy at Canca. Here, course
work centered about geometry, arithmetic, map reading, military theory,
and French. Of these, the latter was given precedence, as most Europeans
could not speak Arabic or Turkish, and many modern technical terms did
not exist in these languages. Equally important, by the 1820s, French influ-

ence was powerful enough to trump the previously mentioned local affinity for Italian. The final product of these studies was a French-style general staff prepared to lead a mass conscript army.[45]

Another scratch built section of the Nizam was its medical and veterinary services. Established in 1827, this branch was the brain child of "doctor-of-fortune" Antoine-Barthélemi Clot (1796–1868). A nobody in France, he was destined for fame and fortune in Egypt. His first five-year contract provided travel money, rations, a uniform allowance, 1524 Spanish dollars per year, the rank of colonel, and a promise that he would not have to change his religion.[46]

Clot helped organize an orderly corps, along with Cairo's famous Qasr al-Aini hospital and Abu Za'bal medical school. He also supervised the hire of other European doctors, both as instructors and for direct service with regiments serving in Greece. Quickly promoted to *bey*, Clot directed an eccentric collection of French, German, Swiss, and Italian medical officers.[47]

While duty offered these men a decent salary of 12,000 piasters per annum, this was not sufficient to attract the very best. Indeed, some surgeons who joined the Nizam were quacks. Also, there was friction between the French and other Europeans. Still, Clot Bey established a system of hospitals that soon extended beyond the military and provided Egypt with significant exposure to western medical thought.[48]

Contemporary reports indicate that, in general, western mercenaries helped the *Wali* with his plans for rapid modernization. About 150 French, Italian, Spanish, and British officers served as instructors in the 1830s. Their efforts proved fruitful, with foreign consuls, travelers, and military leaders issuing positive reports.[49]

Although after Dembinski, no additional efforts were made to mass-hire foreign military talent, the individual contract system still provided for expansion and modernization. This peaked in 1839 when the Egyptian army contained 140,000 regulars. A year later, the big wars were over, and demobilization began.

What can be said about Mehmet Ali's quest for mercenary talent? How can we assess the efforts of his western advisors? Answers to such questions are most easily found in the Nizam's impressive string of victories. Fighting in the Sudan, Arabia, Greece, Anatolia, Palestine, and Syria, it was rarely defeated on the field of battle. Actions like Homs (1832), Koniya (1833), or Nezib (1839) featured Egyptian strategies and tactics equal to those of distinguished Napoleonic generals. In addition, success was the result of superbly disciplined soldiers, who fought in a European manner.

Such troops made it possible for the *Wali* to keep Egypt under his control and establish a dynasty that remained in power until 1952. Also the import of mercenary talent established a long tradition, ranging from American officers of the 1870s, to Russian ones in the 1960s. It is unfortunate that subsequent rulers of Egypt could not match Mehmed Ali's strategic insight with this interest in foreign technology and advisors, for few of these later combinations have been as fruitful.

Notes

1 Prince [Herman], Puckler-Muskau, *Egypt Under Mehemet Ali*, H. Evans Lloyd, trans. (London: Henry Colburn), MDCCCLXV, Vol. I, p. 49.

2 For an excellent nationalist biography, see Afaf Lufti al-Sayyid Marsot, *Egypt in the Reign of Muhammad Ali* (Cambridge: Cambridge University Press, 1984). For a less positive but very well-written account consult Fahmy, *All the Pasha's Men*.

3 Général M. Weygand's *Histoire militaire de Muhammed Aly et de ses fils*, 2 Vols (Paris: Imprimerie National, 1936), provides the only general history of the Nizam in a western language. See also David Nicolle, "Nizam – Egypt's Army in the 19th Century," *The Army Quarterly and Defense Journal*, Vol. 108 (1978): 69–78. Uniformologists may wish to view the color plates in the 1940 edition of Prince Umar Tusun's *al-Jaysh al-Misri al-barri wa al-bahri* [Egypt's Armed Forces on Land and Sea] (Cairo: Matbaat Dar al-Katub al-Misriyah, 1940).

4 Also dubbed "French Mamluks," these men flit in and out of Egyptian military history during the 1810s–1820s. M. Felix Mengin, *Histoire de l'Egypte* (Paris: Chez Arthus Bertrand, 1823), Vol. II, p. 11, places their numbers at only 300. An eyewitness from 1801 noted 500 *Gallo-Egyptiens*, and British efforts "to discourage this unnatural infatuation," William Rae Wilson, *Travels in Egypt and the Holy Land* (London: Longman, 1823), pp. 214–15. See also James Heyworth-Dunne, *An Introduction to the History of Education in Modern Egypt* (London: Luzac and Co., 1938?), pp. 102–3; Edward de Montule, *Travels in Egypt During 1818 and 1819* (London: G. Sidney, 1821), p. 82; P. et H., "Egypte Moderne," in M.J.J. Marcel, *Egypte Depuis la Conquête des Arabes Jusqu'a la Domination Française* (Paris: Didot Frères, 1848), p. 5.

5 *Nizam-i Cedit* is the Turkish version of *Nizam al-Jadid*. The standard account of Selim III and his military reforms remains Stanford Shaw, *Between Old and New: The Ottoman Empire Under Sultan Selim III, 1798–1807* (Cambridge: Cambridge University Press, 1971).

For a quick look at Ali Bey, and an excellent overview of Egypt in the 1700s, see Daniel Crecelius, "Egypt in the Eighteenth Century," in M.W. Daly, ed., *The Cambridge History of Egypt. Volume II. Modern Egypt* (Cambridge: Cambridge University Press, 1998). For more details, see his book, *The Roots of Modern Egypt: A Study of the Reigns of Ali Bey al-Kebir and Muhammad Bey Abu al-Dhahab, 1760–1775* (Minneapolis and Chicago: Bibliotheca Islamica, 1981).

6 Again, Marsot and Fahmy are invaluable to examine interpretations on Mehmed Ali's grand strategy.

7 Mehmed Ali once used these high pay rates as an excuse for his failure to send Nizam officers to help train Ottoman counterparts. He claimed the pay differential would create jealousy and friction. Khaled Fahmy, "The Era of Muhammad 'Ali Pasha," in Daly, ed., *The Cambridge History of Egypt*, p. 158.

8 Jules Planat, *Histoire de la régeneration de l'Egypte* (Paris: J. Barbazet, 1830), p. 104. An ex-officer of Napoleon's Guard Artillery, Planat served as an instructor at the Egyptian staff college in Canca. He provides an important eyewitness account of Mehmed Ali's regime.

9 For reproductions of original letters, dispatches, and reports connected to Egyptian military affairs in the 1820s–1830s, see the works of Georges Douin, Eduard Driault, and Adam Benis. For Cohorn's lengthy critique, see G. Douin, *L'Egypte de 1828 à 1830. Correspondance des consuls de France en Egypte* (Roma: Nell' Istituto Poligrafico, 1935), p. 67. On Boyer, consult Douin, *Une mission militaire Française auprès de Mohamed Aly*, p. 189. Dembinski's report can be found in Benis, *Une mission militaire Polonaise en Egypte*, Vol. I, p. 345.

10 Cited in Darrell J. Dykstra, "Joseph Hekekyan and the Egyptian School in Paris," *The Armenian Review*, Vol. 35 (1982): 174. A superb primary source for

this mission is Rifa'a Rafi' al-Tahtawi, *An Imam in Paris. Account of a Stay by an Egyptian Cleric*, Daniel L. Newman, trans. (London: Oxford University Press, 2004). For more on the school, see Alain Silvera, "The First Egyptian Student Mission to France Under Muhammad Ali," *Middle Eastern Studies*, Vol. 16 (1980): 1–22. See Paddy Griffith, *Military Thought in the French Army, 1815-1851* (Manchester: Manchester University Press, 1989), for a concise appraisal of official military schools in France.

11 Mehmed Ali was not especially hostile toward rank-and-file Mamluks, only their leaders – his main rivals for control of Egypt. Indeed, having wiped out most of the *Amirs* in 1811, he maintained 500 Mamluks, while Ibrahim, his son, kept 300 more. Mainly Circassians, these men and their descendants, held important commands in the Egyptian military through the 1880s. For more on this, see Dunn, *Khedive Ismail's Army*; Thomas Roberdeau Wolfe, *Diary*, Southern Historical Collection, p. 15.

12 As happened at the battle of Navarino (1827) where French warships were sent against Egyptian vessels commanded by French mercenaries. The results of the battle speak for themselves. Roger C. Anderson, *Naval Wars in the Levant, 1559-1853* (Princeton: Princeton University Press, 1952), p. 526. One might also note Giovani Romei, who betrayed his Egyptian masters in the Morea, "Romei to di Rossarol, Modon, 1825," and "di Rossarol to Romei, Zante, 1825," in CO 136/32, PRO, London.

Lists of foreign officers in the Nizam of the 1820s can be found in Douin, *La mission du Baron de Boislecomte, L'Egypte et la Syrie en 1833*, pp. 108–9; Douin, *Une mission militaire*, p. 4, n. 1; Eduard Driault, ed., *L'Expédition de Crête et de Morée (1823-1828)* (Le Caire: Institut Française, 1930), p. 93; Nicolle, "Nizam," p. 70; William Nassau Senior, *Conversations and Journals in Egypt and Malta* (London: Sampson, Low. Marston, 1882), Vol. II, p. 38; Ferdinand Werne, *African Wanderings* (London: Longman, 1852), Vol. I, p. 2.

13 Giovanni Finati provides an early example of this trend, enlisting as an *Arnaut* and fighting against the Wahhaby fanatics in Arabia. See William John Bankes, ed., *Narrative of the Life and Adventures of Giovanni Finati*, 2 Vols (London: John Murray, 1830).

Most Italians, like *Sottotenente* Giuseppe Scarpa (aka Juseff Agha of the 6th Nizam Infantry Regiment), were ex-company grade officers, bumped up to the Egyptian equivalent of major or lieutenant colonel. Their pay rates were less than French, English, or German mercenaries, another factor in their favor. Ersilio Michel, *Esuli Italiani in Egitto, 1815–1861* (Pisa: Domus Mazziniana, 1958), pp. 13–14, provides examples of 750–1250 piasters per month plus uniform, food, and horse allowances. Gabriel Guemard, *Les reformes en Egypte (d'Ali Bey el Kebir à Muhammad Ali, 1760–1848)* (Le Caire: Paul Berbey, 1936), p. 155, notes 125 francs per month. For more on this, see Anouar Louca, *Voyageurs et Ecrivains Egyptiens en France au XIX Siècle* (Paris: Didier, 1970), p. 34, n. 3. For more details on Italians, see Michel, *Esuli Italiani in Egitto*, pp. 12–13, 15–16, 25, 36.

14 Report to Alexander Johnson, in FO 78/3185, PRO. French Napoleonic veterans served as mercenaries or advisors in the Tunisian, Persian, Turkish, and Sikh armies.

15 H. Lauvergne, *Souvenirs de la Grèce pendant la Campagne de 1825* (Paris: Avril de Gastel, 1826), p. 46.

16 Griffith, *Military Thought in the French Army*, p. 8, notes that French pay rates were amongst Europe's lowest. Douin, *Une mission militaire*, pp. x–xi, provides more detail on Sève's Napoleonic career. One could also consult Aime Vingtrinier, *Soliman-Pacha. Colonel Sève. Généralissime des armées Egyptiennes ou*

histoire des guerres de l'Egypte de 1820 à 1860 (Paris: Librairie de Firmin Bidet et Cie, 1886).

Sève was not above embellishing his European career, once claiming he left France a colonel and then telling *The Times* he had served as an officer at Trafalgar. "Ibrahim Pasha," *The Times* (8 June 1846): 6. With his name sometimes entered as Seves, this remarkable man cries out for a modern biography.

17 Benis, *Une mission militaire Polonaise en Egypte*, Vol. I, p. xxxiii.

18 *Bey* connoted a military rank of *miralai* [colonel] or *qaimmaqan* [lieutenant colonel] but also implied civil power. The next step up was a *basha*, which had three grades. See Richard Hill, *Biographical Dictionary of the Anglo-Egyptian Sudan* (London: Oxford University Press, 1951), pp. xi, xiii–xvi. See also Marsot, *Egypt in the Reign of Muhammad Ali*, p. 82. On Sève's early employment, see Douin, *Une mission militaire*, p. xii; Planat, *Histoire de la régeneration de l'Egypte*, p. 14.

19 Gabriel Enkiri, *Ibrahim Pacha (1798–1848)* (Le Caire: Imprimerie Française, 1948), p. 62; Carlos Stone, *Asuntos Militares en Egipto* (Habana: Tipographica de'El EcoMilitaire, 1884), p. 16; Vingtrinier, *Soliman-Pacha*, p. 103.

20 British consul Salt claimed the promotion came on 25 December, "to expressly outrage the religion he [Sève] had renounced." Salt to FO, Cairo, 20 January 1824, FO 78/126, PRO. On Sulyman's next promotions, see Vingtrinier, *Soliman-Pacha*, pp. 257–9.

21 C. Rochfort Scott, *Rambles in Egypt and Candia with Details of the Military Power and Resources of These Countries* (London: Henry Colburn, Pub., 1837), Vol. II, p. 229. It might be noted that Captain Scott did not have a great respect for the French in general.

22 Charles Deval, *Deux Années à Constantinople et en Morée (1825–1826)* (Paris: Nepveu, 1828), pp. 207, 209. For more on religious problems facing western officers, see Pierre Giffard, *Les Français en Egypte* (Paris: Victor Harard, 1883), p. 79; Planat, *Histoire de la régeneration de l'Egypte*, pp. 40–1; Senior, *Conversations and Journals*, Vol. II, p. 28. On 1847 pay, see Helen Anne B. Rivlin, *The Agricultural Policy of Muhammad 'Ali in Egypt* (Cambridge: Cambridge University Press, 1961), p. 326, n. 11.

23 R.R. Madden, *Travels in Turkey, Egypt, Nubia, and Palestine in 1824, 1825, 1826, and 1827* (Philadelphia: Carrey and Lea, 1830), Vol. I, p. 118. President John Q. Adams, who employed English as an executive agent in the 1820s, described his man as having "eccentricities, approaching insanity." John Quincy Adams, *Memoirs*, Vol. VIII, p. 62, as cited in Henry M. Wriston, *Executive Agents in American Foreign Relations* (Gloucester, MA: Peter Smith, 1967), p. 323. English and two fellow Americans, with the appropriate pseudonyms Khalil Agha and Achmed Agha, participated in the invasion of the Sudan, all singing "Hail Columbia" as they sailed up the Nile. George B. English, *A Narrative of the Expedition to Dongola and Sennar* (Boston: Wells and Lilly, 1823), pp. 15–16. For more on western displeasure at those mercenaries who "turned Turk," see Edouard Driault, *Formation de l'empire de Mohamed Aly de l'Arabie du Soudan (1814-1823)* Le Caire: Institue Francaise, 1927); J.R. Wellsted, *Travels in Arabia* [1838 reprint] (Graz: Akademische Druck-u Verlagsanstalt, 1978), Vol. 2, pp. 211–12.

24 Europeans represented a very small minority in Mehmed Ali's Egypt. They numbered about 10,000 in the 1840s, most of whom were Italians or Greeks. On religious discrimination and problems resulting from such, see Heyworth-Dunne, *An Introduction to the History of Education in Modern Egypt*, pp. 114, 158; Planat, *Histoire de la régeneration de l'Egypte*, pp. 40–1; Senior, *Conversations and Journals*, Vol. II, p. 28.

25 In 1833, the Spanish "dollar," a large silver coin, was a major trade currency of

the Middle East and exchanged for twenty piasters. In 1843, it produced twenty-two piasters and was at the same time worth four shillings two pence English. Sir Gardner Wilkinson, *Modern Egypt and Thebes* [1843 reprint] (Wesibaden: n.p., 1981), Vol. I, pp. 28, 102.

Planat, *Histoire de la régeneration de l'Egypte*, p. 41, lists an instructor's salary in 1826 as: 2000 French francs a year, a horse and fodder, two uniforms, and a food allowance of sixty francs per month. Ed. de Cadalvene and J. de Breuvery, *L'Egypte et la Turque de 1829 à 1836* (Paris: Arthus Bertrand, 1836), Vol. I, p. 112, places the figures for 1836 at 2–4000 francs salary plus another 250 francs for uniform purchase and care. Werne, *African Wanderings*, Vol. I, p. 6, with a big mouth, but no previous military experience, claimed he was a *binbashi* [major] for rations, 2500 piasters per month, and "all I could wish for" [i.e. loot]. See also Douin, *Une mission militaire*, p. 66.

Not all Europeans obtained officer slots, some technical branches, like the artillery and sappers, hired Spanish and Italian NCOs. In the navy, British gunners, boatswains, and "top captains" were hired for service on frigates and ships of the line. See "Sketches of a Year's Service in the Egyptian Marine in 1832 and 1833," *United Service Journal* (March 1834): 74.

26 Cattaui Bey, *La Règne de Mohamed Aly d'Apres les Archives Russes en Egypte* (Le Caire: Institut Français, 1931) Vol. I, p. 495; Douin, *Mission*, p. xiv.

27 Hill, *Biographical Dictionary*, pp. 231–2; Lauvergne, *Souvenirs de la Grèce*, p. 10; J. Mangeart, *Souvenirs de la Morée* (Paris: Igonette, 1830), pp. 42–3; Report to Alexander Johnson, in FO 78/3185, PRO.

28 Puckler-Muskau, *Egypt Under Mehemet Ali*, Vol. I, p. 20.

29 General Belliard, *Memoirs du Comte Belliard* (Paris: Berquet et Petion, 1842), pp. 320–1, notes a former French NCO who passed himself as an officer and obtained a major's slot with the Nizam's 9th Infantry Regiment. When his unit was scheduled for service in the Morea, he promptly deserted, returned to France, and became a school teacher!

30 Douin, *Une mission militaire*, pp. xxi, 4; John Marlowe, *Spoiling the Egyptians* (New York: St. Martin's Press, 1975), p. 17; al-Tahtawi, *An Imam in Paris*, pp. 26–7.

31 Baron Pierre François Xavier Boyer (1772–1851) served in Egypt, Santo Domingo, Spain, the Germanies, and France during the Napoleonic wars. An infantry expert, he later commanded a French division in Algeria and was inspector general of the *Gendarmerie* in the 1840s. Douin, *Une mission militaire*, pp. xvii–xix.

32 Boyer obtained an excellent compensation package. British Consul General Salt claimed it was 10,000 Spanish dollars per year, plus expenses, and promotion to *Bey*. In return, the general presented a gift of 500 French muskets plus matching accouterments for Mehmed Ali's bodyguard, Salt to FO, Alexandria, 14 January 1825, in FO 78/135, PRO. See also Guemard, *Les reformes en Egypte*, p. 130; Salt to FO, Cairo, 20 January and 10 October 1824, FO 78/126, PRO.

33 Salt to FO, Cairo, 20 January 1824, FO 78/126, PRO.

34 Douin, *Une mission militaire*, pp. xv, xxi, 9; Driault, *L'Expédition de Crête*, p. 45; Heyworth-Dunne, *An Introduction to the History of Education in Modern Egypt*, p. 115, n. 2.

35 Deval, *Deux Années à Constantinople et en Morée*, p. 198; Douin, *Une mission militaire*, pp. xvi–xvii; Driault, *L'Expédition de Crête*, p. 46; Planat, *Histoire de la régeneration de l'Egypte*, pp. 98, 127.

36 Planat, *Histoire de la régeneration de l'Egypte*, p. 68.

37 See Douglas Daikin, *The Greek Struggle for Independence 1821–1837* (Berkeley: University of California Press, 1973), p. 91, for Greek efforts to induce mercenary desertions.

38 Douin, *Une mission militaire*, pp. 22, 52–3.
39 Scott, *Rambles in Egypt*, Vol. I, p. 166.
40 Heyworth-Dunne, *An Introduction to the History of Education in Modern Egypt*, p. 115. Seguera was promoted to *Liwa* (brigadier) and *Bey* before he returned to Spain in 1837. See A.B. Clot, *Mémoires de A. B. Clot Bey* (Le Caire: Institut Français, 1949), pp. 52–4, 188–9; Driault, *L'Expédition de Crête*, pp. 105, 129–130, 137, 214; Guemard, *Les reformes en Egypte*, p. 157; Heyworth-Dunne, *An Introduction to the History of Education in Modern Egypt*, pp. 185, 188, 190; Planat, *Histoire de la régeneration de l'Egypte*, pp. 129–131; Samir Raafat, "The Spanish Founder of the Egyptian Artillery Academy," *The Egyptian Gazette* (18 February 1997).
41 Murray to FO, Cairo, 12 July 1848, FO 78/757, PRO. See also Douin, *Une mission militaire*, pp. xvi–xvii, 12, 17, 40, 53, 108; Driault, *L'Expédition de Crête*, pp. 83, 105, 129–130, 137, 189, 214; Viscomte de Guichen, *Le Crise d'Orient de 1839 à 1841 et L'Europe* (Paris: Emile-Paul, 1921), pp. 3–4; "Stephen Bey to Artin Bey, Paris, 25 August 1848," in Doss. "Personnel," *Période Mehemet Ali à Said Pacha, Dar al-Wathaiq*, Cairo; Planat, *Histoire de la régeneration de l'Egypte*, pp. 129–31, 133.
42 Polish *émigré* officers were ubiquitous to the world of the 1830s. One commanded the Belgian Army in 1839, while others served in Spanish, Portuguese, and French forces. Others served the Ottoman Empire and the Bey of Tunis.

    Dembinski left an account of this venture, see 'Manuscrit prophétique rédige par moi en 1835 en 1839, et que les événements, qui le passent aujourd'hui en Europe justifiant d'une manière la plus évidente,' 4 September 1855, Carton 42, Dossier 5588 Divers, *Période Mehemet Ali à Said Pacha, Dar al-Wathaiq*, Cairo. See also Benis, *Une mission militaire Polonaise en Egypte*, Vol. I, pp. xxxiv, ixviii–ixix; Edmund Bojerski, "The Poles in Africa 1517–1939, Part II," *Explorer's Journal*, Vol. 35, No. 3 (1957): 27–9; Heyworth-Dunne, *An Introduction to the History of Education in Modern Egypt*, p. 185; A. Kosciakiewicz, *Souvenirs de l'émigration polonaise* (Paris: n.p. 1858), p. 139; Scott, *Rambles in Egypt*, Vol. I, pp. 183–4.
43 Report to Alexander Johnson, in FO 78/3185, PRO.
44 Although service in the Sudan or Arabia was harsh, it could be very rewarding. Witness Joseph Vaissière, who assisted Ibrahim Pasha in capturing the last Wahhaby stronghold of Darriya (1819). Sent back to Cairo with the good news this long war was concluded, he obtained a promotion and gratuity of 50,000 Maria Theresa thalers! Hill, *Biographical Dictionary*, p. 371. Deval, *Deux Années à Constantinople et en Morée*, p. 198, claims five to six European advisors served with every Nizam regiment sent to the Morea, where they obtained 1000–1500 piasters per month.

    For details, see "Armée Egyptienne en 1836," *Magasin Pittoresque* (1836): 348; "Egypte," *La Spectateur Militaire* (August–September 1828): 629; Heyworth-Dunne, *An Introduction to the History of Education in Modern Egypt*, p. 114; Weygand, *Histoire militaire de Muhammed Aly et de ses fils*, Vol. I, p. 159.
45 Planat, one of the original foreign instructors at Canca, provides a detailed list of courses offered and instructors (who were mainly French), *Histoire de la régeneration de l'Egypte*, pp. 92–3, 363–4. See also de Cadalvene and de Breuvery, *L'Egypte et la Turque*, Vol. I, p. 124; W.Y. Carman, *The Military History of Egypt* (Cairo: R. Schindler, 1945), p. 20; Douin, *L'Egypte de 1828*, p. 195; Marsot, *Egypt in the Reign of Muhammad Ali*, p. 168.
46 Planat, *Histoire de la régeneration de l'Egypte*, pp. 358–9, notes chief surgeons obtained 2800 piasters per month in 1829, while pharmacists were paid 1850 piasters. Werne, *African Wanderings*, Vol. I, p. 2, notes a doctor sent into the

Sudan obtained 1000 piasters per month plus rations for himself, a horse, and four servants.

See also Clot's ponderous, but fact-filled *Aperçue général de l'Egypte*, 2 Vols (Paris: Fotin Masson, 1840).

47 Clot, *Aperçue général de l'Egypte*, Vol. II, pp. 394–417; Douin, *Une mission militaire*, p. xiv; Giffard, *Les Français en Egypte*, p. 103; Hill, *Biographical Dictionary*, p. 101; Mangeart, *Souvenirs de la Morée*, pp. 25–6; Werne, *African Wanderings*, Vol. I, pp. 2–3.

For an interesting look at medical service in the field, see Hippolyte Roy, *La vie héroïque et romantique du Docteur Charles Cuny* (Paris: n.p., 1930).

48 For recruiting problems, see Clot, *Aperçue général de l'Egypte*, Vol. II, p. 256. Werne, *African Wanderings*, Vol. I, pp. 59, 60, 150, has only negative comments for Clot and his medical system. This may be Germanic prejudice, but it is supported by another observer, John Lloyd Stephens, *Incidents of Travel in Egypt, Arabia, Petraea and the Holy Land* [1836 reprint] (Norman: University of Oklahoma Press, 1974), p. 452. On pay rates, see Planat, *Histoire de la régeneration de l'Egypte*, pp. 358–9; Werne, *African Wanderings*, Vol. I, pp. 2, 6.

49 "Extremely well equipped and well drilled," Edward B.B. Parker, *Syria and Egypt Under the Last Five Sultans of Turkey* [1876 reprint] (New York: AIMS, 1973), Vol. II, p. 54. Consul Mimaut, 1829, "with great precision," Douin, *L'Egypte de 1828*, p. 132; General Boyer, 1824, "the troops are like our own," Douin, ed., *Une mission militaire*, pp. 9, 37; Consul Muliveire, 1825, "They conduct all the drills with extraordinary precision," Driault, *L'Expédition de Crète*, p. 83.

3 The impact of foreign advisors on Chile's armed forces, 1810–2005

William F. Sater

Foreign nations' militaries have long influenced the development of Latin America's armed forces. This process, which included the training of officers and enlisted personnel, as well as the sale of modern military technology, became quite common in the late nineteenth century. Peru, blithely ignoring the Franco-Prussian War, hired four French officers who, under the leadership of Captain Paul Clément, arrived to revamp its army. Peru's neighbors opted for a Teutonic solution: in 1886, Emil Körner, a Saxon captain who could never expect to reach the rank of major in the Kaiser's army, arrived in Chile.

Other Latin nations, perhaps awed by Germany's 1871 victory over France, also imitated Chile's example: in 1898, Argentina hired a German military mission to establish and man a General Staff College as part of a more ambitious plan to revamp its army. Within a few years, Argentine officers began visiting Germany where some of them observed the Kaiser's army during their annual maneuvers. Beginning in 1906, the Brazilian government, which began sending officers to serve with Prussian units, not only purchased large quantities of artillery from Krupp, but negotiated an agreement that called for a German military mission to reorganize its army. Domestic political pressure and a clever French publicity campaign, however, convinced Brazilian President Hermes da Fonseca to turn away from Germany. Mexico, which paradoxically modeled its military on the French army, also considered embracing German methods and equipment. Bolivia did more than contemplate change: in 1910 it dismissed its French advisors, who since 1895 had revised its system of military education, replacing them with three German officers who were to direct its *Escuela de Suboficiales*, *Colegio Militar*, and *Escuela de Guerra*. Germany did not have a formal military mission in Bolivia until 1910, when a delegation of officers and non-commissioned officers, led by a Major Hans Kundt, arrived to restructure Bolivia's army. Following his service in World War I, Kundt returned to Bolivia, along with future SA leader, Ernst Roehm. Kundt held a variety of posts, including that of minister of war, as well as commander of the Bolivian army. And it was thanks to the German advisor that Bolivia became ensnared in its disastrous war with Paraguay.[1]

Although German military trainers clearly wielded enormous power throughout Latin America – where only Peru remained loyal to its French trainers – nowhere did they seem to exercise as much influence as in Chile. Thanks to the efforts of successive contingents of Prussian army officers, the South American nation became known as the "Prussia of the Pacific."[2] These Prussian officers did more than transmit knowledge or military technology; they would restructure and re-equip Chile's army while teaching its officers and men how to use their new materiel; they also tried to imbue the Chilean army's officer corps with the mores of their Prussian counterpart. But the relationship did not end there: Chile became Prussia's proxy, not simply teaching other Latin-American armies the same lessons it had learned, but acting as a salesman for the same weapons that it had purchased at the urgings of its German advisors.

Powerful as they were, the various German military missions were not the first to train the Chilean army: as early as 1810, foreign officers began enlisting in Chile's army to help the new republic win its independence from Spain. Many of these men remained well into the 1840s. During a second stage of development, which lasted from 1840 to 1885, there was a reciprocal interchange of personnel: the Chilean government hiring a few foreign officers and purchasing equipment, mainly French, while sending individual officers to study in European military schools and even, in some cases, to serve with foreign armies. This exchange of personnel occurred in part as a Chilean response to changing military technology: no longer could a country simply purchase war materiel; the recipient nations had to hire more technically advanced foreign advisors to demonstrate how to use their new weapons. At the onset of the third period, which transpired between 1885 and 1914, Chile acquired enormous quantities of German equipment, engaged German military instructors, and even sent large numbers of its own officers to study in Potsdam's military schools and serve with its units. After 1918, following its defeat in World War I, German influence began to wane; it would disappear after World War II to be replaced by the United States, which emerged as the new principal source of training and equipment.

Unlike other Latin-American nations that employed foreign military missions, Chile exported its newly acquired expertise to other Latin-American nations. This fact made Chile unique as it became the missionary of German military doctrine and, not incidentally, the salesman of its technology. This process also permitted Santiago to cultivate and retain the affection of its neighbors whose support it needed to fend off its diplomatic enemies to the east and the north, Bolivia, Peru, and Argentina.

The presence of foreign officers, mainly from Britain and the United States, also provided the leadership for the embryonic Chilean navy. While the establishment of the *Escuela Naval* eventually allowed Chile to produce commanders to lead its fleet, these new officers still needed specialized training, particularly as the navy began to acquire first steam driven vessels and then armored warships mounting modern cannons. Increasingly, Chile seconded some of its officers to foreign postings, particularly with the Royal Navy and British shipyards, to master the new technology. As the Chilean navy improved, it would also provide technical assistance to other Latin-American fleets. While Germany's influence virtually ended after 1945, Great Britain managed to maintain its ties to the Chilean fleet. Between 1945 and 1960, although the United States provided the Chilean fleet with many vessels, after 1960, English or European shipyards satisfied most of Chile's naval needs. The United States, however, did continue to educate a large number of Chile's naval officers.[3]

The Chilean army

Foreign influence shaped Chile's army virtually from the moment of its creation. Indeed, as many as 10 percent of all officers serving in Chile's pre-1885 army learned their craft in alien lands. Fifteen percent of these officers were natives of Uruguay, Peru, and even Paraguay. Germans, Italians, Englishmen, and Frenchmen and immigrants from other parts of Europe or from the United States constituted an additional 21.5 percent of the officer corps. The largest single foreign contingent, approximately 43 percent, were Argentines, veterans of the Army of the Andes,[4] who having helped win independence from Spain, remained in Chile to serve in its armed forces. While most of them held field grade ranks, three of these men, Gregorio de las Heras, Eugenio Necochea, and Luis Pereira, became generals. Curiously, the second largest group of foreigners to serve in the Chilean army, some 20 percent, were Spaniards. Not surprisingly, the new republic's military incorporated not simply the royalist officers but also the Spanish Army's manuals, such as those for the infantry and the artillery, to regulate its military well into the nineteenth century.[5]

In retrospect, Chile had little choice but to imitate the Spanish army: since the new republic had no independent experience in training warriors, it had to rely upon the Madre Patria's methods. Predictably, the government of Bernardo O'Higgins tried to break this dependency by establishing an *Escuela Militar* to train future officers. Economic problems, however, forced the school to close only to reopen in 1831, this time under the aegis of the conservative Diego Portales. This academy again shut its doors, in part to trim the budget and in part because the army had enough junior officers. The government of General Manuel Bulnes re-established the school in 1842 and it would operate without incident for the next 30 years. In 1876, however, a riot of cadets temporarily shuttered the school that was reconstituted in 1878, just in time for its graduates to join the War of the Pacific. Thanks to this institution, Chile could count on its locally trained officers.

But the advent of new, more complicated military technology forced changes in Chile's army. First, it became clear that while Chilean foundries could cast bronze cannons as early as 1859, they could not produce the newer, and more complicated, iron and then steel barreled guns. Thus, in

1846, Captain Agustín Olvarrieta was seconded to France to study the military art, topography, hydraulic construction, and pyrotechnics.[6]

France became and would remain Chile's premier advisor until close to the end of the nineteenth century. Jorge Beauchef, for example, called for the cadets in the *Escuela Militar* to wear French-style uniforms and to follow French regulations.[7] In a sense, this choice seemed quite logical: Napoleonic France, after all, enjoyed great military currency. Additionally, numerous Frenchmen occupied high places in Chile's army as well as in Chile's political and administrative bureaucracy. The Parisian born Benjamín Viel, for example, served both as a general in Chile's army and as a legislator; while Jorge Beauchef, from the Loire, was a colonel and governor of Valdivia, as well as the first commander of the Escuela Militar.[8]

The need to modernize military equipment ushered in the second phase of foreign influence. Beginning in the 1840s, for example, Chile purchased its uniforms, Minié rifles, and other weapons, including heavy coastal artillery, from France. To insure that these large, expensive guns functioned properly, the Moneda, the seat of Chile's executive branch, hired the services of three French artillery experts while sending 13 Chileans to study in France. Two officers, Francisco Gana and Luis Arteaga, graduated from the Metz Artillery School and then served in the French army. José Donoso first studied both artillery and engineering, before returning to Chile where he labored to build coastal fortifications. Other officers also studied engineering or acquired cartography skills.[9]

The traffic across the Atlantic was not one way. In 1857, two French lieutenant colonels, Juillet and Chamoux, arrived in Santiago to work at the *Escuela Militar* and to train the army's *Regimiento de Artilleria*, as well as the cavalry. Five years later, the army imposed the regulations controlling the Saint Cyr, France's military academy, on Chile's *Escuela Militar*.[10] As weapons became too sophisticated for its local arsenals to produce, the Chilean government systematically replaced the aging Miniés with French-made Gras and then Chassepot rifles.[11] In the late 1870s, it would standardize its small arms by acquiring large quantities of the Belgian Comblain II.

Chile would go to war in 1879 when, for the second time in less than 40 years, it faced a coalition of Peru and Bolivia. Ultimately Santiago's armed forces triumphed, but in the process the civilian government realized that the nation's military needed reforming, particularly with Bolivia and Peru threatening a revanchist war. Not surprisingly, with the memory of Germany's victory in the Franco-Prussian War still fresh, Santiago turned to Berlin for help. As Chile's ambassador to Kaiser Wilhelm II noted, Germany's army "is the best there is in organization and conduct, and if Chile does not wish to lose the land it has conquered [as a consequence of the War of the Pacific], it is necessary that it provide substantial and serious attention to the powerful element which guarantees the life of a nation and is educated and equipped to defend its liberty and sustain progress."[12] Thus, in 1885, President Domingo Santa María won the approval of the Prussian government to hire the services of Emilio Körner, the commoner captain from Saxony, to modernize its land forces.

Körner quickly made his presence felt. Assisted by two other German officers, Captain Hugo Januskowski and Major Gustavo Betzhold, he became the sub-director of the *Escuela Militar*, whose curriculum he modernized. A few years later he helped fashion the *Academia de Guerra*, an institution designed to provide General Staff training to the army's more senior officers.[13]

In January 1891, those political forces who resented what they saw as the heavy hand of the then president, José Manuel Balmaceda, rebelled. Most of the army remained loyal to the embattled chief executive, but Chile's navy sided with the insurgents, transporting the rebels to Chile's north where they established a temporary capital which became the center of the anti-government army. Among those military officers who embraced the Congressional cause was Körner, who became the rebel forces' chief of staff, and in the process, won a promotion to colonel. Körner, who never suffered from a lack of self-esteem, would subsequently proclaim that he had led the insurgent forces to defeat the army of Balmaceda. In fact, the Chilean, General Estanislao del Canto, not Körner, directed the rebel triumph. Körner, however, who emerged from the war as a brigadier general, quickly became the de facto head of the Chilean army.[14]

The new general had some political fences to mend: when he had sided with the revolutionaries, Körner had violated Kaiser William II's direct order not to become involved in the 1891 Revolution. Normally, the Saxon would have been in deep trouble, but Germany's envoys to Chile advocated that Berlin forgive the officer's indiscretion. The reason for this clemency was quite simple: Körner indicated that he would use his influence to purchase German weapons for the new Chilean army.[15]

Körner lost no time achieving this goal. In 1892, at Körner's behest, the Chilean army sold its virtually new Austrian Mannlicher repeating rifles, the weapons which proved responsible for the rebel victories at the battles of Concón and Placilla, replacing these with the carbines and rifles fabricated by the German arms manufacturer, Paul Mauser.

In 1894, Körner visited Germany, where he persuaded Kaiser William II – who did not require much convincing – to send a military mission to Chile. Within months, 31 German officers arrived in Valparaiso, the nation's principal port. Under Körner, Chile tried to become a copy of the Prussian army. By 1906, the nation was divided into four military zones, each defended by a division composed of two infantry brigades, one of cavalry and one of artillery. He also assigned to each division machine gun units, engineer, and supply personnel, as well as mountain artillery. Later, he would make provisions for transportation units as well as those providing communication.

The new commander also created a General Staff, a unit which he initially headed, as well as schools to train non-commissioned officers, teach marksmanship, and provide maps. Subsequently, the army created schools for artillery, engineers, and cavalry officers.[16]

Under a 1900 law, the government replaced Chile's militia system with universal manhood conscription. Henceforth all men between 20 and 45 had to register with the authorities. Those selected, generally by lottery, served one year of active duty followed by nine years in the First Reserve. Once they had completed their initial term, these men passed to the Second Reserve where they remained liable for mobilization until 45. The government could recall veterans who belonged to either Reserve contingent.

Observers watching the revamped Chilean army pass in review could not help but be impressed by what they saw: men wearing German army uniforms, including the infamous *pickelhalbe* helmet, carrying German weapons, goose stepping to the tunes of German martial music played on German musical instruments; the Army even hired a German to teach them to dance. As Prince Henry, Kaiser Wilhelm's brother, gushed, the Chilean army had become a "miniature edition" of the Prussian military.[17]

Some Chileans questioned the beneficial effects of Körner's efforts, but not so the German armament manufacturers. Chile had purchased Krupp cannons before the War of the Pacific and continued to acquire new batteries after the war's successful conclusion. But thanks to the efforts of an utterly venal salesman, Albert Schinzinger, the House of Krupp managed to bribe enough Chilean army officers and local politicians so they purchased Krupp field artillery, mountain guns, as well as coastal defense cannons, even when competing equipment was superior. German companies like Mauser had similar success selling not merely their small arms and small arms ammunition but pistols, harnesses, saddles, and web equipment.

The weapons' sales served as the thin edge of Prussia's economic wedge. Germany became one of the largest purchasers of nitrate. In return, German industrialists provided Chile with railroad equipment, trolley cars, and electrical generating stations; German contractors built public works projects. By 1912, it was estimated that Germany supplied 80 percent of the 60 million marks worth of goods that Chile purchased, often with money borrowed from German banks.[18] The Chilean army appeared to be a clone of the Germans, sometimes with untoward results: Chilean officers visiting France had to flee when the local population, believing that they were Prussian officers because of their uniforms, attacked them.

Not surprisingly, various Latin-American nations turned to the Chileans hoping that they too would become soldiers in the Prussian mold. In short, Chile's army became complicit in Germany's attempt to spread its influence, and its weapons, throughout Latin America. In 1892, Chileans founded and helped staff Ecuador's *Escuela Militar*, its *Escuela de Clases*, and its *Academia de Guerra*. The Chilean government also awarded scholarships to Ecuadorians who wished to attend Chile's *Escuela Militar*, some of whom later served with Chile's army. A Chilean military mission worked in Ecuador from 1901 until 1905. Under its aegis, Ecuador enacted a conscription law in 1905. The Chilean influence in Quito achieved two goals: it prevented the French from obtaining a foothold in the Andean nation and it virtually guaranteed that Ecuador would purchase German arms.[19] Although the Italians sent a team of military advisors in the 1920s, and the Americans after 1947, the Chileans returned in 1956 to lead a military mission and to staff the *Academia de Guerra*.

Other nations also sought Chilean assistance. In 1899, the Chileans responded to a Salvadorian request for military trainers. The first contingent arrived in 1901, and soon Chileans had created and helped staff Salvador's *Escuela Politécnica* – its military academy – as well as a school for infantry and artillery officers. Like the Ecuadorians, Salvadorian officers traveled to Chile where they enrolled in its *Escuela Militar*. Chilean officers became so embedded in the Salvadorian military that a few, including future president of Chile, Carlos Ibáñez del Campo, joined their Salvadorian students fighting against Guatemala. Although German and Italian advisors would subsequently become the dominant military force in Salvador, some Chilean officers returned in 1950 to build the *Escuela de Guerra*.[20]

Colombia was the last country to request and receive a military assistance from Chile. Beginning in 1907, the first of four military missions arrived in Colombia. Beginning in 1906, the Chilean advisors created educational institutions to train officers and non-commissioned officers for the Colombian army, as well as organizations to administer the army; Santiago also agreed to train Colombian cadets in its *Escuela Militar*. Chile's military exercised its greatest influence prior to World War I. Santiago would send another mission in 1958. Colombian officers would also attend various Chilean military schools including the Academia de Guerra and the Academia Politécnica.[21]

By 1911, Chilean instructors had also worked in Nicaragua, Guatemala, and Honduras, although apparently not as part of a military mission. Three officers, acting on their own, served with Bolivia's army in its war with Paraguay in the 1930s. One, Aquiles Vergara, remained, becoming a Bolivian national and eventually retiring with the rank of general. (Ironically, Bernardino Caballero, a young Paraguayan officer graduate of Santiago's *Escuela Militar*, perished in the same Chaco War.) The Venezuelan government also hired a retired general, Carlos Vergara, to restructure the army and to educate some of its officers.[22]

Ironically, at the same time that Chile's neighbors requested help in embracing the German military ethos, problems began to plague Chile's army. First, the system of conscription utterly failed to create a citizen army. Only the uneducated and the poor, those, who one author noted, suffered from "alcohol, the *conventillo* [urban slum housing] and syphilis" seemed to be called to the colors.[23] Worse, once they completed their military service, the recruits disappeared because the authorities did not possess a system to keep track of the army's veteran soldiers. Thus, when the government wanted to mobilize its reserves to celebrate Chile's first centenary, or in 1920, when it feared a war with Bolivia, it could not find enough men with prior service to fill its ranks. Nor did it have sufficient officers to lead the conscript army. Similar problems afflicted the officer class: a combination of slow promotions and wretched pay forced many young subalterns to retire while discouraging others from joining.[24]

A lack of funding compounded the army's personnel problems. Simply put, the Chilean oligarchy that controlled the political system did not appear willing to allocate sufficient funds to recruit, equip, and maintain a large army. Worse, corruption in the ministry of war and the supply process absorbed the army's limited resources while sapping its morale. Seeing civilian politicians and provisioners appropriating or misspending the budget, some military officers imitated Körner's example by taking bribes or selling their influence to the arms merchants. Those who did not often found themselves forced into early retirement.

Once World War I erupted, the Prussian advisors returned to Germany to defend their homeland. Four years earlier, Körner had retired to Berlin where, in 1920, he died. Although many Chileans had tired of the mania for all things German, the army still treasured don Emilio. His remains were repatriated to Chile where the army buried him in a special crypt built in his honor.

By 1920, Chile's political system began to collapse: the traditional political parties, which had come to power through vote buying, fraud, or violence, seemed neither willing nor able to address, let alone cure, the nation's pressing social and economic problems. The military, disgusted by the corruption, became honeycombed with conspiracies, each seeking to overthrow the system. A series of crises demonstrated the utter incapacity of Chile's political elites and system of government: a postwar depression had reduced the world's need for raw materials, driving thousands of Chileans out of work and into the capital where they begged the government for assistance. In that same year, fearing a war with Bolivia, the Chilean government tried to mobilize its army and send it north. The War Scare of 1920, as it came to be called, demonstrated the decay into which the army had fallen: the government could not find, let alone, mobilize, and equip its reservists; a lack of transportation hampered the movement of the soldiers and their equipment to the north, and, once in place, the troops suffered from a lack of weapons and uniforms.[25]

Although some officers, such as Colonel Luis Cabrera, tried to gloss over the problems afflicting the army, the combination of the postwar economic crash and the failed mobilization galvanized the army.[26] Officers began to plot to change the political system in order to make it more responsive to the nation's needs. Two military coups, those of 1924 and 1925, forced an end to civilian government.

Berlin's influence waned after World War I, particularly since the Treaty of Versailles prohibited the German army from sending advisors. The Chileans did, however, hire the services of various individual German officers, who by claiming that since they resided in the Free city of Danzig they were not citizens of the Weimar Republic.

Perhaps tired of subterfuge, in the early 1920s, President Arturo Alessandri sent various officers to study at the US Army Command and General Staff College, Chemical Warfare Arsenal, and Signal School. The Chilean army also diversified its weapons: French Schneiders replaced the Krupp cannons; Japanese Hotchkiss and American Browning machine guns supplanted the German Maxims.

This tendency accelerated after 1940, when the United States became the most powerful military force in the western hemisphere, the only nation that could provide weapons, artillery, and armored vehicles. While some Latin-American nations benefited from Washington's wartime generosity, Chile was not one of them: its refusal to break openly with the Axis, until 1945, discouraged the United States from sending large quantities of weapons. The advent of the Cold War, however, altered this situation. After 1952, a treaty called for the United States to provide not simply weapons, but the technical skills to use them. Increasingly, Chilean officers received training either in US Army Service schools or at the School for the Americas in the Panama Canal Zone.

The overthrow of the regime of Salvador Allende (1970–1973) in 1973 led to the US Congress, and some European nations, to embargo the sale of weapons to Chile. The military government of General Augusto Pinochet responded by encouraging the creation of a domestic arms industry – which produced weapons like cluster bombs – and diversifying its sources of more sophisticated weapons. Today, Chile's army uses German Leopard tanks, Swiss small arms, Italian and South African artillery, and Swiss–Brazilian armored personnel vehicles. Since Chile's return to democracy in 1990, the country has used more conventional means of obtaining weapons.

The Chilean navy

Foreigners seemed to exercise a greater influence on the Chilean navy than its army. In part, this phenomenon may have occurred because since the Spanish navy had never established a strong presence in the Eastern Pacific, these waters "became for the [Spanish] Empire a vast desert, barely utilized by local commerce."[27] Second, the Spanish naval officer corps was so small, particularly after the losses it sustained in the Battle of Trafalgar, that it did not have enough officers or seamen to man its own undersized fleet, let alone command the ships of a rebellious colony. Given Spain's weakness, and Britain's strength, most of the Chilean fleet's senior officers were former Royal Navy officers, including its commander, Lord Thomas Cochrane, as well as men of less rank such as Santiago Bynon, Roberto Forester, Roberto Henson, Raimundo Morris, Carlos Warner, Guillermo Wilkinson, and John Williams. Given the absence of war in Europe, many of these Britons, as well as some Americans, such as Pablo Delano, Eduardo Hyatt and Charles Whitting, remained. One family, that of Robert Simpson, established a naval dynasty that contributed three admirals.[28]

Curiously, the foreign presence in the Chilean fleet remained strong well into the nineteenth century. In part, their involvement was a function of technology: as ships became more complicated, particularly after the adoption of steam power, the Chilean navy needed more technically proficient officers. Although the *Escuela Naval*, founded in 1857, could satisfy the need for deck officers, it did not train engineers. To obtain these technicians, the fleet had to hire foreigners or wait until the newly created *Escuela de Artes y Oficios* began to graduate engineering personnel. By 1863, for example, the fleet had 12 engineers, nine of whom were foreigners.[29]

Just as Chile lacked facilities to produce the new cannons, it could not produce large ships. Beginning in the late 1840s, the firm of Juan Duprat launched a schooner, a sloop, as well two smaller vessels; it even constructed the corvette *Constitución* in 1851. In addition to building these vessels, Duprat, as well as Martín Stevenson, possessed facilities to repair ships, while other shipyards functioned in the ports of Constitución and Chiloé. Later, in 1864, Duprat built a wooden drydock, *Valparaiso*, which could repair steam driven merchant vessels.[30] This facility, however, could not accommodate the navy's larger ironclads.

If Chileans could not manufacture steam driven warships, they clearly could not produce armored clad vessels. Thus, beginning in 1866, when it sought to acquire two corvettes, the *O'Higgins* and the *Chacabuco*, Chile had to purchase armored vessels from British shipyards. Within a few years, Santiago obtained another composite corvette, the *Abtao*, from the United States, and a composite gunboat, the *Magallanes*, from England. In less than a decade, the Chileans purchased two more armored warships, the *Almirante Cochrane* and the *Almirante Blanco Encalada*, from the British shipbuilding firm of Armstrong.

Unfortunately, just as technological changes outstripped the ability of Chile's foundries to produce advanced models of small arms and artillery, these same forces limited the role of local naval facilities to repairing its most modern vessels. In 1877, Chile had to send one of its armored ships, the *Almirante Cochrane*, back to England to replace the zinc plates protecting its wooden hull. Nor could the shipyards in Valparaiso, Valdivia, or Antofagasta resolve less complex problem. During the War of the Pacific, for example, the Chilean fleet had to use divers to scrape away the barnacles from its biggest ships' bottoms. It also became clear that the *Escuela Naval* could not impart the new technology to its midshipmen.

To address this problem, the Chileans began assigning young officers to serve with the Royal Navy. One of these, Patricio Lynch, for example, served with the British fleet during the Opium Wars before returning to Chile. Indeed, at the onset of the War of the Pacific (1879–1884), the Chilean navy had to order Policarpo Toro and Alberto Silva Palma to leave their Royal Navy ships and return home immediately.[31]

The refusal of the United States and Great Britain to sell war materiel to the Chilean government during the War of the Pacific limited but did not stop their nationals from illegally trading in weapons. Chile managed to take delivery of some torpedo boats, thanks, in part to its envoy to Great Britain, Alberto Blest Gana who sent these disassembled vessels – falsely labeled – to Chile.[32]

Chile's victory in the War of the Pacific did not usher in a period of tranquility. Bolivia, and particularly Peru, threatened to unleash a revanchist war. These Andean nations did not constitute Chile's only enemies. Anxious to push its border to the east and to assert its sovereignty over the strategic Strait of Magellan, Argentina began to spend millions to purchase a blue-water navy. Chile believed it had no choice but to respond in kind. Thus during the regimes of Domingo Santa María (1881–1886) and José Manuel Balmaceda (1886–1891), Chile acquired three battleships, the *Captain Prat*, the *Pinto*, and the *Errázuriz*, from France. The rest of the fleet, however, came from English shipyards, particularly those of Armstrong.

Chile's historically close ties to the Royal Navy – which organized the Chilean Navy's *Escuela Naval Superior* in 1911 – reinforced the tendency of Chileans to purchase English vessels. Still, both the United States and German shipbuilders hoped to sell warships to Chile's navy. And Admiral Jorge Montt, the successful leader of the rebel fleet of 1891, seriously considered loosening Albion's grip on the fleet. In late 1906, he indicated to the German naval commander that he would like to send some junior officers to serve with the Kaiser's fleet. He also indicated that he hoped to visit German dockyards with an eye to purchasing some of its warships, including two 12,000 ton battleships.

Although the Kaiser and his diplomatic envoys encouraged Montt's fantasies, Admiral Alfred von Tirpitz, the architect of the new German navy, did not. He had just launched Germany's response to the British dreadnoughts, and he wished to insure that no one would learn about the new ships' specifications. And since Tirpitz considered each "Chilean naval officer a potential British agent," he would not permit them to serve in the Kaiser's fleet or have access to Germany's shipyards. Apparently, the Kaiser seemed willing to bypass Tirpitz: he offered to open up the dockyards but only if the Chileans promised to buy German ships.[33] When they did not, the shipyards remained closed.

The danger of relying upon a single nation for naval weapons, however, became clear in 1914. In 1910, Chile had embarked upon a major naval expansion program, calling for the acquisition of two dreadnoughts, the *Valparaiso* and *Santiago*, six destroyers, and two submarines. (The Chileans would subsequently change the names of the capital ships: the *Valparaiso* became the *Admiral Latorre*; the *Santiago*, *Admiral Cochrane*.) However, when World War I erupted, the British seized those ships it had not already delivered; the Canadian navy acquired the submarines. By the time the conflict ended, the *Cochrane* had become an aircraft carrier, leaving the Chileans with one, very used, battleship, the *Latorre*. As an act of contrition, the British had earlier given the Chileans four US-made submarines, vessels it had ordered but could not take because of the neutrality laws; it also supplied 50 planes for the air force.

The Chilean government used its fleet, like its army, to win friends amongst its neighbors. In 1907, Capitan de Corbeta Alberto Asmussen – who bore a striking resemblance to Britain's King George V – landed in Cartegena, Colombia, where he organized its *Escuela Naval*. Operating from moored ships, the new school graduated a handful of *guardia marinas*, some of whom went to Chile, and others to Spain, to complete their naval education. In 1951, Chile, which sent a team of four officers to train officers for the merchant marine, continued training Colombian personnel until 1959. In 1912, Chile sent a naval expert to assist the Ecuadorian navy. Earlier, in 1907, Chile sold a used destroyer, the *Almirante Simpson*, to Ecuador. Chile sent a naval mission to Paraguay, in 1931, as well as trained midshipmen from Paraguay and Uruguay at its Escuela Naval.[34]

The British continued to influence post-World War I Chile. Although President Arturo Alessandri wanted the United States to assign a naval mission to Chile, the fleet's officers preferred the English. In 1926, the British seconded some officers to Chile where they served as technical advisors. This stratagem permitted the English to operate as if it were a mission without exercising command positions. Only in 1927 did the British and Chilean authorities fuse the advisors into a single entity that would reform the Chilean fleet. Thanks to the British, the *Escuela Naval*, that revised its course of study, also began training both line and engineering officers. The fleet's training manuals were modified, as was the supply system. Various Chilean warships, including the *Latorre*, were sent to England for modernization.[35]

Chile's attempts to purchase two cruisers, in the late 1930s, failed. Although the Italians and Dutch indicated a willingness to provide these items to Chile, the British and Americans managed to sabotage the deal. American influence grew after World War II. Its refusal to sell Chilean surplus ships forced them to acquire these from Canada or Britain. Only in 1951, with the advent of the Cold War, did Washington sell Chile two *Brooklyn* class cruisers. It also provided opportunities to buy some destroyers, as well as some naval aircraft, including helicopters. Approximately 375 Chilean naval personnel attended US civilian and military schools between 1945 and 1975.[36]

In 1960, Chile created (ASMAR) *Astilleros y Maestranzas de la Armada*, Naval Shipyards and Workshops, which permitted Chile to become somewhat independent of foreign weapons producers. ASMAR has manufactured smaller landing craft, a dry dock, as well as a transport, the *Aquiles*. Thanks to these facilities, Chile has diversified its sources, buying mainly surplus British ships – because the United States would not provide them – which its defense industries have modernized, including British *Country* class destroyers and *Leander* class frigates, as well as Dutch frigates, and submarines from France and Germany; it has also produced, under French license, fast attack boats.[37] Additionally, the Chilean fleet has acquired patrol ships from Israel – equipped with Gabriel rockets – Brazil, Holland, Sweden, Norway, and France. The nation's local shipyards produce its own patrol boats and landing ships.

Conclusion

As we have seen, the Prussians trained Chile's army while the British helped form its navy. Motives other than *noblesse oblige* influenced Berlin and London: thanks to the Prussian influence, the Chilean government purchased large quantities of German uniforms, materiel, small arms, coastal as well as field artillery, and technical equipment. And not surprisingly, the establishment of Chilean military missions in Salvador, Ecuador, and Columbia encouraged these host nations to mimic Chile's experience and to adopt German military doctrine and to purchase German military technology. Chile, in short, became a salesman for Krupp and Mauser.

Providing military aid allowed the Germans to shape not simply Chile's armed forces, but to participate in its civilian economy. Building upon the local immigrant population, which was particularly significant in Chile's south, German interests utilized their military advisors to establish a network of banks, as well as cultural and economic institutions, including mining companies, commercial houses, and shipping lines, throughout the country. German nationals also controlled companies providing Valparaíso and Santiago with public transit and the electrical energy. By 1914, Germany had become one of Chile's most important trading partners. This economic involvement gave the German government a means to exercise political leverage. Thanks to the German influence in the army, for example, Chile remained neutral in the 1914–1918 war and only belatedly entered World War II in 1945.

The British, which early established an economic presence in Chile, also became involved in the new nation's naval development. Given England's position as the world's premier maritime power, London would continue to influence Chile's fleet and train its officers. Chile's decision to launch naval missions of its own, as well as to educate a generation of midshipmen from nearby Latin-American nations, magnified Britain's impact, as well as that of Santiago. As we have seen, although the United States became increasingly involved in training both Chile's army and navy in the years after World War II, European influence did not disappear.

Ironically, various Chileans came to doubt the value of foreign missions. As General Arturo Auhmada, an officer who served in the army during the Körner reforms, concluded that the foreign military instructors may have failed: "They," Auhmada noted, "tried to sow foreign seed and what have grown in Chile in special soil, [failed to take root] in land that was without preparation, full of weeds, or in some parts, unsuitable for cultivation."[38]

Still, Chile occupies a unique place among the Latin-American nations: it was the first nation to contract with the Germans to modernize its armed forces. Indeed, by 1900, Chile became known as the Prussia of the Pacific. Even if, in fact, Santiago did not deserve this reputation, it nontheless made its enemies think twice before launching some anti-Chilean adventure. Later, Chile would create military and naval missions of its own, using the military and naval skills that it had acquired from Europe and, to a lesser extent, the United States, to shape the armed forces of its neighbors. These missions enhanced Chile's reputation in Latin America, allowing the government to forge political relationships with neighboring nations and to gain allies in the arena of international conflict.

Notes

1 Frank McCann, *Soldiers of the Patria* (Stanford: Stanford University Press, 2004), pp. 100–1, 200; Marvin, Goldwert, "The Rise of Modern Militarism in Argentina," *Hispanic American Historical Review*, 48:2 (1968), p. 191 (hereafter cited as *HAHR*). Bolivia would also employ missions from Danzig – an artifice which allowed La Paz to hire German trainers – Spain, Czechoslovakia, and Italy. Julio Diaz A., *Historia del Ejército de Bolivia, 1825–1932* (La Paz: Editorial don Bosco, 1971), pp. 641–55; Warren Schiff, "German Military Penetration into Mexico During the Late Diaz Period," *HAHR*, 39:4 (1959), pp. 568–79; Marvin Goldwert, *Militarism and Nationalism in Argentina, 1930–1966* (Austin: The University of Texas Press, 1972), p. 61; León E. Bieber, "La política militar alemana en Bolivia, 1900–1935," *Latin American Research Review*, 29:1 (1994), p. 87.
2 Victor Villanueva, *100 Años del ejército peruano: frustración y cambios* (Lima: J. Mejía Baca, 1971), pp. 63–64; *Historia de la Escuela Militar del Peru* (Lima: n.p., 1962), p. 36.
3 Patricia Arancibia, *La Marina de Chile* (Santiago: Sudamericana, 2005), Vol. I, pp. 98, 123–4, 133–6, 208; Carlos Tromben, *La Armada de Chile desde la alborada hasta el final del siglo XX* (Valparaíso: Imprenta de la Marina, 2001), pp. 1623–33.
4 Sergio Vergara Quiroz, *Historia Social del Ejército de Chile* (Santiago: Departamento Tecnico de Investigaciones, Universidad de Chile, 1993), Vol. I, p. 177.
5 General Miguel Simón Contreras, "Influencia militar española en la formación del ejército de Chile," *Primera jornada de historia militar Siglos*, XVII–XIX (Santiago, 2004), pp. 60, 83, noted that although only 36.4 percent of Chilean army were composed of Spaniards, they dominated the most senior ranks. See also Emilio Körner and J. Boonen Rivera, *Estudios sobre historia militar* (Santiago: Imprenta Cervantes, 1887), Vol. II, p. 257.
6 Pablo Barrientos G., *Historia de la artilleria en Chile* (Santiago: Instituto Geografico Militar, 1946), pp. 141, 145, 160.
7 Hector Aravena, "La Escuela Militar a través de sus 150 años," *Boletin de la Academia Chilena de la Historia*, 76 (1967), p. 144.
8 Vergara, *Historia*, Vol. II, pp. 24, 167; Aravena, "La Escuela Militar," p. 144.
9 Barrientos, *Artilleria*, p. 172; Estado Mayor General del Ejército, *Historia del Ejército de Chile* (Santiago: n.p., 1983), Vol. IV, pp. 52–3.
10 Aravena, "La Escuela Militar," p. 145; José Antonio Varas, *Recopilación de Leyes de 1859 a 1865*, p. 105, cited in Arancibia, *La Marina de Chile*, p. 95; Ejército, *Historia*, Vol. IV, p. 115.
11 Jean-Pierre Blancpain, *Les Allemands au Chili (1816–1945)* (Köln: Bohlau Verlag Koln Wien, 1974), p. 705.

40 *W.F. Sater*

12 A. Matta to Emilio Sotomayor, Berlin, 13 May 1883, *El Mercurio* (Santiago), 11 October 1925 quoted in General Roberto Arancibia Clavel, *La influencia del ejército chileno en América Latina*, Santiago: CSIM, 2002, p. 123
13 Ejército, *Historia*, Vol. VII, p. 325.
14 Emilio Körner, "Die historische Entwicklung der chilenischen Wherkraft," cited in Patricio Quiroga and Carlos Maldonado, *El prusianismo en las fuerzas armadas chilenas* (Santiago: Ediciones DOCUMENTAS, 1988), pp. 196–200.
15 Jürgen Schaefer, *Deutsche Militärhilfe an Südamerika. Militär und Rüstungsinteressen in Argentinien, Bolivien und Chile cor 1914* (Dusseldorf: Bertelsmann Universitätsverlag, 1974), pp. 27–8.
16 Schaefer, *Deutsche Militärhilfe*, pp. 42–51.
17 William Sater and Holger Herwig, *The Grand Illusion: The Prussianization of the Chilean Army* (Lincoln: University of Nebraska Press, 1999), p. 202; Gonzalo Vial, *Historia de Chile* (Santiago: Santilliana, 1981), Vol. I, Tomo 2, p. 787.
18 Sater and Herwig, *The Grand Illusion*, pp. 171–2; Stefam Rinke, "Las relaciones germano-chilenas, 1918–1933," *Historia*, 31 (1998), pp. 218–19.
19 Ferenc Fisher, "La espansión indirecta de la ciencia militar alemana en América Latina del Sur: La cooperación militar entre Alemania y Chile y las misiones militares germanófilas chilenas en los países latinoamericanos, 1885–1914," in *Tordesilla y sus consecuencias: la política de las grandes potencias europeas respecto a América Latina, 1491–1899* (Frankfurt and Madrid: Iberamericana, 1995), p. 247.
20 Arancibia, *La influencia*, p. 339.
21 Arancibia, *La influencia*, pp. 391–475.
22 Ejército, *Historia*, Vol. VIII, pp. 153–4.
23 Dr José Salas, "Sobre la profilaxía de las efermedades venéreas en el Ejército," in *Memorial del Ejército de Chile* (Julio, 1911), p. 36; *El Merurio* (Santiago), 24 July 1911 (hereafter MERS).
24 Sater and Herwig, *The Grand Illusion*, pp. 94, 108–14; MERS, 14–16 July 1910.
25 Carlos Saez, *Recuerdos de un soldado* (Santiago: Ediciones Ercilla, 1933), Vol. I, pp. 31–2.
26 Interview with Colonel Luis Cabrera, MERS, 21 December 1921, cited in Roberto Arancibia Clavel, "La movilización de 1920," unpub. ms, pp. 26–27.
27 Arancibia, *La marina en la historia de Chile*, p. 23.
28 Richard Longeville Vowell, *Campañas y cruceros en el Océano Pacífico* (3rd edn; Buenos Aires: Editorial Francisco Aguirre, 1968).
29 Carlos Tromben, *Ingenieria naval una especialidad centenaria* (Valparaíso: Imprenta de la Armada, 1989), p. 42.
30 Rodrigo Fuenzalida Bade, *La Aramada de Chile desde la alborada al sesquicentenario (1813–1968)* (Valparaíso: Imprenta de la Armada, n.d.), Vol. II, pp. 526–8.
31 M. Salisbury, A Blest, 21 April 1879, Public Record Office, Foreign Office 16/204–116 (hereafter cited as FO).
32 W.P. Moore, Acting Collector, Hull Custom House, 24 July 1979, FO 205/204–10; John Holker *et al.* to Marquis of Salisbury, 8 August 1879, FO 16/204–132 (Temple Bar).
33 Ferenc Fischer, "Un ejemplo de una modernización dependiente: las fuerzas armadas Chilenas y la influencia militar prusiana desde el punto de vista de fuentes alemanas (Segun documentos de la marina, 1905–1914)," in *Europa e Ibero América. Unos siglos de intercambios:actos Europa e Iberamérica* (Sevilla: Asociacón de historiadores latinoamericanistas Europeos, 1992), pp. 736–7.
34 Robert L. Scheina, *Latin America. A Naval History, 1810–1987* (Annapolis: United States Naval Institute Press, 1987), p. 142.

35 Philip Somervell, "Naval Affairs in Chilean Politics, 1910–1932," *Journal of Latin American Studies*, 16 (1984), pp. 394–7.
36 Tromben, *La Armada*, p. 1636.
37 José Maldifassi and Pier Abetti, *Defense Industries in Latin American Countries* (Westport, CT: Praeger, 1994), pp. 102–5.
38 Arturo Ahumada, *El ejército y la revolución del 5 de Septiembre de 1924* (Santiago: n.p., n.d.), p. 38.

4 Buying influence, selling arms, undermining a friend

The French naval mission to Poland and the development of the Polish Navy, 1923–1932

Donald Stoker

The aftermath of World War I in Eastern Europe saw the emergence of a number of independent states from the shattered remains of the German, Russian, Austrian, and Turkish empires. Poland was one of these and, like its compatriots, established naval forces as one of the planks of its national defense. From early in its existence the Polish navy benefited from the assistance of foreign advisors. The help the Polish army received from the French is well known, but few know of the French naval mission to Poland and its impact on the creation of a Polish naval force. But the mission's dispatch to the new state was hardly magnanimous. Beginning in the late-nineteenth century one of the primary purposes of military missions was to sell arms. This practice continued into the period between the world wars, and the French mission to Poland provides an excellent picture of the interconnectedness between military advising, the arms trade, and alliance politics. In Poland the French sought influence, and fought the British for it, but they sought it to sell weapons, often of dubious quality, and to weld Poland to its own strategy for a future, expected war with Germany.

The Baltic and Anglo-French rivalry

In the immediate aftermath of World War I, France and Great Britain (particularly France) struggled to build a cordon sanitaire from the new states in Eastern Europe to box in Germany, as well as separate it from the other pariah nation, Bolshevik Russia. France also sought to construct an alliance system in Eastern Europe to replace the loss of Russia in its strategic calculations vis-à-vis Germany. Poland was the linchpin of French strategy in the region.[1]

But more important was economic penetration and, if possible, domination of the region. One of the arenas of Anglo-French competition was arms sales, including naval armaments, and the path to strengthening one's deal-making hand was the installation of a naval advisor or, even better, an entire naval mission.

Poland's navy and the British advisors

Poland founded its navy on 28 November 1918, a scant 17 days after the Polish declaration of independence. Captain Bogumil Nowotny, a former Austro-Hungarian naval officer, became its first head. He was soon succeeded in 1919 by Rear Admiral Kazimierz Porębski, a veteran of the Tsarist navy. Porębski was not immediately convinced of the possibility of the existence of a Polish navy, which he proved by wearing the uniform of an army general.[2] The initial craft of the reborn naval force were a motley collection of river and coastal vessels of diverse parentage hastily pressed into service.[3]

But the Poles wanted a naval force capable of defending their coastline and sought advisors to organize and train it. From September 1919 to February 1922 Poland enjoyed the services of a short-lived British naval mission and then a British naval advisor. Financial concerns killed both efforts.[4] Sir Horace Rumbold, the British ambassador to Warsaw, predicted, correctly, that the British mission's withdrawal would see the Poles turn to France for naval advice.[5]

The French naval mission – why?

In January 1922 the Poles asked France for an officer to help organize their navy. By July, the request had blossomed into Admiral Porębski requesting an entire naval advisory mission. Initially, the French saw little in the way of strategic possibilities for the weak Polish naval force, but they believed that Porębski's intent was to establish a foundation for 'the strategic cooperation of the French Navy in operations in Poland.'[6] Porębski seems to have been looking for ways to bind the French to Poland, not an unwise decision, and held out naval cooperation as the bait.

The French navy soon proved an eager bridegroom. Poland's geographic position, as well as its desire to build a small fleet, fit perfectly into French naval strategy. In the early 1920s the French navy envisioned having to fight Germany and Italy – without British support. The existence of a Polish fleet provided an additional threat against the Germans. Moreover, in 1922 France signed the Washington naval treaties. These had well-known strictures on capital ships, but they also limited the total tonnage of smaller classes of vessels. In the Polish navy the French found a loophole: small states were not subject to the treaty's strictures. Seeing it as politically inexpedient to allow anyone else to help organize the Polish navy, Raiberti, the French naval minister, assigned then Commander Charles Jolivet the task.[7]

The Poles though, still had to build a navy. They considered a number of plans, most beyond their industrial and financial ability.[8] Eventually basing their decision on a proposal prepared by Jolivet, the Polish parliament appropriated funding for nine submarines, six torpedo carrying and three minelaying. The fact that the French drew up the Polish naval program clearly demonstrates the measure of influence in naval matters that France and its naval mission possessed. Competition for the contracts began immediately, the Poles receiving initial inquiries from firms in France, Great Britain, Italy, and the United States.[9]

The British proved the major French competitor, but their offers foundered on London's refusal to promise basing rights to the vessels in the event of the loss of the port of Gdynia.[10] The French, who had a military alliance with Poland, could make the base offer more easily than the non-aligned British. At this point, French naval influence in Poland solidified, a situation that lasted until 1932.

In March 1925 the Poles decided to build the nine submarines in France over a four-year period and ordered their navy to only entertain bids from French firms. This was the result France wanted for military, industrial, as well as commercial reasons discussed momentarily.[11] The presence of Jolivet and his mission no doubt assured this.

The French deals

After reaching its decision to purchase its submarines from a French firm, the Polish Ministry of National Defense dispatched a mission to Paris. Under the leadership of Admiral Właclaw Kłoczkowski, the organization's members had the task of examining the various construction projects proposed to Poland by French builders and reporting the value of each offering to their government.[12]

The Poles wanted the submarines constructed over a four-year period and allowed 18 months for the completion of each boat, the delivery dates being staggered so as to have one of the vessels reach completion about every six months. The Poles asked that each offering include a rough draft of the design of the proposed submarine, with detailed specifications, and a copy of a contractual agreement. They also preferred to confer the contract on a single French firm or to have one company build the six torpedo submarines and another build the three minelaying boats. The Polish request did not mention price.[13]

Numerous individual French firms and consortia competed for the contracts. They included Les Chantiers Naval Français de Caen, l'Union de Cinq Chantiers Français, Ateliers de la Gironde, les Forges et Chantiers de la Méditerranée, les Chantiers de St. Nazaire, les Chantiers de France, as well as a group composed of Chantiers Augustin-Normand, Chantiers de la Loire, and Schneider. Some of the French firms encouraged the French navy to involve itself directly in the negotiations for the contracts. Its representatives agreed to provide technical data but preferred that the Polish government handle any contractual matters, as well as instigate any preliminary discussions. The French navy also refused to examine in detail the validity of the projects submitted by the competing firms. The service's leadership believed that the time involved for such an endeavor would detract from the effort it needed to devote to its own new construction. Additionally, the navy wanted to limit its involvement because it did not feel qualified to deal with the financial questions that such circumstances inevitably produced.[14]

The great number of French firms interested in the contracts did not set well with Paris. The government consistently urged them to unite in an effort to thwart competitors from other countries, but the pleas had limited effect. In the end, it seems that all the government could do on this matter was to instruct Jolivet to remain neutral when deciding between the contenders.[15]

The Poles wanted two types of submarines, standard torpedo-armed boats displacing 700 tons and minelaying vessels of 950 tons. The torpedo submarines envisaged were actually superior to those of the French navy in many respects, including radius of action, stability, buoyancy, and diving time. In regard to the minelaying vessels, French naval officials expressed some doubt that they could have the armament, speed, and radius of action required by the Poles and still meet the 950 ton limit. Outlining requirements that went beyond what many of the contractors thought they could deliver was part of the naval strategy of Admiral Jerzy Swirski, who became head of the Polish navy in 1925. Swirski, realizing that Poland would never have very many vessels, insisted that Polish ships be qualitatively superior to other models in their respective classes.[16] Moreover, the same realization led the Poles to demand simple and robust submarines in the hopes of having the maximum number at sea simultaneously. In the period prior to World War II, large navies generally only expected to have one-third of their submarines on station in the combat area. The other two-thirds would be either undergoing repair or journeying to or from the operational zone. This did not suit the needs of the Poles as they wanted to avoid having their ships laid up for extended periods undergoing maintenance and repair. Also tied to this concern was the knowledge that it would take Polish crews quite some time to acquire the technical expertise to deal with the most complicated machinery. A simple design would also help alleviate some maintenance issues.[17]

Admiral Kłoczkowski and his mission examined all of the offers, weeding out any unsuitable proposals.[18] By September 1925 the Poles had narrowed the competition to three groups of builders: Les Chantiers Navals Français de Caen, l'Union de Cinq Chantiers Français, and the Normand/Loire/Schneider group.[19]

The Poles first struck Chantiers Navals Français from the list, even though their case had been strongly lobbied by the Polish Ambassador to Paris, Alfred Chłapowski. Chłapowski argued that financial concerns made Chantiers Navals Français a good choice because the deal could then be financed by the Paris-Bas Bank. Chłapowski neglected to mention that this bank owned a significant interest in Chantiers Navals Français. The ambassador pushed hard for his chosen builder, insisting that quality would be assured, that they were 20 percent cheaper than the Normand group and that the faults of this firm, which had apparently been pointed out by the French navy, were hardly serious ones. Moreover, he asked that if the committee could not give them the full order, perhaps it could give them part of the order if they would work with firms of the defense ministry's choosing.[20]

Chłapowski's pleas fell on deaf ears. Chantiers Naval Français was eliminated from the competition for the submarines for, among other reasons, two of the same points that struck another contender from the list: no experience building submarines and the advice of Admiral Jolivet, the head of the French naval mission.[21] In all of this the obvious question is, Why did Chłapowski push so hard for Chantiers Navals Français? One author suggests that French internal corruption played a part in the eventual purchase decision,[22] and indeed he is correct, but corruption goes two ways.

One of the other remaining bidders, L'Union de Cinq Chantiers Français de Constructions Navales, had no formal, legal existence, being simply a marriage of opportunity among three of the firms competing for the submarine contracts. The trio, Société des Forges & Chantiers de la Méditerranée, Société des Chantiers et Ateliers de St. Nazaire, and Société des Ateliers et Chantiers de France, united in the quest for the contracts at the end of 1924 but intended for their relationship to be a temporary one. Between them, the three firms had five shipbuilding yards in France, hence the name. They campaigned for the contracts partially on the basis of the reputation and experience of their chief engineer, Monsieur Doyère, who had served as the director general of naval construction for the French naval ministry. While in the employ of the French navy, he had served as the chief engineer overseeing some of the latest French submarine designs, as well as their construction.[23]

The Union de Cinq Chantiers submitted the low bid among the final three competitors. It was 7.5 percent lower but did not win them the contract. They believed that one of the weaknesses of their hand was that despite the experience of their engineers and workers, they had never built a submarine. The firm's competitors used this as a weapon against them in what soon shaped up into a nasty fight between the various French rivals. The other French firms sarcastically branded Cinq Chantiers 'Chantier n'ayant pas construit' (the builder who has never built). Because of this the firm, despite the technical superiority of its boats, had decided that it had to offer a lower price to compete.[24]

Lastly, the Poles considered the Normand/Loire/Schneider group. This combination had the only experience in submarine construction among the three finalists. Schneider had built 15 such vessels, Normand, one other. The three firms entered into an agreement to divide any work derived from the orders. If they won the contract, Loire would build either the standard torpedo-equipped submarines or the minelaying boats, Normand would construct the other class, and Schneider, the engines for at least one of the categories. To the Poles, who wanted to avoid any risk in the matter, the Normand group seemed the best choice. Jolivet also encouraged the Commission to select this experienced group if Poland wanted to reduce the possibility of adverse results.[25]

On 11 September 1925 General Sikorski, in his capacity as the minister of military affairs, decided to confer the contracts for the nine submarines on the Normand/Loire/Schneider consortium. One of the defeated contenders, Union des Cinq Chantiers Français, had contributed greatly to its own failure by a disastrous effort to apply pressure on General Sikorski. They organized a press campaign against the general and supplied parliamentary deputies with a memorandum that violently attacked Chantiers Navals Français de Caen and denounced the firm's inexperience in building submarines. They also attempted to vilify Admiral Swirski in the press by having articles run in the Sunday papers for a number of weeks that accused Swirski of incompetence and dishonesty and that asked how General Sikorski could have tolerated the Admiral for so long. Attacking Swirski was doubly stupid. He played a key role in influencing Poland's final decision and certainly had General Sikorski's ear. Jolivet had never given specific counsel to the Poles to exclude this firm's proposal, but he did, in a secret conference, approve Sikorski's intention to confer the contract on the more experienced Normand group.[26]

In some respects, it comes as a surprise that the Normand consortium received the contract. Their initial price exceeded that of the other firms by 18 percent. Realizing that this placed them in an inferior position in regard to the competition, they immediately reduced the price by about 10 percent, thereby making the difference more acceptable to Sikorski and the Commission.[27] Fortunately for the Normand group factors other than price played a role in the awarding of the contract. The Polish desire to take no chances on purchasing a vessel from a firm that had never previously constructed submarines played a critical role. Political and economic considerations also contributed.

Meanwhile the French government, undoubtedly unaware that a decision had already been made, tried to take an active hand in managing the competition. On 14 September 1925 Monsieur de Sorbier, the director of commercial affairs for the foreign ministry, tried to get the representatives of Chantiers Navals Français and the Normand/Loire/Schneider consortium to reach an understanding that would enable both groups to share in the Polish submarine contracts and insure the order went to the French.[28] Competition from multiple French firms always worried Paris. They preferred for French businessmen to form an entente and submit a joint proposal, thus easing the task of the local French political representative in making recommendations and undercutting non-French competitors. De Sorbier's effort failed, and the discussion between the firms was later described as 'rather animated' because the French builders had little interest in combining forces.[29]

But not everything was settled, and Alfred Chłapowski, the Polish ambassador to Paris, still had a part to play. Early in the process he had attached great importance to satisfying the Paris-Bas Bank and, as previously mentioned, made unsuccessful demands that the order for the submarines go to the Chantiers Navals Français de Caen, which was at least partly owned by Paris-Bas. He had not changed his mind and returned to the matter in October, journeying to Warsaw to try and influence the decision Sikorski and Swirski had already made.[30]

In addition to having the support of the bankers, Chantiers Naval Français counted a number of members of the French government among its stockholders. Connected to this was Poland's then ongoing effort to secure a large loan from Paris. The Polish Minister of Foreign Affairs, bowing to pressure from Chłapowski, also campaigned on their behalf. Sikorski was unwilling to abandon his decision, but he also proved unable to sufficiently deflect the desire of the Minister of Foreign Affairs. An effort to have the French navy render an opinion as to the best builder also failed, as the navy preferred to maintain its neutrality.[31]

When Ambassador Chłapowski arrived in Warsaw, he met in a closed-door session with General Sikorski. Admiral Swirski waited in the room outside. Sikorski came out and asked Swirski, 'Which ships are in the program next?' Obviously, the General meant the naval program. But Swirski had no naval program beyond the plan to build the nine submarines. He had assumed that these would keep the Polish navy occupied for sometime. Seizing the opportunity, Swirski instantly replied: 'Two large destroyers.' General Sikorski agreed immediately, provided that the order went to Chantiers Navals Français. Swirski gladly approved. The result: the Poles got two destroyers, and pleased the Paris-Bas Bank, which meant that Warsaw got its loan. Chantiers Navals Français was also happy, as were the corrupt French officials who had shares in their yards, which at the time had been lying idle.[32]

The result not only satisfied the Minister of Foreign Affairs, but also allowed Sikorski and Swirski to avoid the inherent risk involved in awarding the contract for the submarines to a firm that had never built them. Chantiers Navals Français eventually received not only the contract for the two destroyers, but also that for the floating dock destined for Gdynia. The Poles ordered the two destroyers in January 1926, and they were laid down in the summer. The order for the three minelaying submarines came in April. The number of submarines had been reduced from nine for budgetary reasons, and none of Swirski's efforts could reverse the decision, especially after Marshal Josef Piłsudski's 1926 coup. British diplomatic observers complained that the French firms received the orders only because of a large French loan to Poland and a 'lavish bestowal' of Legions of Honor. The smell of the entire matter makes one lean toward the earlier assessments of governmental corruption.[33]

Even though the Poles made the deal, they did not do so without harboring some concerns. In a situation similar to that with the submarines the

Poles did not want to take any risks with the construction of the destroyers. In an effort to avoid any future problems the Polish government, through the auspices of Jolivet, asked that the projected destroyers be constructed based upon the plans of a similar 1,500 ton French type that had been built previously by Chantiers Navals de Caen.[34]

Jolivet might not have known about the Sikorski–Swirski meeting and must have seen the final compromise as a last-ditch effort at obtaining the order for French industry. He believed that if the destroyers had been ordered separately, the contract would not have gone to a French firm, but have enriched the coffers of a British or Italian yard. Competitors from both nations reared their heads at various times during the period in which the Poles investigated the French offers. Jolivet considered the Italians a threat because of their low prices. The British presented a danger in other ways. In April 1925 Armstrong Whitworth & Co. attempted to sell Poland two submarines nearing completion in the firm's yards. Sikorski declined the offer, in spite of an offer by the admiralty to provide training. The tonnage of the two vessels proved too great for Poland's needs.[35]

With the conclusion of the submarine deal Jolivet wrote: 'Thus ended the laborious negotiations.' But things were not quite over as the Poles, the French government, the builders, and the consortium of bankers eventually brought in to finance the deal, wrangled over payment conditions. But this was to come and not unusual. This also did not keep Jolivet from criticizing the French industrialists involved in the competition, complaining that he could not praise the actions of some of those who did not receive the contracts. He also believed that these same unnamed individuals did not respect the fact that their actions injured the overall cause of France,[36] an obvious allusion to the Union des Cinq Chantiers.

Jolivet also condemned the lack of unity on the part of the builders, a discord that the French officer believed had cost French industry 20,000,000 francs. He calculated this loss based on the knowledge that the Poles did not reach their decision solely on the basis of cost. Jolivet believed that the price agreed upon was too low and as a result would generate in Poland a mistrust of French builders regarding the quality of their wares. The Poles paid 10 percent less for their submarines than the French navy and received a better boat. Jolivet did not believe the Poles needed to know this and that the French firms made a costly financial error in not charging a higher price for, in Jolivet's opinion, the Poles would 'well expect to pay more dearly.'[37]

It was not until 2 August 1926 that the Poles signed the contracts for the destroyers. Construction of the first ship began on 1 November 1926, the work on the second a year later.[38] Along with the submarines and destroyers came a need for other naval items such as mines and torpedoes. As the Poles reviewed the various offerings from shipbuilders they also negotiated with other French arms suppliers. Sautter-Harlé was one. In late 1924, even before the passage of the naval program, Sautter-Harlé began talks with the Polish government to supply submarine mines for the proposed vessels. The firm asked the French foreign ministry for support and an official endorsement. The Foreign Ministry did agree to approach the Polish government on their behalf, but they would not do it in a manner that would hinder other firms that might be interested in the contracts, nor would they allow the direct intervention of Admiral Jolivet on Sautter-Harlé's behalf, citing as their reason the 'character of his mission in Poland.' Despite this refusal, the Foreign Ministry did specifically request that the French navy give some support for the offers of Sautter-Harlé, as well as any other French firms competing in Poland, if the opportunity arose. This entire matter boiled down to the Foreign Ministry agreeing to notify the Poles that Sautter-Harlé was indeed a reputable house. The Foreign Ministry went on to suggest to Sautter-Harlé that in the event of a rivalry developing between competing French firms that they should consider reaching an 'understanding' regarding competition for the contracts.[39] Again, we see the French government pushing its firms to collude on prices in an effort to insure that the orders passed to France and not into foreign hands.

The Poles embarked upon a comparison of exterior-mounted and interior-mounted submarine mines of the Maurice Callot and Paul Chailley types. They concluded that the Callot models, an internal type, were much better. French technical advisors agreed with the Polish decision, citing the harsh climatic conditions of the Baltic as the basis for the formulation of their decision.[40]

Further activities of the French naval mission

In addition to pursuing Polish armaments contracts the French also played an active part in the establishment of the Polish naval training school at Torun. A French officer, Commander de Lavergne, in collaboration with the commander of the school, prepared a list of items necessary for the instruction of young officers. The list included many basic items such as training manuals, maps, charts, and other educational tools. The school had a great shortage of instructional materials because of the Polish navy's lack of money.[41]

Admiral Jolivet urged his superiors to act quickly on the matter, stating that most of the material could be drawn from French depots and arsenals and be ceded to the Poles at a minimum price as obsolete material. He argued that the material was indispensable to the development of a competent Polish navy. Jolivet also deplored the great lack of French naval training material in the possession of the Poles. The instruction manuals held by the new navy tended to be of German or Russian origin. Jolivet wanted to inspire the teaching of naval history at the new school based upon the bibliography used in French naval colleges. This, he hoped, would help the Polish navy develop a spirit similar to that of its French counterpart. Additionally, the Poles planned to include the study of French as a part of their program of instruction, as well as prepare translations of some if not all of the French manuals.[42]

Jolivet also suggested to his superiors that the French navy receive ten Polish officers per year as students, a request made at the behest of the Polish navy. He also encouraged his superiors to hurry the transfer of the *Desaix* (a hulk the Poles wanted as a training vessel), not only because the failure of such a move would hurt the training of the Polish navy, but because French influence would suffer as well. The French navy agreed to the Polish request to send officers to France for training and soon, four Polish cadets served annually on the French training ship *Jeanne d'Arc*. Other Polish officers regularly studied at French naval specialty schools, attending special courses in gunnery, torpedoes, hydrology, and so on. Some also attended the Ecole de Guerre in Paris or the Centre des Hautes Etudes Navales.[43]

The changing nature of the French naval mission and Polish politics

Under Admiral Jolivet's direction the French naval mission exerted a great amount of influence over the development of the Polish navy. But he died unexpectedly on 17 June 1926. Subsequent French discussion of the mission's fate reveals much about French opinion on the usefulness of such missions.[44]

To the diplomats, the mission provided 'beneficial influence' and served as a 'tool for securing contracts for French industry,' but Laroche, France's Ambassador to Poland, also suggested that it could be reduced. Jolivet's untimely passing presented an opportunity to reevaluate the benefit to France of encouraging the 'exaggerated ambitions of the Polish Navy' and ensuring that the Poles focused upon the development of their army, some-thing more in the common interest of the two states.[45]

This evoked an immediate argument from the French navy. The naval minister soundly opposed any shrinking of the mission and disagreed heartily with Laroche's stance. He argued for a more equitable division of Poland's military budget between the land and sea services and went on to remind them of the military agreements between the two states. The alliance of 1921, and a subsequent accord of November 1924, foresaw coop-eration between the French and Polish navies. The caveats for this coopera-tion were the completion of the port at Gdynia and the fulfillment of Poland's naval program. These factors were not independent of the develop-ment of the ground forces because troops were certainly needed to protect Gdynia, as were destroyers, submarines, and minesweepers. Ships were necessary to keep the port open, and the French navy did not have sufficient forces to do this. Therefore, the Minister insisted, the French navy needed the Polish fleet in order to carry out its assigned part of France's strategy. The efforts that the Poles made to develop their navy 'cannot be qualified as exaggerated,' and it would be better to 'encourage' rather than moderate Polish naval building efforts. Moreover, the personnel of the mission played an indispensable instructional role guiding the organization and training of the Polish navy.[46]

French admiralty opinion seems to have won out, though the records are incomplete. The French sent Captain Richard as Jolivet's successor in November 1926 but were careful to appoint someone of less than Flag status so as not to disconcert Admiral Swirski, the head of the Polish navy, and Marshal Piłsudski, who, it was said, disliked being advised by someone of high rank. Commander Raymond Cellier succeeded Richard in December 1929.[47]

In 1927 the naval mission was made autonomous. The French ambassador seems to have extracted some kind of promise from Piłsudski regarding the continuance of the naval mission. As always, the French feared British encroachment and worried that Britain might try to substitute themselves for the French in Poland, something that would injure French influence, and which the French viewed as even more likely after the military mission departed.[48]

But the Polish navy had enemies closer to home. In 1926 Marshal Piłsudski seized power in Poland, a change that did not bode well for the navy. The building program embarked upon in 1925 had already been cut from nine to three submarines because the Polish currency was rapidly falling in value. The advent of the Piłsudski regime made additional naval building very unlikely. Initially, the Marshal expressed no interest in naval matters and worked on the principle that since such decisions had been made before his assumption of power, and made badly, they did not merit pursuit. For the navy, the question of funding became an uncertain one. The doubts of the Polish High Command regarding the usefulness to Poland of a navy in wartime, as well as the question of the navy's ability to guard its own base in the event of hostilities, also raised questions. These elements combined to prevent any immediate new construction.[49]

Despite his initial unwillingness to allocate the funds the navy wanted, Piłsudski did authorize the drawing up of plans for a new naval program. He recruited three generals to produce a naval program that he would then put before the Polish parliament. The new plan differed little from that of the 'small program' of 1925 and met with even less success. Parliamentary resistance and the lack of money in government coffers prevented the voting of sufficient credits for new construction. A French official wrote that throughout the 1920s and early 1930s the feelings of the Polish navy drifted regularly from hope to despair. He compared the force's situation to that of the four seasons. In the summer the various departments received their orders to prepare their budget provisions for the next year; this was the good season. They composed a budget and the navy was hopeful. But the autumn came quickly. Marshal Piłsudski or the parliament intervened, cutting the credits. The winter arrived, and the navy passed it in the 'doldrums.' Spring soon returned, and with it a revival of the navy's hopes for expansion, and with this, the appearance of the suppliers and salesmen.[50]

For several years the navy had to remain content with the purchases it had made in 1925–6. The three submarines and two destroyers ordered from

French yards in the mid-1920s arrived in Poland over the next few years. The French builders took an inordinate amount of time completing the vessels, all arrived much later than had been planned. The first of the destroyers, *Wicher* (hurricane), arrived 20 months late. Its sister ship, *Burza* (squall), did not see completion until 1932, 32 months late. Numerous construction defects and the bankruptcy of the builder, Chantier Navales Français, account for much of the delay. The three submarines, *Rys* (lynx), *Wilk* (wolf), and *Zbik* (wildcat), also arrived from their French builders only after many delays. Both the destroyers and the submarines suffered from many mechanical difficulties, and their poor performance did not set well with Polish officials. It also contributed to a lack of confidence in French shipbuilding and a reluctance to purchase additional French vessels when money later became available.[51]

Some additional French deals

In 1932 the Polish navy tried again to get funding for new construction. They wanted 14,231,000 złotys, of which about 9,000,000 złotys would have been destined for foreign orders. Poland envisaged purchasing three 1,200 ton, 36-knot destroyers and five 700 ton, 17-knot minelaying submarines. The remaining 5,000,000 złotys would finance the construction of minelayers by Polish government yards in Modlin and Gdynia.[52] At some point elements of this initiative met with some measure of success and the Poles began looking for builders.

The French navy greeted the news with much enthusiasm, and why they were interested gives us another insight into some of the strategic thinking of the French navy in the interwar period. They wanted the Polish navy to expand because this meant the growth of an allied naval force that ran little chance of having its fleet reduced by any naval limitations treaties, something that the heads of any large navy could expect in this era of naval disarmament agreements. Moreover, if France failed to get the order, another state would and thus deprive France of the business. The contracts would also help address France's unemployment problem. Indeed, the matter was seen as one that interested the 'national defense, foreign policy, and economic activity of France.'[53] Clearly, foreign arms sales were an element of French interwar strategy that helped meet its military, political, and economic goals. And the people who helped sell these arms were the members of the French advisory missions.

Nothing came of the more ambitious elements of the navy's plan, but the improvement of Poland's economic situation in 1933 did see the authorization of a segment of the navy's program. The Polish navy received the funds to order four minesweepers from Polish yards.[54] This same period also saw the Poles embark upon technical studies for the construction of a large minelayer that they hoped to order before 1 April 1933. Despite Polish dissatisfaction with earlier warships purchased from France, the order for the minelayer went to the French builder Chantiers Navales Français but only after some ruthlessly hard bargaining on the part of the Poles. The Poles were 'tough bargainers,' and negotiating a business agreement with them was never for the faint hearted.[55]

The Poles demanded economic compensation from France in return for placing the order with a French firm. At one point, Admiral Swirski threatened to withdraw from all Polish obligations to Chantiers Navales Français if the French government did not provide a satisfactory response by 15 April 1933. Swirski also revealed to the French that he had already embarked upon preliminary discussions with Scandinavian builders who had yards lying idle and that if the French did not provide a satisfactory decision by the above date, he would have no choice but to commit Poland to an unnamed Scandinavian firm.[56] This might have been a bluff on Swirski's part to worry the French and extort more concessions from them, one he successfully executed, though the Poles certainly needed the concessions from France as badly as the French did the order.

France's economic difficulties gave the Poles a strong negotiating position. The Poles also benefited from the timing of their decision. It came during a period in which the French had been pressuring the Polish government to order a new submarine as a means of supporting the strapped French shipbuilding industry. Swirski did not follow through on his threat to break off the talks on 15 April. They dragged on, endlessly, from January to the end of April, nearly collapsing on more than one occasion.[57]

Lieutenant René Papillon, the French naval attaché for the region, worried about the impact of a French failure to conclude a deal for the minelayer. He believed that within the next year the Polish navy planned to request the credits necessary for the purchase of two 1,200 ton torpedo boats and six 700 ton submarines. The contracts for these would be worth 250,000,000–300,000,000 francs. Papillon believed that if France could not bring the negotiations for the minesweeper to a successful conclusion, it would have less of a chance of capturing the contracts for the new naval purchases, that is, if the government approved them. The loss of these orders to a foreign builder, in Papillon's eyes, would surely deal a great blow to the influence that the French navy then had with its Polish counterpart.[58]

France and Poland finally concluded an accord on 28 April 1933. In return for placing the order for the minelayer in France, the Poles received import credits that amounted to about 17,000,000 francs, approximately one half of the cost of the minelayer.[59]

The arrangement did not last long. In November 1933, the Poles cancelled the deal with Chantiers Navals Français and announced that they would have another French firm build the minelayer. This shocked the French. Why the Poles made this decision is unclear, but in February 1934 they conferred the order on Augustin-Normand. The price was 33,000,000 francs, and in return for getting the contract Augustin-Normand agreed to buy a number of the components from Polish firms.[60] This willingness to do business in Poland undoubtedly contributed to the Polish government's sudden change of mind.

The French yard continued its tradition of inefficiency by not delivering the vessel until 1938. The ship, *Gryf*, proved a poorly designed one, as the Poles had tried to build her for use as a training vessel, a state yacht, and a minelayer. The deal received much criticism in Poland, not only for the poor quality of the ship, but also for its cost, which approached that of a small destroyer.[61]

The final act: the end of the French naval mission

The purchase of *Gryf* marked the end of the first period of Poland's association with French naval builders. Long before the conclusion of the deal though, cracks had begun to appear in the political relationship between Poland and France. On 1 May 1932 the Polish government, in accordance with the terms of their agreement, gave the required three months notice regarding the termination of the French naval mission to Poland. Despite their number having been reduced considerably the previous year, the ending of the mission came as a surprise not only to its personnel, but also to the Polish officers working with them. The brusque manner in which the Poles ended a relationship dating to 1923 offended the members of the mission, as well as the French Embassy, and harsh words were exchanged. The ending of the naval mission coincided with the expiration of the contract for the French military mission to Poland. The Poles gave measures of economy as the reason for cancellation, and some in the Polish government believed that the mission had become unnecessary. Also driving the Polish action was the French government's refusal to supply the second installment of a loan that would have allowed the completion of Poland's Upper Silesia–Gdynia railway. Economic and political disagreements between the two states also strained the relationship. Important among these was the French approval of a change in the military status of Germany. Some British observers speculated correctly that the decision to terminate the mission came directly from Marshal Piłsudski.[62]

In July 1931 the Poles made their first moves toward killing the mission, deciding at the end of the year on its phased reduction. By January 1932 Piłsudski had decided to eliminate the military mission. His reason for doing so foreshadows a great shift in Polish policy and reveals the reasoning behind much of what Poland did in foreign policy and military matters for the rest of the 1930s. Piłsudski, in the later part of 1931, redirected Poland's foreign diplomacy and began putting more pressure on Lithuania and Czechoslovakia, presumably to resolve their diplomatic and territorial disputes with Warsaw. He also moved to become more independent of the League of Nations and Poland's ally, France. In regard to the French missions, the Poles had simply decided that they had 'grown up' and no longer had any use for an entity that in the eyes of foreigners made it appear as if the 'Polish Army is under the tutelage of France.' To the Poles, getting rid of the military mission was a matter of 'dignity.'[63]

The French believed the mission's dissolution 'enfeebled' French influence but saw no way around the matter other than supporting the appointment of a general as military attaché. On the heels of this came Piłsudski's decision to kill the naval mission as well, the Marshall arguing, correctly in the mind of some French observers, that not only could Poland not afford the mission, but that it needed to concentrate on developing its army.[64]

Following the departure of the French missions, Franco-Polish relations suffered another serious blow. In September 1932 Germany withdrew from the Geneva disarmament conference after the refusal of its demand for equality in armaments. By December 1933 the resolve of the European powers, including France, had melted away, resulting in the granting to the Nazi regime this privilege continually refused by the Weimar Republic. Poland deeply resented the sudden volte-face in French policy. Poland's more independent foreign policy now began to include a warming in relations with Germany. This culminated in the signing of a German–Polish treaty of non-aggression in January 1934.[65]

The ineptness of French firms, and the increasingly strained economic and political relationship between Warsaw and Paris, cost the French their best customer in the Baltic region. The breakdown in relations between the two states is not surprising when one considers France's poor treatment of its allies in general,[66] and Poland in particular. The French looked at Poland, as well as the other states of the cordon sanitaire, and Eastern and Central Europe in general, as cash cows and places to supplement their own military strength while, most importantly, turning a profit. The years 1931–2 even saw accusations from the Polish public that France was financially exploiting the Poles.[67] This was a bad policy. To be magnanimous in their treatment of their allies in regard to arming them would have been costly to France, in a financial sense. But it was more costly, politically, diplomatically, and in the end also economically, to exploit them while simultaneously counting on their military support. After the cancellation of the French naval mission the Poles followed an independent course in their foreign policy and in regard to their naval armaments. They abandoned French builders, but only for a short time.

Conclusion

The departure of the French naval mission severely weakened the influence that France had exerted over the Polish navy and the contracts connected with it. The experience of the French naval mission to Poland demonstrates the importance of missions in the eyes of both the sending and the receiving powers. Placing a mission provided the perfect basis upon which to build influence. This mission could shape the emerging service in ways that it deemed profitable, not only to the new state, but also as support for the political, military, and economic strategies of the nation providing the mission. Often, but not always, naval missions and their heads, or individuals holding the position of naval advisor, prove instrumental in directing the course of naval development, and which nation wins the potentially lucrative orders.

Ultimately though, the connection made possible by the French naval mission's dispatch did not prove as permanent or as profitable economically, militarily, or politically as France desired. When one considers that the dispatch of the French naval mission was more about serving French interests than Polish ones, this should come as no surprise.

Notes

1 For an examination of this rivalry in the Baltic see Stoker, *Britain, France, and the Naval Arms Trade in the Baltic, 1919–1939*. This chapter is based upon material in this book. Michael Jasinki provided translations of the Polish language sources used in both.

2 J. Unrug, 'Wie die polnische Kriegsflotte entstanden ist 1918–1939,' *Marine Rundschau* 63 (1966): 199; Rear Admiral Jerzy Swirski report, 14 May 1919, Polish Institute and Sikorski Museum (hereafter PISM), London, file MAR A II 1/7; Michael A. Peszke, *Poland's Navy, 1918–1945* (New York: Hippocrene, 1999), p. 14.

3 Unrug, 'Wie die polnische Kriegsflotte entstanden ist,' pp. 199–200; *Conway's, 1906–1921* (London: Conway Maritime Press, 1985), p. 419; Jürg Meister, 'Die polnischen Flußflottillen, 1919–1939,' *Marine Rundschau* 66 (1969): 230–9; Oskar Halecki, *A History of Poland*, 3rd ed. (New York: Roy Publishers, 1961), pp. 286–7.

4 Poland. Annual Report, 1920, 18 March 1922, Foreign Office (hereafter FO) 371/8143, National Archives of the United Kingdom, Kew, London; Flint to FO, 29 September 1920, FO 371/5411; Barstow to FO, 15 October 1920, FO 371/5411; Christopher Bell, *The Royal Navy: Seapower and Strategy Between the Wars* (Stanford: Stanford University Press, 2000), pp. 153–5; Crookshank, 'Memorandum on Polish Affairs, 1919–1921,' in Kenneth Bourne, D. Cameron Watt and Michael Partridge (eds), *British Documents on Foreign Affairs: Reports and Papers from the Foreign Office Confidential Print* (Frederick, MD: University Publications of America, 1996) (hereafter *BDFA*), pt. II, ser. F, Vol. 52, p. 194; Stoker, *Britain, France, and the Naval Arms Trade*, pp. 42–4; Wharton to Graham[?], 16 July 1921, FO 371/6807; Wharton, 'Report on the Polish Navy and Mercantile Marine,' 15 November 1921, FO 371/6842.

5 Rumbold to Curzon, 30 March 1920, in Rohan Butler and J.P.T. Bury (eds), *Documents on British Foreign Policy, 1919–1939* (London: HMSO, 1961), ser. 1, Vol. 11, pp. 271–2.

6 Sosnkowski to Dupont, 22 January 1922, Archives du Ministère des Affaires Etrangères (hereafter AMAE), Pologne 45; d'Ythurbide to Panafieu, 23 July 1922, ibid.

7 Peter Jackson, 'Naval Policy and National Strategy in France, 1933–1937,' *Journal of Strategic Studies* 4 (2000): 130, 134; signature illegible (hereafter s.i.), Ministre de la Marine (hereafter MM), to Ministre de l'Interieur, stamped 7 November 1931, AMAE, Pologne 315; Raiberti to Ministre de la Guerre, 4 August 1922, AMAE, Pologne 45.

8 Stoker, *Britain, France, and the Naval Arms Trade*, pp. 85–6.
9 Jolivet to MM, 29 September 1925, SHM, 1BB[7] 132 Pologne; attached note, ibid.; Panafieu to le Ministre des Affaires Etrangères (hereafter MAE), 25 December 1924, AMAE, Pologne 42.
10 Muller to Chamberlain, 28 January 1925, FO 371/10999; Muller to Chamberlain, 9 February 1925, ibid.; Walker to FO, 28 February 1925, ibid.; Muller to Chamberlain, 14 April 1925, ibid.
11 Warsaw to MM, 28 March 1925, SHM, 1BB[7] 128 Pologne; President du Conseil MAE to MM, 28 March 1925, SHM, 1BB[7] 132 Pologne; Jolivet to MM, 31 March 1925, SHM, 1BB[7] 132 Pologne; Laroche to French Minister Warsaw, 12 December 1924, AMAE, Pologne 42; Salaün to MAE, 10 December 1924, AMAE, Pologne 42.
12 Salaün to MM, 3 July 1925, SHM, 1BB[7] 132 Pologne; Kłoczkowski to MM, 6 July 1925, ibid.; MM to Chłapowski, 5 August 1925, ibid.
13 Polish Embassy R.H.[?] to Directeur Général de la Sté. Anonyme des Forges et Chantiers de la Méditerranée, 20 April 1925, SHM, 1BB[7] 132 Pologne; Société des Forges & Chantiers de ..., Société des Chantier & Ateliers de St. Nazaire, Société des Chantiers & Ateliers de ... to Gevant, Départment de la Marine de Guerre Polonaise, 25 May 1925, ibid.; Ambassade de Pologne report, 8 April 1925, ibid.
14 Vice Amiral to Contre Amiral, Chef de la Mission Navale Française en Pologne, 7 May 1925, SHM, 1BB[7] 132 Pologne; Jolivet to MM, 29 September 1925, ibid.; attached note, ibid.; MM to Chłapowski, 9 April 1925, ibid.
15 Ste. Ame des Chantier et Atelier de St. Nazaire note, 28 April 1925, AMAE, Pologne 42; Blanchet note, 11 May 1925, ibid.; MAE to MM, 3 June 1925.
16 Cabinet Militaire report, 'Direction Centrale des Constructions Navales,' 8 April 1925, SHM, 1BB[7] 132 Pologne; MM to Chłapowski, Polish Ambassador 9 April 1925, ibid. Details on the relevant technical requirements can be found in Vice Amiral, Chef d'EMG de la Marine to Contre-Amiral, Chef de la Mission Navale Française en Pologne, 7 May 1925, ibid.; Swirski, 'Plany I Zamierzenia Ruzbudowy Marynarki Wojennej w Okresie 1920–1926' (hereafter 'Plany'), PISM, Swirski Papers, MAR AII 7/7.
17 Vice Amiral, Chef d'EMG de la Marine to Chef de la Mission Navale Française en Pologne, 7 May 1925, SHM, 1BB[7] 132 Pologne.
18 Union de Cinq Chantiers Français de Construction Navales report, 'Note Sur la Sousmission Pour la Commande des Sous-marins Polonais,' n.d., SHM, 1BB[7] 132 Pologne; 'Note de l'amiral Jolivet,' n.d., ibid. Jolivet's note also states the following: 'The commission does not have to approve the recommendation of Admiral Kłoczkowski. If the latter has made promises he has overshot his ability to help.'
19 Attached note in Jolivet to MM, 29 September 1925, SHM, 1BB[7] 132 Pologne.
20 Union de Cinq Chantiers Français de Constructions Navales sur la Mer du Nord, La Manche, L'Atlantique, La Méditerranée report, n.d. [probably 1925], SHM, 1BB[7] 132 Pologne; Swirski report, 11 September 1925, annex in Panafieu to MAE, 16 September 1925, AMAE, Pologne 42.
21 Swirski report, 11 September 1925, annex in Panafieu to MAE, 16 September 1925, AMAE, Pologne 42.
22 Peszke, *Poland's Navy*, pp. 21–2.
23 Union de Cinq Chantiers Français de Constructions Navales sur la Mer du Nord, La Manche, L'Atlantique, La Méditerranée report, n.d. [1925?], SHM, 1BB[7] 132 Pologne; Société des Forges & Chantiers de ..., Société des Chantiers & Ateliers de St. Nazaire, Société des Chantiers & Ateliers de ... to Gevant, Départment de la Marine Polonaise, 25 May 1925, ibid.

24 Union de Cinq Chantiers Français de Construction Navales, 'Note sur la Sousmission pour la Commande des Sous-Marins Polonais,' n.d., SHM, 1BB⁷ 132 Pologne; attached note in Jolivet to MM, 29 September 1925, ibid.

25 Union de Cinq Chantiers Français de Construction Navales, 'Note sur la Sous-mission pour la Commande des Sous-marins Polonaise,' n.d., SHM, 1BB⁷ 132 Pologne; 'Sous-Marins Polonais,' n.d., ibid.; attached note in Jolivet to MM, 29 September 1925, ibid.

26 Jolivet to MM, 29 September 1925, SHM, 1BB⁷ 132 Pologne; Société Anonyme des Ateliers et Chantiers de la Loire to MM, 16 October 1925, ibid.; Swirski, 'Plany,' PISM, Swirski Papers, MAR AII 7/7; 'Note de l'amiral Jolivet,' n.d., ibid. The Union did tie for first in the decision of the Commission regarding the torpedo submarines, but their inexperience prevented their receiving the contract.

27 Ibid.; 'Compte-rendu de la séance de la Commission Militaire du 12 Octobre 1925,' ibid., records a difference of seven and one half per cent in the price after reduction.

28 'Note,' n.d., SHM, 1BB⁷ 132 Pologne.

29 Ibid.; 'Note pour Monsieur Berthelot,' 14 September 1925, AMAE, Pologne 42.

30 'Visite de l'Ambassadeur de Pologne,' 12 October 1925, AMAE, Pologne 42; Swirski, 'Plany,' PISM, MAR, AII 7/7.

31 'Compte-rendu de la séance de la Commission Militaire du 12 Octobre 1925,' and Société Anonyme des Ateliers et Chantiers de la Loire to MM, 16 October 1925, SHM, 1BB⁷ 132.

32 Swirski report, PISM, Swirski Papers, MAR AII 7/7.

33 Jolivet to MM, 29 September 1925, SHM, 1BB⁷ 132 Pologne; 'Compte-rendu de la séance de la Commission Militaire du 12 Octobre 1925,' ibid.; Société Anonyme des Ateliers et Chantiers de la Loire to MM, 16 October 1925, ibid.; Poland. Annual Report, 1926, 3 October 1927, FO 371/12580; *Conway's All the World's Fighting Ships, 1922–46* (London: Conway Maritime Press, 1980), pp. 349–50; Peszke, *Poland's Navy*, pp. 21–2; Przemsyslaw Budzbon, '*Wicher* and *Burza*, Big Ships of a Small Navy,' in John Roberts (ed.) *Warship IV* (London and Annapolis: Conway's Maritime Press, 1980), p. 59; Swirski report, PISM, MAR AII 7/7.

34 Jolivet to MM, 29 September 1925, SHM, 1BB⁷ 132 Pologne.

35 Ibid.; Muller to Chamberlain, 14 April 1925, FO 371/10999. For the negotiations see AMAE, Pologne 42.

36 Jolivet to MM, 29 September 1925, SHM, 1BB⁷ 132 Pologne.

37 Ibid.

38 Capitaine de Frégate Fernet, note for Vice Admiral, 23 November 1926, SHM, 1BB⁷ 132 Pologne.

39 Le President du Conseil to Sautter-Harlé, 5 January 1925, SHM, 1BB⁷ 132 Pologne; MAE to MM, 17 January 1925, ibid.; MAE to Sautter-Harlé, 2 January [1925?], AMAE, Pologne 42; MAE to Sautter-Harlé, [5?] January 1925, ibid.

40 Salaün to Jolivet, 6 February 1925, SHM, 1BB⁷ 132 Pologne; Telegramme Officiel no. 2 to MM, 27 January 1925, ibid.; MM to French Embassy, note for Admiral Jolivet, Telegramme Officiel, no. 876, 31 January 1925, ibid.

41 Jolivet to MM, 26 January 1925, SHM, 1BB⁷ 132 Pologne.

42 Ibid.; EMG, Bulletin de Renseignements no. 1256, 29 January 1927, ibid.; de Lavergne to MM, 26 October 1926, ibid.

43 Jolivet to MM, 26 January 1925, SHM, 1BB⁷ 132 Pologne; EMG, Bulletin de Renseignements no. 1256, 29 January 1927, ibid.

44 Laroche to MAE, 17 June 1926, AMAE, Pologne 45.

45 Laroche to MAE, 21 June 1926, AMAE, Pologne 45; MAE to MM, 29 June 1926, ibid.
46 s.i., MM to MAE, 16 July 1926, AMAE, 16 July 1926.
47 Leygues to MAE, 18 November 1926, AMAE, Pologne 45; s.i., French Chargé Poland to MAE, 16 July 1926, ibid.; Laroche to MAE, 27 December 1929, ibid.
48 French Ambassador Poland to MAE, 26 November 1927, AMAE, Pologne 43.
49 'Programme Naval – Budget,' n.d., SHM, 1BB⁷ 132 Pologne; 'Divers Non Dates, Marine Future' [late 1920s to early 1930s], ibid.; *Conway's, 1922–46*, p. 347.
50 Organization General de la Marine,' n.d., SHM, 1BB⁷ 132 Pologne; 'Programme Naval – Budget,' n.d., ibid.; 'Rapport de fin de Mission de la Mission Navale Française en Pologne,' 20 July 1932, ibid.
51 Charpeutier[?] to Chef du 2éme Bureau, received 19 July 1930, SHM, 1BB⁷ 132 Pologne; *Conway's, 1922–46*, pp. 347, 349–50.
52 BI no. 8, 9 December 1932, SHM, 1BB⁷ 132 Pologne.
53 s.i., MM to Ministre de l'Interieur, stamped 7 November 1931, AMAE, Pologne 315; 'Note pour le Ministre,' 3 December 1931, ibid.
54 'Rapport de fin de Mission de la Mission Naval Français en Pologne,' 20 July 1932, ibid; SHM, 1BB⁷ 132 Pologne; *Conway's, 1922–46*, pp. 347, 351.
55 Attaché Naval report, 9 November 1932, SHM, 1BB⁷ 132 Pologne; *Conway's, 1922–46*, p. 347; David E. Kaiser, *Economic Diplomacy and the Origins of the Second World War: Germany, Britain, France, and Eastern Europe, 1930–1939* (Princeton, NJ: Princeton University Press, 1980), p. 94.
56 Papillon to MM, 10 April 1933, SHM, 1BB⁷ 132 Pologne.
57 Piotrs S. Wandycz, *The Twilight of French Eastern Alliances, 1926–1939: French – Czechoslovak – Polish Relations from Locarno to the Remilitarization of the Rhineland* (Princeton, NJ: Princeton University Press, 1988), p. 345; Papillon to MM, 16 May 1933, SHM, 1BB⁷ 132 Pologne.
58 Papillon to MM, 4 April 1933, SHM, 1BB⁷ 132 Pologne; Papillon to MM, 16 May 1933, ibid.
59 Papillon to MM, 16 May 1933, 1BB⁷ 132 Pologne.
60 Bargeton to French Ambassador Warsaw, 29 November 1933, AMAE, Pologne 315; Laroche to MAE, 27 November 1933, ibid.; Laroche to MAE, 22 February 1934, ibid.; Laroche to Barthou, 5 May [1934?], ibid.
61 Papillon to MM, 16 May 1933, 1BB⁷ 132 Pologne; *Conway's, 1922–46*, pp. 347, 351.
62 'Rapport de fin de Mission de la Mission Navale Française en Pologne,' 20 July 1932, ibid.; Erskine to Simon, 27 May 1932, FO 371/16314; Erskine to Simon, 27 May 1932, ibid.; Vereker to Seymour, 5 July 1932, ibid.; Wandycz, *Twilight*, pp. 233–4.
63 Bressey to MAE, 29 July 1931, AMAE, Pologne 318; Maginot to MAE, 11 September 1931, ibid.; Laroche to MAE, 13 January 1931, ibid.; R. Ahmann, '"Localisation of Conflicts" or Indivisibility of Peace": The German and Soviet Approaches Towards Collective Security and East Central Europe 1925–1939,' in R. Ahmann, A.M. Birke, and M. Howard (eds), *The Quest for Stability: Problems of West European Security, 1918–1957* (London: Oxford University Press, 1993), p. 210.
64 MAE to Laroche, stamped 10 February 1932, AMAE, Pologne 318; Laroche to MAE, 30 April 1932, ibid.; Laroche to MAE, 18 July 1932, ibid.
65 Josef Korbel, *Poland Between East and West. Soviet and German Diplomacy Toward Poland, 1919–1933* (Princeton, NJ: Princeton University Press, 1963), pp. 277–86.
66 Michael Geyer, 'The Crisis of Military Leadership in the 1930s,' *Journal of Strategic Studies* 14 (1991): 460.
67 Ahmann, 'German and Soviet Approaches,' pp. 205–6.

5 Uneasy intelligence collaboration, genuine ill will, with an admixture of ideology

The British Military Mission to the Soviet Union, 1941–1945

Alaric Searle

Although until recently historians have only shown limited interest in the history of military advising, some attention has been devoted to the British Military Mission to the Soviet Union, 1941–5. Nonetheless, much of what has been written is incomplete and tends to concentrate on Britain's Military Mission No. 30 within the wider context of diplomatic and intelligence relations with the Soviet Union.[1] The most important study covering the mission examines its role in intelligence exchange with the Soviet military together with the United States Military Mission in Moscow.[2] But, unfortunately, there has hitherto been no single attempt to provide a complete history of the British Military Mission to the Soviet Union. Moreover, considering the diverging judgments which have been passed on the mission in the available literature, our understanding of its successes, failures and leading personalities still remains confused. This is particularly so in the case of Bradley F. Smith's study, *Sharing Secrets with Stalin*, which at times appears dismissive and patronizing towards the British mission, yet in some places also suggests it was fairly successful in gleaning intelligence.

If a number of historical question marks still surround Britain's Military Mission No. 30, one area in particular does not seem to have received the attention it deserves: that of *ideology*.[3] A thorough examination of the documents available strongly suggests that ideology, and the suspicions which ideology generated, was probably the major factor dominating the relationship between the members of the military mission and the Russian military officers with whom they liaised during the course of the Great Patriotic War. There were, in fact, two ideologies within this relationship: on the one hand, Communism, or Bolshevism as it was better known among members of the political and military elite in Britain, and on the other, 'anti-Bolshevism', in many ways just as much an ideology as Communism.[4] Not only did Red Army officers and Soviet officials take exception to the part previously played in the Allied intervention of 1919–20 by individuals with whom they were involved as part of wartime military cooperation,[5] British officers, too, carried with them attitudes acquired immediately after the First World War.[6]

In examining the relationship between members of a military mission and the 'host officials' with whom they cooperate, there are many factors which can be identified as exerting an influence on behaviour. The British Military Mission to the Soviet Union had a number of aims, and as a component part of a broader policy to provide the country with military supplies, it certainly had its role to play in the war effort. However, without the element of ideology, it is impossible to understand the officially defined goals of the mission, the positions adopted by the six heads of mission, the reactions of British officers and men to life in the USSR and the policy disputes which arose in London over the role of the mission. Indeed, in any wider view of the history of military advising, it can be argued that ideology has been an important – yet underrated – factor which holds the potential to regulate the relations between a military mission and the host nation. This chapter is, therefore, as much a case study in the role of ideology in the activities of a military mission as it is, specifically, an analysis of Britain's Military Mission No. 30 in the Soviet Union, 1941–5.

I

Important for any appreciation of British policy in relation to the military mission is quite obviously the general attitude of Britain's armed services towards the Soviet Union during the interwar period.[7] From the moment the Bolshevik revolution occurred, the military, together with the ruling political, diplomatic and social elites, felt threatened by Communism. The Bolshevik revolution was, though, but one head of a hydra of revolution: in addition to the Red threat, there was the problem of the Sinn Fein 'revolutionaries' in Ireland and nationalist movements in India and the Middle East. These threats were on the one hand strategic: war at the backdoor in Ireland, the unstable situation in India and the challenge of the Soviet Union to the Empire. But the 'revolutionary movements' of Bolshevism, militant Irish nationalism and 'Mohammedism' all combined to generate a feeling of insecurity which was intensified in the early postwar years by a fear of Bolshevik revolution in Britain itself.[8]

Not surprisingly, relations with the Soviet Union were always going to be strained, so that even after Germany began serious rearmament in the mid-1930s, hostility towards the USSR remained. That the First World War had left the British Empire overextended, with too many military commitments, a fact which became all too obvious in the 1930s,[9] further increased the distaste of British officers for Bolshevism. A closer look at British strategic planning and talks with Soviet staff officers in the period from early 1939 until the German invasion of Russia on 22 June 1941 makes plain just how strong this feeling was.

The attitude of the Chiefs of Staff towards the Soviet Union in this period was characterized by political hostility and considerable professional scepticism towards Russian military capabilities. This dismissive attitude is reflected in an intelligence summary of information on the Red Army of November 1939 which concluded that the 'consensus of opinion is that the value of the Red Army for war remains low'.[10] However, despite all the negative assessments, there was still fear of a possible Soviet threat to British interests in the Middle East.[11] The full extent of this fear can be seen in a Chiefs of Staff Committee report for the War Cabinet dated 8 March 1940. One of the assumptions was, 'Should Allied-Soviet hostilities commence … we must expect Germany to be ready to provide such military aid as the Soviet may be willing to accept.' Although the final conclusions of the report rejected the idea that Britain could assist the early defeat of Germany through action against Russia, it reflected the long-standing obsession with the danger from 'the dissemination of subversive propaganda and the stirring up of disorder and rebellion' by the USSR. It also made clear the signatories' (C.L.N. Newall, Dudley Pound and Edmund Ironside) worries of possible threats to Iran, Iraq, Afghanistan and India.[12]

Following the disastrous defeat of the British Expeditionary Force (BEF) in France in June 1940, there was no clear sign of a major turnaround in British military attitudes towards the Soviet Union, hardly surprising given that the USSR and Germany were still alliance partners, however unholy an alliance that may have been. The suggestion made in October 1940 by Russian officers that staff talks be conducted with the British did, however, lead to a positive though cautious response in the War Office.[13] The final decision to send a military mission to the Soviet Union was, in fact, one to which Britain had been slowly drifting shortly before the *Wehrmacht* launched Operation Barbarossa. In response to a request by the war cabinet to give 'preliminary consideration' to dispatching a military mission, it was agreed at the 210th Chiefs of Staff Committee meeting held on 13 June 1941 that 'if a Mission or Delegation were sent to Russia, all three Services should be represented on it'. The Chiefs of Staff Committee also instructed the Joint Planning Staff and the Joint Intelligence Sub-committee to consider 'the general principle of sending of a "Mission" or "Advisers" to Russia if she were attacked by Germany' and also what 'the composition and functions' of such a mission would be.[14]

The report produced by the Joint Planning Staff on 19 June is a most revealing document. Although it was pointed out that the mission could 'provide the Russians with the benefit of our experience in fighting the Germans up to date', at the same time, the 'Russians would however be likely to demand information from us which it would be undesirable to provide.' Even though it was generally assumed that the Germans would succeed in defeating the Red Army within a relatively short period of time, it was nonetheless noted that, in the event of Russian resistance being 'more prolonged than we expect', the mission would help in the coordination of

British and Russian strategy against Germany. Yet, enthusiasm was any-thing but overwhelming. The compilers of the report noted that, on balance, the main advantage would be intelligence gathering, but that they felt that the value of the mission would disappear 'in the face of Russian mistrust'. This negative attitude on the part of the Joint Planning Staff hardly augured well for the success of the mission, which – it was recommended – ought to receive the title of British Liaison Mission, 'in order to avoid political com-plications'. Nonetheless, the functions of the mission were identified with a good deal of pragmatism: the provision of intelligence on both Russian and German operations; the coordination of British and Russian strategy against the Germans; and in the event of a defeat of the Red Army in the Western regions of the country, to stimulate resistance in those parts of the country where forces were still in existence.[15]

The day after the completion of the report, the Chiefs of Staff met to con-sider its recommendations. The chiefs 'agreed that no further action was required until it was known whether the Russians would accept such a Mission'.[16] The German attack on the USSR two days later changed the situ-ation dramatically. The Chiefs of Staff Committee now found itself over-taken by events and on 24 June had to rubberstamp the directive which led to the appointment of Lieutenant General Noel Mason-MacFarlane as head of the Mission which, due to the urgency of this situation, was already being prepared for departure.[17]

Even after the German attack, the Chiefs of Staff attitude towards a wartime alliance with the USSR remained dominated by their lack of faith in the ability of the Red Army, Air Force and Navy to withstand the German onslaught. There is little doubt that this military assessment could not be so easily disentangled from their ideological distaste for Commun-ism. However, even if the Germans were only to be temporarily preoccupied in the Soviet Union, this still seemed worth exploiting to Britain's advant-age. Thus, the Chiefs of Staff saw opportunities emerging but far less for assistance to Russia and rather more as one further means of supporting Britain in its fight against Germany.[18]

II

Noel Mason-MacFarlane's tenure of the position of head of Military Mission No. 30 was probably the most turbulent of all the six heads of mission, in part due to the speed with which he changed his attitude towards the capacity of the USSR to resist the German invasion. This not only put him irrevocably on the side of Sir Stafford Cripps, the controver-sial British ambassador in Moscow, it also laid him open to the suspicion of too much sympathy with the Russians. At the same time, he was placed in the difficult position of having to pass on Russian requests for military aid at a time when Britain was not in a position to provide very much. Yet, despite his own distaste for Communism, MacFarlane quickly developed an independence of mind and belief in the Russian cause which was most unwelcome in Whitehall.[19]

While doing his utmost to carry out the major tasks of the mission, Mac-Farlane rapidly reached realistic assessments of what would be possible to achieve vis-à-vis the Russians, provoking sharp exchanges between himself and his superiors. On 10 July, he wrote in a secret cipher telegram to the War Office: 'I am very disturbed at our insistence on approaching Russians at once on subject of letting us co-operate over preparations for demolition [of] Caucasus oil fields.' He thought that an approach of this nature 'would be a great psychological mistake'.[20] He also showed some insight into Russian psychology. At the end of August 1941, for instance, he stated bluntly in a cipher message: 'Under existing circumstances Russians will never reveal their own dispositions and intentions. Apart from other considerations they mistrust our security principally on account of press and B.B.C.'[21]

Particularly interesting was one response of the Chiefs of Staff to further unwelcome views. In a message to MacFarlane in mid-July, they noted: 'We are disturbed at suggestion in your M.I.L. 11/7 that Russians are convinced we are not pulling our weight.' There then followed the statement that 'our present difficulties are largely due to Russian action in 1939 and for last 12 months we have been fighting alone against heavy odds'. The Chiefs of Staff bristled at the possibility that the Russians might make 'quite impossible demands for action by us', while the references to the only recently extinguished alliance between Germany and the Soviet Union showed a considerable degree of continuing ideological mistrust towards the USSR on the part of senior military officers.[22]

Nonetheless, even though MacFarlane had become convinced within a short period that the Russians could hold out, this did not make his task any easier as Red Army resistance began to stiffen. But many of the difficulties which were experienced under his leadership were problems which continued throughout the duration of the war, no doubt reinforcing already existing anti-Communist tendencies on the part of some members of the mission. On the one hand, there was the constant surveillance by the Soviet security services, all of which made it virtually impossible to maintain any contact with the inhabitants of Moscow. By and large, social life was restricted to embassies and the flats or hotel rooms of other mission members. The Russian officers with whom the mission had contact were afflicted by the widespread attitude in the USSR towards foreigners: one of deep suspicion.[23] According to the mission's chief interpreter under MacFarlane:

> Cooped up as we were in restricted surroundings, with little or no normal intercourse with local people ... and often watched and followed by plain clothes police, the outcome would have been collective insanity had it not been for the indomitable spirit of Mason-Mac and one or two others.[24]

Another problem which MacFarlane faced was the unwieldy structure of the mission, with three separate service chiefs for the military, naval and air sections, who in some ways duplicated the work of the service attachés who were also present in Moscow. At a meeting at the Kremlin on 30 June 1941, for example, Molotov and the deputy chiefs of the Red Army and Naval staffs received MacFarlane, Rear Admiral Geoffrey Miles and Air Vice-Marshal A.C. Collier, together with the service attachés.[25] At the same time, the mission was split up geographically, with a considerable number of personnel stationed at the ports of Murmansk and Archangel, not all of whom were naval. There was a contingent of army and air-force technicians who were required to assist in passing on tanks and aircraft in working condition, after they had been delivered by British convoys. Moreover, the Russian staffs were constantly making all kinds of demands for information, such as for advance lists of the quantity of stores and equipment which were to be delivered in each convoy, and frequent objections were made to the number of British personnel serving in Russia.[26]

In addition, MacFarlane's command suffered from the evacuation of all British mission and embassy staff from Moscow to Kuibyshev in mid-October 1941.[27] Even though the military mission was able to return in January 1942, the embassy staff remained stranded in Kuibyshev, complicating the coordination of policy between mission and embassy. Even in April 1942, the Foreign Office advised the British ambassador not to put pressure on the Soviet government for a return of the embassy to the capital and to rely simply on 'prolonging' the length of his visits to Moscow to keep in touch with the military mission.[28] However, for the mission, a return to Moscow also meant a return to the daily frustrations of dealing with the Otdel, the Soviet organization responsible for liaising with the British officials. In fact, the nature of this daily business led MacFarlane to note in a cipher message of March 1942, reporting on an encouraging visit to the northern ports, that 'the trip ... emphasized how much easier things are when you get away from Moscow'.[29]

But if MacFarlane's visit to the northern ports had shown that the situation there was positive, and relations with the local Russian commanders good, the work of the British Tank Detachment continued to be a source of intense irritation.[30] Information obtained in early January 1942 by a member of the military section of the mission, Lieutenant Colonel Hugo, indicated that British bren-gun carriers had already been employed for reconnaissance purposes in conjunction with motorcycles and that British tanks had been contributing positively to the situation at the front line.[31] Yet, despite this, the Russians continued to make no use of British technical experts stationed at Moscow, Gorki, Archangel and Kazan, and the Red Army Tank Directorate took two months to respond to a request by Mason-MacFarlane in October 1941 for discussions. While the Russians were aware of the importance of British maintenance work carried out on tanks delivered to Archangel and Murmansk before they were sent on by rail, the work-

ings and machinations of Soviet bureaucracy conspired to sabotage an effective use of the available British technical personnel.[32]

MacFarlane's 'indomitable spirit' in the face of such difficulties did,
however, gradually undermine his position at home. At the Moscow conference in late September and early October 1941, he had been extremely outspoken at a meeting on 2 October between Lord Beaverbrook and Stanislaw
Kot, General Wladyslaw Sikorski's representative in Moscow. Likewise, he
had to some extent been a victim of the lukewarm attitude of the Chiefs of
Staff towards the mission. They seemed unable or unwilling to understand
his exasperation after the mission, and the embassy staff had been evacuated
to Kuibyshev in October. MacFarlane was also caught up in the disputes
over policy in the Cabinet, which were in full swing in the wake of the
Moscow conference. Above all, in late 1941 and early 1942, the infighting
in London created an atmosphere in which it was politically expedient to
blame the head of mission for any difficulties which arose in military cooperation with the Russians.[33]

III

In fact, the very discussions surrounding MacFarlane's replacement indicated
the divisions and confusion over British policy vis-à-vis the mission. Despite
his reasonably good relations with the Russians in early 1942, including a
long and friendly talk with Marshal Boris Shaposhnikov on 23 February,[34] in
late March the question of MacFarlane's replacement was raised at a Chiefs
of Staff Committee meeting after some prompting by the Foreign Office.[35]
But the deliberations over his successor dragged on for so long that by the
time he was informed on 8 May 1942 that he was to be replaced (and to be
taking up an appointment as Governor and Commander-in-Chief Gibraltar),
the question of his successor had still not been settled. In a final message to
the War Office, he reminded the military secretary that, when selecting his
successor, it ought to be borne in mind that 'the Soviet Staff are extremely
suspicious of officers who were either in Russia during the revolutionary war
period or who have been prominently identified with intelligence work'.
After a farewell dinner given by officers of the mission on 15 May, he
departed from Moscow Central Airport on 19 May.[36]

As it turned out, Rear Admiral Geoffrey Miles, already serving in the
USSR, was entrusted with the position of head of mission. This decision,
which reversed the earlier intention to recall Miles before the winter of
1942, seems to have been viewed as a convenient, interim solution, since it
meant that 'Miles would be taking over a "running" show with which he
was well acquainted.'[37] The period of Miles' tenure as head of mission can be
seen as an interregnum in the history of Military Mission No. 30. In early
June, Miles reported back to London that there seemed to be signs of an
improvement in relations with the Soviet military, one of the rays of light
being progress in cooperation with the Russian Tank Directorate in

Moscow. However, by mid-July, there were the first signs that he was running up against the sort of frustrating difficulties his predecessor had encountered.[38] The problem was quite simply that the new head of mission lacked the initiative, dynamism and insight of Mason-MacFarlane.

Needless to say, Miles displayed the sort of mistrust of the Russians which typified the British personnel serving with the mission. In a telegram at the beginning of June 1942, he argued: 'I can see no reason why we should continue these one sided arrangements for ever and give Soviet Mission [in the UK] something for nothing. It certainly does not help the military section here.'[39] Still, it was in many ways an unfortunate time to be head of mission. The War Office remained jittery over anything which might rock the Anglo-Soviet boat and was quick to advise Miles in July 1942 against pursuing a request to inspect Moscow's anti-aircraft defences due to the 'obvious preoccupation' of the Russian General Staff with the German summer offensive.[40] Nonetheless, many of Miles' messages to Whitehall displayed a general sense of helplessness in the face of the difficulties he was encountering, and he made frequent requests for 'guidance' on various issues, in particular on that most thorny of all problems: how to deal with Russian questions on the formation of a 'Second Front'.[41]

During a visit to Britain, Miles reported on 29 September 1942 at a Chiefs of Staff Committee meeting in Whitehall that there appeared to be a food shortage among the civilian population and that he thought the Russians might ask for food supplies and oil to be sent with the next convoys. He also noted that Murmansk 'had been considerably devastated by enemy air action' but continued to complain about the difficulty of obtaining information from the Russians, even though he had been allowed to inspect the port.[42] In February 1943, he made the demand that the British government should take 'concerted action' in order that 'Soviet information and experience' be obtained in a timely fashion, yet justified his request by pointing out that the American military attaché, Brigadier General J.A. Michela, had suggested he follow his policy of pursuing the issue of increased diplomatic pressure at a higher level. Not surprisingly, the reply from the Chiefs of Staff was extremely icy.[43]

At the beginning of the following month, Miles was informed he was to be replaced, no doubt as a result of his hapless approach to adhering to official policy.[44] Indicative of his lack of success was the fact that when he finally left Moscow by air on 22 March 1943, following the announcement on 17 March that his successor would be Lieutenant General Giffard Martel, no representative of the Soviet General Staff came to the airport to see him off.[45]

IV

Martel arrived at an aerodrome near Moscow on 5 April 1943 at 7.30 A.M. and was met by high-ranking officers of the mission and two Red Army officers, Major General Dubinin and Colonel Evstigneev.[46] He had been sent to

Moscow with two letters in his pocket, one from Churchill addressed to Stalin, the other from Alan Brooke addressed to the Chief of Staff of the Red Army, at that time Marshal A.V. Vasilevsky. Both letters praised Martel as a distinguished officer with an excellent military record.[47] According to Martel, on his arrival in Moscow, he felt that the chances of success of his mission would be slight. He asked the advice of members of the mission and officials on the Embassy staff and was told he would have to be tough with the Russians. In his own – perhaps rather exaggerated – view, he took this policy to heart and enjoyed some initial successes.[48] Martel's own extremely positive, postwar view of his performance as head of mission has been more or less discounted by Bradley Smith, who sees him as being too blunt and accuses him of making a series of mistakes.[49] Is Smith correct or did Martel actually achieve something?

There is no doubt that during the first four months of his tenure of the post of head of mission that Martel enjoyed a number of successes in gaining access to information and senior Red Army officers. Having met Marshal Vasilevsky on 21 April, two days later he was granted permission to visit the front line in the Kursk/Oriel region. During the visit, which took place between 11 and 19 May, he was able to gather a considerable amount of order of battle material and gain impressions of the strengths and capabilities of the Red Army. Martel also met R.Ya. Malinovsky at the latter's headquarters. After Malinovsky had explained the situation at the front with the aid of a large map, Martel demanded in an outraged tone that the Russian dispositions, which were covered by a piece of paper, be revealed to him. The Red Army commander was taken aback but then pulled the piece of paper aside. According to Martel, this confrontation led directly to the full cooperation of the Red Army in his tour of the front line, and he achieved a number of other successes shortly afterwards in gaining access to the Russian General Staff.[50]

Throughout his time as head of mission, Martel did prove to be extremely effective in the way in which he collated military information, processed it and passed it back to London. Periodic reports which summarized experiences and important information attest to his professional and energetic approach. What is interesting is that his pronounced anti-Communist attitude did not interfere with his military judgment when it came to making use of the intelligence and general impressions, which he gathered from conversations and meetings. One field in particular illustrates Martel's professionalism better than any other: that of armoured warfare. In June 1943, for instance, he compiled an insightful report on the organization and methods of the Russian armoured forces, based on observations gathered during his visit to the front the previous month and a long discussion with the head of the Red Army Tank Directorate in Moscow on 15 June. In September 1943, he sent a report drawing lessons from the Russian front for future Allied operations in Europe on the basis that the experience in Russia would be more relevant than that of the British in North Africa.[51]

Moreover, he showed that he was perfectly capable of being insubordinate. As a result of comments made in his 'Report No. 3 from the British Military Mission to the U.S.S.R.', the Chiefs of Staff Committee communicated the strong objection which the Foreign Office had taken towards criticisms by Martel of their ministry. After a largely implausible explanation about certain 'shortcomings' not being attributable to officials in the Foreign Office, the letter closed with the recommendation that in future 'you will ... ensure that any criticism you may have to make in future reports are more impartially distributed'.[52] However, and as later correspondence made abundantly clear,[53] Martel was not mistaken in attributing to the Foreign Office what he saw as a policy of 'appeasement' towards the Russian military authorities.

At the beginning of September, in a report which summarized information gained from 'long discussions with the General Staff at Moscow' in July and August, Martel was still fairly optimistic. Although he noted that it would be necessary to take a firm line when the Russians were being 'particularly tiresome', he pointed out at the same time that problems in 'domestic relations' (visas, difficulties over mail and the treatment of British personnel arrested by the Russian authorities) had been no fault of the Russian military, who had in fact been helpful 'at all times' in such matters.[54] The War Office also seemed satisfied. At the end of June, the Vice Chief of the Imperial General Staff (VCIGS) had written to Martel stating that there was 'no doubt that during the short time you have been there you have been able to get us an enormous amount of information'.[55] 'Pug' Ismay wrote him a personal letter towards the end of September 1943, commenting that 'I like your reports and appreciations of the Russian situation so much and feel that, despite your misgivings, you are doing a grand job of work.'[56] Furthermore, in an estimate of the information supplied by Martel between July and October made by MI3 in the War Office, the conclusion was reached that 'there has been a very satisfactory flow of information'.[57]

By the end of September 1943, however, Martel felt that relations with the Russians were beginning to turn sour. Partly a result of the effects of a clash between Martel and the new head of the Air Section (appointed in June 1943), Air Marshal Sir John Babbington,[58] the deterioration may well also have been exacerbated by frustration caused by decisions made in Whitehall. As a result of the progressive worsening in relations between the mission and the Soviet authorities in the final months of the year, opinion in Whitehall began to turn against the head of mission. Still, this was as much due to pressure being exerted by the Foreign Office as it was to the War Office's dissatisfaction.[59] Hence, considering the evidence, Bradley Smith's view of Martel's leadership as inept seems misplaced. For instance, Martel had sent clear and perceptive warnings of the necessity of reducing the size of the mission as early as May 1943, stating in one cipher telegram: 'Am investigating possible reductions in size of mission. Russians dislike large missions. Undesirable to force an increase on Russians at moment when they are co-operating well.'[60]

Towards the end of 1943, Martel was becoming increasingly frustrated at the uncooperative attitude of the Russian military, not least of all due to his wish to gather information on German army methods before the invasion of northern Europe. Since his visit to the front line in May, there had been no further opportunity to witness active operations. He found it particularly galling that in the second half of the year, the Soviet Military Mission in London had made 60 visits to see units and bases of the British army, navy and air force and over 100 visits to armament factories, while a Russian general had been able to observe British combat operations in Italy.[61] In January 1944, Martel continued his pressure on the Chiefs of Staff in order that he be allowed to adopt a tougher line. He sent a request to this effect to the VCIGS on 12 January; a similar request 'suggesting a firmer attitude' was sent on 25 January. On 28 January, the CIGS sent a message to Moscow that he was to be recalled. Martel left the Soviet Union just over a week later by air on 7 February 1944.[62]

The recall had obviously been discussed in advance; a letter of 10 January 1944 from Martel to the VCIGS makes clear that the former was aware that he was to be leaving the USSR shortly. His recall – which he may well have deliberately set out to provoke – seems to have been due to his constant demands for greater firmness and the feeling that he was not being allowed to take the strong stand he felt necessary. But it was certainly not due to the depression which tended to grip other members of the mission. In his letter of 10 January to the VCIGS, he wrote that he was 'keeping fit and boxing and can so far take on any of the youngsters here. One has to do something like this to counteract the depressing influence of dealing all day with these astonishing Bolsheviks.'[63]

Back in London, Martel made plain to the military authorities in White-hall, not least of all the Chiefs of Staff Committee, that the position of the mission could only be improved if it were instructed to take a firm line, were supported by 'the authorities in this country' and by exerting pressure on the Soviet Military Mission in London. He pointed to recent American successes as proof of his point of view, as well as noting that his own experience had shown that 'The Russian does not resent plain truthful speech. He despises the bootlicking methods which we sometimes employ.'[64] While these views represented the thinking of many senior British officers, no one had stated them before, or did so later, quite as bluntly as Lieutenant General Giffard Martel.

V

Well over a week after Martel's departure, the War Office informed the British ambassador in Moscow of the appointment of Lieutenant General Brocas Burrows as new head of the military mission; he subsequently arrived in Moscow on 30 March 1944.[65] Until Bradley F. Smith's study, Burrows only appearance on the historiographical stage was a brief walk-on part during the Moscow conference of October 1944.[66] In fact, he is portrayed by Smith in his study of Anglo-American intelligence cooperation with the Soviet Union as a virtual cliché of an anti-Communist British general. Specifically, he notes how Burrows insisted on being presented to Stalin wearing medals which he had earned during the Allied intervention in the Russian Civil War. Still, the references he makes to Burrows' period as head of mission are rather inconclusive. On the one hand, he notes that 'Burrows got off to an especially rocky start regarding intelligence-sharing matters', but, on the other, certain aspects of British intelligence relations with their host counterparts 'were warmer during the spring and summer of 1944 than they had been in the chilly winter atmosphere of 1943–4'.[67] To what extent, then, did Burrows fit the ideological role model provided by his predecessor Martel?

Of considerable interest is an assessment by him of the attitude of the Soviet leadership towards its Western Allies before his first month in Moscow had been completed – in other words, before he had really had time to assess the situation properly. Burrows thought that the Soviet government had been active in trying to prevent close cooperation between the Soviet military forces and their Western Allies because 'a close comparison would display all too soon the bareness of the Soviet military cupboard'. For Burrows, the overconfidence of Soviet military commanders was due to the fact that they knew nothing about the capabilities of the armed forces of their allies, this being mainly due to the activities of the secret police. He was also of the opinion that without 'Allied supplies of all types', the Red Army would have been unable to have resisted the German invasion. He ended his communication by warning that the Soviet authorities were now nervous about the second front and likely to try and downplay its significance. Burrows' memorandum reveals a great deal about his anti-Soviet attitudes and is interesting for the way in which he looked forward mainly to the postwar portrayal of the military achievements of the Allies, rather than current operations, going as far as to recommend a press campaign in the wake of the landing in Europe which would highlight the anticipated Anglo-American achievements.[68]

As in the case of other high-ranking British officers, this negative assessment of Soviet military capabilities seems to have been dominated, and more probably driven, by a strong anti-Communist political stance. It can be ascertained from Alan Brooke's diary that Burrows was in a negative frame of mind before he even set off for Moscow. According to the entry for 17 February 1944:

> After lunch I had an interview with Brocas Burrows who is off to Moscow ... and found that the Foreign Office had been briefing him on such a conciliatory basis that he did not imagine he was to get anything back out of the Russians.[69]

This attitude does not seem to have changed much during the course of Burrows command of the mission. Further evidence can be seen in his reactions towards a suggestion which began to receive attention at the beginning of July 1944. On being informed by Major General John R. Deane, head of the United States' Military Mission, that Stalin had told W. Averell Harriman, the American ambassador, 'he thought the time had arrived to form in Moscow a military committee to coordinate matters of military importance concerning the Allies', Burrows sent a cipher telegram to generals Hastings Ismay and John Alexander Sinclair asking whether they agreed in principle. Burrows himself saw in the idea a way of rescuing the British Military Mission from its impasse, commenting that 'it is vital that this combined staff should be formed in Moscow'.[70] The reaction of the Chiefs of Staff was, predictably, one of suspicion. Sir Charles Portal suggested that both Deane and Burrows should visit London to discuss the idea further, while it was agreed that Burrows should not commit the chiefs to the functions of the proposed committee.[71]

By the beginning of August, Burrows was back in Britain for consultations with the Chiefs of Staff. He submitted a very revealing paper – which was read by the VCIGS, Lieutenant General Archibald Nye – dealing with the issue of the proposed combined committee, and still seemed at this stage convinced of its potential value. Although he went on to complain about the lack of cooperative attitude on the part of the Soviet military, he explained this as being partly due to the lack of centralization in their battlefield intelligence system. His disapproval of the Foreign Office policy was made plain in the statement: 'In my opinion there is only a very remote possibility that the Military Mission in MOSCOW will be allowed any access to the Red Army at any level if the present policy of complete appeasement continues.' The message was an old one: the lack of freedom to bargain was interpreted by the Russians as a weakness and put the mission in an impossible position.[72] It is clear from the wording of this memorandum that a political stance had taken precedence over military analysis.

On 2 August 1944, Burrows attended a Chiefs of Staff meeting at which the idea of the combined committee was discussed, but the chiefs remained unenthusiastic. Alan Brooke noted afterwards in his diary, 'I feel that it is highly unlikely that Stalin will ever agree to any such organization being established.'[73] A further meeting took place on 16 August, at which Burrows referred to the combined committee as 'an opportunity', yet at the same time warned that he thought the Russians would try to use it to obtain advance information on Anglo-American plans. Two days later, in a communication to Washington, the Chiefs of Staff stated that they were 'wholly opposed to the creation of a United Chiefs of Staff Committee'.[74] With that, the idea was effectively killed, even though the Foreign Office continued to pursue it long after it had become clear that it was stillborn.[75]

On his return to Moscow, in addition to the usual and frustrating wrangles over the exchange of intelligence material, in particular order of battle details, Burrows seems to have performed reasonably competently when it came to the general management of intelligence exchange. Bradley Smith is unable to reach a conclusion as to whether Burrows' tenure of the position was ineffective due to the general's own failings or because of the incoherence of official British policy. While he was dealt a poor hand, Burrows does though appear to have rubbed the Russians up the wrong way, and the most obvious contributory factor was clearly his openly anti-Communist attitude.[76] Moreover, as Burrows probably foresaw, the failure of the Combined Committee ended his attempt to rejuvenate the work of the mission. On 18 October 1944, it was announced on the BBC that he had been appointed commander-in-chief, West Africa. On 25 and 29 October, he paid two final visits to General Kutuzov and then departed from Moscow on 1 November.[77]

VI

The final phase of the British Military Mission in Moscow can best be described as lacklustre. Following the departure of Burrows, the head of the naval section, Admiral E.R. Archer, took over as chief of mission. His period in office can be viewed as decidedly uneventful.[78] It was fitting for the continuing impromptu nature of British policy that Whitehall decided three days before VE-Day that the status of the mission could be enhanced if a higher ranking officer were to become its head. Thus, Lieutenant General J.A.G. Gammell was sent to replace Admiral Archer, but not in time to attend the formal surrender ceremony organized by the Red Army in Berlin.[79] In fact, as the ever fewer and more laconic entries in the war diary indicate, in the final months of the war, the mission ceased to hold any of its previous significance. At the beginning of May 1945, one of Admiral Archer's last dispatches noted that relations with the Russians had deteriorated considerably in the preceding weeks.[80]

On 1 August 1945, the Chiefs of Staff informed Gammell how to react should the Soviet Union declare war on Japan. In particular, he was instructed to show a willingness to provide intelligence on enemy forces in areas under the command responsibility of the Chiefs of Staff, although he was to refrain from volunteering material on British equipment or 'our own intentions, distribution or Order of Battle'.[81] But as the first Cold War frost began to form, the last head of Military Mission No. 30 could only watch as Anglo-Soviet relations began to seize up, even before the final defeat of Japan. It seems cruelly symbolic that the war diary of the mission contains no entries for the penultimate month of its presence in the Soviet Union.[82] At some point towards the end of September 1945, Gammell left Moscow, finally ending the existence of the mission in the USSR.[83]

The last six months of the mission had made plain that latterly it had become effectively irrelevant to the conduct of the war in the East. Still, despite all the frustrations of the six heads of mission, there seems little doubt that certain successes were achieved in the exchange of intelligence, especially details on order of battle and German equipment. Likewise, one cannot underestimate the contribution of the mission to managing the arrival and maintenance of vital British supplies, including tanks and aircraft. The uneasy intelligence cooperation did though obviously favour the Russians, who showed – other than during fairly brief periods – little desire to recipro-cate. However, since Britain's aim in mid-1941 had been to keep the Red Army in the field fighting the Germans, one of the central goals surrounding the dispatch of the mission was achieved. But the question under considera-tion here is less, Was the mission a success? and much more, What role did ideology play in the work of Britain's Military Mission No. 30?

One of the most important observations which can be made is that there was a clear correlation between a strong anti-Communist conviction and a negative perception of the fighting abilities of the Red Army. This is clearly noticeable in the decision making of the Chiefs of Staff Committee in 1941.[84] In many cases, anti-Communist attitudes led to completely unrealis-tic ideas as to how the British Military Mission should become involved in the war in the East, the suggestion that mission members should assist the Russians in the demolition of the Caucasian oil fields being one glaring example. Moreover, it is interesting to note that the two heads of mission who came to the most realistic and positive assessment of the fighting abili-ties of the Soviet forces, Mason-MacFarlane and Martel, made a clear differentiation between ordinary Soviet citizens, and also Russian officers and men at the front, and those Soviet state and military officials whose main job appeared to be obstruction and surveillance.[85]

Essentially, the influence of ideology led to a three-cornered fight in British policy-making circles in relation to the military mission. On the one hand, the Foreign Office tended to play down the mission's difficulties in favour of nurturing 'good relations' with the Soviet Union. Not surprisingly, this led to clashes not only between the Foreign and War Offices, but also between the Chiefs of Staff and the heads of mission – after all, the chiefs could hardly ignore the instructions of the War Cabinet. Yet, this was not the only cause of friction between the Chiefs of Staff and the heads of mission. The ideological influence on the chiefs' view of the situation in Russia caused intense disputes between them and the two most competent heads of mission, MacFarlane and Martel. Although these two generals were certainly anti-Communist, their military professionalism led them to a prag-matic attitude when dealing with Soviet state and military authorities. Instead of the suspicious, mistrusting anti-Communism of the early interwar period, which certainly survived in the War Office during the war, they reached an appreciation of what made Soviet officials and the Soviet system tick. The very different postwar careers of MacFarlane, who in 1945 was elected as a Labour Member of Parliament,[86] and Martel, who became one of the most prominent military Cold War publicists,[87] cannot detract from the quite similar views which they held about the Soviet Union as a result of their wartime experiences.

Thus, it can be argued that ideology can seriously distort the perspective of the situation of a military mission as seen from the decision making centre at home. Senior military officers of average ability appointed to serve as head of mission (men such as Miles and Burrows) are likely to be affected by any prevalent ideological leanings in the armed forces. However, senior officers with a certain flair for independent thought (such as MacFarlane), or the assessment of foreign military capabilities (such as Martel), are capable of putting aside their ideological predispositions and reaching sound assessments of the capabilities of the host nation's armed forces and the best approach to military collaboration with them. In short, managing the effects of ideology, and selecting officers with the ability to work against prevailing ideological attitudes, can decisively influence the effectiveness of a military mission. In the case of the British Military Mission to the Soviet Union, the impact and effects of ideology on decision making were never seriously addressed, so that the mission was never able to achieve its full potential.

Notes

1 Joan Beaumont, 'A question of diplomacy: British Military Mission 1941–45', *RUSI Journal*, 118 (1973), pp. 74–7, although it has merits, it is too brief and incomplete to qualify as a reliable overview. Still useful for the history of the mission until December 1941, especially within the wider diplomatic context, is Gabriel Gorodetsky, *Stafford Cripps' Mission to Moscow, 1940–42* (Cambridge: Cambridge University Press, 1984), while there is a considerable amount of information to be found in F.H. Hinsley, *British Intelligence in the Second World War: Its Influence on Strategy and Operations. Volume II* (London: HMSO, 1981). There are, though, only two cursory references in John Erickson, *The Road to Berlin: Stalin's War with Germany*, Vol. 2 (London: Weidenfeld & Nicolson, 1983), pp. 191, 511, indicating the scale of neglect which was shown by historians towards the history of the mission until recently.

2 Bradley F. Smith, *Sharing Secrets with Stalin: How the Allies Traded Intelligence, 1941–45* (Lawrence: Kansas University Press, 1996).

3 For various definitions and discussion, see Göran Therborn, *The Ideology of Power and the Power of Ideology* (London: Verso, 1980); Kurt Lenk, 'Ideologie/Ideologiekritik', in Dieter Nohlen (ed.), *Wörterbuch Staat und Politik* (Munich: Piper, 1991), pp. 229–32; Erwin Häckel, 'Ideologie und Außenpolitik', in Wichard Woyke (ed.), *Handwörterbuch Internationale Politik* (Opladen: Leske & Budrich, 2000), pp. 148–54.

4 On this issue, see Markku Ruotsila, *British and American Anticommunism Before the Cold War* (London: Frank Cass, 2001).

5 The head of the Soviet Military Mission to Great Britain (1941–4), Admiral N.M. Kharlamov, mentions a Major Swan of the British Army in his memoirs, who had been suggested as a representative of the British General Staff in Moscow, but who apparently turned out to have served as a British commander in Archangel during the Allied intervention; Kharlamov claims he succeeded in blocking the appointment. See N. Kharlamov, *Difficult Mission. War Memoirs: Soviet Admiral in Great Britain During the Second World War* (Moscow: Progress Publishers, 1986), pp. 114–15.

6 It is worth pointing out here that part of the reason for the anti-Communist attitude of British officers was that they regarded the Bolsheviks as having

betrayed the Allied cause during the First World War, allowing the Germans to concentrate forces for the March 1918 offensive. On this point, see Giffard Martel, *The Russian Outlook* (London: Michael Joseph, 1947), pp. 34–5.

7 Useful here are Keith Neilson, '"Pursued by a bear": British estimates of Soviet military strength and Anglo-Soviet relations, 1922–1939', *Canadian Journal of History*, 28 (1993), pp. 189–221; James S. Herndon, 'British perceptions of Soviet military capability, 1935–9', in Wolfgang J. Mommsen and Lothar Kettenacker (eds), *The Fascist Challenge and the Policy of Appeasement* (London: George Allen & Unwin, 1983), pp. 297–319.

8 Correspondence between leading British army officers in 1920/1 indicates that they viewed Bolshevism as a threat to British society at home as well as to the security of the Empire. For examples, see Liddell Hart Centre for Military Archives, King's College London, Field Marshal Sir A.A. Montgomery-Massingberd Papers, 8/16, Colonel W.L.O. Twiss to Montgomery-Massingberd, 30 June 1921, Lieutenant General W. Braithwaite to Montgomery-Massingberd, 11 July 1921, and Montgomery-Massingberd to Colonel C. Evans, 12 July 1921.

9 See here David Dilks, '"The unnecessary war"? Military Advice and Foreign Policy in Great Britain, 1931–1939', in Adrian Preston (ed.), *General Staffs and Diplomacy Before the Second World War* (London: Croom Helm, 1978), pp. 98–132.

10 The National Archives of the United Kingdom, Kew (hereafter, TNA), WO193/642, M.I.2(b), SECRET. The Red Army, memorandum, 22 November 1939.

11 TNA, WO193/646, Soviet Union. Memorandum Respecting the Soviet Threat to British Interests in the Middle East, SECRET, 28 October 1939.

12 TNA, WO193/646, COS (40) 252, War Cabinet. Chiefs of Staff Committee, Military Implications of Hostilities with Russia in 1940. Report, SECRET, 8 March 1940.

13 TNA, WO193/648, COS (40) 842, War Cabinet. Chiefs of Staff Committee, Staff Talks with the Soviet [sic], 18 October 1940.

14 TNA, WO193/645A, War Cabinet. Chiefs of Staff Committee, extract from minutes of meeting, 13 June 1941.

15 TNA, WO193/645A, SECRET. JP (41) 465. Proposed Mission to Russia, 19 June 1941.

16 TNA, WO193/645A, War Cabinet. Chiefs of Staff Committee, extract from minutes of meeting, 20 June 1941.

17 TNA, WO193/645A, War Cabinet. Chiefs of Staff Committee, extract from minutes of 210th meeting, 24 June 1941, and War Cabinet. JP (41) 482. Joint Planning Staff, Mission to Russia, 24 June 1941.

18 Sheila Lawlor, 'Britain and the Russian entry into war', in Richard Langhorne (ed.), *Diplomacy and Intelligence During the Second World War: Essays in Honour of F.H. Hinsley* (Cambridge: Cambridge University Press, 1985), pp. 168–83, esp. 180–3.

19 A brief summary of Mason-MacFarlane's work as head of the Military Mission can be found in Ewan Butler, *Mason-Mac: The Life of Lieutenant-General Sir Noel Mason-MacFarlane* (London: Macmillan, 1972), pp. 130–44. There is more detail and context in Smith, *Sharing Secrets*, pp. 48–118, but Gorodetsky, *Stafford Cripps' Mission*, pp. 177–267, is more balanced.

20 TNA, WO193/644, cipher telegram, 30 Military Mission to War Office (hereafter, WO), 10 July 1941, and reply by WO to 30 Military Mission, n.d. [11 July 1941].

21 TNA, WO193/644, cipher telegram, 30 Military Mission to WO, 31 August 1941.

22 TNA, WO193/644, Foreign Office (hereafter, FO) to Moscow. Chiefs of Staff for MacFarlane, 14 July 1941.

23 A.H. Birse, *Memoirs of an Interpreter* (London: Michael Joseph, 1967), pp. 57–60, 66–8; for similar impressions of life in Russia, also Martel, *The Russian Outlook*, pp. 77–9.

24 Birse, *Memoirs*, p. 68.

25 TNA, WO178/25, 30 Military Mission. War Diary, entry for 30 June 1941.

26 Martel, *The Russian Outlook*, pp. 80–1; TNA, WO208/1787, cipher telegram, Military Mission to WO, MIL/2510, 24 January 1942.

27 Vividly described in Gorodetsky, *Stafford Cripps' Mission*, pp. 251–4.

28 TNA, WO 178/26, 30 Military Mission. War Diary, entries for 11, 22 and 25 January 1942, WO193/645A, cipher telegram, No. 499, FO to Kuibyshev, 10 April 1942.

29 TNA, WO193/645A, cipher telegram, MacFarlane to Director of Military Intelligence, MIL/3998, 30 March 1942.

30 Recent research is starting to suggest that the contribution to Russian combat strength of British tanks and bren-gun carriers in late 1941 and early 1942 has hitherto been underestimated. For a useful contribution, see Alexander Hill, 'British "Lend-Lease" Tanks and the Battle for Moscow, November-December 1941 – A Research Note', *Journal of Slavic Military Studies*, 19 (2006), pp. 289–94. See also the remarkable collection of photographs of British Valentine, Matilda and Churchill tanks in Red Army service, in M. Kolomyjec I. Moszczanskij, *Lend Lease*, Vol. I (Warsaw: Waydawnictwo Militaria, 2001).

31 TNA, WO208/1792, MacFarlane to Director of Military Intelligence, 7 January 1942.

32 TNA, WO208/1797, MacFarlane to Under Secretary of State for War, 11 February 1942, enclosing translation of memo to Lieutenant General A.P. Panilov, British Tank Personnel in USSR, 6 February 1942.

33 Gorodetsky, *Stafford Cripps' Mission*, pp. 236–7; Smith, *Sharing Secrets*, pp. 112–15.

34 TNA, WO193/645A, cipher telegrams, 30 Military Mission to WO, 24 February and 2, 6 and 14 March 1942.

35 TNA, WO193/645A, Chiefs of Staff Committee, extract from minutes of meeting, 25 March 1942.

36 TNA, WO178/26, 30 Military Mission. War Diary, entries for 8, 11, 15 and 19 May 1942.

37 TNA, WO193/645A, Chiefs of Staff Committee, extracts from minutes of meetings, 25 March and 11 May 1942.

38 TNA, WO193/645A, cipher telegrams, 30 Military Mission to WO, 8 June and 18 July 1942.

39 TNA, WO193/645A, cipher telegram, head of Military Mission to WO, 3 June 1942.

40 TNA, WO208/1810, cipher telegram, WO to Military Mission, 12 July 1942.

41 TNA, WO208/1810, cipher telegram, 30 Military Mission to WO, 7 July 1942, WO193/645A, cipher telegrams, 30 Military Mission to WO, 3 June and 18 July 1942, Chiefs of Staff Committee, extract from 194th meeting, 1 July 1942.

42 TNA, WO193/644, Chiefs of Staff Committee, extract from 275th meeting, 29 September 1942.

43 TNA, WO193/645A, cipher telegram, Miles to Chiefs of Staff, MIL/8360, 16 February 1943, reply by Chiefs of Staff, 20 February 1943.

44 TNA, WO193/645A, cipher telegram, FO to Miles, reply to telegram of 1 March 1943.

45 TNA, WO178/27, 30 Military Mission. War Diary, entries for 17 and 22 March 1943.
46 TNA, WO178/27, 30 Military Mission. War Diary, entry for 5 April 1943.
47 Imperial War Museum, London (hereafter, IWM), Lieutenant General Sir Giffard Martel Papers, GQM 4/4, fol. 266, A.J. Brooke to Chief of Staff, Red Army, n.d., fol. 271, Winston Churchill to Josef Stalin, 27 March 1943.
48 IWM, Martel Papers, GQM 4/4, fol. 2–5, SECRET AND CONFIDENTIAL. Notes on Russia, n.d.
49 Smith, *Sharing Secrets*, pp. 179–80, accusing him of 'heavy-handedness' and having 'patronized and quarreled with senior members of his own mission'.
50 IWM, Martel Papers, GQM 4/4, fol. 267–8, SECRET. Record of meeting with Marshal A.V. Vasilevski, 21 April 1943; Martel, *The Russian Outlook*, pp. 47–60.
51 IWM, Martel Papers, GQM 4/4, fol. 200–3, MOST SECRET. The Russian Armoured Force, No. 30 Military Mission, 21 June 1943, fol. 129–30, SECRET. Some observations on battle lessons and some particular references to armoured warfare, No. 30 Military Mission, 6 September 1943.
52 IWM, Martel Papers, GQM 4/4, fol. 127, MOST SECRET, Nye to Martel, 18 August 1943.
53 IWM, Martel Papers, GQM 4/4, fol. 85, MOST SECRET AND PERSONAL, Nye to Martel, 22 November 1943.
54 TNA, WO208/1835, Report No. 4 from the British Military Mission in Russia, 2 September 1943, [signed] Martel.
55 IWM, Martel Papers, GQM 4/4, fol. 180, CIGS/DO/103, Nye to Martel, 28 June 1943.
56 IWM, Martel Papers, GQM 4/4, fol. 114, Ismay to Martel, 22 September 1943.
57 TNA, WO208/1835, M.I.3/6895/68, information obtained by 30 Military Mission from the Russians, MI3.c., 24 October 1943.
58 See IWM, Martel Papers, GQM 4/4, fol. 149, Martel to Alan Brooke, 31 August 1943, fol. 127–69 for other documents relating to the dispute and, for an account of the affair, fol. 2–5, Notes on Russia, pp. 4–5.
59 Smith, *Sharing Secrets*, pp. 142–61, 177–80.
60 TNA, WO193/645A, cipher telegram, Chiefs of Staff from Martel, 20 May 1943.
61 IWM, Martel Papers, GQM 4/4, fol. 32, Brief. Difficulties which the British Military Mission have encountered during the last six months, n.d. [late 1943].
62 TNA, WO178/27, 30 Military Mission. War Diary, entries for 12, 25 and 28 January and 7 February 1944.
63 IWM, Martel Papers, GQM 4/4, fol. 61, Martel to Nye, 10 January 1944.
64 IWM, Martel Papers, GQM 4/4, fol. 19–21, War Cabinet. Chiefs of Staff Committee, COS (44) 49th Meeting, 16 February 1944, fol. 17–18, SECRET. The British Military Mission and its relations with the Russians, n.d. [1944].
65 TNA, WO178/27, 30 Military Mission. War Diary, entries for 20 February and 30 March 1944.
66 Winston S. Churchill, *The Second World War. Vol. VI: Triumph and Tragedy* (Reprint, London: Society, 1956), pp. 201–2; Arthur Bryant, *Triumph in the West 1943–1946* (London: Reprint Society, 1960), pp. 237–40, 242–3, 246. See also Martel, *The Russian Outlook*, p. 135.
67 Smith, *Sharing Secrets*, pp. 180–1, 192.
68 TNA, WO178/27, Lieutenant General M.B. Burrows to Under-Secretary of State for War, WO, 21 April 1944, [memo. entitled] Russian Attitudes Towards the War Efforts of Their Allies.
69 Bryant, *Triumph in the West*, p. 121.

70 TNA, WO193/671, cipher telegram, 30 Military Mission to AMSSO, 2 July 1944.
71 TNA, WO193/671, extract from minutes of the COS (44) 219th (O) meeting, 3 July 1944, and extract from minutes of the COS (44) 221st (O) meeting, 5 July 1944.
72 TNA, WO193/671, TOP SECRET. [Lieutenant General Burrows] Notes for the Chiefs of Staff, British Military Mission to the USSR, 1 August 1944.
73 Bryant, *Triumph in the West*, p. 196.
74 TNA, WO193/671, extract from minutes of COS (44) 277th (O) meeting, 16 August 1944, and cipher telegram, AMSSO to JSM Washington, 18 August 1944.
75 TNA, WO193/671, extract from minutes of COS (44) 360th (O) meeting, 7 November 1944. Meeting to be held on 29 December 1944. Note on COS (44) 1055 (O). Tripartite Military Commission in Moscow and minutes of the COS (45) 9th meeting, 9 January 1945.
76 Smith, *Sharing Secrets*, pp. 205–7, 210–11, 216, 223–6.
77 TNA, WO178/27, 30 Military Mission. War Diary, entries for 18, 25 and 29 October and 1 November 1944.
78 The war diary of the military mission does not even mention the promotion of Archer to head of mission, merely noting that on 7 November 1944, he attended a reception given by Molotov. TNA, WO178/27, 30 Military Mission. War Diary, entry for 7 November 1944.
79 Smith, *Sharing Secrets*, pp. 243–4.
80 TNA, WO178/27, 30 Military Mission. War Diary, entry for 2 May 1945.
81 TNA, WO208/1787, cipher telegram, AMSSO to 30 Military Mission, 1 August 1945.
82 TNA, WO178/27, 30 Military Mission. War Diary, August 1945.
83 TNA, WO208/1787, cipher telegram, 30 Military Mission to WO, 21 September 1945, indicates that Gammell was preparing a farewell meeting with General Antonov at some time between 27 and 30 September. The Soviet Military Mission to Great Britain was disbanded in early October. Kharlamov, *Difficult Mission*, p. 229.
84 Anti-Communism in Whitehall is a prominent theme in the memoirs of the head of the Soviet mission to Britain, 1941–4. Kharlamov identifies Admiral Dudley Pound in particular as one of the most ardent anti-Communist senior officers. Kharlamov, *Difficult Mission*, pp. 37–8, 111–13.
85 IWM, Lieutenant General Sir Noel Mason-MacFarlane Papers, reel 2, MM31, untitled summary of experiences in Russia, n.d.; Martel, *The Russian Outlook*, pp. 51–3, 66–71.
86 Butler, *Mason-Mac*, pp. 199–217.
87 For his post-1945 views, see G. le. Q. Martel, 'When we are rearmed', *Freedom. The Journal of the Fighting Fund for Freedom*, 70 (1952), pp. 1–2, and 72 (1952), pp. 1–3; G. le. Q. Martel, 'The shadow of the Russian bear', *Daily Mail*, 22 September 1949. See also his memoirs, *An Outspoken Soldier* (London: Sifton Praed, 1949), pp. 333–60, and his book, *East Versus West* (London: Museum Press, 1952).

6 American advisors to the Republic of Korea

America's first commitment in the Cold War, 1946–1950

Bryan R. Gibby

American military advisors assigned first to the American zone of occupation in Korea (1946–1948), and then later to the United States Military Advisory Group to the Republic of Korea (KMAG; 1948–1950), found themselves tackling not only traditional roles of training and organization, but also more crucial ones like nation building and counter-insurgency. Indeed, the success and survival of a non-Communist state on the Korean peninsula hinged upon the political, cultural, and military talents of the officers and men assigned to the Korean Military Advisory Group. They were responsible to build from scratch – following the surrender of the Japanese Empire in August 1945 – a functional government with an effective domestic security and defense establishment. A myriad of problems and challenges, not the least of which were severe economic dislocation, a complete absence of a modern military experience, and a language alien to the Americans, worked against their success. Nevertheless, patience, focused training, and professional dedication on the part of individual advisors succeeded in stabilizing the Republic of Korea (ROK) government, developing an indigenous defense capability, and defeating a chronic, communist-inspired insurgency. In fact, the success of ROK forces in combating guerrillas likely influenced the decision of North Korea's Kim Il-sung to launch a conventional invasion that threatened to engulf the ROK and triggered America's first major military commitment of the Cold War.

The unexpectedly rapid collapse of Japanese military power on 14–15 August 1945 caught the Americans by surprise. The Soviet Union had already declared war on Japan the week prior and had begun offensive operations in Manchuria, which quickly flowed across the Yalu and Tumen Rivers into northern Korea. American forces, on the other hand, were not prepared nor positioned to occupy their respective zone until after Japan's formal surrender on 2 September 1945. Advance elements of the US XXIV Corps, comprising three infantry divisions, finally disembarked at Inchon on 8 September. Over the next few weeks, the remaining occupation troops arrived to disarm and repatriate Japanese military and colonial officials and their dependents.

The Americans' ignorance of Korean geography and culture, and their unpreparedness to deal with the effects of colonial exploitation, war, factionalism, and subsequent ideological division made the task of governing extremely complex. From the very start, the United States Army Military Government in Korea (USAMGIK) was one step behind popular expectations for economic improvement, political emancipation, and social stability. The dizzying effects of this heady mixture of liberation, nationalism, and anti-colonialism – one author rightly calls it "revolution"[1] – caused the Americans to temporize. As Bonnie B.C. Oh points out, "the policy [of the Military Government] was comprised of reactive, incremental stop-gap measures."[2] Nowhere is this assessment more accurately descriptive than in the American Military Government's initial attempts to create stability through an indigenous national military organization. American patronage of this organization, first known as the Korean Constabulary and subsequently as the Republic of Korea Army (ROKA), insured the state's independence and survival.

The KMAG was an accidental creation born out of the frustration inherent in any military venture lacking firm political guidance. Policy misunderstandings and outright blunders such as retaining Japanese occupation officials as "advisors," relying on the Japanese-trained National Police for domestic order, and enforcing an anti-fraternization order criminalizing social contact with Koreans led to a souring relationship between the military government and prominent nationalist Koreans. Originally, American policy was to establish trusteeship with Soviet, British, and Chinese participation. However, when the latter two countries showed a lack of interest or capability, the polarization between the communist-dominated north and the American-controlled south forcefully emerged.

Anxious to relieve US forces of internal security duties, Lieutenant General John R. Hodge, in mid-November, initiated the first steps to establish a Korean national defense force by creating the Office of National Defense within the Military Government to oversee both the Bureau of Armed Forces and the Bureau of Police, later combined as the Bureau of National Defense. Hodge hoped the subsequent creation of a Korean military organization under the control of the Military Government would reduce the potential for violence and remove a great military and political burden from the Americans.[3] Initially, Americans controlled both bureaus, but over time, authority transferred to Koreans with the Americans taking a more active role as advisors. Thus, the American advisory mission was born.

In mid-November, an incident in the village of Namwon, North Cholla province, underscored the desirability of a Korean military security force to support the Korean National Police and the Military Government. The incident began when local police attempted to enforce an ordinance to turn over all Japanese property held by self-styled "People's Committees." The local committee naturally refused, and when the police arrested several of its leaders, spontaneous riots erupted. American reports claimed that up to 1,000 civilians besieged the Namwon police station, which American troops had to defend. After warning the crowd to disperse, the troops fired in the air and marched forward with leveled bayonets. In the scuffle, a number of Koreans were killed or injured (including one policeman stabbed to death), and up to 50 agitators were arrested.[4] The bloody confrontation at Namwon underscored the need to transition security functions to a Korean national defense force.

Colonel Arthur Champeny, the first director of National Defense, conceived the establishment of a Korean National Constabulary to act as a reserve for the National Police. Champeny's plan, dubbed the "Bamboo Plan," envisioned a Constabulary of 25,000 men with light infantry-type weapons and given basic infantry tactical training. Hodge approved Champeny's concept and directed the Constabulary to begin activating units in January 1946.[5]

It was in the arena of officer recruitment and selection that American officers assigned to the director of National Defense first confronted the challenges in building an indigenous military. The Americans began the process by seeking qualified candidates who would likely be compatible with American military doctrine and culture. The material that the Americans had to work with for selecting officers was raw. For the level of responsibility they would assume, potential Korean officers were young and inexperienced in the art and science of modern warfare as understood and practiced by the Americans. The most promising candidates (those with some kind of military experience) came from varied and incompatible political and military backgrounds: Imperial Japanese Army (IJA) or its surrogate Manchukuo Army, the Korean nationalist "Restoration Army" (*Kwangbok-kun*), and the Nationalist Chinese Army. It was an unenviable task to choose the officers who only months before had been fighting against each other but would now be the standard bearers for a new national Korean army.

Without any type of system in place to recruit officers, the Americans simply invited representatives of militia groups and any Koreans with military experience to apply for commissions. A number of men assembled at the old Capitol Building in late November, where Colonel Reamer Argo, Champeny's deputy, explained the Constabulary program and encouraged them to join. Gradually, word spread that the Americans were accepting applications at the Methodist Theology Seminary at Sudaemun and at the Japanese military post at Taenung. Aspirants who showed up were interviewed by Lieutenant Colonel John T. Marshall (first chief of the Constabulary) and Major David Rees. The Americans invited suitable candidates to remain, and as American advisors reported to receive their regimental assignments, they picked up three or four newly minted Korean officers. By such an informal procedure, the first six of eight planned regiments of the Constabulary were formed.[6]

On 14 January 1946, the Korean National Defense Constabulary was officially established with an authorization for 25,000 men.[7] With an approved plan and officer training already in progress, the Americans then tackled soldier recruitment, equipment, and training. Recruitment progressed slowly; by the end of April 1946, the entire Constabulary numbered only 3,000 men. American observers noted that there seemed to be little enthusiasm "for a Korean army as such."[8] In fact, many Koreans identified the Constabulary too closely with the Japanese-era colonial police, which had become a hated institution. The American and Korean officers attempted to disguise reality by implying that the Constabulary was actually the precursor organization to a national army and by marching recruits in formation. However, the Military Government offered little incentive for young Korean men to join the Constabulary, whose conditions for food, discipline, and treatment "fell somewhere between the harsh standards of the Japanese army and the treatment of Japanese POWs."[9] Not surprisingly, recruitment became much easier once the National Police began to crack down on leftist groups, whose members flocked to enlist in an organization starved for manpower and subsidized by the Americans. As more and more men of questionable political loyalty found refuge in the Constabulary, it called into question the Constabulary's stated purpose to reinforce police authority.

Despite initial problems with equipment, training, and culture that were a holdover from the hated Japanese regime, the Koreans and Americans had taken the first steps to forming a national defense organization. As more and more units began to congeal as battalions and regiments, the advisors (who at this point functioned as de facto commanders) then had to face the growing and complex challenge to train this pseudo-military Constabulary. Although simple enough administratively, training Korean soldiers proved to be much more difficult than training American ones.[10] Since Constabulary units had a first duty to support police forces – a frequent requirement as popular discontent fueled by food shortages and poor harvests exploded into violence – and each Constabulary "regiment" was at a different level of organization and competence, training regimes had to be improvised. Prudent advisors recognized the value of both on-the-job training and cooperative training with neighboring American units. These techniques were inefficient, frustrating, and perhaps not even that effective, but they were a start, and the Americans were confident that overall conditions would improve with time.[11]

Still, there was too little time and way too much to accomplish. Each advisor, who typically oversaw one Constabulary regiment (which could have subordinate units spread over an area as large as 350 square miles), was responsible for recruitment, induction, organization, administration, and training. Each of these duties ordinarily commands the attention of a full staff section in any modern military. For young majors and captains, the challenge could be overwhelming. Each advisor essentially relied on his own ingenuity and knowledge to discharge his duties for training in "methods of internal security."[12] There were, however, several special factors that influenced, and would continue to influence, the training of the Korean Constabulary and the future ROKA. Among these were the educational level and general health of soldiers, the lack of suitable training materials and training areas, awkward language issues, and the ability of individual advisors to persuade and lead their Korean counterparts.

Soldier health and education continually influenced the fortunes of the Constabulary. By American standards, Koreans had a low level of general health. Nearly one-third of recruits and inductees were rejected because of various health problems such as tuberculosis, intestinal disorders, and other communicable diseases. For a population that had lived on the margin for so long, the rigors of soldiering often left many Constabularymen at higher risk of illness, which compromised training and readiness. Also, from a Western perspective, the Koreans ranked low educationally. Although the Koreans prized learning, a high level of functional illiteracy meant that many of the standard training procedures used in the American army were ill-suited to training Korean soldiers. All training had to be presented in a visual format and reinforced through demonstration, rote memorization, and repetitive drill. Such measures can be effective for introductory tasks such as rifle manual of arms or basic military movement, but they are time consuming and mindless; add to this mixture the inability to communicate except through an interpreter, and the result would test the patience and flexibility of advisor, trainer, and trainee. For more complex tasks, or for technical skills training, illiteracy was a major handicap.[13]

Few advisors believed Koreans lacked aptitude to be soldiers. On the contrary, one senior advisor said that the Koreans' ability to learn military arts depended in great part on their "educational level, ability of the leaders, and efficiency of the training program." Furthermore, considering that Koreans "[were] not accustomed to telephones, radios, modern weapons and mechanical equipment to have obtained as much information in as short time as they have, it appears that they have an inherent aptitude for training and learning new methods." More important in determining the effectiveness of Constabulary training was usually the availability of training materials and space. Advisors fortunate to be close to American occupation troops could leverage their contacts for additional ammunition, equipment, and training space. In more remote areas, advisors had to rely on make-shift training aids and less realistic exercises.[14] Training manuals also were in short supply, and there was never a completely satisfactory program to translate and publish American manuals. In August 1948, as economic conditions improved (paper shortages precluded earlier action), the Constabulary headquarters did make prodigious efforts to get field and technical manuals translated into Korean and issued to field units.

In May 1946, Colonel Terrill ("Terrible") E. Price became Director, Department of National Defense, which shortly was renamed the Department of Internal Security. Because of the many political and economic problems plaguing the country, there was little enthusiasm for putting resources into a Korean army. Price was lucky to get five additional officers assigned to the Constabulary between June and August. These officers immediately were sent to command the Constabulary regiments forming in the field.[15] The situation these officers found defied their definition of what an army should be: training ranges and facilities were decrepit or non-existent; weapons, uniforms, supplies, and ammunition were scarce; Constabulary recruits (they could not be called "soldiers" yet) barely met Western standards for fitness and health. It was a nightmare assignment for most officers, who found themselves literally at the end of a long supply line stretching from San Francisco, to Honolulu, to Tokyo, then finally, to Korea.[16]

In this environment, personal relationships became crucial to success. The Constabulary advisors had to cement a social and professional bond with their Korean counterparts just as quickly and effectively as they did with fellow officers assigned to nearby occupation units. Additionally, the American Constabulary officers assumed roles as salesmen, mediators, auditors, and commanders. One particular officer distinguished himself as the catalyst for making the Constabulary a viable organization that one day would mature into the ROKA. Captain James H. Hausman, a reserve officer who fought the Germans in Europe, arrived in Korea in August 1946. His first assignment was as commander of the Eighth Regiment, based at the north-central city of Chunchon. He did not stay there long because Colonel Russell Barros, chief of the Constabulary, recognized Hausman's talent for administration and organization and brought him back to Seoul to be his executive officer.[17] Over the next four years, Hausman shepherded the Constabulary's expansion to 50,000 men, helped purge its ranks of communist subversives, negotiated for the "lease" of American weapons and ammunition, and navigated the dangerous political waters between the rising nationalist Syngman Rhee, the Korean National Police, and the American Military Government. Hausman probably did more than any other American to establish a professional bedrock that would become the moral support of the future ROKA. He set the standard for other officers who would forge bonds of trust between KMAG and the ROKA, bonds that proved strong enough to reform, rebuild, and recommit the ROKA to its decisive role as guardian of an independent southern state. Hausman accomplished this extraordinary feat by a complete immersion in the culture and language of Korea. In so doing, he emerged in the eyes of many Koreans and fellow advisors as the father of the ROKA.[18]

Getting the Constabulary to its future authorized paper strength of 50,000 was no mean task. Because the Constabulary competed for resources and manpower with the National Police and the other military government departments, efforts to screen out undesirable recruits failed in the face of mounting pressure from Colonel Price, who insisted on speed. Later, Hausman admitted that a thorough screening process would have been time consuming but in the long run beneficial. Leftist infiltration into both the officer corps and the ranks reduced the Constabulary's effectiveness and exposed it to charges from the National Police that the Constabulary was merely a haven for Communists.[19]

The first military challenge came soon enough, during the Autumn Harvest Uprisings. Progress in the transfer of power from American administrators to Koreans could not paper over the social and economic inequities that appeared to perpetuate Japanese colonial structuralism in the countryside, particularly in the southern provinces. In October 1946, popular discontent with American policies, along with an economic crisis fuelled by rice shortages and the constant influx of displaced persons, exploded into violence. Mobs generally limited their actions to labor stoppages and attacks against the National Police, but the Americans interpreted the rebellion as a communist-inspired bid to subvert the Military Government. As a result, Military Government policy tilted toward support for a crackdown on suspected communists. Conservative Korean political leaders and parties received a boost in American eyes, while more moderate figures were shut out of the Military Government's inner circle. The second consequence was to emphasize the impotence of the Constabulary as a reserve force to keep law and order. The National Police, who bore the brunt of the rebellion, resented the Constabulary's failure to be of much help. Hence, the uprising highlighted the most unpleasant aspects of the occupation as American troops had to use force to maintain order in the Korean hinterlands – a task that the Constabulary should have handled.[20]

In December, Major General Lerch (the Military Governor of Korea) reversed an earlier decision to limit Constabulary recruitment, propelling the Constabulary into a period of time that "brought about the most important events in [its] history." One month after the United States referred the problem of Korean unification to the United Nations in the fall of 1947, generals Hodge in Seoul and Douglas MacArthur in Tokyo had to admit the inevitable: the Constabulary would have to become the national military organization of the south, despite Soviet diplomatic protests. To beef up the Constabulary and to make it look more like an army, Hodge agreed to expand the Constabulary to 50,000 men and to provide heavy infantry weapons, light artillery, and light armored vehicles.[21]

While it appeared that the Constabulary finally had earned high-level recognition as an embryonic military force, the truth of the matter was quite different. The number of advisors within the Constabulary remained inadequate, though it did increase from less than two dozen to 90 officers. It was further decided that an American brigadier general ought to be assigned to the Department of Internal Security (which replaced the Department of National Security) as the head of an advisory organization. Yet, in terms of the structure of the Constabulary, no provisions were made to field the various support units necessary for a modern army to function. Tactical proficiency was feeble. Facilities, training areas, logistics, transportation, and other infrastructure remained backward or non-existent. Additionally, no system existed to train specialists to employ the heavier weapons being added. Nevertheless, in December 1947, the Constabulary moved forward to consolidate its regiments into brigade-sized organizations and to prepare to take over the defense of the southern half of the peninsula.[22]

Before that could happen, however, a full-fledged insurrection broke out as communist agents attempted to derail or at least delegitimize the national elections scheduled for 10 May 1948. Violence began on the southern island of Cheju, with attacks against registration and polling booths, government officials, and police. Although the elections proceeded as scheduled, by summer government control of the island was in doubt. More ominously, it became clear in Seoul that the Constabulary was being compromised by a steady stream of leftists and communist sympathizers joining the ranks.

It was against this backdrop that major changes were in the offing, politically and militarily. The elections south of the 38th parallel resulted in the convention of a National Assembly, which elected Syngman Rhee as its first president on 20 July.[23] On 15 August 1948, Syngman Rhee proclaimed the inauguration of the ROK. In a near-simultaneous series of changes, the USAMGIK terminated its operations, and the American advisors (90 altogether) previously assigned to the DIS were subsequently reassigned to the Provisional Military Advisory Group (PMAG), with Brigadier General William L. (Lynn) Roberts as chief.[24]

The formation of the PMAG in August 1948 established the first formal structure for the Americans to advise the Koreans. However, PMAG remained a fringe organization in the USAFIK hierarchy, and it had to compete for personnel, equipment, and attention. Despite these organizational handicaps, within two years these advisors developed a national army in Korea. Considering the organizational, technical, and leadership problems they faced, it was a minor military miracle. The ROK was not collapsing like Nationalist China, and the Republic's military problems, though still severe, appeared to be lessening with the passage of time.

The dominant personality of PMAG was Brigadier General Roberts. Roberts replaced Colonel Price as the chief of DIS (later renamed PMAG) and immediately made his mark on the American and Korean organizations under his purview.[25] Roberts's immediate task was to supervise the organization, training, and advice of a foreign army whose size grew from 50,000 to nearly 100,000 soldiers, in just two years of peace and war. Roberts had a solid though undistinguished record as an infantry officer in World War I and as a commander of armored forces in the European Theater of Operations from 1944 to 1945.[26] He had seen war and had plenty of experience with training raw troops. Roberts was a capable administrator and a strong leader who made an indelible impression on the advisory mission. His confidence, appreciation for training, and zealous pursuit for support to the ROKA created a legacy that endured to the very end of the war.

As soon as Roberts arrived (20 May 1948), he attacked the problems of organization and training the Constabulary. First, he streamlined the DIS and Constabulary headquarters to free up advisors for the field and to flatten the bureaucracies involved. He also established a number of provisional schools to train officers and men to use new American weapons and equipment. Roberts also traveled extensively. On 12 July, Roberts, along with several staff officers, descended on Taegu to inspect the Weapons School and the headquarters of the second and third brigades.[27] From this experience, Roberts observed some of the critical weaknesses in training, drill, and discipline that he expected advisors to correct. Additional advisors began to flood the field, but Roberts was picky in field assignments.[28] Eventually, Roberts fleshed out PMAG's authorized strength to 248 advisors, but these were still inadequate to fulfill all the functions necessary for the formation of a new army. In this way, Roberts moved quickly to bring order to the chaotic conditions he found in Korea, imposing upon both the KMAG and the ROKA his standards for leadership, training, and administration. These standards insured that the ROKA would survive its turbulent birth – years filled with institutional disarray, uncertainty, insurgency, and low-scale but persistent fighting along the thirty-eighth parallel.[29]

The most critical quality General Roberts brought to PMAG was firm leadership. Gruff in manner and unafraid to express his views, Roberts imbued his subordinates with a sense of urgency. He keenly felt the responsibility for making the Constabulary into an efficient and militarily competent organization. The most important decision Roberts made was to establish KMAG's signature standard, which became to be known as the "counterpart system." This system, which paired one American advisor to one Korean officer at each level of command from division to battalion, lasted throughout the war years, with some modification. Of course, the counterpart system was not foolproof, and it did not eliminate all friction that could be expected in this unique military marriage of radically different customs, perceptions, and experiences. Because he expected advisors to offer counsel and unsolicited guidance to their counterparts, Roberts searched hard to find and assign experienced officers as field advisors down to the battalion level.[30] To reinforce that standard, and to insure that the Americans clearly understood their place in the military chain, Roberts emphasized, "Advisors do not command – they ADVISE." He directed his advisors to beware trying to "convert the Korean into an American." Their mandate and foremost responsibility was simply "to organize and train, in a democratic way, a small but efficient organization ... capable of maintaining internal security."[31]

Unfortunately, Roberts had to wait to get the experienced men he knew he needed. Advisory duty in Korea was generally unpopular; those officers who did volunteer were young and lacked formal training in how military missions should function.[32] To help these officers understand their roles as advisors, Roberts published an *Advisor's Handbook* in the fall of 1949. In this handbook, Roberts and his staff laid out standards of leadership, expectations for advisors, and procedural techniques to assist the field advisor in all his endeavors as partners in command with his counterpart.

Roberts believed in personal, direct leadership. He told an assembled group of advisors, "[G]et under the skin of your counterpart – get his confidence by your honesty, your ability, your guidance – this may become a 'command' team even if not in name."[33] Roberts recognized that credibility was the only capital he could freely spend, and he understood that credibility would only have an influence if exercised in person. This point became even more critical as the army had to dedicate more time to anti-guerrilla and counter-infiltration operations in place of formal training. Roberts expected his advisors to make a virtue out of necessity. In an August 1949 memorandum he wrote, "Whenever a hot spot [incident] highlights the operations and training [activities] in a division zone or area, I expect the senior advisor to go into action" and see to it that Korean officers "milk" the incident dry of its training value.[34] Too frequently, Korean officers spent valuable time indulging in the perquisites of rank, rather than being focused on tactics or training.[35] Basic tasks such as maintaining accurate intelligence and operations situation maps rarely occurred, and Roberts expected the advisors to fix that. Further, he noted that the best advisors would keep good notes, share information with fellow advisors, and of course, be sure to "prevent mistakes."[36]

By the fall of 1949, KMAG was operating on a firmer basis than it had been just a few months prior. At the same time, the ROKA was conducting many more daily operations, primarily against guerrillas. Roberts continued to sing his old refrain for the counterpart system. Personal observation and involvement had no satisfactory substitutes. Officers who failed to accompany their unit on combat missions not only missed the best opportunity to gain respect, they also failed in their duty to observe, critique, train, and advise. Roberts also expected his advisors to render full and factual reports. Any officer who had to go to Seoul was expected to make an office call with the chief and to report on his local situation, to include the status of training, the competence of his counterpart, logistics, and enemy activity. This dialogue of instruction and feedback was valuable in keeping Roberts informed of local conditions and activities.[37]

He often acted on the input from his subordinates and was prepared to back them fully in disputes involving high-ranking Korean officers and government officials. On 19 April 1949, Major Arno Mowitz, the senior advisor to the second brigade, wrote Roberts to recommend the relief of the brigade command, Colonel Chae Wan-gai, for his "continuous failures to perform his duties as Brigade Commander." Mowitz reported that Chae's lack of interest in his responsibilities as a commander manifested itself in apathy, absenteeism, and a preoccupation with "social gatherings."[38] Roberts forwarded Mowitz's recommendation with his concurrence to the ROK defense minister *the same day*, adding,

Last summer I made an inspection of the [2nd] Brigade in [Taejon] and found it in the poorest condition in the army ... I believe that [Colonel Chae] has shown he is not deserving of this or any other command.[39]

The colonel was replaced.

In another instance, Roberts asked a lieutenant who had just returned from Cheju-do how best to deploy the reconstituted ninth regiment for training. First Lieutenant Charles Wesolowsky disagreed with Roberts's idea to centralize the regiment's encampment and instead suggested a series of company-sized patrol bases along the island's perimeter to establish a visible presence among the islanders and provide training in scouting and patrolling, small unit tactics, and marksmanship while in the field. Roberts briefly considered the idea and then told Wesolowsky that he was immediately reassigned to Cheju-do to implement the plan.[40] It is a credit to Roberts's professional competence to know when to defer to the judgment of an officer many years his junior. He was smart enough to realize they were the ones who had to live and fight with their counterpart. He not only enforced the counterpart system on his advisors, he allowed them the flexibility to make it work.

Roberts recognized that the Korean Constabulary and Army had significant defects that would not be overcome quickly, and he constantly reminded advisors to look to the long-term. He acknowledged that the advisors would "be called upon to exercise the utmost ingenuity" in training and mentoring. Many Korean officers, particularly those with backgrounds in Japanese service, did not approach training in the ways that their American mentors did. These officers' preference for lecture and group demonstration contrasted with the American model of explanation, demonstration, and practical exercise. The resulting tactical demonstrations usually impressed KMAG observers as being unrealistic and "for show" rather than suitable for combat. Roberts was concerned about this condition, and he directed the advisors to be active in showing their counterparts effective training techniques. It was important for the development of the officer corps that advisors show that officers would not lose face by getting close to the ground and dirty, "teach[ing] as much by example as by expert knowledge."[41]

At the same time, the advisors needed to remain objective and focused on tactical fundamentals.[42] Roberts's considerable combat experience told him that the success of American arms was due to "great attention to the smallest detail." It *was* important how individual soldiers moved on the battlefield. At the squad level, marching fire was far superior to the *banzai* charge. Advisors needed to exert all their powers of logic and demonstration to "kill off all ideas of *banzai*." The Chief also directed his advisors to be intimately familiar with all weapons in the Constabulary inventory – rifles, machine guns, carbines, and automatic rifles. They had to teach Koreans to employ units as units, not to fragment them attempting to accomplish too much at once. Roberts was impatient with half-stepped measures, and he urged his advisors to get out with the troops and "sneer at their parade ground tactics." Roberts reminded advisors to emphasize realistic training, such as patrolling techniques, which were particularly useful against guerrillas.[43] Set-piece demonstrations, while useful when dealing with large audiences, could not substitute for the rigorous training modern warfare demanded. It was necessary for soldiers and units to go out and practice what they saw and learned.

Of course, advisors had to find ways to get training value out of counter-guerrilla operations, which became increasingly prevalent in 1949. Roberts expected advisors to witness and render advice upon everything their units did, including combat. After one anti-guerrilla operation conducted by the Eighth Regiment near Kuman-ni, Roberts received an operations summary and critique from the regiment's senior advisor. Roberts distributed the report along with his endorsement of the advisor's actions to encourage similar personal involvement of advisors in combat situations.[44] Roberts also expected that advisors would read, digest, and disseminate the lessons catalogued in such reports to their own units. Nothing could substitute for actual field work, and he expected advisors to use their experience and judgment to make units tactically proficient and their officers professionally competent.

Administratively, Roberts read every report and acted on relevant conclusions or requests. He expected weekly updates from the advisors, and he in turn made sure to issue germane responses. Although he may have tended to equate bureaucratic efficiency with advisory success, he at least did not fall into the managerial trap of demanding reports he would never read. In addition to reports on training and operations, Roberts was interested to know if Korean officers resisted or disregarded advice or if they used military supplies for other than military purposes. Distractions such as unauthorized travel, personal service to high-ranking officers, and black marketing not only deprived the army of money and training time, they reflected badly on the officer corps as a whole. Such abuses had to be reported and eliminated. If permitted to endure, he was sure that these practices would undermine the credibility of KMAG and the legitimacy of the military mission to foster a professional army and officer corps.[45]

While the advisors focused on unit training, Roberts continued to push his staff to promote Korean officer training, education, and professionalization. During Roberts's tenure, Captain Hausman shepherded a program to send high-quality Korean officers to US army schools. On 14 August 1948, six officers attended the Advanced Infantry Course at Fort Benning, Georgia.[46] Although a small start, this program continued until the summer of 1953, with only a short break from mid-1950 until the summer of 1951. This was an investment that successfully returned hundreds of officers trained in American doctrine, tactics, service support, and operations. Upon their return, these graduates provided a fruitful leaven for the Korean counterpart schools, and they proved exceptionally competent in brigade and division positions.

Sometimes the Chief had to speak frankly, and he was not shy to provide unsolicited advice to his counterpart, an unfortunate officer who did not enjoy Rhee's confidence and could not enforce his directives on much of the army. Nonetheless, Roberts sought to stiffen his resolve to squash practices inimical to the efficient management of the army. Late in 1948, he delivered a stern rebuke when subordinate commanders bypassed positions in the chain of command. In Roberts's judgment, to permit such practices demonstrated a poor appreciation for military effectiveness, while sowing confusion and inefficiency:

> [Your] office knows the correct way. If your army is to become efficient, you should listen to correct advice by those who are more experienced. The U.S. is furnishing some 200 advisors at great expense, but their usefulness is being curtailed by the necessity of ironing out needless difficulties put in their way by such practices throughout the Korean Army.[47]

Roberts also had the opportunity to speak to the senior tier of the Korean officer corps on a number of occasions.[48] In April 1950, he addressed all the division commanders and gave them a broad tongue-lashing: "By this time you too know that I do not pull punches, that I call spades, spades. You [will] know what I mean when I'm thr[ough]." For the next half an hour, he admonished the senior leadership of the ROKA to economize ammunition and fuel expenditures, treat civilians with dignity and humanity, improve relations with the local and national police, assess honestly good and bad officers, insure that officers receive the same technical education as the soldiers, stamp out graft and dishonesty, focus on training rather than personal comfort, status, or enrichment, resist the temptation to fatten administrative functions and symbols of office at the expense of infantry soldiers, produce timely and accurate reports, coordinate and cooperate with neighboring units during operations, and train and allow staffs to function. Roberts concluded:

> I must finish now. I may have talked about many things which are wrong. Believe me when I tell you I have seen more correct things than wrong, and I know there is vast improvement .... I see great strides in training; every month sees a graduation from our many schools .... Every unit is hard at work daily. Our troops operating against guerrillas are successfully terminating those operations; there are very few guerrillas left today .... All these add up to progress and excellence. I think you have reason to be proud.[49]

If Roberts had let his optimism run ahead of reality publicly, he at least saw no need to sugarcoat the truth as he saw it when dealing with his Korean counterparts.

Up to his last day of duty, Roberts remained focused on fundamentals: marksmanship, leadership by example, simple tactics, planning, and assessment. He confided to his advisors, "If these few items are taught honestly and well during the summer, this army will become one fine group."[50] After two years at the helm of the PMAG and KMAG, advisors under Roberts's direction were doing what they were supposed to do. Frequent inspections identified deficiencies and focused advisor attention to correct those deficiencies. They did everything they could to exploit field operations of any training value whatsoever, be it patrolling techniques, marksmanship, staff procedures, or bivouacs. Promising Korean officers went to US army schools in the States to prepare them to take over many of the technical functions performed by the Americans, namely training administration, staff functions, and schools.

Advisors in the field

Roberts's rhetoric and drive could have no effect the advisors working with units in the field. These men constituted the soul of the American military mission to Korea. Eventually, this group evolved and acquired more mature officers, but by August 1948, the majority of advisors were from varied backgrounds and branches with one common trait. Most were recently commissioned lieutenants without combat experience. They knew nothing about running armies, let alone fighting a war. These officers, regardless of their willingness, background, or talents, were the men that would take the Constabulary through its toughest times and growing pains, to include battle. Their responsibilities as organizers, trainers, mentors, and fighters, insured the survivability of the Constabulary, the ROKA, and eventually the ROK.

One of their toughest tasks was to organize Constabulary units from scratch. To raise a new unit was a difficult undertaking, as it embodied all of the challenges of language, unfamiliarity with the environment, inexperience, and lack of resources. The history of the Cavalry Regiment illuminates these factors and the dramatic impact that individual advisors could have on their counterparts. First Lieutenant Robert G. Shackleton, a West Point graduate (class of 1946), was one of the officers affected by the 7th Infantry Division levy that assigned him to the Department of Internal Security in April 1948. Although not unwilling to go to advisory duty, he was shocked to learn that as an infantry officer with only one year of troop duty, he was to become the senior advisor to the 1st Reconnaissance Troop, a true-to-life cavalry formation with horses, saddles, and armored cars. When Shackleton protested that he had no experience with either cavalry or armor, the director of the DIS, Colonel Terrill Price, curtly informed him that he "*was* and would *remain* the cavalry advisor." When the lieutenant attempted to find out more about his new posting, Price lost his patience and erupted, "Lieutenant, talk to Captain Hausman. I've got my problems, you've got yours.

Now get out." Impressed only by the disorganization, discouragement, and lack of direction at the DIS headquarters, Shackleton set out to organize his new command.[51]

Shackleton found the Reconnaissance Troop (actually still a Constabulary infantry company) billeted not far from Seoul. Immediately upon assuming his duties to advise two officers and 200 men, the unit embarked on a program of training, recruitment, and expansion lasting from May to September 1948. Initially, progress was very slow. Neither of the Korean officers spoke English well, which made Shackleton's advisory role problematic. Military terms and concepts like "machine gun" or "phase-line" had no natural Korean equivalent and so had to be improvised – and not necessarily in a standardized way. Shackleton recalls that he often resorted to "pidgin English" to express his views.[52] In the Reconnaissance Troop, Shackleton had to face additional problems dealing with people who lacked any knowledge about motor vehicles. One advisor recalled his frustration that even items as simple and ubiquitous as spark plugs were novelties to the Koreans and known as "bolts that spit fire."[53]

Fortunately for Shackleton, he encountered a civilian, Chang Bong-chung, who spoke marvelous English and wanted to join the Constabulary. Shackleton enlisted him on the spot and relied on Private Chang as his interpreter. When an English-speaking lieutenant joined the Troop later in the summer, Shackleton's language problems were minimized.[54]

Trying to get the most out of official training, which prior to 1948 consisted mostly of small arms practice and basic tactical skills congruent with "methods of internal security," was a constant challenge, as Shackleton spent most of his time worrying about old and worn weapons, poorly conditioned vehicles, and lack of training space. At one point, due to poor sanitation and mess facilities, up to 60 percent of the unit was sick. Even when the majority of the men were healthy, Shackleton found it impossible to rely on a published training schedule for he was never sure when equipment would arrive or what he could expect to receive. Constant shifting of billets back and forth across the Han River further aggravated the training situation.[55]

Noticeable improvement began in late summer. Roberts's presence energized PMAG, and his personal inspections impressed and lifted the morale of the advisors and Korean soldiers. Shackleton also received reinforcements. Second Lieutenant Ralph Bliss, an active 19-year-old cavalry officer, was a welcome addition to the Reconnaissance Troop. Bliss was glad to be assigned to a real mounted unit, but he looked in vain for the horses. Enough vehicles had arrived to constitute a mechanized capability, but the half-tracks and jeeps were poorly reconditioned surplus items with almost no reservoir of spare parts. The Troop's motley collection of weapons consisted of carbines, .45 caliber pistols, some .50 caliber machine guns, and a few air-cooled .30 caliber machine guns.[56]

Both Shackleton and Bliss remember the campaign to recapture Yosu from rebellious Korean soldiers in October 1948, as a watershed event for the Reconnaissance Troop. Although the Troop suffered nearly a quarter of its strength killed or wounded, the Americans discovered themselves to be more openly accepted by their Korean counterparts, as if their shared experience had constituted some sort of test. Shackleton also noted that the soldiers themselves appeared to carry themselves more confidently in light of their baptism by fire. Shortly after Yosu, the Troop was redesignated the Cavalry Regiment, and it redeployed to a former Japanese cavalry garrison post near Seoul. Here, Shackleton seized an opportunity to collaborate with an American cavalry troop that was preparing to redeploy. For the first time, training began to assume the formality that Shackleton recognized. American sergeants teamed up with interpreters to provide individual instruction on radios, motor maintenance, scout tactics, and mounted movement. The Koreans learned quickly and became especially adept with their vehicles. Shackleton proudly remembered that in just over a year, men who had never set foot inside a motor vehicle, much less repair one, were able to plan and conduct a lengthy road march from Seoul to Chuminjin (on the east coast) without breakdowns or accidents. Much of the movement was at night, further testifying to the proficiency of the officers, NCOs, and soldiers. Following this major tactical movement, Shackleton and Bliss felt they had arrived. The regiment had a new commander, Colonel Lee Ryong-moon, a competent officer, veteran of the IJA, and broadly experienced in military administration. The versatile and reliable M8 armored scout car, armed with a 37-mm cannon and a coaxially mounted .30 caliber machine gun replaced the regiment's ramshackle fleet of jeeps and half-tracks. "I began to see light at the end of the tunnel," Shackleton recalled, and he was confident that the Regiment, with its base of training, combat experience, and *esprit*, was on its way to being a first-class outfit.[57] Both advisors were justifiably proud of the regiment's achievement – a transformation of raw and inexperienced recruits into trained and disciplined soldiers.[58]

The story of the Cavalry Regiment was symptomatic of the challenges of training Korean troops on the mainland. Fortunately for Bliss and Shackleton, the process worked out all right, as the Cavalry Troop demonstrated its mettle under fire. Perhaps nowhere was the overall advisory challenge more acute than on Cheju-do, a volcanic island far removed from the mainland and infested with bandits and communist inspired rebels. The Ninth Regiment, recruited on Cheju-do, was considered by many to be the Cinderella of the Constabulary, first to get abused, last to get support.

Violence on Cheju-do began in April 1948 and was only suppressed by stern measures taken by the Constabulary's Eleventh Regiment, hurriedly transported from Pusan. A general calm settled over the island during the summer months, even though Constabulary operations and intelligence reports indicated the presence of rebels among the island residents. Retraining the Ninth Regiment involved small-scale field exercises, patrols, and marksmanship.[59] However, the Americans never had enough interpreters or printed materials to help them teach Korean soldiers the rudiments of tactics, weaponry, or field craft. One advisor recalled having to work directly with the troops, using a combination of written instructions, slow speech, and hastily drawn diagrams to make his point.[60]

First Lieutenant Minor Kelso (West Point class of 1946) found a disheartening situation in his Third Battalion, located near the port of Mosulpo, Cheju-do. The regimental advisor, First Lieutenant Charles Wesolowsky, had just compiled and distributed a weekly training schedule along with 46 American field manuals. But, like other units on the mainland, the battalions on Cheju lacked basic building blocks for militarily effective units:

> The equipment was in a poor state of repair. The individual soldier did not have all of the normal basic equipment. The rifles were rusty. The troops knew little about their weapons. There was very little practice firing. I recall no inspection by higher headquarters.[61]

In fact, Kelso's first inspection of his unit revealed that although it paraded smartly, it was not ready to train, and it would be a long while before it could fight. The battalion had a mixture of US and Japanese weapons, with less than 40 rounds available for the American rifles and ten for the carbines. The only men who appeared to have even fired a weapon were the officers and a few noncommissioned officers.

Weapons training began on 11 August when Kelso visited each company and demonstrated the care, cleaning, and assembly of the M1 rifle to the Korean officers and NCOs. Three days later, the battalion went to the range to practice firing. Kelso dryly noted by 1,000 that morning there had been "considerable delay with no firing at present." Eventually, the officers got organized enough to send 600 men through the range, firing both the M1 and Japanese rifles. Kelso noted that Captain Hahn competently demonstrated proper techniques and positions, but he was alarmed at the lack of safety awareness, "a factor that received little attention from either enlisted men or officers." His personal intervention likely saved several soldiers' lives. He was also dismayed at the poor scores, "however, for men (and particularly men from the farm, etc.) who had never fired before, the results were as could be expected with only eight rounds fired per M-1 and five per Jap[anese] rifle."[62]

A month later Kelso transferred to Kwangju, where he became the senior advisor to the Fourth Regiment. Even with several months under Roberts's emphatic regime, Kelso found the state of training in the brigade in shambles. Kelso confronted the brigade commander about this sorry affair and demanded that training programs include English translations and activities at the company level.[63] Before anything could be done, though, the Fourth Regiment was committed to suppress mutinies at Sunchon and Yosu, actions that highlighted the poor state of training among officers and soldiers alike.

Training remained a weak spot for the ROKA until the 1950 invasion. Korean officers, even those with combat experience, still had to unlearn tactics and techniques that were incompatible with American methods and weapons. For example, Japanese tactics as practiced on mainland Asia, "suggest[ed] that battle, whenever possible, was reduced to a drill."[64] The heavy emphasis on small group action over individual initiative or higher unit objectives meant that offensive tactics lacked cohesion and coordination and often degenerated into futile and bloody frontal efforts. Since the Japanese did not practice the same degree of combined-arms coordination between tactical units as the Americans did, elementary tactics such as fire and movement, support by artillery, or support by fire were completely alien to Koreans.[65] Roberts never had enough advisors to spread across the force (the scarcity of American noncommissioned officers was especially hurtful), and the operations tempo after November 1948 kept army units in the field instead of following any comprehensive training program that would have addressed these problems.

If KMAG advisors were not so successful in training the Korean army, they did make a significant impression on their counterparts nonetheless. The mentor relationship between American and Korean officers was crucial to developing a professional officer corps, as many advisors reflexively understood. All the material support, training, and advice in the world would make no difference if Korean officers simply failed to grasp the tenets of modern military practices. The Americans were attempting a cultural as well as military transformation among their counterparts. For example, advisors had to showcase American military traits such as direct and honest communication, flexibility, and initiative. These were Western military values without direct equivalents in Korean culture. Professionalism included being willing to learn from experience, either direct or vicariously from the advisor. It also meant being flexible and self-correcting. Nearly every advisor had to come to terms with the unique trait that did more perhaps to interfere with the formation of a professional culture than any other – "face."[66]

Face manifested itself in many ways. One observer called it "purely a question of that compound of pride, self-respect, and vanity." It also touched upon social status, perceptions of power, and Confucian hierarchical values. Maintaining face among peers was as important as with social inferiors. All Koreans stood to lose "face" if proper "protocol" was not observed – a cultural nuance that put more than one advisor into a tight spot.[67] Any advisor who caused his counterpart to lose face was on a fast track to failure. Sometimes, issues of face led to humorous situations that illuminated the potential for frustration between the different cultures.

The general reluctance for Koreans to admit mistakes in judgment or to relay bad news rankled the Americans, particularly when the stakes were much higher than personal prestige. Some advisors accused Korean officers of even supplying misinformation to avoid losing face with superiors or their counterpart, or refusing to change or modify orders, lest their original judgment be suspected of being wrong.[68]

Therefore, for any criticism to be effective (and a means of furthering mutual professional respect), it had to be given in private. To embarrass an officer by contradicting or correcting him, particularly in front of his subordinates, was a surefire way to discover the erection of an impenetrable wall.[69] The shrewd advisor recognized the value of social and informal contacts with his counterpart as a method of building a relationship of trust. One advisor indicated that he had success by maintaining formality at the command post and informality at the "hooch." In this way, the Korean officer would not feel pressured always to be correct in front of his staff. He could try to extend his own ability, confident that any tutorial would come at the end of the day and in private.[70] In this way, a bond of trust developed that would permit a Korean officer to ask for advice without being ashamed of his ignorance.

Because Korean officers and soldiers were neophytes with little appreciation or understanding of logistics as practiced by the American Army, advisors spent a lot of time teaching and coaching the fundamentals of maintenance and supply. One advisor remembered:

> Maintenance was a hell of a problem at first. You must remember that there were few vehicles in Korea before the war [1950], discounting Japanese Army, except oxcarts ... As a result of this, the Korean didn't know one was supposed to keep oil in the engine, anti-freeze in the radiator, inflated tires, etc.[71]

However, once Korean soldiers were shown how to take care of their equipment, they generally did so, as long as the advisor held his counterpart to that standard. This meant visiting the local markets to check for unauthorized sale of military supplies, spot-checking individual units, and at times even withholding authorization for supplies as a means to encourage compliance with an advisor's "suggestions."[72] Logistics advisors sometimes ran even greater risks than their combat brethren on account of the general lack of knowledge about military things. One advisor witnessed a Korean civilian in an ammunition "factory" manually filling and crimping .30 caliber cartridges with black powder and primer, all the while with a lit cigarette dangling from his mouth![73]

If the advisors had to work hard to teach the value of logistics discipline to their counterparts, they had to take an entirely different approach toward personnel discipline. The Americans flatly disapproved of the physical punishment meted out by Korean sergeants and officers. In addition to being abusive, discipline was often applied inappropriately during training. Reluctant to tell his counterparts how to run their army, Lieutenant Shackleton nevertheless took special care when dealing with Korean soldiers to model more productive techniques to teach and train.[74] Captain Edward J. Stewart witnessed one Korean lieutenant smack a soldier on the head when he failed to fire his weapon properly. Stewart made the lieutenant fire the rifle, while Stewart smacked *him* on the head to make his point.[75] It was an uphill battle to displace these deeply ingrained methods, which were not only unmilitary but counter-productive to the goal of developing a profes-sional army.[76] Most disheartening of all was to see "army justice" and "discipline" applied to civilians who were suspected of harboring or aiding the enemy or to witness true indiscipline as when soldiers deliberately used deadly force against noncombatants.[77] The brutality of the Cheju-do cam-paign and the carnage attending to the recapture of Sunchon and Yosu were beyond the capability of the Americans to understand, much less prevent at the time.[78]

Even with these strains and stresses, KMAG always enjoyed good overall relations with Korean officers. This relationship was an anchor for the greater trials that would come, and it was in no small measure responsible for the rebirth of the Korean army later during the war. During the initial years of the Constabulary, the Americans chose officers with care, tending to favor candidates with military experience gained in the IJA or its anti-guerrilla surrogate, the Manchukuo Army. These officers brought with them Japanese habits and tactical concepts that did not neatly mesh with Amer-ican standards, and they often did not care for the administrative require-ments of soldiering.[79] Despite these drawbacks, the Americans prized these veterans, and they formed a core of loyal and patriotic officers, who never relinquished their attachment to all things American.[80]

Though technically the advisors' least important role, participation in combat operations was the one assignment that carried the most risk and had the potential for the greatest gain. How much (or little) an advisor had to do personally was a good gauge of a Korean officer's or unit's competence. General Roberts made it very clear that the advisors' role was to prepare their counterparts to do for themselves what they could no longer rely upon the Americans to do – defend their country. Advisors had no official combat role to perform and they had no command authority over Korean troops, nevertheless, many found themselves participating in actual operations against Communist guerrillas, bandits, and even North Korean security and army forces. In June 1949, just a month after some severe fighting along the thirty-eighth parallel, Roberts reminded his advisors that though their chief task was training, they needed to be prepared to assume a wartime function. "This army," he told them, "even to do its defense mission, will, in my opinion, need your stabilizing advice."[81]

Although not formally in command in the months prior to the conven-tional invasion, advisors often found themselves at the forefront of action. Usually, brushes with the enemy were brief but sharp. Some engagements were humorous misadventures, such as one officer's surprise encounter with a clothesline while chasing rebels on Cheju-do. Others were more serious. Kelso's first combat experience was during the effort to recapture Sunchon (October 1948). Kelso was accompanying Colonel Kim Paek-il, the task force commander, when rifle fire came from his left. He and the nearby

Korean troops drove into a ditch on the side of the road. When he looked up, he saw the bespectacled Colonel Kim, unperturbed and standing in the middle of the road. Somewhat embarrassed, Kelso got up too, now appreciating that Koreans often did not shoot straight. Later, Kelso again found himself in the thick of the fighting, when he personally directed the firing of an 81-mm mortar at a rebel machine gun position. When the first round destroyed the rebel site, "a great cheer came up from the soldiers. The American lieutenant was [now] in good standing."[82]

Kelso's experience was echoed by many other advisors who, by virtue of their responsibilities to render advice on all situations, found themselves leading troops and directing operations. On Cheju-do, Wesolowsky and his fellow advisors took active roles in searching out guerrillas (called "raiders" in official reports). Immediately following his arrival, Constabulary troops conducted an ineffective two-week operation to sweep the island from south to north, up Halla-san mountain, an extinct volcano. Because the raiders had been tipped off by local informants, the troops only fought heat, thirst, and fatigue. Figuring that the intelligence and reporting system was likely compromised by civilians sympathetic to the raiders, Wesolowsky and his fellow lieutenants changed tactics and directed their units to rely on frequent foot patrols and coast guard craft to disrupt and maybe surprise and capture some raiders. This change in method did not enjoy much success either, but it shows the degree to which American officers had to remain involved in the daily operations of the units they were only supposed to advise.[83]

In the heat of battle, advisors had not only to think quickly, they also had to communicate their advice and insure it was understood. Obviously advisors had to form close bonds with their interpreters. Good interpreters were treasured like gold. An advisor's effectiveness depended on him being able to understand a situation, give pertinent advice, and – when required – assistance to implement that guidance. Too often, of *how* the advisor's question was translated, and of *how* the ensuing discussion unfolded, the advisor remained ignorant. He had to trust his interpreter not only to interpret correctly the English–Korean exchange, but also to capture the nuances inherent in any verbal communication, particularly those bearing on a fluid tactical situation. Under the pressure of battle, this might be too much to expect.

Major Howard Trammell recalled, "Fortunate indeed, was the advisor who had [an interpreter] who could really translate and interpret."[84] In some cases, the bond between advisor and interpreter was one of life or death. Lieutenant Kelso personally intervened to prevent the execution of a relative of his interpreter. On a second occasion, Kelso bluntly told one Korean officer that he specifically did not want his interpreter shot as a suspected Communist. As it turned out, the Korean officer was himself a Communist, and he cleverly knew how to sabotage any effective linkage between the advisor and the troops.[85]

By any measure, Korea was a tough assignment. Considering the extra burden of being the only American living and working with Koreans without any linguistic or cultural preparation, little material support, and a motivated but demanding boss, it is amazing that so many advisors not only were successful, but even thrived in this most challenging environment. Not all officers, however, were cut out for this kind of duty.[86]

Ignorance, insensitivity, racist attitudes, and dissatisfaction with an advisory assignment had no place in KMAG. Advisors stuck in their own rut of cultural and military superiority could not expect to get very far, and they were completely ineffective.[87] Advisors who did make conscious efforts to accommodate themselves to Korean language, manners, and food quickly learned the secret for a productive relationship with their counterparts. Professional courtesy and genuine friendship, along with a willingness to respect the judgment of the Korean officer, who was, after all, in charge, could carry an advisor far when he was called to render hard advice.[88] It was not uncommon for lieutenants to advise battalion and regimental officers in training and combat operations. If their youth seemingly disqualified them from interaction on the basis of social equality, their professionalism, courage, and cultural sensitivity nearly always made up the difference.[89] Fortunately, the Americans demonstrated early their commitment to the counterpart partnership. As a result, most Korean officers had a high opinion of Americans in general, especially those who followed the example set by men like Hausman. They trusted these officers, even if they did not always follow their counsel. It could only be on this moral basis of trust that Korean officers would allow foreigners so much latitude to make their army.[90]

Taking "provisional" out of the MAG

By 1 January 1949, the Constabulary had become the Korean army, and it boasted a total strength of 64,588 officers and men.[91] As the ROKA continued to expand, PMAG also grew, from just over 100 officers to 234 officers and men in the spring of 1949. To reflect the growing responsibilities of PMAG, the US ambassador to the ROK, John Muccio, received in April a telex message from the Department of the Army granting authority for an official advisory group subordinate to Muccio's American Mission in Korea (AMIK).[92] Washington also authorized an increase in personnel, which allowed Roberts to plan for a redistribution of officers so that an advisor would be present at all the military schools and down to battalion level.[93]

On 1 July 1949, the day after the last American combat troops left Korea, the KMAG officially assumed duties as the military mission in Korea. Its mandate was

> to develop ROK security forces within [the] limitations of [the] Korean economy, by advising and assisting [the] ROK in training such forces involving Army, Coast Guard, and National Police and by insuring effective utilization [of] US military assistance [to] these forces.[94]

For an army now expanded to eight divisions, it was a tall order by any measure for the 492 officers and men assigned to KMAG.

One of the greatest criticisms that can be leveled at Roberts was the failure early to provide a systematic mission overview to his advisors. Not until June 1949, did Roberts begin to consolidate his ideas on the advisory mission and draft a presentation that he called his "Orientation speech," which he gave frequently to new and old KMAG soldiers. For many advisors, this was the first time they caught a comprehensive glimpse of what the boss wanted them to do. A few months later, KMAG demonstrated its growing organizational maturity by publishing the *Advisor's Handbook* and providing a copy to every American in KMAG. The *Handbook* symbolized a giant leap over the provisional methods prevalent in the days of DIS and the PMAG. In the *Handbook* were specific instructions covering every aspect of an advisor's job, such as personnel, logistics, and training. The advisor also received guidance on how to interact with the KMAG staff in Seoul.[95] Perhaps most importantly, the *Handbook* contained Roberts's "command philosophy," in which he had the first and last words of advice and instructions to incoming advisors. Roberts clearly articulated his vision, expectations, and potential pitfalls as an advisor. The *Advisor's Handbook* was a valuable distillation of experience, judgment, and practical application. At last, KMAG had a standard, and Roberts expected KMAG to live up to it.

As war clouds loomed ominously in the spring of 1950, serious weaknesses still remained in the overall advisory structure. Prior to 1950, KMAG got little attention, other than what Roberts could squeeze out of official visitors and journalists, because in the eyes of the real decision-makers in Tokyo and Washington, the advisory effort was secondary to providing for the US troops still stationed in Korea, and those with occupation duties in Japan.[96] The Korean army's school system for recruits was still not adequate to train all of the army's soldiers. Without a centralized replacement training center, individual training remained a unit function, which counter-guerilla operations often displaced. Korean officers, in Roberts's opinion, still had a long way to go toward approaching American standards of professionalism and tactical competence. He lamented in May 1950 that too many had too much tendency to cling to "old ways" – a euphemism for Japanese methods.[97]

Roberts also worried about the physical state of the ROKA. KMAG's last great initiative prior to June 1950 was to build up the ROKA's stocks of weaponry and supplies. Although Roberts looked askance at Rhee's persistent requests for tanks, combat aircraft, and heavy artillery (which he felt were economically and logistically unsupportable without substantial increases in military aid), he was not blind to the fact that the ROKA was weak on firepower and logistics support. While publicly touting the ROKA's accomplishments, he continued to lobby for greater military assistance. Washington's cost consciousness, however, approved a paltry sum of $10 million in military aid, which only began to arrive in Korea by the time war broke out in June 1950.[98] The effects of attrition and expansion strained the ROKA's fragile logistics system to the breaking point. As of 5 May 1950, KMAG estimated that the ROKA had 15 percent of its weapons and 35 percent of its vehicles unusable due to maintenance shortfalls. Roberts warned his advisors "[t]he significance of this situation is that unless prompt, effective and vigorous measures are taken to conserve available resources, the Army will be dangerously reduced in firepower, mobility, and logistical support."[99] Even more disturbing was the assessment that ammunition stocks continued to decrease from 19,000,000 rounds of small arms ammunition in December 1949 to a point that only six days of combat supply existed for the front line divisions in June 1950.[100]

But Roberts was no stooge. Some battles he could not or would not fight, such as publicly exposing the ROKA's weaknesses in equipment, firepower, or leadership. He did not endorse Rhee's requests for tanks and heavy artillery, nor did he fall in line with the outlandish estimates produced by the Ministry of National Defense.[101] Officially, and knowing full well that Washington was not willing to expend the resources in Korea, Roberts ducked the issue by asserting such requests were unnecessary because not only was the Korean terrain unsuitable for such heavy equipment, but that the ROKA was "the best little army in Asia" and fully capable of handling any potential opponent.[102] Privately, though, Roberts was aware that the Koreans simply did not have the economic capacity to afford, the military expertise to use, nor the technical ability to maintain the equipment Rhee demanded. Although subsequent events would cause many to question his motives and judgments, Roberts's decisions in this regard were in fact entirely consistent with his mission to "advise the Government of the Republic of Korea in the continued development of the Security Forces ... now in being, consistent with the limitations of the Korean economy."[103] As for the inability of the military to use or maintain more modern equipment, Roberts had plenty of empirical evidence to support his position.

Given time, most American advisors were confident that conditions in the ROKA would improve.[104] The history of the MAG up to the summer of 1950 appeared to bear out that conclusion. The advisors' achievement in the first two years of the Republic's existence was unique in America's involvement in Asia.[105] They established enduring credibility with their Korean counterparts in an environment defined by an alien culture and language, limited practical experience, and inadequate manning and resources. Their high military standards commended them to those Korean officers who eventually became senior commanders, and they built up interpersonal "capital" with the future leaders of the ROK government and military. General Lim Sun-ha, one of the first officers of the Constabulary, and later a division commander in the ROKA during the conventional war, still remembers how impressed he and his fellow officers were with the Americans. Officers such as Colonel Champeny, Lieutenant Colonel Barros, and Captain Hausman made their mark with their work ethic and willingness to get into the details, a habit that former officers of Japanese service found unusual. Their example resulted in a push by Korean officers to learn US military drill and customs and to acquire US uniforms and equipment – indeed, Koreans perhaps went overboard in their desire to do everything like the Americans, to the point of copying unit insignia.[106] Although Roberts had expressly forbade the advisors from trying to turn the Koreans into Americans, the Koreans themselves saw imitation as the only way to be who they wanted to be. KMAG had become the ROKA's figurative "older brother."

Just prior to leaving Korea in June 1950, General Roberts published a farewell letter to KMAG and the ROKA. In this letter, Roberts reflected on his two years in "a most important and satisfying assignment." He acknowledged the many challenges that KMAG faced in trying "to superimpose Western methods on you and your army," but he also underscored his faith in those methods to turn the Korean Army into a modern military force. He urged Korean officers to keep their American counterparts informed so that the advisors could best perform their job to advise and support the ROKA. Roberts praised the Korean officer corps saying, "Your strength lies in your attention to duty, your willingness to work, your bravery, your loyalty to your country..." His final words of advice to his Korean counterparts reminded them of his high regard for the soldiers who made up their army that "will endure great hardships if properly lead."[107] How little did he, or his audience, know the prescience of that sentiment.

Conscientious, efficient, and sternly professional, Roberts did fail in one crucial aspect. Although many of KMAG's shortcomings – personnel, materials, space, and time – were beyond his control, Roberts did run KMAG as a personal fiefdom, with each member expected to report directly to him. As a result, when war did come and the chief was midway across the Pacific Ocean en route to the States and retirement, too many advisors were unsure of what they were supposed to do in the face of a *real* war. KMAG had not progressed much beyond a formalized ad hoc organization. It remained undermanned, under supported and underappreciated by its own army and leaderless at the moment of greatest danger. Furthermore, his private warnings about ROKA had not surfaced, buried by the tide of acceptance his public comments prompted.[108] The unfortunate result was that when it really mattered, KMAG's potential was less than the sum of its parts.

Nonetheless, KMAG's early advisory triumph insured the political, institutional, and military survival of the ROK. Charismatic Americans like Russell Barros and James Hausman played key roles in keeping the Constabulary independent of the National Police and in trying to instill in its officer corps a sense of patriotic duty and professionalism. How the Constabulary performed its duties also weighed heavily on the Americans for the future viability of a South Korean state. Between August 1946 and September 1948, the Constabulary faced severe tests in surviving internal subversion, political imbroglio, and expansion. The Constabulary survived more because of the fractured nature of the armed opposition to American Military Government and (after 15 August 1948) the ROK, than because of any real fighting ability. In fact, during the Constabulary's greatest challenge, the Yosu-Sunchon mutiny of October 1948, Americans had to get uncomfortably close to exercising command and control of Korean units, and the failure to consummate the government's victory over the mutiny would have long-term consequences for the ROKA until well into the Korean War. However, the experience gained by both American and Korean officers became the foundation for the successful prosecution of anti-guerrilla campaigns in 1949 and the first six months of 1950.

The officers and enlisted men detailed as KMAG advisors carried their counterparts through the tough times of sedition, rebellion, and war; occasionally, they found themselves as de facto leaders of the Korean military. Problems that previously had been considered in abstract terms were now theirs to solve. Haphazard organization, training, and logistics combined with challenges in understanding Korean history, language, and culture to make the problems of advice and assistance nearly impossible to fathom, let alone ameliorate. Individual initiative and resourcefulness of the advisor had to make up for many of these deficiencies. To their credit, these men did the best they could given the environment of poverty, insurrection, corruption, and isolation. This was the organization that, in final form, had a mere 12 months to prepare the Korean army to survive and thrive on its own. Had KMAG failed, no amount of American support would have saved the ROK from destruction in 1950. They made an army and insured its survival.

Notes

1 Bruce Cumings, *The Origins of the Korean War*, vol. 1, *Liberation and the Emergence of Separate Regimes* (Princeton, NJ: Princeton University Press, 1981), xx.
2 Bonnie B.C. Oh, "Introduction: The Setting," in *Korea Under the American Military Government, 1945–1948*, ed. Bonnie B.C. Oh (Westport, CT: Praeger, 2002), 2.
3 Korea Institute of Military History, *The Korean War*, vol. 1 (Lincoln: University of Nebraska Press, 2001), 63. Hereafter referred to as KIMH, *KW*.
4 Headquarters, U.S. Army Military Government in Korea, *History of the United States Army Military Government in Korea*, part III, vol. 2, September 1945 – June 1946, pp. 198, 241. Copy available at the U.S. Army Center for Military History Library, Fort McNair, Washington, DC (hereafter referred to HUSAMGIK).
5 KIMH, *KW*, 65–66; Robert K. Sawyer, *Military Advisors in Korea: KMAG in Peace and War*, ed. Walter G. Hermes (Washington, DC: Office of the Chief of Military History, 1962), 13.
6 Lim Sun-ha to Allan R. Millett, 29 December 2003 and 1 January 2004.
7 KIMH, *KW*, 66.
8 Headquarters, KMAG, Historical Report, 1, U.S. Army in Korea and Military Advisory Group Korea, Historical Reports, 1949, Army – AG Command

Reports, 1949–1954, Record Group 407, National Archives and Records Administration II, College Park, Maryland; KIMH, *KW*, vol. 1, 70.

9 Allan R. Millett, "The Forgotten Army in the Misunderstood War: The *Hanguk Gun* in the Korean War, 1946–53," in *The Korean War 1950–53: A 50 Year Retrospective*, ed. Pete Dennis and Jeffrey Gray (Canberra: Army History Unit, Department of Defense, 2000), 1–26.

10 Lim Sun-ha, Major General, ROKA (ret.), interview by Allan R. Millett, Yongsan, Seoul, Republic of Korea, 30 November and 1 December 1994, transcript, provided to the author.

11 Sawyer, *Advisors in Korea*, 24–5, 90; Robert Shackleton, telephone interview with author, 29 November 2003, notes.

12 Sawyer, *Advisors in Korea*, 23–4.

13 Not until after 1953, did the ROKA institute a literacy program for trainees.

14 Sawyer, *Advisors in Korea*, 25.

15 KMAG Historical Report, 1949, 1–2.

16 Shackleton interview.

17 Millett, "Captain James H. Hausman and the Formation of the Korean Army, 1945–50," 513; Sawyer, *Advisors in Korea*, 23.

18 Lim Sun-ha recollection in Allan R. Millett, *Their War for Korea* (Washington, DC: Brassy's, Inc., 2002), 80ff.; Edgar S. Kennedy, *Mission to Korea* (London: Derek Verschoyle Limited, 1952), 174; Millett, "Captain James H. Hausman," 527.

19 James H. Hausman to Allan R. Millett, 13 December 1994.

20 Cumings, *The Origins of the Korean War*, 352–9.

21 KMAG Historical Report, 3; KIMH, *KW*, vol. 1, 69–70.

22 KMAG Historical Report, 3; KIMH, *KW*, vol. 1, 69–70.

23 Harry S. Truman, *Memoirs by Harry S. Truman*, vol. 2, *Years of Trial and Hope* (Garden City, NY: Doubleday & Company, Inc., 1956), 327.

24 Sawyer, *Advisors in Korea*, 35.

25 KMAG Historical Report, 3–4.

26 Roberts commanded an armored Combat Command as a spearhead for Patton's Third Army during the Battle of the Bulge; Charles B. MacDonald, *A Time for Trumpets* (New York: William Morrow, 1984).

27 KMAG Historical Report, 4.

28 Harold S. Fischgrund, email to the author, 8 February and 18 February 2002.

29 Minor L. Kelso, telephone interview with author, 5 December 2003, notes; Eighth Army, Special Problems, 2. When KMAG became operational in July 1949, its manpower authorization was raised to 500.

30 Harold Fischgrund to author, 8 February and 18 February 2002.

31 Office of the Chief of the KMAG, *Advisor's Handbook*, 17 October 1949, 2, Mowitz Papers, USAMHI.

32 Of the 106 officers assigned to PMAG on 17 August 1948, 63 were in the grade of lieutenant. Headquarters, USAFIK, Special Orders no. 176, 17 August 1948, Korean War Collection, The Ohio State University, Columbus, OH.

33 Brigadier General William L. Roberts Speech to All Tactical Advisors – KMAG, 23 June 1949, Roberts's Speeches to Americans and Koreans, AG File 333 1949, Provisional Mil. Adv. Group (1948) and Korean Mil. Adv. Group (1949–1953), RG 554.

34 KMAG Headquarters Memorandum, "Hot Spots," Inclosure 2 to *Advisor's Handbook*.

35 William L. Roberts to Major General Charles L. Bolté, 19 August 1949, 3, Assistant Chief of Staff (G-3), Plans and Operations 091 (Korea), Decimal File

1949–1950, Records of the Army Staff, Record Group 319, National Archives and Records Administration II, College Park, Maryland.

36 Ibid.

37 KMAG Headquarters Memorandum, "Operations Report," Inclosure 3 to *Advisor's Handbook*.

38 Major Arno P. Mowitz to Brigadier General William L. Roberts, 19 April 1949, Box 8, Mowitz Papers, USAMHI.

39 Brigadier General William L. Roberts to ROK Defense Minister Shin Ung-kyun, 19 April 1949, Box 8, Mowitz Papers, USAMHI.

40 Charles Wesolowsky to Allan R. Millett, 26 March 1996.

41 Roberts, Speech to All Tactical Advisors, 3–6.

42 *Advisor's Handbook*, 10, Mowitz Papers.

43 William L. Roberts, Memo, "Various," Inclosure 1 to *Advisor's Handbook*, Mowitz Papers.

44 William L. Roberts, Memo, "Operations Report," Inclosure 3 to *Advisor's Handbook*, Mowitz Papers.

45 *Advisor's Handbook*, 5, Mowitz Papers; Roberts, Speech to All Tactical Advisors, 3.

46 KMAG Historical Report, 4.

47 Roberts to the Supreme Chief of Staff, ROKA, 29 November 1948, AG File 300,000 General 1948 to 250 Discipline 1948, PMAG (1948–49) and KMAG (1949–1953), RG 554.

48 Il-Song Park, "The Dragon from the Stream: The ROK Army in Transition and the Korean War, 1950–1953" (PhD dissertation, Ohio State University, 2002). Roberts lectured regularly on tactics at the ROKA Staff College.

49 Roberts speech to Korean Army Division Commanders, 10 April 1950, Roberts's Speeches to Americans and Koreans, AG File 333 1949, PMAG (1948) and KMAG (1949–1953), RG 554.

50 Roberts, Speech to All Tactical Advisors, 6.

51 Robert Shackleton to Allan R. Millett, 11 April 1997; Shackleton, telephone interview, notes.

52 Shackleton to Millett, 11 April 1997; Sawyer, *Advisors in Korea*, 63.

53 Edward J. Stewart, telephone interview with author, 1 May 2003, notes.

54 Private Chang eventually obtained a commission and commanded a tank battalion in 1953, rising to the rank of Major General in the Korean Army; Shackleton to Millett, 11 April 1997; Shackleton, telephone interview.

55 Shackleton to Millett, 11 April 1997; Shackleton, telephone interview, notes.

56 Bliss to Millett, 13 February 1997.

57 Shackleton, telephone interview, notes.

58 Unfortunately, this fine unit never lived up to its potential as a mounted reconnaissance force as it was mismanaged, committed piecemeal, and destroyed in the early days of the Communist invasion of June 1950. Shackleton to Millett, 11 April 1997.

59 Charles Wesolowsky to Allan R. Millett, 26 March 1996.

60 Edwin M. Joseph, U.S. Army Service in Korea Questionnaire, 2, USAMHI.

61 Minor L. Kelso to Allan R. Millett, 12 October 1995.

62 Minor L. Kelso, PMAG Personal Diary, August–November 1948, entries 11 and 14 August 1948, copy furnished to author.

63 Entry 15 October 1948, Kelso diary.

64 H.C. Brookheart, "Japanese Infantry Tactics," *Military Review* 26 (November 1946): 39.

65 Ibid., 38, 40–2; Roberts to Bolté, 19 August 1949, 5.

66 Howard A. Trammell, "Korean War Notes," 17, Howard A. Trammell Papers, U.S. Army Military History Institute, Carlisle, Pennsylvania.

67   Kennedy, *Mission to Korea*, 103.

68   Sawyer, *Advisors in Korea*, 65.

69   Sometimes advisors learned that occasionally "the Korean way was best" and spared themselves the trial of trying to repair their advisory relationship just to demonstrate superior knowledge; Alfred H. Hausrath, *The KMAG Advisor: Role and Problems of the Military Advisor in Developing an Indigenous Army for Combat Operations in Korea* (Chevy Chase: Johns Hopkins University, 1957), 48.

70   Ibid., 50.

71   Trammell, "Korean War Notes," 21, USAMHI.

72   *Advisor's Handbook*, 4–5, 14–15, 30–32; Cowey, telephone interview, notes.

73   Stewart, telephone interview, notes.

74   Shackleton, telephone interview, notes.

75   Stewart, telephone interview, notes.

76   Kelso to Millett, 12 October 1995.

77   Kelso diary, 26–28 October 1948; *Advisor's Handbook*, 4.

78   Trammell, "Korean War Notes," 7; Kelso to Millett, 12 October 1995.

79   Lim Sun-ha, Major General, ROKA (ret.), interview by Allan R. Millett, Yongsan, Seoul, Republic of Korea, 30 November and 1 December 1994, notes.

80   Millett, *Their War for Korea*, 81–2; Roberts to Bolté, 19 August 1949, 2.

81   Roberts, Speech to all Tactical Advisors, 2.

82   Entry 26–28 October 1948, Kelso diary.

83   Charles Wesolowsky to Allan R. Millett, 16 September 1995.

84   Trammell, "Korean War Notes," 15–16, USAMHI.

85   Kelso to Millett, 12 June 1995.

86   Trammell, "Korean War Notes," 18–19; Hausrath, *The KMAG Advisor*, 2, 21, 31–7.

87   Fischgrund to the author, 8 February 2002.

88   Hausrath, *The KMAG Advisor*, 45.

89   Ibid., 44.

90   *Advisor's Handbook*, Mowitz Papers; William L. Roberts, Farewell Letter to Korean Army, 1 June 1950, AG File 300.6 1950, Provisional Mil. Adv. Group (1948) and Korean Mil. Adv. Group (1949–1953), RG 554.

91   KIMH, *KW*, vol. 1, 73–74; 2,730 officers and 61,858 enlisted men, KMAG Historical Report, 5.

92   Sawyer, *Advisors in Korea*, 45; MacArthur, *Reminiscences* (New York: McGraw-Hill, 1964), 320.

93   KMAG Historical Report, 5.

94   KMAG Historical Report, 7; Inclosure 1 to KMAG Historical Report, 1.

95   *Advisor's Handbook*, 4–24.

96   See the report of Philip C. Jessup, Ambassador at Large, Memorandum, 14 January 1950, *FRUS* (1950), 7: 5ff for an account of a high-profile visit to the ROK.

97   Marguerite Higgins, "U.S. Army Mission Called Success in South Korea's Fight on Reds," *Herald Tribune*, 30 May 1950.

98   KIMH, *KW*, vol. 1, 88; *FRUS* (1949), 7: 1095.

99   General Roberts to all KMAG Advisors, "KA [Korean Army] Logistical Situation," 5 May 1950, *FRUS* (1950), 7: 93.

100 Kim Chum-kon, *The Korean War: 1950–1953* (Seoul: Kwangmyong Publishing Company, 1980), 208; Roberts to Bolté, 19 August 1949, 9. See also Roberts to Bolté, 13 September 1949, 2, Plans and Operations (091) Korea.

101 Roberts figured that the "best rule" for evaluating ROKA reports and estimates was to "divide by ten." Roberts to Bolté, 19 August 1949, 7. Regarding tanks, the Minister of National Defense requested tanks weighing 46 tons;

Roberts pointed out that Korean bridges were only rated at 30 tons, and at any rate, even if Washington was ready to accede to their request for tanks, the Koreans had neglected to ask for tank ammunition. Roberts to Bolté, 13 September 1949, 2.

102 Millett, "Forgotten Army," 21.

103 KMAG Table of Distribution, AG File 400.34 1949, RG 554.

104 Sawyer, *Advisors in Korea*, 90.

105 For America's first attempt at a military mission in Asia, see Richard P. Weinert, "Original KMAG," *Military Review* 45 (1965): 93–99.

106 Lim, interview; General Isaac D. White, Senior Officers Oral History Program, 426, USAMHI.

107 General Roberts's Farewell Letter, 1 June 1950, AG File 300.6 1950, PMAG (1948) and KMAG (1949–1953), RG 554.

108 The most revealing information is found in Roberts's correspondence with Major General Charles L. Bolté, plans and operations officer of the US Army G-3. The KMAG chief clearly outlined the ROKA's structural, training, tactical, and leadership weaknesses. He also took care to highlight progress, but his report is at best cautiously optimistic. See Roberts to Boltè, 19 August 1949.

7 The French–Algerian War, 1954–1962

Communist China's support for Algerian independence

Donovan C. Chau

The People's Republic of China (PRC) has been interested and active in Africa for over half a century.[1] Since its establishment in 1949, Communist China has sought to engage the entire world as a respected, global power. When did China first become involved in Africa?[2] How was it operating in Africa and what did it achieve? One of China's earliest efforts at meddling in African affairs was its support for Algerian independence during the French–Algerian war (1954–1962). China was operating in North Africa, despite being a newly established nation. China's support for Algerian independence has not been examined independently or in great detail. China's military assistance to Africa has been overlooked as well. Garnering a greater understanding of Chinese activities in Algeria, therefore, will help clarify current and future analyses of Chinese actions – including military assistance – in Africa.

The PRC was a staunch supporter of African independence movements and governments from the French–Algerian war to the end of the apartheid era in South Africa. Over the course of four decades, China provided political, economic and military support to numerous movements and countries. The list is seemingly endless: attempting to train and arm guerrillas from West Africa in Ghana; training and arming Jonas Savimbi and UNITA (União Nacional para a Independência Total de Angola or the National Union for the Total Independence of Angola) in Angola; equipping and arming rebels in the Congo; gaining an eventual monopoly on military assistance to the Tanzanian military and security forces as well as training and arming resident guerrilla movements and providing continued military, economic and development assistance to the Sudan and Zimbabwe.[3] But support for the Algerians during the French–Algerian war was the first example of tangible military assistance.

Communist China's foray into North African politics was initiated at the Afro-Asian conference held in Bandung, Indonesia, in April 1955, just as the Algerian nationalist movement was gaining momentum.[4] According to Alistair Horne, the National Liberation Front (*Fronte de la Libération Nationale* or FLN) gained an invitation to the Conference after 'energetic lobbying.'[5] 'Although the Algerians, with no recognized government behind them, attended as 'unofficial' delegates, their presence at Bandung was sufficient to achieve a notable victory on the international scene.'[6] Delegates from the United Arab Republic (UAR) first introduced China to the independence struggle in French Algeria.[7] Conference delegates later 'adopted unanimously an Egyptian [UAR] motion proclaiming Algeria's right of independence, and called upon France to implement this forthwith.'[8] In his speech at the closing session, moreover, PRC Premier Chou En-lai declared that China extended its 'full sympathy and support to the struggle of the people of Algeria, Morocco and Tunisia for self-determination and independence.'[9] It was this initial contact at Bandung that set in motion PRC support for Algerian independence.

East through the UAR

To gain access to Algeria and support Algerian independence, the PRC established relations with two North African countries, the UAR and Morocco. As W.A.C. Adie wrote, 'China's positions in Egypt, Morocco and later Iraq were mainly important as means of access to Algeria.'[10] After the Bandung Conference, the PRC moved aggressively to establish relations with the UAR.[11] While the Bandung Conference was ostensibly held to promote peace and cooperation in Asia and Africa, China successfully exploited the forum to promote its broader international interests, including support for Algerian independence. Thus, China's first contact with the UAR at Bandung spawned interaction with the African continent as a whole.

Through its initial contact with Africans at Bandung, China used a series of contacts and agreements with the UAR to facilitate access on the African continent. PRC–UAR talks on cultural cooperation were held in May 1955, a month after Bandung.[12] On 10 August, a PRC contract to buy Egyptian cotton was signed in Cairo. Twelve days later, an agreement was signed for Egyptian purchase of Chinese steel.[13] In October, the two countries signed a three-year trade agreement including notably a provision for opening a PRC trade office in Cairo and vice versa. A formal agreement on cultural cooperation was later signed in April 1956. Soon thereafter, on 30 May 1956, Cairo withdrew recognition of Nationalist China (the Republic of China on Taiwan) and established full diplomatic relations with Communist China. Alaba Ogunsanwo stated clearly, 'From Cairo, China's diplomats observed the situation on the continent.'[14] Cairo became China's first base from which to assess and operate on the African continent and a node through which to support Algerian independence.

The PRC exploited its presence in the UAR to further its objectives in Africa. The operations of one individual illustrate Cairo's geographic importance: 'After the establishment of the Cairo Embassy in 1956, the Commercial Officer, Chan Hsiang-Kang, succeeded in establishing trade relations with Tunisia, Libya, Nigeria, Ghana, Ethiopia and Tanganyika in 1957.'[15] Chan benefited from the UAR's geographic position and, later, the presence of numerous African nationalist leaders in Cairo. In December 1957, for example, the establishment of the Permanent Secretariat of the Afro-Asian People's Solidarity Organization (AAPSO) in Cairo:

> gave the Chinese a base from which to make direct contacts with dissidents from both North and Tropical Africa, without going through the European Communist Parties or the Soviet-controlled international front organizations, such as the WPC [World Peace Council] and WFTU [World Federation of Trade Unions].[16]

China contributed annual funds to the AAPSO, demonstrating its commitment to African nationalism. 'The Cairo Embassy thus became the first basis for Chinese activity in Africa.'[17]

Relations between the UAR and China later became strained because of the latter's support of Iraq and Syria. Because of its diverse presence in the UAR, however, China was in a position to formally squabble while maintaining contacts with groups in Cairo. The New China News Agency (NCNA) also established its first office on the African continent in Cairo in 1958.[18] Although the PRC moved elsewhere to enter the Algerian battlefield, Cairo remained a strategic location for Chinese operations on the continent.

West through Morocco

West of the UAR and Algeria was Morocco, independent since 1956. Prior to gaining its independence, the territory played an instrumental role in establishing French colonial power in Africa.[19] Like the flurry of diplomacy with the UAR, China quickly established relations with Morocco: 'Trade agreements between the PRC and Morocco were signed on October 13, 1957, and on October 27, 1958, and finally full diplomatic relations were established on November 1, 1958.'[20] As Richard Lowenthal and Wei Liang-tsai both attest, thereafter, 'Morocco became one of Peking's major trading partners in Africa.'[21] While Lowenthal and Wei may have been correct, China's trade with Morocco was not as significant as Morocco's strategic location west of Algeria. 'In [1957] cultural and trade contacts were established with Morocco, and through Morocco and other channels China extended financial and other aid, plus training, to the *Front de Liberation* (F.L.N.) in Algeria.'[22] Morocco was the means by which China was able to support Algerian independence tangibly.

Further analyses of PRC intentions in Morocco reveal a common theme — Morocco as a western point of entry into Algeria. According to Fritz Schattan, after establishing full diplomatic relations with Morocco, 'China was more interested in Algeria than Morocco.'[23] Due to geography, Morocco was 'the only State in North Africa which offered Peking any chance of exerting influence on the Algerian war.'[24] China's 'diplomatic activity was concentrated largely in the strategically placed Peking consulates in Tangiers, and in Oujda on the Moroccan-Algerian border.'[25] Sources indicated that the PRC used Oujda 'as a base to support the Algerians against the French.'[26] According to Lowenthal, furthermore, the PRC consulate in Oujda was the 'principal base of exiled FLN forces in Morocco.'[27] After the Moroccan government banned the domestic Communist Party, the PRC was willing to cease contact with any of its members in order to continue providing assistance to Algerian nationalists. 'Thus, support for revolutionary activity in Algeria received priority [over the global Communist movement].'[28] Time and again, in Africa China prioritized strategic ends over ideological pursuits.

PRC operations in Morocco and the UAR laid the path to China's direct role in the Algerian war for independence. Exploiting the presence of African nationalists in Cairo and the Moroccan border posts with Algeria allowed China to support Algerian independence directly.

The FLN

From the onset, Algerian nationalists aligned with Communist China politically. 'The War of Independence contributed to a set of beliefs that emphasized Algeria's identification with the newly independent, less-developed countries.'[29] Like other wars of national liberation, Algerian nationalists used guerrilla warfare techniques – particularly organizational methods.[30] China exploited the existing organizations to support the Algerian independence movement.

Created in October 1954, the FLN was an outgrowth of Ahmed Ben Bella's the Revolutionary Committee of Unity and Action (*Comité Révolutionnaire d'Unité et d'Action* or CRUA) in Cairo.[31] The leaders of the independence movement were a group of nine CRUA members known as the historical chiefs (*chefs historiques*). They included Ait Ahmed, Mohamed Boudiaf, Belkacem Krim, Rabah Bitat, Larbi Ben M'Hidi, Mourad Didouch, Moustafa Ben Boulaid, Mohamed Khider and Ben Bella. Leadership of the Algerian revolution was experienced and recognized.

The CRUA also organized a military network in Algeria comprising six military regions (or *wilaya*). The military regions' leaders and their followers became known as the 'internals.' Ben Bella, Khider and Ait Ahmed formed the 'External Delegation' in Cairo 'to gain foreign support for the rebellion and to acquire arms, supplies, and funds for the *wilaya* commanders.'[32] The renamed FLN took responsibility for the political direction of the CRUA; the National Liberation Army (*Armée de Libération Nationale* or ALN) was the FLN's military wing. 'The contribution of the CRUA leaders lay mainly in their development of unity and cohesion rather than in their organizational creations. They had infused pre-existing structures with a new sense of purpose and cooperation.'[33] Experienced political and military organizations were therefore present when China began supporting Algerian independence.

Another significant organization related to Algerian independence was the Political and Administrative Organization (*Organization Politique et Administrative* or OPA). Located in both rural and urban environments, OPA cells performed financial and administrative duties; they also disseminated FLN propaganda and supplied intelligence reports. Known as 'the backbone of the nationalist movement,' the OPA's primary duty was 'to undermine the French administration at every level, gradually replacing it with officials and institutions of the revolutionary party.'[34] As a result, the OPA helped manage and sustain the Algerian nationalist movement.

Support for the FLN

In one of Communist China's initial political ploys, Premier Chou En-lai called for negotiations in June 1956 between France and the Algerian resistance on the basis of full recognition of the national aspiration of the Algerian people.[35]

> Peking regarded the Algerian *Front de la Libération Nationale* (FLN) as an avant-garde anti-colonialist movement and sought to shape it, along the lines of the Viet-Minh movement in Indo-China, into an instrument of revolutionary strategy against France and against the West generally.[36]

FLN leaders, it was believed, decided on an 'Indochinese discussion' as well.[37] Reports speculated that captured French Algerian soldiers in Vietnam were being converted into Algerian revolutionaries.[38]

China also communicated its message through mass public demonstrations. For example, in November 1957, the PRC celebrated a 'national day of solidarity with the Algerian people.'[39] Utilizing the first Afro-Asian People's Solidarity Conference, held in Cairo from December 1957 to January 1958, China exploited international organizations to reaffirm support for Algerian independence.[40] Soon after, in March 1958 (designated 'Algeria Day' by the Afro-Asian People's Solidarity Conference), the PRC held a 'Support Algeria' rally in Peking. A resolution adopted at the rally pledged 'full support for the just cause of the people of Algeria and of Africa as a whole in their efforts to secure and safeguard their national independence.'[41] Burhan Shahidi, chairman of the China Islamic Association, stated at the rally, 'the Chinese people regard the Algerian people's struggle and victories as their own.'[42] In Peking, Premier Chou En-lai and Foreign Minister Chen Yi received Ibrahim Ghafa, representative of the FLN, and Atef Daniel of the Arab People's Conference. In this four-month span, China used mass rallies and public statements to demonstrate full PRC support for Algerian independence in addition to making direct contact with the FLN. Public

PRC support demonstrated to the Algerian nationalists the nature of Chinese support, adding a psychological element to PRC operations.

PRC material support began a month later. In April 1958, China sent 500,000 *yuan* via the All-China Federation of Trade Unions (ACFTU), China Islamic Association and the Asian Solidarity Committee to the FLN.[43] In an article published in the *Peking Review* that same month, the PRC gave moral support to the Algerian cause: 'Now North Africa is in the forefront against colonialism. Fighting heroically, Algeria has become their beacon light in this struggle.'[44] Although meagre, PRC financial contributions combined with public support served as tangible evidence of PRC interests in Algeria. China's support for the Algerian cause became more tangible later that same year.

The PRC was the first Communist country to offer to establish official diplomatic relations with the Provisional Government of the Algerian Republic (*Gouvernement Provisionel de la République Algérienne* or GPRA) after its formation by Ferhat Abbas in 1958.[45] China recognized the newly formed GPRA after Foreign Minister Chen Yi informed Algerian Foreign Minister Mohamed Lamine Debaghine of the decision in a September message. In greetings sent to Premier Ferhat Abbas, Premier Chou En-lai declared, 'As in the past the Chinese people will firmly stand by the heroic and indomitable Algerian people.'[46] Giving the GPRA immediate recognition was a calculated political move by China. Public support for and recognition of the newly created Algerian government was another psychological boost for the Algerians.

By the end of the year, the PRC began communicating more frequently with the GPRA through exchange visits. An Algerian ministerial delegation led by Ben Yossef Ben Khedda arrived in Peking in December 1958.[47] On 5 December, a mass rally was staged in Peking where Burhan Shadidi, once again, voiced PRC support for the Algerian struggle.[48] The PRC reinforced the need to continue armed struggle, providing both political and moral support to the independence cause. At a 7 December banquet in honour of the visiting delegation, Vice Premier and Foreign Minister Chen Yi pledged China's full support for the Algerian people's struggle for independence.[49] Prior to the arrival of the Algerian delegation, Minister of Information Mohammed Yazid suggested that the delegation would negotiate for material support – including the possibility of military supplies.[50] Notably, Mahmoud Sherif, Minister of Armaments and Supplies, was one of the delegates sent.[51] While in China, the Algerian delegation spent a day with a People's Liberation Army (PLA) infantry division stationed near the capital and had 'a number of discussions with prominent generals of the Peking Defence Ministry.'[52] While specific evidence of PRC assistance was not revealed, Ben Khedda's visit illustrated China's use of exchange visits to communicate and negotiate.

After a second Algerian visit to China that same month, the fruit of PRC-Algerian exchange visits was the symbolic Sino-Algerian communiqué, signed on 20 December 1958. It stated, 'During the talks, the two parties studied *concrete methods* [emphasis added] to strengthen relations between the two countries and affirmed the principle of establishing diplomatic and cultural relations between the two countries.'[53] The communiqué concluded by indicating 'their determination to further strengthen friendly co-operation between the two countries.'[54] That same day at a reception held in honour of the visiting Algerian delegation, Chen Yi gave a speech and stated, 'The Algerian people's struggle against French imperialism is a component part of the anti-imperialist struggle of the Arab and African peoples.'[55] Chen Yi's speech along with the communiqué laid the PRC foundation for continued support for Algerian independence.

Active support

By the end of 1958, 'Active support for the FLN ... now became the heart of Red China's African policy.'[56] Evidence indicated that China was already quite active supporting Algerian independence. For example, it was reported that 'Algerian soldiers were trained in China, and between 1959 and 1962 ... the PRC supplied arms worth about $10 million to the Algerians.'[57] More specifically, the PRC allegedly financed Algerian arms purchases in the Middle East and Europe by 'an interest-free loan' method and trained selected Algerian officers in China as early as spring 1959.[58] In October 1959 in Baghdad, while announcing that he had sent ten planeloads of arms and £500,000 to the Algerians via Libya, Iraqi President General Kassem 'also indicated that the Chinese had given other aid to the Algerians of which he had no personal knowledge.'[59] Clearly, China was intent on providing the FLN with whatever support needed – from weapons and equipment to funds and training – to achieve independence.

In 1959, China continued its direct and indirect support for Algerian independence. In February, the Afro-Asian Youth Conference opened in Cairo.[60] Liu Hia-yan, head of the Chinese delegation, noted that this was the first time numerous youth from Asia and Africa had come together. Chou En-lai sent a message of greetings to the Conference, hoping it would make a contribution to Afro-Asian unity much as the Bandung Conference and the Afro-Asian People's Solidarity Conference had. The following month, the Chinese Red Cross Society sent 15,000 *yuan* to the Moroccan Red Crescent Society and 10,000 *yuan* to the Tunisian Red Crescent Society 'as contributions to the Algerian refugees now in exile in those countries.'[61] While relatively small, the assistance conveyed China's support for those affected by war. Later in the year, Chou En-lai sent a message of greetings to Prime Minister Ferhat Abbas on the first anniversary of the founding of the GPRA, reiterating PRC support for the Algerian people's struggle for national independence.[62]

That same year, an Algerian military delegation 'headed by Omar Oussedik, Secretary of State, and an experienced guerilla fighter' arrived in Peking.[63] The delegation visited China until May, touring military academies and installations across eastern, southern and northeastern China, and Chen Yi and Mahmoud Sherif signed another Sino-Algerian communiqué.[64] The previous month, Tunisian President Habib Bourguiba stated that he would not oppose China supplying arms to the FLN.[65] In addition, later a military mission of ten FLN officers led by Omar Oussedik told the Belgian News Agency that twenty Algerians were being trained as pilots in China.[66] At a mass rally held in Peking for 'Support Algeria Week,' visiting Secretary Oussedik spoke about the Chinese supporting 'the Algerian people [to] combat the coalition of imperialist powers.'[67] Five hundred representatives of the PLA were also at the rally. 'In a farewell message, its leader Omar Oussedik declared that his delegation was returning home with far richer experience and a new firmer determination to battle the French colonialists.'[68] According to reports in autumn 1959, China had spent between $3 and $10 million for weapons, propaganda and administration for Algerian rebels.[69] The 1958 and 1959 Algerian military delegation visits to China reinforced PRC support for Algerian independence in addition to helping the Algerians strengthen their military capabilities.

While providing military assistance, China continued to communicate directly to the Algerian people. In November 1959, an Algerian Workers General Federation delegation visited Peking to discuss means to assist Algeria in the war against France.[70] Chou En-lai and Liu Chang-sheng, vice chairman of the ACFTU, invited the delegation to the PRC.[71] On 31 December 1959, Liu Ning-i, Chairman of the ACFTU, sent a letter to the Secretariat of the Foreign Mission of the Algerian General Federation of Workers, paying respect to the fifth anniversary of the Algerian people's war against France.[72] In addition, the ACFTU and Chinese National Women's Federation sent 'medicines and children's clothing worth fifty thousand *yuan*' in December in response to the worldwide appeal to help Algerian refugees.[73] The following March – on China's designated 'Algeria Day' – the Chinese Committee for Afro-Asian Solidarity issued a special statement of support, as did organizations of workers, women and youth. Paying respect to their 'Algerian brothers,' the messages stated Algeria was at 'the forefront of the struggle against imperialism and colonialism.'[74] With exchange visits, public messages of support and the distribution of funds, China used a combination of means to support Algerian independence.

At the same time, China continued to assist the Algerians militarily. In 1960, PRC equipment was reportedly found on the Algerian battlefield.[75] By spring, another high-level Algerian delegation visited China and was received by Chairman Mao Tse-tung.[76] At a banquet for the Algerian delegation, Vice Premier Ho Lung declared:

> the Chinese people have always stood firmly by the African peoples in their struggle for national independence, and will continue to stand shoulder to shoulder with them in the future to bring the struggle against imperialism and colonialism to its conclusion.[77]

A report following the Algerian delegation's visit hinted at additional military assistance to the FLN: 'The Algerians have sent a mission of three high-ranking members of the Provisional Government to Communist China to discuss material aid ... for nationalist guerrilla forces in Algeria.'[78] Another communiqué in May affirmed China's continued support for Algerian independence and, conversely, Algeria's 'full support' for China's recovery of Taiwan.[79] That same day, Belkacem thanked China for its 'tangible aid' and 'material sacrifices.'[80] As China continued its support for Algerian independence, for the first time the Provisional Algerian government voiced its support for PRC interests – agreeing with China's position with regard to Taiwan.

US analysis at this time began to recognize PRC activities in North Africa. 'In Africa, the USIA [United States Information Agency] reported, Red China [was] concentrating on "anti-colonialist" propaganda and support of the Algerian Nationalist movement. Chinese Communist diplomatic missions have been set up in Morocco and Guinea, it said.'[81] Left unsaid was that the Moroccan mission served as direct transit points in support of PRC operations in Algeria. By July 1960, the PRC became the first Communist government to accept permanent representation from the GPRA, offering the Algerians even closer relations.[82] That same month, a Chinese commentator likened the Algerian struggle to the PRC struggle, citing the peasant aspects of both: 'Without the active participation of this huge peasant force, there could be no powerful national independence movement in Africa. The war for national independence in Algeria, for instance, is basically a peasant war.'[83] Through such public pronouncements, China created a common bond based on shared experiences, thereby strengthening relations.

In the summer of 1960, the intimacy of PRC–FLN relations was further revealed: 'A close relationship is developing between Communist China and the government in exile of the Algerian rebels [of] the FLN, in Tunis.'[84] Chinese 'technicians' and 'specialists' were entering North Africa.

> Chinese technicians and specialists in various fields [were] flooding into Libya, Tunisia, Morocco and the newly independent nations to the south. They [were] promoting trade, cultural and scientific and technical exchanges at every level, with special emphasis on students and young intellectuals.[85]

PRC technicians and specialists served as another means of communicating China's message of support to the African people (as well as gathering intelligence on local environments). In September, Chairman Liu, Premier Chou and Vice Premier and Foreign Minister Chen Yi sent greetings to GPRA leaders on the second anniversary of its establishment. Premier Chou noted that the militant friendship and cooperation between the two peoples was being 'continuously developed and consolidated.'[86] At the same time, China sent a military mission led by Deputy Chief of Staff of the PLA General

Chang Tsung-hsun to Cairo, creating speculation that China might offer large-scale security assistance to the FLN.[87] In addition, Prime Minister Ferhat Abbas accepted Premier Chou's invitation to visit the PRC for National Day celebrations. These events demonstrated the considerable extent of China's relations with the Algerian independence movement.

An Algerian delegation led by Prime Minister Abbas visited China from 29 September to 6 October 1960, attending the eleventh anniversary celebration of the founding of the PRC.[88] On 29 September, the delegation attended a banquet in their honour where Premier Chou voiced PRC support for the Algerians.[89] In reply, Premier Abbas stated Algeria's intention, like China's, to spread their revolution throughout the region.[90] Thus, Algerian and Chinese interests in Africa had become entwined. On 30 September, Chairman Mao and Chairman Liu received Abbas and the delegation. At the invitation of the Chinese-African People's Friendship Association (CAPFA), a twenty-four-member Algerian art troupe also attended the National Day celebration.[91] China and Algeria signed another joint communiqué on 5 October, which stated, 'The Chinese Government reiterated its firm stand of rendering *unfailing assistance and support* [emphasis added] to the just struggle of the Algerian people.'[92] In reply, the Algerian government voiced support for China, expressing 'full support for the Chinese people's just struggle to liberate their own territory.'[93] In his farewell speech at the Peking airport, Abbas concluded, 'We are returning home with the conviction that the People's Republic of China stands resolutely by the Algerian people against imperialism and that it will not cease to support the Algerian people, materially and morally, until they attain independence.'[94] And in an interview with an Italian communist newspaper at the end of the month, Abbas said China would provide 'multiform aid' to the Algerian rebels 'on a material and on a diplomatic plane.'[95]

To demonstrate China's level of development, the PRC participated in the October 1960 International Fair in Tunis with a 2,160 square meter pavilion of industrial and agricultural exhibits. The Algerian Minister of State, Said Mohamadi, visited the PRC pavilion and endorsed China's path in the visitor's book.[96] Once again, China used a foreign venue to influence the Algerian leadership. On 1 November, seven Chinese people's organizations sponsored a rally to commemorate the sixth anniversary of the Algerian revolution.[97] In the same month, observers in Tunis predicted that China's 'multiform aid' to the FLN would consist of arms, money and technicians.[98] These same observers expected Chinese technicians to help breach the frontier line that was isolating the interior of Algeria from nationalist arms and men in Tunisia, in addition to serving as ideological warfare counsellors (guerrilla warfare advisors).[99] Also, an NCNA correspondent reported that FLN officers were studying Mao's works and using Chinese guerrilla methods.[100] Once again, Communist China combined public statements of support with tangible material aid.

Independence achieved

Communist China continued to voice support for Algerian independence until it was achieved. On the 'National Day Against Partition' (5 July 1961), China expressed full support for the Algerian people's recent resistance to the colonists' attempt to carve up their country.[101] PRC organizations including the Committee for Afro-Asian Solidarity, the ACFTU and the CAPFA 'declared that Sahara is the inalienable and sacred territory of Algeria and that the scheme of French imperialism to separate the Sahara from Algeria is a gross violation of and encroachment on the sovereignty and the territorial integrity of Algeria.'[102] Later, Chairman Liu and Premier Chou sent a greeting to Premier Ben Youssef Ben Khedda on the third anniversary of the establishment of the GPRA. The message expressed confidence that the 'militant friendship' between the two peoples would grow firmer with each passing day.[103] Two months later, Premier Chou sent another message to Premier Ben Khedda on the anniversary of the beginning of the Algerian war.

In addition to vocal political support, China's military assistance to Algeria continued apace. According to the Central Intelligence Agency (CIA), 'The Chinese supplied approximately $15 million, beginning in 1959, to support Algerian nationalist military activity.'[104] While the figure may be inexact, it was clear that China provided material support – funds, arms and equipment – as well as public support – communications in print, mass rallies and exchange visits – to the FLN. Finally, in 1962, Algerian nationalists achieved their aspiration of national independence.

On 20 March 1962, Premier Chou sent a letter of congratulations to Premier Ben Khedda on occasion of the Algerian–French ceasefire agreement.[105] The letter read in part:

> The conclusion of the agreement between Algeria and France is the result of armed struggle waged heroically by the Algerian people for more than seven years, and of their perseverance in negotiations on an equal footing and on the basis of armed struggle.[106]

In addition, the letter stated: 'The close and militant friendship between the Chinese and Algerian people is based on reliable foundations.' Since 1956, the PRC had provided multiform support for Algerian independence. So it was with satisfaction that, in July 1962, the Algerians achieved independence from France. On 3 July 1962, Chairman Liu and Premier Chou sent a message to Prime Minister Ben Khedda congratulating him on Algeria's independence, and Foreign Minister Chen Yi announced China's decision to recognize independent Algeria.[107]

Conclusion

From Bandung in 1955 to Algiers in 1962, China was a robust supporter of Algerian independence, using a variety of political, economic and military means to help Algerian nationalists gain independence. China's approach was calculated and systematic, and military assistance was a crucial instrument of PRC influence. China's involvement in Algeria demonstrates its multifaceted use of all the resources of the country to influence and affect events in Africa, without relying on any single means. This case also illustrates the patient, long-term perspective of China's leaders, particularly when dealing with events in Africa. China's support for Algerian independence, above all, reveals that its political objectives took precedence over all of its other objectives. Before judging China's current and future activities in Africa, therefore, it would be prudent to examine the historical record of China's involvement in Africa, studying the character and intent of past Chinese actions.

Notes

1 The PRC will be used interchangeably with Communist China/China throughout this chapter.
2 I differentiate here between historic China and Communist China.
3 For case studies on the Ghanaian and Tanzanian examples, see Donovan C. Chau, 'Grand Strategy into Africa: Communist China's Use of Political Warfare, 1955–1976,' PhD dissertation, University of Reading, United Kingdom, 2005.
4 In general, the 'Bandung Conference' was a gathering to unite African and Asian nations and peoples. For more, see George McTurnan Kahin, *The Asian-African Conference: Bandung, Indonesia, April 1955* (Ithaca, NY: Cornell University Press, 1956).
5 Alistair Horne, *A Savage War of Peace: Algeria 1954–1962* (New York: Viking Press, 1994), p. 130.
6 Ibid., pp. 130–1.
7 The short-lived UAR (created in 1958 and dissolved in 1961) comprised modern-day Egypt and Syria. However, Egypt was referred to as the UAR prior to 1958 and until 1970. Egyptians introduced a resolution on French North Africa, including Algeria, during the Bandung Conference, Kahin, *The Asian-African Conference*, p. 17.
8 Horne, *A Savage War of Peace*, p. 131.
9 'Asian-African Conference Closes,' *Survey of China Mainland Press*, No. 1033 (1955), p. 10, translated by the American Consulate General in Hong Kong and originally published in *NCNA*, 24 April 1955.
10 W.A.C. Adie, 'Chinese Policy Towards Africa,' in Sven Hamrell and Carl Gösta Widstrand, eds, *The Soviet Bloc, China and Africa* (Uppsala: The Scandinavian Institute of African Studies, 1964), p. 50.
11 Wei Liang-tsai, *Peking Versus Taipei in Africa 1960–1978* (Taipei, Republic of China: Asia and World Institute, 1982), p. 104.
12 Also in 1956, the PRC sent cultural missions to the Sudan, Morocco, Tunisia and Ethiopia. Alaba Ogunsanwo, *China's Policy in Africa 1958–71* (London: Cambridge University Press, 1974), p. 9.
13 Adie, 'Chinese Policy Towards Africa,' p. 50.
14 Ogunsanwo, *China's Policy in Africa*, p. 9.

15 Ibid., p. 37.
16 Adie, 'Chinese Policy Towards Africa,' p. 51.
17 Richard Lowenthal, 'China,' in Zbigniew Brzezinski, ed., *Africa and the Communist World* (Stanford, CA: Stanford University Press, 1963), p. 152.
18 Chang Ya-chun, *Chinese Communist Activities in Africa – Policies and Challenges* (Taipei, Republic of China: World Anti-Communist League and Asian Peoples' Anti-Communist League, 1981), p. 5.
19 See, for example, Dwight Norman Harris, 'French Colonial Expansion in West Africa, The Sudan, and the Sahara,' *American Political Science Review*, Vol. 5, No. 3 (1911), pp. 353–73; and Archibald Cary Coolidge, 'The European Reconquest of North Africa,' *American Historical Review*, Vol. 17, No. 4 (1912), pp. 723–34.
20 *Communist China in Africa* (Taipei, Republic of China: Asian Peoples' Anti-Communist League, 1961), p. 32; Wei Liang-tsai, *Peking Versus Taipei in Africa*, p. 106; Adie, 'Chinese Policy towards Africa,' p. 51; 'China and the World: China-Morocco Diplomatic Relations,' *Peking Review*, Vol. I, No. 36 (1958), p. 22; 'Foreign Trade New: Sino-Morocco Trade Agreement,' *Peking Review*, Vol. I, No. 36 (1958), p. 22.
21 Lowenthal, 'China,' p. 165; Wei Liang-Tsai, *Peking Versus Taipei in Africa*, p. 106. Peking is the same as Beijing.
22 W. A. C. Adie, 'China and the Bandung Genie,' *Current Scene*, Vol. III, No. 19 (15 May 1965), p. 6.
23 Fritz Schatten, *Communism in Africa* (New York: Praeger, 1966), p. 198.
24 Ibid.
25 Ibid. The border town of Ouida is also spelled Oujda.
26 Lowenthal, 'China,' p. 165; Ogunsanwo, *China's Policy in Africa*, p. 30; Wei Liang-tsai, *Peking Versus Taipei in Africa*, p. 106.
27 Lowenthal, 'China,' p. 165.
28 Ogunsanwo, *China's Policy in Africa*, p. 30.
29 Jean A. Tartter, 'National Security,' in Helen Chapin Metz, ed., *Algeria: A Country Study* (Washington, DC: Federal Research Division, Library of Congress, 1994), p. 238.
30 For a theoretical discussion on the French perspective of *la guerre révolutionnaire*, see George A. Kelly, 'Revolutionary Warfare and Psychological Action,' in Franklin Mark Osanka, ed., *Modern Guerrilla Warfare: Fighting Communist Guerrilla Movements, 1941–1961* (New York: Free Press, 1962), pp. 425–38.
31 Horne, *A Savage War of Peace*, p. 79.
32 Anthony Toth, 'Historical Setting,' in Helen Chapin Metz, ed., *Algeria: A Country Study* (Washington, DC: Federal Research Division, Library of Congress, 1994), p. 44.
33 Alf Andrew Heggoy, *Insurgency and Counterinsurgency in Algeria* (Bloomington: Indiana University Press, 1972), p. 86.
34 Heggoy, *Insurgency and Counterinsurgency in Algeria*, pp. 102, 120. Undermining the French administration could be considered the 'insurgents' oil spot' strategy as well. I thank Dr Christopher C. Harmon for sharing this perspective.
35 'Our 600 Million Back Up Algerian People,' *Peking Review*, No. I, Vol. 6 (1958), p. 21.
36 Schatten, *Communism in Africa*, p. 198.
37 Georges Beuchard, *L'Equivoque algérienne* (Paris: Nourvelles Editions Debresse, 1949), p. 34.
38 Without citing any source directly, Horne wrote: 'Employing subtlest techniques of psychological warfare, the Viet-Minh suggestively quizzed the Algerians captured there: 'Since you are such good soldiers, why do you fight for

the colonialists? Why don't you fight for yourselves and get yourselves a country of your own?' Horne, *A Savage War of Peace*, pp. 78–9.

39 Adie, 'China and the Bandung Genie,' p. 6.

40 *Communist China in Africa*, pp. 2–3. Twenty-seven African states and regions attended the conference. Tung Feng, 'The Bandung Spirit Thrives,' *Peking Review*, Vol. I, No. 9 (1958), p. 7.

41 'Our 600 Million Back Up Algerian People,' p. 21.

42 Kuo Mo-jo, member of the Chinese–African Solidarity Committee and a Chinese peace leader, was also on hand, ibid.

43 Adie, 'Chinese Policy Towards Africa,' p. 51; 'China and the World: Friendly Aid to Algeria,' *Peking Review*, Vol. I, No. 7 (1958), p. 18; Ogunsanwo, *China's Policy in Africa*, p. 43.

44 Tung Feng, 'The Bandung Spirit Thrives,' p. 7.

45 The provisional government was created on 19 September 1958; Peking granted recognition on 22 September. Wei Liang-tsai, *Peking Versus Taipei in Africa*, p. 105.

46 'China and the World: China Recognizes Algeria,' *Peking Review*, Vol. I, No. 31 (1958), p. 25.

47 *Communist China in Africa*, p. 32; Ogunsanwo, *China's Policy in Africa*, p. 51.

48 'China Welcomes Algerian Delegation,' *Peking Review*, Vol. I, No. 41 (1958), p. 15.

49 'China and the World: Algerian Delegation in China,' *Peking Review*, Vol. I, No. 42 (1958), p. 20.

50 Lawrence Fellows, 'Algerians Seek Aid from Peiping,' *New York Times*, 1 December 1958, p. 8.

51 'China and the World: Algerian Delegation to China,' *Peking Review*, Vol. I, No. 39 (1958), p. 19.

52 'China and the World: Algerian Delegation in China,' p. 20; Schatten, *Communism in Africa*, p. 198.

53 'Sino-Algerian Communique,' *Peking Review*, Vol. I, No. 43 (1958), p. 24. Evidence of 'concrete methods' may be perceived from the last day of the delegation's stay when they visited a Peking gymnasium. The Minister of Armaments and Supplies revealed that the Algerian government would send a football team and other 'sportsmen' to China, 'Sportsmen Patriots,' *Peking Review*, Vol. I, No. 4 (1958), p. 23.

54 'Sino-Algerian Communique,' p. 24.

55 'To the Victory of the Algerian People!' *Peking Review*, Vol. I, No. 43 (1958), p. 24.

56 John K. Cooley, *East Wind Over Africa: Red China's African Offensive* (New York: Walker and Company, 1965), p. 155.

57 Wei Liang-tsai, *Peking Versus Taipei in Africa*, p. 105.

58 Lowenthal, 'China,' pp. 162–3.

59 Adie, 'Chinese Policy Towards Africa,' p. 52; Ogunsanwo, *China's Policy in Africa*, p. 53.

60 'China and the World: Afro-Asian Youth Conference,' *Peking Review*, Vol. II, No. 6 (1959), p. 18.

61 'China and the World: Briefs,' *Peking Review*, Vol. II, No. 13 (1959), p. 23.

62 'China and the World: Solidarity with Fighting Algeria,' *Peking Review*, Vol. II, No. 39 (1959), p. 28.

63 Ogunsanwo, *China's Policy in Africa*, p. 52. Minister of National Defense Marshal Peng Teh-huai invited the delegation.

64 Adie, 'Chinese Policy Towards Africa,' p. 51. The details were not explicit, though the Minister of Armaments and Supply cosigned the document.

65 Statement made in *Newsweek* and cited in Adie, 'Chinese Policy Towards Africa,' p. 52. In addition to cross-border arms transfers:
    Still later the ALN-FLN sent young recruits to their sanctuaries in *Tunisia*

and in *Morocco* [emphasis added]. There they were able to train the men and keep them out of the hands of the various French institutions of counterrevolutionary education.
Heggoy, *Insurgency and Counterinsurgency in Algeria*, p. 138.

66 Adie, 'Chinese policy Towards Africa,' p. 52.
67 'National Support for Algerian Independence,' *Peking Review*, Vol. II, No. 14 (1959), pp. 16–17.
68 'China and the World: Algerians' Visit Ends,' *Peking Review*, Vol. II, No. 19 (1959), p. 25.
69 *Reuters* cited in *Communist China in Africa*, pp. 41–2. Zartman cited the PRC giving $10 million in arms shipments to Algeria in 1959. William Zartman, 'Tiger in the Jungle,' *Current Scene*, Vol. II, No. 2 (1962), p. 2. The British Broadcasting Corporation (BBC) reported that China had granted a US$10 million credit for military equipment and the financing of administration and propaganda and had also agreed to supply large quantities of US weapons seized during the Korean War, cited in Ogunsanwo, *China's Policy in Africa*, p. 53.
70 'China and the World: Ties with North Africa,' *Peking Review*, Vol. II, No. 47 (1959), p. 21.
71 *Communist China in Africa*, pp. 33–4.
72 Ibid., p. 33.
73 Appeal issued by 'committee for solidarity with the workers and people of Algeria, conference of International Trade Union in solidarity with the People of Algeria, September 1958,' Ogunsanwo, *China's Policy in Africa*, p. 45.
74 'China and the World: "Algeria Day"' *Peking Review*, Vol. III, No. 14 (1960), p. 32.
75 Adie, 'Chinese Policy Towards Africa,' p. 52.
76 Ibid., p. 53. The Algerian delegation visited China from 30 April to 3 May, 7–9 May and 13–20 May 1960. 'Welcome to Algeria's Delegates,' *Peking Review*, Vol. III, No. 18 (1960), p. 5.
77 'China Hails Fighting Algeria,' *Peking Review*, Vol. III, No. 19 (1960), p. 13.
78 Thomas F. Brady, 'North Africans Turning to East,' *New York Times*, 5 May 1960, p. 9; 'Chinese Penetration of Africa,' *Afrique Nouvelle (Dakar)*, 10–16 June 1965, p. 34. Latter found in *Translations on Africa*, No. 230, *Joint Publications Research Service*, 31368, 2 August 1965, pp. 33–9.
79 'Sino-Algerian Joint Communique,' *Peking Review*, Vol. III, No. 21 (1960), pp. 16–17.
80 Adie, 'Chinese Policy Towards Africa,' 53.
81 'Africa Hears Red Chinese Propaganda,' *Washington Post Times Herald*, 31 May 1960, A7.
82 Adie, 'Chinese Policy Towards Africa,' p. 53.
83 Feng Chih-tan, 'The Awakening of Africa,' *Peking Review*, Vol. III, No. 27 (1960), p. 13.
84 Marquis Childs, 'The New Entry in Africa: China,' *Washington Post Times Herald*, 10 August 1960, A14.
85 Ibid.
86 'China and the World: Sino-Algerian Friendship,' *Peking Review*, Vol. III, No. 39 (1960), p. 27.
87 'Cairo Visit Implies Peking Aid to Algeria,' *Washington Post Times Herald*, 25 September 1960, A4.
88 *Communist China in Africa*, 34.
89 Premier Chou stated: 'We will do everything we can to support the Algerian people's struggle for national liberation,' later adding, 'We have done so and will continue to do so in the future,' 'Premier Chou En-lai's Speech at Banquet

in Honor of Premier Abbas Ferhat,' *Peking Review*, Vol. III, No. 40 (1960), pp. 41–2.

90   'Speech by Premier Abbas Ferhat at Peking Banquet,' *Peking Review*, Vol. III, No. 40 (1960), p. 44.

91   'Premier Abbas Ferhat in Peking,' *Peking Review*, Vol. III, No. 40 (1960), p. 40.

92   'Sino-Algerian Joint Communique,' *Peking Review*, Vol. III, No. 41 (1960), p. 16.

93   'Sino-Algerian Joint Communique,' p. 17.

94   'Premier Abbas Concludes Visit in China,' *Peking Review*, Vol. III, No. 41 (1960), p. 18.

95   Arnaldo Cortesi, 'Algerian Implies Reds Offer Arms,' *New York Times*, 31 October 1960, p. 8.

96   'China and the World: Chinese Show at Tunis Fair,' *Peking Review*, Vol. III, No. 43 (1960), p. 21.

97   'China Firmly Supports Algerian People's Just Struggle,' *Peking Review*, Vol. III, No. 45 (1960), p. 26.

98   Algerians quoted Mao Tse-tung as saying that the PRC would provide 'multiform and growing help' to the FLN, Thomas S. Brady, 'Lag in Peiping Aid to Algeria Likely,' *New York Times*, 5 November 1960, p. 2.

99   Ibid.

100 Adie, 'Chinese Policy Towards Africa,' p. 53.

101 'China and the World: No Carve-up of Algeria,' *Peking Review*, Vol. IV, No. 28 (1961), p. 22.

102 Ibid.

103 'China and the World: Algerian Anniversary,' *Peking Review*, Vol. IV, No. 38 (1961), p. 22. The following month, a PRC commentator wrote that the Chinese had 'extended [the Algerians] active support from the very beginning,' Mao Sun, 'A Righteous Cause Will Triumph,' *Peking Review*, Vol. IV, No. 45 (1961), p. 10.

104 Central Intelligence Agency, *Chinese Communist Activities in Africa*, Memorandum, 30 April 1965, p. 8, memorandum in *CIA Research Reports Africa, 1946–1976* (Frederick, MD: University Publications of America, 1982).

105 'Premier Chou En-lai Greets the Algerian People's Victory,' *Peking Review*, Vol. V, No. 12 (1962), p. 5.

106 In a March *People's Daily* editorial, the Algerians were commended for using 'the revolutionary double tactics of combining armed struggle with negotiations.' 'The Algerian People's Great Victory,' *Peking Review*, Vol. V, No. 12 (1962), p. 6.

107 'China Recognizes the Republic of Algeria,' *Peking Review*, Vol. V, No. 27 (1962), p. 9.

8 Relegated to the backseat

Farm Gate and the failure of the US air advisory effort in South Vietnam, 1961–1963

Edward B. Westermann[1]

In describing the problems that he faced in conducting revolutionary war in China, Mao Tse-tung remarked:

> The only way to study the laws governing a war situation as a whole is to do some hard thinking. For what pertains to the situation as a whole is not visible to the eye, and we can understand it only by hard thinking; there is no other way.[2]

Without doubt, the prosecution of counterinsurgency operations requires a great deal of "hard thinking" as the American experience in the Republic of Vietnam (RVN) between 1961 and 1963 so aptly demonstrates. The nature of peoples' war as a political, social, economic, and military struggle illustrates the profound complexity associated in combating insurgencies whether clad in the armor of communism, nationalism, or religious ideology.

The American air advisory experience in South Vietnam offers a number of insights into the strengths and weaknesses of military power in the insurgency environment. First, it highlights the specific roles and missions that airpower offers against guerrilla or insurgent forces. Second, it also exposes the limits of third party support to a country involved in this type of warfare. Third, it warns against an over reliance on military technology when faced with "war in the shadows." Finally, and perhaps most importantly, it demonstrates the critical importance of cultural awareness and linguistic abilities among advisory forces.

Establishing a capability

In an attempt to expand service capability in the counterinsurgency role, General Curtis E. LeMay, Chief of Staff of the US Air Force, ordered the establishment of a small Special Air Warfare Command (SAWC) in early

1961.[3] Although several leading participants in the SAWC later attributed the support of the services as mere "lip service" and a "passing fad," LeMay apparently established the fledgling command for several reasons.[4] Despite his oft-stated predilection for "strategic airpower," he recognized the need for an air force capability to support Third World governments in the counterinsurgency role.[5] Likewise, a conviction took root within the Air Staff that "if the Air Force failed to provide adequate air support to the Army, the Army would furnish its own [air force]"; a belief heightened by the Army's development of helicopter and light aircraft assets.[6]

The first step in building an Air Force counterinsurgency capability occurred with the selection of Colonel Benjamin H. King to head the new 4400th Combat Crew Training Squadron (CCTS) at Eglin Air Force Base, Florida. It was from the ranks of the 4400th CCTS that the initial cadre of the USAF Farm Gate advisory effort to South Vietnam would be drawn. One indication of the rush to establish the unit involved King's interview for the position in the early hours of a Saturday morning and the almost total lack of guidance he received on the unit's mission after assuming command.[7] Officially established on 14 April 1961, the 4400th (codenamed Jungle Jim) included 124 officers and 228 airmen and an assortment of vintage aircraft. According to LeMay, the unit was created in order to "jump-start the Air Force's special air warfare program."[8] In his testimony to Congress, he described the mission of the 4400th as involving "counterinsurgency and unconventional and psychological warfare operations."[9]

The unit's aircraft consisted of an array of World War II era and propeller-driven aircraft, including 16 C-47s, eight B-26s, and eight T-28s. In one respect, the advanced age of the aircraft proved a problem. King recalled, "We had no training program. We had no one ... that at the time he arrived was fully qualified in the type airplane that we had assigned."[10] However, these propeller-driven aircraft constituted the perfect platforms for supporting Third World countries as they could operate from austere locations with little supporting infrastructure. Their ability to operate "low and slow" provided a major advantage for spotting and attacking insurgents operating in areas of heavy ground cover as did their capability to land and take off from short, unimproved runways.

Ostensibly, the mission involved training indigenous forces to fly these aircraft in preparation for counterinsurgency operations. In truth, the training and advisory mission was from the start a "cover" for the unit's real mission. LeMay told King that the unit's primary job involved the ability "to conduct combat operations ... under extremely austere operating conditions anywhere in the world, and to be a responsive force, either overtly or covertly, to support United States policy."[11] The pilots that joined the unit were all volunteers and under the impression that they would be conducting "cloak and dagger" operations by infiltrating and exfiltrating agents and supplies from denied areas.[12]

From its inception, the 4400th enjoyed a special status made outwardly visible by the unit's distinctive uniform consisting of an Australian bush hat, fatigues, scarf, and combat boots personally selected by LeMay.[13] A more substantive manifestation of the unit's unique mission included the routine practice of taking aircrews from their post-flight debriefings and placing them in the swamps of the Florida panhandle for a three-day escape and survival trek.[14] The distinctive aircraft, uniform, and training of the "air commandos" reinforced the perception of an elite unit preparing for special missions. Certainly, King interpreted the unit's charter in this light. In fact, LeMay later admitted, "They [4400th CCTS] went over there [Southeast Asia] to fight right from the start. We knew it, nobody ever said that though." He also disclosed that this information was common knowledge among the Joint Chiefs of Staff (JCS) and that it was merely policy consider- ations that prevented "the announcement that this outfit was going over to go into combat."[15]

The formation of the 4400th under the pretext of providing an advisory capability proved important in several respects. First, it showed that despite the Kennedy administration's stated objectives and Secretary of Defense Robert McNamara's subsequent statements, the USAF created the Farm Gate program with the intention of capitalizing on US capabilities and employing US pilots in a direct combat role.[16] Second, the unstated assump- tion that combat operations constituted the real goal of the unit certainly influenced the way in which the men approached their "advisory" duties with their South Vietnamese counterparts. For example, upon their arrival in Vietnam, Farm Gate pilots "were not happy to discover that training the Vietnamese Air Force (VNAF) was their primary mission."[17] Third, the actual charter established for the Farm Gate program demonstrated an expanded US commitment to the Diem regime.

In response to a recommendation by the JCS to strengthen the American air commitment and South Vietnam's President Ngo Dinh Diem's agree- ment to accept combat units, President John F. Kennedy authorized the deployment of a detachment of the 4400th on 11 October 1961 "to serve under the MAAG [Military Assistance Advisory Group] as a training mission and not for combat at the present time."[18] Two days later, King departed with two other USAF officers to brief Admiral Harry D. Felt, the Commander in Chief Pacific Command (CINCPAC) on the unit's cap- abilities. Felt initially appeared skeptical of the 4400th's ability to conduct counterinsurgency missions, especially with its assigned aircraft. King's team, however, convinced Felt of the soundness of their approach and the team left for Vietnam to meet with the commander of the Air Force MAAG section. Upon arrival, King evaluated several potential airfields, eventually selecting the airstrip at Bien Hoa near Saigon based on its accessibility to the capital and its central location for air operations. During his trip to Pacific Command (PACOM) headquarters and Vietnam, King recalled "It was never mentioned that we would have the responsibility of training VNAF [the Vietnamese Air Force]."[19]

The first aircraft that reached Bien Hoa in November with their USAF markings replaced by VNAF insignia "found a rundown French air base with a flight surface consisting of a single pierced-steel-plank runway 5,800 by 150 feet."[20] From the beginning of operations, King's unit, Detachment 2 Alpha, 4400th CCTS, operating under the classified designation of Farm Gate suffered from a confused command relationship. Orders and directives emanated from a plethora of organizations including PACOM and Pacific Air Force (PACAF) headquarters through 13th Air Force and the 2nd Advanced Echelon (ADVON) as well as the MAAG and Tactical Air Command headquarters.

For his part, King, operating on personal instructions from LeMay, believed that he worked for the Country Team Chief, Ambassador Frederick E. Nolting, Jr., and the Central Intelligence Agency's chief of station in Saigon. As a result, King repeatedly ran afoul of Brigadier General Rollen H. Anthis, 2nd ADVON commander, during discussions of the 4400th's primary mission. Based on his conversations with LeMay, King continued to maintain that the "training of the [Vietnamese] nationals was a cover story" while Anthis "was very emphatic ... that our mission over there was to assist the VNAF in establishing a capability."[21]

A message of 6 December 1961 from Major General Thomas S. Moorman, Jr., vice commander in chief of PACAF, appeared to resolve the issue concerning the nature and objectives of the Farm Gate program. The message described Farm Gate as a "covert operation" that utilized the "training function as cover ... in support of RVNAF actions against the Viet Cong within the borders of SVN [South Vietnam]." Moorman continued, "This [mission] will include all feasible operational activity, overt and covert, and will be in addition to advisory and training functions." Addressing the command relationships, Moorman's message vested command authority with CINCPAC for the "operational control of all Farm Gate operational missions flown with USAF crew-members [*sic*]."[22] In practice, the commander of PACAF exercised operational control over Farm Gate aircrews through his subordinate commanders at 13th Air Force and the 2nd ADVON. In other words, Moorman's message should have resolved the issue of daily control of Farm Gate in favor of Anthis; however, among the air commandos, the issue of Anthis' authority remained a point of contention until the summer of 1963.[23]

In addition to describing the nature of the Farm Gate program, Moorman's message also outlined the following objectives:

1   Deny Viet Cong supply routes and concentrations in South Vietnam.
2   Establish armed air patrols of SVN borders and shorelines, to include river, highways, rail, and trail traffic suppression, day and night.
3   Seek out and destroy/disrupt Viet Cong Command/Control organization.
4   Seek out and destroy any Communist airlift effort into SVN.

5   Develop and implement an aggressive program of offensive air operations, to complement and to set the pattern for VNAF operations, to neutralize all manifestations of communist actions and strengths in SVN.[24]

On the one hand, the objectives established an ambitious charter for a relatively small unit operating a limited number of vintage aircraft. On the other hand, these objectives also underlined the primary focus of the 4400th on direct combat operations to counter the Viet Cong insurgency, a point underlined by the glaring omission of a *specific* objective concerning the training of VNAF personnel.

Despite the omission of the training aspect of the program, Moorman did address the relationship between US and Vietnamese forces. For example, US operations and intelligence personnel were to augment their Vietnamese counterparts at the VNAF Operations Center at Tan Son Nhut airbase on the outskirts of the capital. Furthermore, USAF personnel received instructions to "conduct coordinated planning with the ARVN and VNAF." Finally, Moorman ordered that VNAF personnel accompany Farm Gate crews during operational missions in order to utilize the "'training through operations' technique," a point again moderated by the remark that the unit's training and advisory mission with VNAF constituted a "cover story" for the employment of American forces in operational missions within South Vietnam.[25]

The JCS also weighed in on the issue of training versus operations in a message designed to "insure no misunderstanding in the authority granted for the use of Jungle Jim [Farm Gate] aircraft."[26] The JCS message emphasized the program's "principal purpose" involved the *training* of VNAF personnel. Despite this pronouncement, Admiral Felt, the commander of Pacific Command, maintained the position that Farm Gate aircraft could conduct "all kinds of conventional combat and combat support flights" contingent upon the presence of a VNAF observer on board.[27] This example highlighted two major issues facing the program from its inception. First, the tortured chain of command and lines of authority resulted in competing and conflicting statements on the unit's mission. Second, this conflicting guidance essentially relegated the training and advisory role to a subordinate role in the eyes of the unit's leadership and its pilots.

Flawed by design

The secondary role assigned to the training and advisory missions by senior USAF leaders profoundly influenced the way Farm Gate pilots approached their duties. In several respects, the 4400th was ill prepared to undertake an advisory mission. For example, it was only after King and his men arrived in Vietnam that the unit "began to think seriously about setting up a training program for foreign nations."[28] While the unit's aircrews proved to be expert operators, they had little understanding of the culture or the history of their Vietnamese hosts and this lack of cultural awareness significantly handicapped the advising effort. Likewise, the inability of advisors to speak Vietnamese, or even French, provided a major obstacle to any planned advisory and training mission. One army advisor later observed that during the war "thousands of Vietnamese learned English ... but only a handful of the many thousands of Americans who received language training ever learned to really speak Vietnamese."[29] In fact, one senior Vietnamese general could not recall a single instance "in which a US advisor effectively discussed professional matters with his counterpart in Vietnamese."[30]

In addition to acting as a bar to communication, the language barrier also contributed to the de facto isolation of the 4400th from their VNAF counterparts at Bien Hoa. Colonel Robert L. Gleason, a former Farm Gate commander, later remarked, "We [US personnel] went to one side of the base, sat there with our own cantonment, maintenance and operations, VNAF down on that side of the base ... and so forth and so on."[31] Another pilot recalled "we really didn't have a great deal to do with the Vietnamese," and he could not recall a single instance of a joint gathering or party between USAF and VNAF personnel at Bien Hoa during his entire tour in 1963.[32] Likewise, the fact that Farm Gate personnel were sent on temporary duty to Vietnam for periods of six months provided an added obstacle to establishing close relationships with their VNAF counterparts or building continuity in any training program.[33] General Anthis recognized the need for continuity in working with the South Vietnamese Air Force and went so far as to recommend tour lengths of 18–24 months instead of the initial 179-day temporary duty and later one-year assignments in country.[34]

Training the VNAF

By the end of 1961, the VNAF certainly required US assistance in a number of areas, including equipment, training, infrastructure, logistics support, and maintenance. One of the most pressing needs involved increasing the size of the air force and the number of trained aircrew and mechanics. In November, the South Vietnamese Air Force consisted of approximately 100 fixed-wing aircraft, including a propeller-driven ground attack version of the A-1H (AD-6), TO-1D observation aircraft, C-47 transports, and an additional 17 helicopters.[35] In order to augment VNAF strike capabilities, the US navy (USN) delivered 15 T-28C's on 11 December 1961, and by the end of the month, USAF trainers under the aegis of the MAAG began formal training for Vietnamese pilots and maintenance, electronic, and ordnance personnel. In addition, PACOM supported plans for the creation of a second A-1H squadron in order to increase the VNAF fighter strength to a total three squadrons; however, these plans immediately ran into the problem of finding and training a sufficient number of qualified pilots.[36]

A message from PACOM underscored the "[k]ey to build-up of VNAF ...

is to increase number of qualified pilots AS[A]P, with the objective of replacing USAF pilots flying with VNAF and turning job over to VNAF completely."[37] USAF and USN Military Training Teams provided the cadre for the initial aircraft qualification programs with Farm Gate personnel slated to provide advanced air-to-ground training for VNAF pilots.[38] Despite the evident need for instructors to train VNAF students, Farm Gate pilots only "grudgingly" embraced this role, but King did send four T-28 pilots to the South Vietnamese air base at Nha Trang to provide flight training.[39]

On 15 January 1962, Anthis briefed Secretary McNamara on the initial progress of the Farm Gate program and optimistically reported that American pilots were training their Vietnamese counterparts in a variety of missions, including night attack and night reconnaissance, flare drops, outpost air support, and aerial resupply. Additionally, Anthis predicted that the VNAF would be an "Air Force" within a year at which point General Emmett O'Donnell, Jr., the PACAF commander, cautioned, "You can't make an air force overnight."[40] With respect to training, O'Donnell's pessimism proved well founded. In order to create an additional VNAF T-28 strike squadron, 30 USAF C-47 pilots moved into VNAF squadrons to allow Vietnamese pilots to transition to the T-28.[41] Although offering a short-term advantage, this program robbed Peter to pay Paul and failed to address the shortage of pilots. It also had an unintended negative consequence, resulting in the VNAF closing down its flying training school at Nha Trang.[42]

O'Donnell's comment highlighted another key point in the creation of an air advisory mission. Regardless of the sophistication of the aircraft chosen, the development of an air force requires a number of supporting technological and infrastructure initiatives. For example, communications and air traffic control systems are critical to insuring flight safety and facilitating operational responsiveness. Likewise, maintenance of aircraft and their associated communications, navigational, and propulsion systems is vital for achieving high sortie rates. Unfortunately, finding and training the specialized maintenance personnel in the Vietnamese armed forces "required for aviation technology presented an unending challenge to South Vietnamese authorities."[43] In fact, as late as May 1963, Brigadier General M.B. Adams, Assistant Chief of Staff, Plans, Military Assistance Command-Vietnam, informed McNamara that a phaseout of USAF flying units was possible; however, he warned "the RVN Armed Forces would not be able to provide the technical support, maintenance, and communications for the VNAF if USAF support personnel were relieved."[44]

Problems with communications and air traffic control provided major barriers for effectively controlling and employing VNAF and US aircraft. The state of communications in South Vietnam proved abysmal. Although Bien Hoa was located only 20 miles from Saigon, King recalled that communications were so poor that "you were a damn sight better off to get in an airplane and fly down there and talk than try to talk over the phone."[45] In response to this problem, the USAF airlifted the 5th Tactical Control Group into South Vietnam in early January 1962 and the unit set up a tactical air control system within a period of only 14 days.[46] One stopgap measure to improve communications involved using a Farm Gate C-47 as an airborne radio relay connecting the ARVN command post and the Joint Operations Center at Tan Son Nhut with strike aircraft.[47] Despite these efforts, one report noted, "the root of the entire [communications] deficiency lies in the lack of suitable radio equipment."[48]

Despite these setbacks, the USAF and VNAF made progress, and the establishment of a Joint Air Operations Center at Tan Son Nhut and two auxiliary air operations centers (AOCs) at Da Nang and Pleiku constituted a major step in improving the coordination of aircraft operations. Unfortunately, even in this endeavor, some US support personnel displayed a lack of cultural awareness and sensitivity to Vietnamese pride. For example, Americans usurped their Vietnamese counterparts and "simply took over the control centers."[49] Despite the creation of the AOCs and the use of airborne radio relays, "limited and failure-prone communications between the centers and the airfields" continued to plague operations until the installation of a new communications system in September 1962.[50]

The US penchant to seek increased efficiency at the cost of allowing the Vietnamese to retain control of operations became a hallmark of US participation in Vietnam and constituted a fatal weakness in the advisory effort. General Maxwell Taylor observed:

> It was a natural reaction of many Americans to want to take over for themselves the tasks of the Vietnamese. Many times I have seen a young military officer, arriving for just one year of service attempt to energize a Vietnamese counterpart who had been in the field for the last eleven years.[51]

Even as late as 1971, US advisors fell victim to this mindset as one lieutenant serving with the ARVN noted, "As an American military man, schooled in the direct, aggressive approach to problem-solving, I was going to get the job done, with or without the help of the Vietnamese."[52] Although promoting short-term success, this approach created a "superior–subordinate" relationship rather than an advisory relationship and eventually sacrificed long-term rapport by alienating South Vietnamese military leaders and creating a dependency relationship.

The primitive communications infrastructure was not the only bar to rapid decision-making. Bureaucratic and domestic political considerations, including the need to receive ARVN approval for missions, often resulted in long delays in striking targets and significantly degraded operational response times. Approval for striking targets often required the concurrence of local and regional Vietnamese political and military leaders and even

President Diem himself.[53] In some cases, the authorization for missions came down from the 2nd ADVON two to three days after the initial request while even the fastest approvals required between two and six hours.[54] This cumbersome approval process severely handicapped effective aerial operations and points to a key issue of insurgency warfare. The Viet Cong relied on stealth and speed in their campaign against the RVN. Likewise, agility and responsiveness constituted a major strength of airpower; however, the procedural and physical obstacles to rapid decision-making prevented Farm Gate personnel from taking advantage of the unit's major strength.

Poor infrastructure provided another impediment to effective operations. Aerial operations rely on the use of fixed, improved airfields, aircraft ramps, hangars, petroleum, oil, and lubricants and logistics facilities, air traffic control structures, and meteorological services. For combat aviation units, requirements also include weapons supply points and storage areas, intelligence support, and base security forces. In late 1961, this infrastructure and these types of facilities existed, if they existed at all, in the most rudimentary forms. In fact, the few suitable airfields in South Vietnam quickly became overcrowded by the growing US air presence and by the transfer of aircraft to the VNAF.[55]

Farm Gate goes to war

While Anthis continued to underline the training aspect of the Farm Gate mission, the reality of daily operations combined with the nascent state of VNAF training increasingly led to greater US participation in combat operations. Brigadier General Heine Aderholt, one of the most flamboyant and successful of the air commandos, complained:

> Either the 2nd Advanced Echelon in Saigon didn't understand or didn't give a damn, the Farm Gate boys started flying close air support for the Vietnamese army ... [t]hat should have been a job for the VNAF and its A-1s, not the Americans.[56]

This focus on combat operations led to the continued relegation of VNAF pilots and their training to a position of second rank.

Early Farm Gate operations reflected the scope of the problems facing King and his unit upon their arrival at Bien Hoa. While initially focusing on gaining familiarity with the area and the established procedures at Bien Hoa, the unit's first "mission" involved observing a flight of VNAF attack aircraft make bombing and strafing runs. Although armed, the Farm Gate T-28s did not participate in the attack. As the 4400th under King's command attempted to embark upon combat operations, the tortured command relationship with the 2nd ADVON became apparent. Although willing to accept Anthis' authority on issues concerning administration and support, King rejected 2nd ADVON's attempts to control operational combat missions on the "covert side of the house."[57]

Despite back-channel communications through the American embassy to LeMay, King and his unit found themselves at the mercy of 2nd ADVON, especially for intelligence and flight authorizations. After speaking with the Director of Operations at 2nd ADVON headquarters in Saigon, King left the meeting with the impression that the headquarters would not grant Farm Gate aircraft permission for any *daylight* strike operations. Consequently, King acquired some parachute flares and began experimenting with using a C-47 as a flare ship to support night operations. Later, after receiving intelligence information on a Viet Cong supply area, a flight of Farm Gate T-28s attacked a group of sampans and "obliterated the target," proving the unit's ability to serve as a night rapid reaction force.[58]

The ability of Farm Gate pilots to fly combat missions at night proved significant in two respects. First, the VNAF pilots did not fly at night and they remained reluctant to conduct nighttime strike missions even as late as 1963.[59] Second, the unwillingness of VNAF aircrews to fly at night ceded a major advantage to the insurgents as the Viet Cong often used the cover of darkness to launch their attacks against isolated villages and garrisons throughout the South. Therefore, Farm Gate operations at night provided an important increase in available firepower to both ARVN and US Special Forces contingent upon rapid forwarding and approval of air support requests from the field.[60]

Flying nighttime strike missions to isolated hamlets required both skill and courage. Locating the target area alone often proved difficult and placed a premium on map reading and dead reckoning skills for navigation.[61] One technique used by friendly forces to identify Viet Cong troop concentrations involved igniting cans of oil pointed in the direction of the enemy attack. Using the burning markers as an orientation point, the C-47 flare ship would provide illumination for the T-28s to attack.[62] The high standards required of Farm Gate pilots included the expectation that "pilots should be trained to the extent that their proficiency will enable them to destroy one shack with one bomb," an impossible standard for pilots operating primarily at night.[63] Although important, strike missions proved less critical than aerial supply and transportation in countering the insurgent threat.

Mule Train

The requirement for airlift to support isolated outposts and hamlets constituted one of the most pressing requirements for supporting ARVN forces and their US army advisors early in the war. Farm Gate, with its complement of C-47s, possessed a limited capability to conduct resupply efforts, but these aircraft could not meet the demand for aerial transport and resupply. As a result, LeMay ordered the deployment of a detachment of Fairchild C-123 transport aircraft to South Vietnam in January 1962.[64] Sixteen C-123s, complete with aircrews, maintenance, medical staff, loadmasters, and air base personnel, began arriving for temporary duty at Tan Son Nhut in early January under the code name Mule Train. Although not technically part of the Farm Gate program, Mule Train operated under the command of 2nd **ADVON** and constituted an additional pillar of the American air support effort in South Vietnam. In fact, orders and messages from PACAF headquarters routinely treated the missions of both programs as part of a single effort.[65]

A week after arriving in Vietnam, Mule Train aircraft were averaging three airlift missions per day with over 500 sorties flown by the end of February, transporting 3,600 passengers and delivering 695 tons of cargo.[66] The standards expected of the airlift crews proved as stringent as those demanded from their Farm Gate counterparts and called for precision in the delivery of air dropped heavy cargo and airborne forces to "pinpoint targets," including "small clearings in the jungle, swamps, or rice paddies." Furthermore, Mule Train aircrews required the skill to fly into and out of "short, rough, and marginal airfields" on a routine basis.[67]

With the approach of the rainy season in the spring of 1962, Mule Train became a "very valuable asset" and missions gained added importance as secondary roads became nearly impassable mud holes.[68] However, it was the ability of the aircraft to allow US and ARVN forces to avoid Viet Cong ambushes along road and waterways throughout the country that constituted a major benefit of the effort. A top secret Air Force historical study in 1964 remarked that "inland surface transportation in the RVN was extremely limited because of Viet Cong operations. Consequently, airlift operations achieved a relative importance seldom experienced in more conventional environments."[69] Over 40 years later, US forces relearned the same lesson in Iraq.[70]

The ability of the Viet Minh to conduct ambushes along the paths, waterways, and roadways throughout the country was legendary and made famous by the journalist Bernard Fall in his classic work, *Street Without Joy*.[71] The Viet Cong proved every bit as skilled in the art of the ambush as their predecessors as the following account demonstrates:

> The VC ambush was perfectly placed and timed, hitting my column from the dense bamboo to our right, exploding a captured American Claymore mine and raking the trail with AK-47 fire. Bright green tracers slashed through the shade, cutting leaves and chipping wood.... Now I heard the distinctive crack of AK fire from our left front. The VC had just sprung the leg of their L-shaped ambush.[72]

In this case, artillery and air support helped limit casualties to one dead and two wounded; however, the description of the ambush highlights the important role played by concealment in allowing the Viet Cong force to achieve tactical surprise, a scenario repeated a thousand-fold in the paddies and jungles of Vietnam throughout the war.

Based on the poor physical infrastructure and the geography of South Vietnam, and the threat posed by Viet Cong ambush, the importance of tactical airlift in supporting ARVN forces continued to increase throughout the first two years of the Mule Train program. For example, the airlift force doubled from 16 to 32 C-123s in June 1962 and a third squadron moved into country in April 1963. In recognition of the challenging flying environment and the combat conditions experienced during these missions, General LeMay ordered the re-designation of the units from tactical airlift squadrons to "assault airlift" squadrons in the spring of 1963.[73]

Ranch Hand

In addition to their use in a mobility role, transport aircraft proved their value in non-traditional roles. Recognition of the problem posed by the heavy foliage found along many of South Vietnam's road and waterways led to the creation of a Combat Development and Test Center in Vietnam in the summer of 1961. Among other projects, the center began to search for herbicides to destroy Viet Cong food sources and to "deprive the Viet Cong of assembly and ambush areas."[74] After early small-scale efforts at defoliation using C-47s and H-34s, the USAF settled on C-123 aircraft equipped with aerial spray systems and defoliant agents. The aircraft deployed from Pope Air Force Base in North Carolina and were flown by aircrew who had volunteered but had not been selected for the original Farm Gate mission. In fact, it was only at their en route stop at Clark Air Base in the Philippines that the aircraft and aircrew technically separated from the Farm Gate mission and adopted the code name Ranch Hand.[75]

In mid-January, Ranch Hand aircraft, escorted by VNAF fighters and using a VNAF L-19 observation aircraft as a forward air controller (FAC), flew six defoliation missions.[76] The results of the missions, however, proved disappointing as the vegetation failed to die. Based on this inauspicious start, the cancellation of the Ranch Hand program appeared to be "imminent."[77] However, an investigation of the missions revealed that "most of the plants had been dormant, and the herbicide ... worked only on actively growing plants."[78]

The results of the investigation provided the program with a reprieve and led to further testing. Later missions in October directed at mangrove forests along the waterways of the Ca Mau peninsula stripped over 90 percent of the foliage in the targeted areas, initiating an expanded effort throughout the country. The success of these defoliation missions resulted in requests from the Vietnamese to use the aircraft against suspected Viet Cong food supplies. President Kennedy subsequently approved a limited program targeting guerrilla food sources, but the State Department insisted on the right to approve targets for each mission.[79]

Early in the program, Ranch Hand aircraft, in addition to their spraying activities, also provided logistics support by moving troops and materiel. By 1967, however, the spray missions dominated the effort with aircraft flying an average of 20 spray missions a day. Between 1965 and 1970, Ranch

Hand aircraft sprayed approximately "41 per cent of South Vietnam's mangrove forests, 19 per cent of the uplands forests and 8 per cent of all cultivated land" primarily using the controversial dioxin-based Agent Orange.[80] The tactical and operational success of these missions in stripping away the Viet Cong's advantage of concealment once again highlighted the utility of airpower in an auxiliary role in the counterinsurgency environment, though the aftereffects of the defoliation operations on the physical health of US and Vietnamese citizens alike constituted the effort's most enduring legacy.

Evaluating early US air support

The decision to create the Farm Gate, Mule Train, and Ranch Hand programs and deploy these units to South Vietnam within a period of only two months provides several important insights into the nature of US military and political objectives in the early stages of the conflict. First, all three programs offered complementary capabilities designed to improve the operational situation in South Vietnam by providing tactical level support to Vietnamese forces. Second, the initial performance of these units provided a significant adjunct to ARVN forces and especially to a South Vietnamese Air Force suffering from limited resources, political restraints, and a lack of operational freedom. Third, the requirement for a fairly robust infrastructure ranging from bases to supply depots to communications and navigational aids highlighted the intrinsic complexity and demands of any air advisory effort, including those employing relatively unsophisticated aircraft. Finally, and perhaps most importantly, the prosecution of these programs demonstrated that the advisory mission took a backseat to the employment of these aircraft under US control.

Taking a backseat

The requirement for VNAF observers onboard USAF aircraft served merely as a cover to legitimize US participation in combat operations and served as a political foil to mitigate the US's clear violation of the Geneva Accords.[81] In the early stages of the program, pilots, especially those in the two-seat T-28, protested the requirement for VNAF personnel to accompany them. One Farm Gate commander complained:

> The requirement that a VNAF pilot be a member of the T-28 crew, always riding in the backseat, has been unsatisfactory to both VNAF and USAF personnel.... Qualified VNAF pilots do not like this duty, and the VNAF crew member is often unqualified. Little training is provided, and the VNAF man often becomes violently ill in flight.[82]

This comment once again highlighted the minimal utility of the training provided under this construct in which the VNAF "student"/observer essentially served as ballast. An attempt by PACAF headquarters to remove the restriction in July foundered, as did a request that "USAF crews in Farm Gate aircraft be allowed to lead or act as wingman with VNAF aircraft."[83] In truth, the requirement for VNAF observers did at times seem to approach the absurd, as was the case during a night mortar attack against the Soc Trang airfield on 10 September 1963, during which the Viet Cong pinned down the VNAF T-28s. Four air commandos, however, made it to their aircraft and drove off the attackers. After the attack, these Americans received commendations for their bravery and reprimands for failing to have a VNAF observer on board.[84]

If the observer program essentially proved a façade, in one area, at least, USAF air advisors initiated efforts to begin working more closely with their VNAF counterparts. While VNAF pilots onboard USAF aircraft seemed a waste of resources, such was not the case for VNAF FACs. The program to train VNAF FACs offered one positive example of an effort to train and advise VNAF personnel. A two-day seminar involving USAF and VNAF personnel in February 1962 addressed problems and procedures involved with forward air control and resulted in an agreement "to develop and jointly conduct a formal FAC course."[85] In truth, the program was the product of necessity as Farm Gate aircraft required the presence of a Vietnamese FAC prior to conducting attacks.[86]

Flying "low and slow" in L-19s, Vietnamese FACs played a key role in Farm Gate missions based on their intimate knowledge of the local terrain. Still, the ultimate test of their effectiveness rested on their ability to guide strike aircraft onto the target; a skill that required both reliable radios and clear verbal communications. The absence of Vietnamese and French-speaking USAF pilots placed the onus on VNAF FACs to learn English, again highlighting the problem caused by the American neglect of linguistic skills in the "advisory" effort. Likewise, the limited number of VNAF FACs provided an additional obstacle for expanded cooperation.[87]

The renewed emphasis on improved training and coordination between USAF and VNAF crews was not entirely coincidental. On 21 January 1962, Farm Gate aircraft accidentally attacked a village in Cambodia, killing several civilians and raising concerns at the "highest level" of the US government. In the wake of the attack, PACAF headquarters warned:

> If we are to avoid the imposition of highly limiting controls on the application of Farm Gate, we must take every effort to avoid another incident and, in addition, demonstrate the effectiveness of our control and ability to discriminate in the selection and designation of targets as well as in the conduct of air strikes.[88]

The concerns expressed at PACAF headquarters proved justified as Secretary McNamara tightened guidelines for US aircrews in Vietnam. One reflection of the discrimination exercised by Farm Gate aircraft is apparent in the return of over half of T-28 strike sorties with unused ordnance in 1962.

Despite the increased restrictions on operations, Farm Gate aircraft provided much needed firepower in support of ARVN forces on several occasions. For example, two T-28s supported by a C-47 flareship scrambled during the night of 1 March 1962, in response to the distress call of a Vietnamese outpost 30 miles north of Saigon. Using napalm, rockets, and machineguns, the T-28s played a key role in breaking the assault. Two days later, a B-26 assisted two Vietnamese AD-6s in a strike aimed at a Viet Cong assembly point 105 miles northeast of Saigon. Caught in the open, the Viet Cong suffered 12 killed.[89] The missions not only highlighted the value of rapid responsiveness in counterinsurgency warfare, but they also signaled an expansion of operations, including daytime strikes.

A review of the types of missions flown by Farm Gate aircraft in early 1962 clearly demonstrates that not only VNAF personnel, but the training mission as well, took a backseat to operational sorties. For example, Farm Gate aircraft, including T-28s, B-26s, and C-47s, flew 254 operational missions but not a single training sortie in January and February. Table 8.1 provides an overview of the number of operational and training sorties flown by Farm Gate aircraft between January and November 1962.[90]

Operational missions constituted an astounding 92 percent of Farm Gate sorties, with training sorties comprising only 8 percent.

With respect to Farm Gate operational sorties, the types of armaments employed provided an important adjunct to existing capabilities as VNAF aircraft faced a temporary prohibition against carrying bombs in the wake of a failed coup attempt by two disgruntled VNAF pilots against the Diem regime in February 1962.[91] Farm Gate pilots became especially adept at the employment of napalm. The incendiary proved useful in burning through heavy jungle cover. In August alone, crews flew eight missions using napalm, including three day strikes and five night missions. Additionally, C-47 crews conducted flight tests involving the release of napalm in "fuzed barrels dropped in a string from the C-47 via the roller rail system." The major weakness in this procedure involved the relatively low altitude of the aircraft, only 50–100 feet, which made them susceptible to ground fire. In

Table 8.1 Overview of the number of operational and training sorties flown by Farm Gate aircraft

Aircraft type	Timeframe	Operational sorties	Training sorties
T-28	Jan.–Nov. 1962	1,589	205
RB-26	Jan.–Nov. 1962	1,042	74
SC-47	Jan.–Nov. 1962	699	29
Total:		3,330	308

addition to napalm, RB-26 crews experimented with incendiary cluster bomb devices and 260 pound fragmentation bombs. Finally, the introduction of the 100 pound white phosphorous bomb proved "excellent for use in the jungle since it penetrates the canopy before detonation and does not dissipate its effects, as napalm does, on the top layers of foliage." Aircrews also believed that the white phosphorous bomb had the added advantage of producing "considerable psychological effects when used at night."[92]

Psychological operations

The conduct of psychological operations (PSYOP) provided an additional task for some Farm Gate crews in 1962. Special Operations forces enjoyed a long history of conducting PSYOP, but the mission tended to be viewed as a bastard son by conventional forces, a fact highlighted by the Air Force's inactivation of the career field in 1958.[93] Early Farm Gate PSYOP missions centered on using C-47s equipped with loudspeakers and leaflets to broadcast messages and to provide information to persons in regions controlled by the Viet Cong, an area estimated at 40 percent of the South Vietnamese countryside by March 1964.[94]

On early missions between December 1961 and February 1962, however, marginal speaker quality required the pilot of the aircraft to fly at 500 feet and 100 knots, thus making the aircraft extremely vulnerable to anti-aircraft and small arms fire. In fact, a C-47 conducting a leaflet drop on February 11 crashed for unknown reasons leading to the death of the eight Americans and the VNAF observer on board.[95] As a result of the loss of the aircraft and the difficulty in measuring the effectiveness of the effort, General LeMay argued in March for the return of the mission to the VNAF.[96]

The consequences for failing to train

The lack of a dedicated and widespread training program for VNAF pilots constituted a fundamental weakness in the air advisory effort and the entire "training through operations" concept. Assigning VNAF crewmembers to sit in the backseat of a T-28 or to "observe" operations in the B-26 or C-47 provided little to no real training advantage. Real training involved the assignment of pilots to provide actual flight instruction to VNAF pilots, an initiative that took place only on a very limited scale. Instead Farm Gate pilots "demonstrated" the techniques of operational flying and evaluated the state of Vietnamese training and standardization.[97] This approach not only failed to increase capability within the VNAF, but it also promoted a dependency relationship that kept the VNAF on the sidelines as "second stringers."

The small size of the VNAF pilot base compounded the problem of inadequate training by the end of 1962. One report observed, "The existing VNAF pilot base is severely taxed now to accomplish the VNAF tasks and is completely inadequate to permit significant VNAF expansion." The report continued, "Training programs are in being to broaden the now meager VNAF pilot base, but this program will not produce the assets to significantly increase the VNAF pilot base until late 1964."[98] One solution to this problem involved Secretary McNamara's order to more than double the number of Vietnamese pilots in stateside training programs from 130 to 300. Although the MAAG retained responsibility for training the Vietnamese in-country, the small military training teams from the USAF and the USN proved inadequate to meet the demand for qualified VNAF aircrew.[99] By October 1962, McNamara increasingly sought the creation of a "wholly adequate Vietnamese Air Force" and he felt that "Farm Gate ought to train Vietnamese rather than operate."[100]

Expanding Farm Gate

At the end of 1962, the US air advisory effort found itself between a rock and a hard place. The requirement for air support within Vietnam continued to increase, however, the number of qualified VNAF pilots and available aircraft proved insufficient to meet these demands. PACAF reported in October 1962 that the operational sortie rate of the VNAF had almost quadrupled from the start of the year but identified "the extreme shortage of pilots" as the "major deterrent" to an expansion of the VNAF.[101] As a result, PACAF recommended that "USAF effort in SVN be further augmented ... to pick up slack during conversion and expansion of pilot base in VNAF."[102] Based upon the recommendation of the JCS, President Kennedy, with the concurrence of McNamara and the State Department, approved the expansion of Farm Gate in December 1962.[103]

The expansion of Farm Gate demonstrated the growing reliance upon air support in battling the Viet Cong.[104] However, at a more profound level, it represented the failure of the US air advisory to prepare VNAF to fight their own war as both Kennedy and McNamara continually advocated. This failure proved all the more damaging in that many Farm Gate personnel gave their VNAF counterparts good marks for skill and capability when fully trained.[105] In fact, Aderholt described the VNAF as "great pilots" and he argued that "It [the war] should have been dealt with as an insurgency, and it should have been the Vietnamese's fight and not ours."[106]

The "lessons" of Farm Gate

In the final analysis, the US experience with Farm Gate between 1961 and 1963 highlights several important issues concerning advisory efforts in general, and air advisory missions specifically. First, the program demonstrates the need for a variety of skills among advisors including the need for cultural awareness, linguistic fluency, and the requirement for continuity of personnel and close interaction between advisory and host nation personnel.

Second, the program reveals the importance of a clear-cut chain of command and an explicit mission statement. Third, the US experience demonstrates the value of less-sophisticated technology when training and advising military forces that may lack the technological and physical infrastructure to support state of the art weapons systems or in situations where less technically sophisticated equipment provides a more effective platform for supporting operations in an insurgency environment. Finally, the program underlines the critical part played by airpower in a supporting role during counterinsurgency operations; a case where firepower may prove less important than capability to gain information or move troops and equipment.

The lack of cultural awareness and linguistic abilities constituted a major weakness for effective training and advising by Farm Gate personnel and was symbolic of a larger failure in the entire US effort during the war in Southeast Asia.[107] Waiting for development of English-speaking VNAF personnel and the return of VNAF pilots from stateside training programs provided one clear indication of the absence of cultural awareness and language abilities and created a major obstacle to close interaction between the Americans and the Vietnamese. Likewise, a tendency to speak "derogatorily" of their Vietnamese counterparts and treat them "like so many undereducated and underprivileged children" further inhibited the growth of close personal relationships.[108] The American attitude could also be particularly insulting to experienced VNAF pilots with extensive combat experience. As King correctly observed, "[W]ho the hell were we to tell them how to run a combat operation when they had people in their organizations who had flown a thousand or two thousand combat sorties within the theater."[109]

A further complicating factor involved the deployment of American personnel for temporary duty assignments ranging from 30 to 179 days, a practice that prevented continuity in both training programs and the development of close personal relationships between the two air forces. As General Anthis remarked:

> Continuity is necessary in working with the South Vietnamese ... they work on a friendship or personal basis, in many cases, rather than just the fact that we were there to assist and work with them. What the VNAF people were experiencing was that about the time they got acquainted with the US airman well, learned to respect and trust him, he was gone and the Vietnamese had to start all over again and get reacquainted with a new person.[110]

In addition to problems with developing a close liaison with the Vietnamese, Farm Gate suffered from dissonance concerning its primary mission, as well as a dysfunctional argument over operational command authority. In the case of the former, the initial Farm Gate cadre saw themselves as aerial secret agents and their missions as being closely tied to "cloak and dagger" operations; a perception reinforced by close contacts with the Central Intelligence Agency in Vietnam, as well as by LeMay's marching orders to King.[111] This perception eventually led to lower morale among Farm Gate pilots and increased frustration as pilots found themselves placed in a training role that significantly differed from their initial expectations.[112] The lack of a clearly understood mission also created confusion throughout the entire chain of command on the exact nature, activities, and objectives of the program. Brigadier General John W. Roberts, a former wing commander in Southeast Asia, concluded "There were a lot of people who didn't understand it [the Farm Gate mission].... The people that didn't understand the mission were privy only to the overt part of that mission. The misunderstandings of that role were quite rampant." He continued, "I had no problem with what FARMGATE [*sic*] was supposed to do. It was just a matter of sometimes getting a question answered from higher level. We at PACAF did not have the answers. We knew what the questions were, but we didn't have any answer[s]."[113] Finally, the tug of war between Farm Gate and the 2nd ADVON concerning command authority exacerbated the confusion and acted as a major "detriment" to the program.[114]

The USAF air advisory mission also underlines the importance of selecting and employing the appropriate technology when fighting in an insurgency environment. In this case, the use of World War II era propeller-driven aircraft proved especially effective due to their ability to operate from austere bases, their relative ease of maintenance, and their ability to fly low and slow. The belief by some USAF officers that jet aircraft, with their improved speed and range, constituted the most effective weapons systems catalyzed a "propeller versus jet" debate. For his part, Aderholt warned, "My God, we are in trouble if we think that jet technology and high performance fighters have made less advanced capabilities obsolete."[115] Likewise, General Pritchard noted his concern about the USAF obsession with advanced technologies at the expense of more appropriate aircraft for the insurgency environment by remarking, "I think we're more concerned now about how we retain our 24-wing, 14-carat fighter force, than how we accomplish these other things."[116]

Finally, the missions conducted by Farm Gate, Ranch Hand, and Mule Train aircrews once again highlight the critical importance of airpower when used in a supporting role, including the transport of troops, equipment, and supplies or the gathering of intelligence. The ability of C-47s and C-123s to resupply garrisons in isolated and inaccessible areas and to bypass Viet Cong ambushes proved a major contribution of the early US air effort.[117] Likewise, the use of the RB-26 as a photoreconnaissance platform provided major advantages to US and Vietnamese forces in finding and identifying Viet Cong enclaves or troop movements.[118] In fact, the significance of photoreconnaissance in Vietnam clearly demonstrated the great importance of intelligence, surveillance, and reconnaissance assets in counterinsurgency warfare. Although the ability of aircraft to bring firepower to bear should not be underestimated, neither should one neglect the other equally important capabilities provided by airpower in the counterinsurgency arena.

Conclusion

The experience of Farm Gate and the US air advisory effort between 1961 and 1963 was in fact emblematic of the larger American effort in Vietnam. From its inception, the program pursued conflicting aims, the effort to improve the firepower available to ARVN forces and to increase the effectiveness of the VNAF proved at odds with one another. The failure to concentrate on developing a dedicated training program for improving the size and quality of the VNAF led to an ever greater reliance on US forces. The traditional American impatience in obtaining results led to a self-fulfilling prophesy in which the "motivation and leadership" provided by Farm Gate personnel received the credit for the VNAF's "growing professionalism" while criticisms continued concerning the number of VNAF operational sorties and the professional competence of the VNAF that "is still far below that of the USAF."[119] Ironically, a PACAF report in October 1962 perfectly identified the dilemma faced by US forces:

> This Hq [headquarters] recognizes that FARM GATE must not be permitted to become a crutch to compromise VNAF development, but it is the only air support unit with the capability to increase its performance quickly to meet the expanding requirements.[120]

In concentrating on operations instead of training and by relegating the VNAF literally to the backseat, the Farm Gate program did become, in fact, a crutch – one of the United State Air Force's own making.

In retrospect, one former Farm Gate commander opined:

> We should have had a bona fide Vietnamese pilot and we should have had our butts in the rear seat as soon as he was halfway competent; and had we done this in each of the several squadrons, I think that [the] VNAF would have achieved confidence a hell of a lot faster than they did.[121]

This pilot's hindsight may have been 20/20; however, once relegated to the backseat, it proved difficult for both the VNAF and the USAF to change places.

Notes

1   I would like to thank Joe Caver, Toni Petito, Tom Hughes, James Kiras, and Rich Muller for their assistance during the writing of this article.
2   Mao Tse-tung, *Six Essays on Military Affairs* (Peking: Foreign Language Press, 1972), p. 12.
3   Monro MacCloskey, *Alert the Fifth Air Force: Counterinsurgency, Unconventional*

Warfare, and Psychological Operations of the United States Air Force in Special Air Warfare (New York: Richards Rosen Press, 1969), p. 148.

4 USAF Oral History Interview (hereafter ORI) #218, Major General Gilbert Pritchard, 21 August 1969. K239.0512–218, USAF Historical Research Agency (hereafter AFHRA).

5 USAF ORI #592, General Curtis LeMay, 8 June 1972. K239.0512–592, AFHRA.

6 James Corum and Wray Johnson, *Airpower in Small Wars: Fighting Insurgents and Terrorists* (Lawrence: University Press of Kansas, 2003), pp. 244–5.

7 USAF ORI #219, Brigadier General Benjamin King, 4 September 1969. K239.0512–219, AFHRA.

8 Warren Trest, *Air Commando One: Heine Aderholt and America's Secret Air Wars* (Washington, DC: Smithsonian Institution Press, 2000), p. 121.

9 MacCloskey, *Alert the Fifth Air Force*, pp. 148–9.

10 USAF ORI #219, King, K239.0512–219, AFHRA.

11 Ibid.

12 USAF ORI #415, Major General Rollen Anthis, 30 August 1963. K239.0512–415, AFHRA.

13 Robert Futrell, *The Advisory Years to 1965* (Washington, DC: Office of Air Force History, 1981), p. 79.

14 Michael Haas, *Apollo's Warriors: United States Air Force Special Operations During the Cold War* (Maxwell AFB, AL: Air University Press, 1997), p. 223.

15 USAF ORI #592, LeMay, K239.0512–592, AFHRA.

16 Robert McNamara, *In Retrospect: The Tragedy and Lessons of Vietnam* (New York: Times Books, 1995) pp. 29, 62.

17 Haas, *Apollo's Warriors*, p. 228.

18 Futrell, *The Advisory Years*, p. 80. See also USAF ORI #489, Ambassador Frederick E. Nolting, Jr., 9 November 1971. K239.0512–489, AFHRA. Ambassador Nolting remarked:

President Diem on many occasions told me that he, as much as he was tempted from time to time to ask for American combat forces in difficult situations – he didn't think that a struggle won with foreign troops would be viable out there [in Vietnam].

19 USAF ORI #219, King, K239.0512–219, AFHRA.

20 Futrell, *The Advisory Years*, p. 81.

21 USAF ORI #219, King, K239.0512–219, AFHRA.

22 Message signed by Major General Thomas S. Moorman, Jr., Subject: Concept of Employment of Farm Gate, 6 December 1961, K717.1623, part 1, AFHRA.

23 Trest, *Air Commando One*, p. 127.

24 Message signed by Major General Thomas S. Moorman, Jr., Subject: Concept of Employment of Farm Gate, 6 December 1961, K717.1623, part 1, AFHRA.

25 Ibid.

26 Futrell, *The Advisory Years*, p. 83.

27 Ibid.

28 USAF ORI #219, King, K239.0512–219, AFHRA.

29 Stuart A. Herrington, *Stalking the Vietcong: Inside Operation Phoenix: A Personal Account* (New York: Ballantine Books, 1982), p. 253.

30 Ronald Spector, *Advice and Support: The Early Years* (Washington, DC: Center of Military History, 1983), p. 286.

31 USAF ORI #218, Pritchard, K239.0512–218, AFHRA.

32 USAF ORI #357, Major Roy Lynn, 9 Sept. 1970. K239.0512–357, AFHRA.

33 USAF ORI #219, King, K239.0512–219, AFHRA.

34 USAF ORI #240, Major General Rollen Anthis, 17 Nov. 1969. K239.0512–240, AFHRA.

35 Carl O. Clever, *Support Activities*, part VI [Project Contemporary Historical Evaluation of Counterinsurgency Operations (CHECO)], May 1964, K 717.0413–30, AFHRA, p. 20. Corum and Johnson, *Airpower in Small Wars*, p. 235. By 1965, the A-1 "Skyraider" became the mainstay of the VNAF fighter force with six operational squadrons and a total of 146 aircraft.
36 Clever, *Support Activities*, pp. 20–2.
37 Ibid., p. 23.
38 Ibid., pp. 21, 23.
39 Futrell, *The Advisory Years*, p. 127.
40 Clever, *Support Activities*, pp. 17–18.
41 USAF ORI #240, Anthis, K239.0512–240, AFHRA.
42 USAF ORI #415, Major General Rollen Anthis, 30 Aug. 1963, K239.0512–415, AFHRA.
43 Corum and Johnson, *Airpower in Small Wars*, p. 250.
44 Clever, *Support Activities*, p. 19.
45 USAF ORI #219, King, K239.0512–219, AFHRA.
46 USAF ORI #415, Anthis, K239.0512–415, AFHRA.
47 Report from Detachment 2 Alpha to Commander, 2nd ADVON, 5 June 1962. K526.549–2, AFHRA.
48 Report entitled: "Development of New Tactics and Techniques," 14 January 1962. K526.549–2, AFHRA.
49 John Schlight, *A War too Long: The History of the USAF in Southeast Asia* (Washington, DC: Air Force History and Museums Program, 1996), p. 9.
50 Futrell, *The Advisory Years*, p. 107.
51 Maxwell D. Taylor, *Responsibility and Response* (New York: Harper & Row Publishers, 1967), pp. 50–1.
52 Herrington, *Stalking the Vietcong*, p. 64.
53 USAF ORI #415, Anthis, K239.0512–415, AFHRA.
54 USAF ORI #219, King, K239.0512–219, AFHRA.
55 Corum and Johnson, *Airpower in Small Wars*, p. 250.
56 Trest, *Air Commando One*, p. 123.
57 USAF ORI #219, King, K239.0512–219, AFHRA.
58 Ibid.
59 USAF ORI #357, Lynn, K239.0512–357, AFHRA. Admittedly, some reports cite the support of VNAF C-47 flareships during night missions.
60 USAF ORI #219, King, K239.0512–219, AFHRA.
61 Message from PACAF headquarters to Tactical Air Command, 28 February 1962, K717.1623, AFHRA.
62 USAF ORI #240, Anthis, K239.0512–240, AFHRA.
63 Message from PACAF headquarters to Tactical Air Command, 28 February 1962, K717.1623, AFHRA.
64 Clever, *Support Activities*, p. 5.
65 Message signed by Major General Thomas S. Moorman, Jr., Subject: Concept of Employment of Farm Gate, 6 December 1961, K717.1623, part 1, AFHRA.
66 Futrell, *The Advisory Years*, p. 108.
67 Message from PACAF headquarters to Tactical Air Command, 28 February 1962, K717.1623, AFHRA.
68 Message from PACAF headquarters to Tactical Air Command, 10 March 1962, K717.1623, AFHRA.
69 Clever, *Support Activities*, p. 4.
70 Steven Komarow, "Pentagon Boosts Number of US Air Missions," *USA Today*, 15 March 2006. www.usatoday.com/news/world/iraq/2006–03–15-air-missions_x.htm.

71 Bernard B. Fall, *Street without Joy: Indochina at War, 1946–54* (Harrisburg, PA: Stackpole, 1961).
72 Tommy Franks, *American Soldier* (New York: Regan Books, 2004), p. 74.
73 Clever, *Support Activities*, pp. 8–10.
74 Futrell, *The Advisory Years*, p. 73.
75 Haas, *Apollo's Warriors*, p. 250.
76 Message from PACAF headquarters to the Chief of Staff of the USAF, 15 January 1962, K717.1623, AFHRA.
77 Report entitled "Comments on Notes on Secretary of Defense Meeting," 13 March 1962. K717–1623, AFHRA.
78 Futrell, *The Advisory Years*, pp. 113–16.
79 Ibid., pp. 116–17.
80 Haas, *Apollo's Warriors*, pp. 253–4. Based on the health issues for US forces and the indigenous population associated with the spraying program, and North Vietnamese claims of chemical and biological warfare, the Ranch Hand program became one of the most controversial efforts of the war.
81 Memorandum for General Martin [PACAF Commander] from Colonel John B. Kidd, 20 February 1963. K717.1623, AFHRA. The Geneva Accords prohibited the participation of third party military forces in combat operations in Vietnam. Although not a signatory power to the accords, the United States agreed in principle to accept the stipulations of the agreement.
82 Report from Detachment 2 Alpha to Commander, 2nd ADVON, 5 June 1962. K526.549–2, AFHRA.
83 Message from PACAF headquarters to Chief of Staff of the USAF, 6 July 1962. K717.1623, AFHRA.
84 Haas, *Apollo's Warriors*, p. 229.
85 Message from PACAF headquarters to USAF headquarters, 13 March 1962. K717.1623, AFHRA.
86 Futrell, *The Advisory Years*, pp. 144, 174.
87 Message from PACAF headquarters to USAF headquarters, 13 March 1962. K717.1623, AFHRA.
88 Futrell, *The Advisory Years*, p. 120.
89 Ibid., p. 121.
90 Message from PACAF headquarters to USAF headquarters, dated 1 December 1962. K717.1623, AFHRA. Totals do not include information for the last day of November.
91 USAF ORI #415, Anthis, K239.0512–415, AFHRA.
92 Draft report entitled "FARMGATE [*sic*] TACTICS AND TECHNIQUES," January 1963(?), K526–549–2, AFHRA.
93 Futrell, *The Advisory Years*, p. 122.
94 Message signed by Major General Thomas S. Moorman, Jr., Subject: Concept of Employment of Farm Gate, dated 6 December 1961, K717.1623, part 1, AFHRA. See also Memorandum from the Secretary of Defense Robert S. McNamara to the President Lyndon B. Johnson, subject: South Vietnam, dated 16 March 1964, Texas Tech Virtual Archives, item# 0240102022. www.vietnam.ttu.edu/virtualarchive.
95 Futrell, *The Advisory Years*, p. 122.
96 Report entitled "Comments on Notes on Secretary of Defense Meeting" signed by Brigadier General John B. Henry, Jr., 13 March 1962. K717–1623, AFHRA. See also Futrell, *The Advisory Years*, p. 123.
97 Futrell, *The Advisory Years*, pp. 127, 131.
98 Message from PACAF headquarters to 2nd Air Division, 22 November 1962. K717.1623, AFHRA.

99   Clever, *Support Activities*, pp. 23–31.
100 Futrell, *The Advisory Years*, p. 133.
101 Message from PACAF headquarters to Tactical Air Command, 12 October 1962. K717.1623, AFHRA.
102 Message from PACAF headquarters to 2nd Air Division, 22 November 1962. K717.1623, AFHRA.
103 Futrell, *The Advisory Years*, p. 134.
104 Message from PACAF headquarters to Tactical Air Command, 12 October 1962. K717.1623, AFHRA.
105 USAF ORI #240, Anthis, K239.0512–240, AFHRA.
106 Trest, *Air Commando One*, p. 124.
107 See Robert K. Brigham *ARVN: Life and Death in the South Vietnamese Army* (Lawrence: University Press of Kansas, 2006).
108 Herrington, *Stalking the Vietcong*, p. 253.
109 USAF ORI #219, King, K239.0512–219, AFHRA.
110 USAF ORI #240, Anthis, K239.0512–240, AFHRA.
111 USAF ORI #219, King, K239.0512–219, AFHRA.
112 Haas, *Apollo's Warriors*, p. 228.
113 USAF ORI #405, Brigadier General John W. Roberts, 2–3 March 1971. K239.0512–405, AFHRA.
114 USAF ORI #219, King, K239.0512–219, AFHRA.
115 Trest, *Air Commando One*, p. 12.
116 Colonel Robert L. Gleason as quoted in USAF ORI #218, Pritchard, K239.0512–218, AFHRA. Emphasis in the original.
117 Clever, *Support Activities*, p. 4.
118 Message from PACAF headquarters to Tactical Air Command, 29 October 1962. K717.1623, AFHRA.
119 Message from PACAF headquarters to Tactical Air Command, 13 October 1962. K717.1623, AFHRA.
120 Message from PACAF headquarters to Tactical Air Command, 12 October 1962. K717.1623, AFHRA.
121 Colonel Robert L. Gleason as quoted in USAF ORI #218, Pritchard, K239.0512–218, AFHRA.

9 Ruminations of a wooly mammoth, or training and advising in counterinsurgency and elsewhere during the Cold War

John D. Waghelstein

From something between riding with Lawrence of Arabia and trying to control a yard full of puppies, my time spent training, equipping, advising, and leading indigenous forces has been memorable. Hopefully, in addition to providing me with lots of stories, some even worth a round or two, some of this may be of value to the next practitioner of the occult. I am going to do this in chronological order because it is easier to overcome my creeping senility that way.

My experience as an advisor began with the Cuban Missile Crisis in 1962. I was a senior Infantry First Lieutenant, had just finished the US Army Language School's Spanish Course, and was assigned to D Company of the 7th US Special Force Group based at Ft Bragg, North Carolina. Our company was slated to begin deployment to the Panama Canal Zone in December as part of the soon-to-be activated 8th Special Action Force (SAF) for Latin America. The 8th was to be the "stick" of President John Kennedy's carrot and stick counterinsurgency effort, the Alliance for Progress being the "carrot." Shortly after my arrival at Ft. Bragg, I began training as the Executive Officer of one of the A Detachments preparing to head south.

When the Soviet missiles were discovered in Cuba in October, we were alerted, briefed, and deployed to train and lead Cuban exiles in the invasion of Cuba. Having recently commanded a U.S. Basic Training Company, I was at home making soldiers out of recruits but was unprepared for the pace of training the Cubans. We put the Cubans through the most intense training program I experienced in 30 years of active service. We were to take them in as the landing's first wave, and there was an obvious need to get them ready as soon as possible. We attached one 12-man Special Forces A Detachment to each of the battalion's six companies, a degree of "adult supervision" I never witnessed again.[1]

The training of the Cubans provided me several personal benefits. Total immersion sharpened my Spanish, and my training skills improved in a number of areas. I was given the mission of training all 48 of the battalion's machinegunners with unlimited ammunition and little time. In about two weeks and after more than one million rounds, I had 12 (four men per team) of the best trained and highly motivated gun crews in the world, at least I thought so. We all thought we were going to war and the Cubans thought they were going home; every class began with the Cuban National Anthem and ended with *Navidad en Cuba*.

I was then given the reconnaissance platoon to train. Drawing on my Army Ranger School experience, I developed a training program and pushed the Cubans day and night in small unit operations, scouting, reconnaissance, combat patrolling and in night ambush techniques. But it was all for naught. JFK and Krushchev cut a deal that ended the invasion preparations and we were pulled out. Though it did not sit well with us to abandon the Cubans, the "No-Go" drove home the point that we were but tools in the foreign policy toolbox. We might have been less disappointed if we had known the Soviets had tactical nukes in Cuba.

The lessons I learned from this experience were:

- Motivation and resources can overcome time constraints and motivation leads by far.
- If you are fluent enough to think in another language too, you can get inside your advisee's head.
- Cultural sensitivity, foreign language proficiency and maturity make U.S. Special Forces ideally suited for training non-US personnel.

My next experience in the business of advising took place in Panama.[2] Based at Ft. Gulick in the Canal Zone, the 8th SAF had the hemisphere's counterinsurgency mission, and Panama provided a superior training environment. In addition to the triple canopy jungle, isolated beaches, and the Chagres River, we also had the Canal's lake system and access to the interior of the Republic of Panama west toward the Costa Rican border and into the really heavy jungle east toward the Darien. We trained extensively with the Panamanian *Guardia National* (GN), as that US assisted force was called in the pre-Noriega era. We were also asked to provide aggressor forces for the US army's School of the Americas based next door to us at Ft. Gulick. During the numerous field-training operations our detachments conducted in those years, we got to know the jungle and the Panamanians well.

In 1963, we conducted a training exercise in Panama's Mandinga Peninsula and nearby San Blas Islands. My detachment's task was to train, organize, and assist a guerrilla force, a role reminiscent of our traditional World War II-era missions. For guerrillas, we had GN soldiers, and for insurgent infrastructure, we recruited resident Panamanians including San Blas (Cuna) Indians. The GN played their parts well as we developed their tactical skills. While the Indians were not a problem, there was an unforeseen issue. There was a long history of abuse of the Cuna by the Spanish, Colombian, and more recently by the Panamanian government that left a legacy of distrust not easily overcome by the presence of *gringos* playing war games. It was not until we talked to the Indians that we heard of the incidents that had soured the Panamanian–San Blas relations.

Some years earlier, in the process of trying to capture a Colombian boat involved in a smuggling operation, a GN customs cutter fired on the smuggler and accidentally shot and killed a San Blas Indian girl. The Indians reacted swiftly, swarmed over the government boat, killed several of the crew, including the pilot, disarmed the rest of the GN police, stripped them, laid them out on the beach, and after threatening to fricassee them all, ransomed them back to the government for a dollar apiece. We were unaware of this incident or of the long history of friction in the area. But we quickly solved the problem with our Panamanian "guerrillas" by replacing their GN insignias with US ones and experienced no problems for the remainder of the exercise.

We found the Cunas to possess talents at a premium in an insurgency as they were adept in smuggling and illicit trading with their kin up the coast in Colombia. They were excellent scouts, knew the mainland and the peninsula well though they only farmed the mainland and lived on the healthier islands. They were incomparable small boat handlers and were highly dependable and honest. With Indian support, we set up supply caches and supply routes and established safe houses and developed intelligence and transportation networks, the Indians providing boats and crews that gave us an additional method of moving besides hacking through the jungle. Living with the Indians was a terrific experience, and the exercise provided some useful lessons:

- Dig deeper than the intelligence community's production. Put someone on the ground.
- Examine the economic, ethnic-racial, and other "non-military" issues that can bite you.
- Every training exercise, no matter how unique, contrived or artificial, should be mined for problem-solving opportunities. Duress "in the bush" trumps the classroom or garrison.
- Your friends' strengths and weaknesses are as important as your enemies'.

In 1964, I commanded a Mobile Training Team (MTT) sent to the Dominican Republic to train the DR's counterinsurgency forces. We were the *Tropas Especiales* (Special Troops) based at San Cristobal, about 25 miles west of Santo Domingo. We used the dead ex-dictator Trujillo's ranch at *Casa Caoba* (Mahogany House) for a training area. We taught small arms, heavy weapons, patrolling, ambushes and raids, communications, first aid, and demolitions.

The Dominican military wanted lots of new equipment. New toys and the latest gizmos were seen as the true measure of a modern military. What they really needed, along with the training, was extensive physical conditioning, leadership, and someone to care for their welfare. The troops were eager, and when the Dominican Officers saw us doing physical training with their troops, they reluctantly joined in. We transferred this new-found closeness to a more hands-on role by the DR officers during training which not surprisingly led to higher esprit and morale.

During our mission, we organized a number of medical patrols into the countryside. These were excellent training opportunities for our team medics and added to the Dominican medics' experience as well. Additionally, our USSF Intelligence Sergeants, who were cross-trained as medics, had the opportunities to check the pulse of the *campesinos*. Without being intrusive, it was a simple matter to determine what the countryside was thinking. Mothers getting medical treatment for their children are surprisingly candid as well as grateful. We got the kind of intelligence worth its weight in gold in a real counterinsurgency situation.

During one such patrol, I was invited into the humble home of a poor farmer. He had pictures of FDR and JFK on the wall of his hut, and over a cup of coffee, he asked me when the United States was going to come back to the island to "fix things."[3] He had a low opinion of his government's ability to deliver. My impression was that although dirt-poor, he was tuned into what was going on beyond his village's borders.

One day during the training, my team sergeant and I were invited to a luncheon at San Cristobal's Military Club. During the after-dinner speeches I was stunned to hear several retired ex-Trujillista officers complaining about the country's current political leadership. It was evident that this "San Cristobal Group," as it was called, was deeply involved in the coming attempt to overthrow the government. What made this particularly unsettling was the presence of many of the Dominican active-duty officers we were working with. The US embassy dismissed my incident report as the usual muttering of those left out at the feeding trough.

In three months, we produced a pretty fair battalion capable of conducting small unit operations in a counterinsurgency environment. We were then directed to conduct a series of three-week training programs for several other companies from the capital city. This turned out to be an equal-opportunity event as several of these units were on the other side of the soon to erupt Dominican Crisis of 1965. While we were training these companies, some of their officers aired their discontent with the situation. They said many of the younger officers were not prepared to join the putsch being prepared by the old dictator's acolytes. They were well aware of the role of the Special Troops officers in the "San Cristobal Group" but believed it was time Dominican officers started thinking about the future of the country and the reforms necessary to end the corruption. In my out-briefing to the embassy, I said the Dominican army was split, trouble was brewing, and the lid would blow when the coup was attempted. I said it would happen within the next 60 days. I was wrong – it took 90 days. The scenario was as I had predicted with the Dominican army divided. When it blew, the US embassy was nearly empty, most on vacation, including the ambassador and the MAAG chief. The US should not have been caught by surprise but we were. So:

- Sophisticated modern equipment is not a "must." You can produce a fairly competent counterinsurgency force with training, boots, rations and radios.
- Training opportunities are also intelligence-gathering opportunities.
- The countryside knows more than you might think. Passive techniques often work best in finding out what is going on.
- Good intelligence is not always well received and when received, does not necessarily get acted upon.
- Any embassy, including its intelligence entities, can be complacent. An environment where violence is not evident does not mean there is not trouble coming.

In 1965, I volunteered for my first tour of duty in Vietnam. I went from the 8th to the 5th Special Forces Group to take command of Detachment A-101, and the camp at Khe Sanh sited just below the Demilitarized Zone (DMZ) near the Laotian border. Along with many other SF camps, our mission was to conduct surveillance and interdiction missions along the border. The SF teams led the Civilian Indigenous Defense Group (CIDG) soldiers in those missions. Huong Hoa Districts's Bru *Montagnard* tribesmen were first-rate material. There was also a company of lowland Vietnamese along with a detachment of Vietnamese Special Forces (LLDB) assigned to the camp. Additionally, I was fortunate to command a company of *Nungs*, ethnic Chinese mercenaries recruited mostly from Saigon's Cholon district. This ethnic mix was potentially a problem. The day I arrived, some of the *Montagnards* and *Nungs* were training their weapons on the LLDB team house, the result of some personal disagreement. I defused the situation and never had another such incident but was keenly aware of the racial issues.

Leading the CIDG was a joy and an education. The "Yards" were solid performers as were the *Nungs*. I was less impressed with the quality of the lowland Vietnamese as they were poor soldiers, generally unreliable and unhappy at being in the highlands. The US Special Forces were well prepared to accomplish their mission of leading *Montagnard* tribesmen and other indigenous minorities in the conduct of interdiction and special operations in the border regions of Laos and Cambodia. We were, however, too few in number to have a serious impact on the course of the war. The real war was being fought and lost in the rice-paddies of the lowlands and the Mekong Delta. I was fortunate in this assignment and learned much about dealing with diverse ethnic groups and their issues.

In addition to my role as commander of the Special Forces Detachment at Khe Sanh, I had an additional duty of Huong Hoa District advisor. I was to assist my counterpart on the business of fighting the war. That meant, fire-power, air support, and "army business." I was warned by my other boss, the MACV Quong Tri Province Adviser, to stay away from the non-military side of the war. All that "other stuff" was not in my charter, and if I got involved in the "political" side of the war, I would be in "big trouble" and ran the risk of a truncated career.

My counterpart was a major in the Vietnamese Army (ARVN) and one of the finest officers I ever served with. Not only did he work well with the pre-dominantly *Montagnard* population, he had none of the usual lowland Viet-namese prejudices regarding the hill people. He ran the best district I saw in two tours there, he made the *Montagnard* chieftain his deputy and worked tire-lessly to address the social, political, and economic issues which made his dis-trict a dangerous place for the Viet Cong. He also provided me with an education in the intricacies of counterinsurgency at the grassroots level. I got much more from this Vietnamese officer I was supposed to advise than he ever got from me. In Southeast Asia, we were dealing with a smart, well-organized, and highly motivated opponent, an opponent who understood the complexity of the struggle. Insurgency in Vietnam was a different business from the Latin-American brand and required applying *all* the elements of national power, not just the military. In the end we lost, but the lessons I learned were as follows:

- There are ethnic/cultural issues that can affect the mission.
- Fighting someone else's battle is a non-starter. If they do not have the stomach for the fight or the wisdom to out-reform the revolutionaries, they will lose.
- Reform must be a part of the solution, not an end-product of winning the military struggle.
- You can get so heavily involved that you cannot exert leverage on your client.
- To be a truly effective advisor, one must be able to function in all facets of the struggle, not just the military ones.

In 1967, I was posted to Cochabamba, Bolivia to advise Bolivia's Airborne Battalion and to double as an instructor at their two service schools, *Escuela de Armas* (School of Arms) and *Escuela de Clases* (NCO School). During one of my classes at the *Escuela de Armas*, the Bolivian equivalent of Fort Benning's Infantry School, I was asked about my experiences in Vietnam and what I thought was the most effective weapon in that war. I turned the question back to the class and got the usual responses of air power in general, B-52s in particular, as well as artillery, helicopters, and other weapons systems that delivered firepower on the target. When it was my turn, I expressed my belief that hardware and weapons were more likely to cause collateral damage and therefore were often counterproductive in insurgency wars. I further surprised the class by offering the Viet Cong's five-man agitation-propaganda team as my choice. Bigger is not always better but small can be.

The best example of both modest and effective took place in Bolivia. When Che Guevara's little adventure was discovered in Camiri, the Bolivian government and our embassy asked Washington for a massive infusion of hardware including aircraft, artillery, tanks, and armored personnel carriers. Southern Command (SOUTHCOM) met to determine our response, and it was an overage-in-grade 8th Special Forces Lieutenant Colonel named "Red" Weber who said that the Bolivians were not likely to achieve results with hardware that they could neither use nor maintain, the recommended a low-tech solution. What we did provide was a 15-man Special Forces MTT to train a Bolivian Ranger battalion. Two weeks after their graduation, Che and his dream of creating "other Vietnams" were dead.

That we could succeed in Bolivia, with an essentially military response to Che's purely military threat, was the major weakness of all the "Castroesque" insurgencies of the 1960s and early 1970s. Unlike the VC in Vietnam, the Cubans and their clones were unwilling to invest in time, infrastructure and other preparation; they were unable to tap into the civilian population for wider support. In Bolivia, the Indians that Che & Company were trying to recruit had already had their revolution (1950–52) and viewed the Cuban-led adventurers as a threat rather than a solution. Besides, the dummies spoke Spanish, not Quechua or Aymara, and Cuban Spanish at that.

Finally, there was the issue of the Bolivian army. Recruited from the poorest of the peasantry, but unlike some other armies in the region, their induction was viewed as a step up. The army was a chance to advance, to become literate, and the *campesinos* saw it was their army's duty to protect the reforms of the revolution of the 1950s. The troops, the toughest I have ever seen, were knowledgeable in field-craft and were treated with respect by their officers, and we were invariably welcomed in the *pueblos* of the country-side. When we entered a village, we were greeted with a cool drink, offers of help, and information on the guerrillas.

And so:

- Better trained troops were the solution to armed guerrillas, at least until the opposition got smarter.
- Advising and assisting sometimes means saying no.
- Keep the US profile small. If the client will do the job, help, but stay in the background.
- Too close and too much stuff means less leverage.
- Insurgents make mistakes and are neither omniscient nor omnipotent.
- If the people see the army as part of the solution and not as a threat, the guerrillas lose.

In 1979, I took command of the 2nd Battalion of the 7th Special Forces Group. Because of President Jimmy Carter's force reductions in the aftermath of Vietnam, we found ourselves earmarked to support not only SOUTHCOM, our traditional area of orientation, but also Pacific and Atlantic Commands. This overstretched environment meant some wide-ranging training opportunities. We conducted the *Dancer* exercises in the Caribbean for Atlantic Command, numerous missions and training exercises in Panama for SOUTHCOM, and *Foal Eagle* in Korea for Pacific Command. Training with the Republic of Korea (ROK) Special Forces was an unforgettable experience. One notable difference between our respective modus operandi was that in a war with North Korea, the ROKs did not plan for extraction after they completed their initial missions. They planned to stay. Living within enemy artillery range gave them a dissimilar point of view. Because my battalion was expected to conduct real world missions in Northern Asia, we also got to train in Alaska. *Exercise Brimfrost* gave me, with my southern hemisphere perspective, an unexpected and instructive glimpse of how to train and fight in Arctic conditions.

Coincidental to our missions were those of the 19th and 20th National Guard Special Forces Groups. If we ever went to war, these two units were earmarked to participate. As their active-duty SF counterpart, I was expected to assist in their training and to evaluate their capabilities. It made for an interesting challenge. These guard units had some really talented people. Many of their communications specialists were Vietnam veterans and were better and faster than some of my junior radio operators. Many had served in Recon or LRRP units in Southeast Asia and still knew a few tricks. We worked with them in Panama, Alaska, and Korea. While neither unit was "foreign" in the usual sense, there were some interesting cultural aspects to deal with.

The 19th's Group Headquarters was in Salt Lake City and had a battalion based in Provo, Utah. As you might expect, both the headquarters and the battalion were predominantly Latter Day Saints. They had extensive linguistic capabilities by virtue of their missionary experience which made the Mormons effective communicators in a number of areas of the world. They were solid citizens, but the headquarters had some difficulty in communicating with its two other battalions. The Colorado-based battalion was definitely not composed of "Saints" but did seem to include a high percentage of beer drinkers and bikers, mostly on Harleys. Once they were in the field, they did well, but it was while waiting to go to the field that they presented a bit of a challenge. Their "peacetime pastimes" appeared to be trying to piss off the Mormons at headquarters and how to steal the 19th Group Headquarter colors. The other battalion was based in West (by God!) Virginia. Looking back, it seems as if someone had a warped sense of humor in combining the Utah, Colorado, and West Virginia elements under the same headquarters. The mountaineers in the West Virginia battalion were the most colorful group I ever worked with. Not surprisingly, their field-craft, scouting, and patrolling abilities were excellent; they were good "shade-tree mechanics" and they could communicate better than anyone else, particularly in the mountains. I often think that some of this highly valued military expertise was the result of their "peacetime pastimes" associated with distilling and "running" and avoiding pursuing Treasury Agents. As to lessons learned:

- Battalion Command is the best job in the world for a Lieutenant Colonel.
- Assess the unit you're advising with as much objectivity as you can muster.
- Keep your sense of humor.

In late 1981, I was selected for promotion to Colonel and ordered to take command of the US Military Group in El Salvador the following March. This was to be the single most demanding assignment in my 30 years of active duty. I was getting my Spanish buffed up a bit at The Army Language School in Monterrey, California (hey, somebody has to sacrifice!), when I received a call one Friday afternoon in February from the State Department telling me the US Ambassador to El Salvador, Deane Hinton wanted to see me. I got on the next flight to Washington, DC, and met my soon-to-be-boss at State that Sunday morning. He started the meeting with the comment that what he really expected in a "MIL-GROUP" commander was someone who could "manage the program," that is, keep track of the massive amount of paperwork required by our Security Assistance (SA) program, a program I always felt had been designed in Moscow to thwart our efforts. I said that if he thought that was the primary role of his MIL-GROUP commander, he would be better served by finding a senior administrative sergeant recently graduated from the SA school to do the paperwork and that I could seek employment elsewhere. He asked me what I thought was the proper role of the military mission chief. I took the bait, for that was Ambassador Hinton's style, and launched into a somewhat lengthy monologue on how to conduct a counterinsurgency. After about an hour or so he stopped me and said, "I don't know if you really believe all that or if you're just trying to make me feel better, but I'll see you next month in San Salvador." On arrival, I hit the ground running and, with the Ambassador's support, never looked back.[4]

As I had concluded years before, fewer, but better trained troops, was the solution to the armed guerrillas in the *sierra*. I was now able to implement some of these ideas in El Salvador's counterinsurgency campaign. The desire for more "stuff" was still out there as was the desire to supply it. In 1982, the Defense Department's vested interests were pushing more helicopters, artillery, and hardware on the Salvadorans who were more than happy to accept. I remember that in the Vietnamese experience, this giving and taking reflected more than simply bureaucratic pressures at work. In the giving and taking, the bonds between the patron and client are tightened, and it becomes tougher to exercise pressure to change. The sponsor has less leverage to reform the social, political, economic, or military aspects of a struggle if there is a large and apparently open-ended or endless commitment. America wrote a check on its national treasury in Southeast Asia and found it had less to say about how things should go than the expenditure of its human and material treasure should have warranted.

In Latin America, we were able to keep it cheap in part because priorities were elsewhere. For those of us in that side-show arena, this was a blessing and we were able to keep it small and still win. The point that almost everyone was missing was that in an insurgency the hearts and minds of the target population was still the only piece of "key terrain" that was important. In order to secure it, the military needed to be out among the population, on patrol, in small numbers, showing the flag and talking to the villagers, not flying over them at 5,000 feet. I was able to keep the number of helicopters at a minimum and pressed that the infantry battalions get accustomed to walking to work. And we were able with minor success to hold off on high-performance aircraft and heavier artillery for the same reasons. These goodies are counterproductive, road-bound, lead to "collateral damage" and stressed out our clients' already wobbly maintenance systems.

In El Salvador, I was fortunate to have a boss who understood the correlation between efficiency, human rights, and hardware, and he provided a heat-shield against those techno-buffs in Washington who constantly pushed hardware over other considerations. As it had been years before in Bolivia and elsewhere, it was cheap, low-tech stuff – rations, boots, and radios – that helped to make the El Salvadoran Armed Forces (ESAF) effective in the field. Finally, and best of all, the congressionally imposed 55-man-limit on our MILGP helped keep the war as essentially a Salvadoran effort. Whenever the left-wing opposition and the press began keening over another Vietnam in the making, we countered with the magic number of 55 *gringos* in country, hardly comparable to Southeast Asia and its half-million US troops.

The prototype for what I wanted to do in El Salvador was Colonel (later Major General) Edward G. Lansdale's support of Ramon Magsaysay's success in the Philippines against the Huk insurgency of the early 1950s. I had read Lansdale's book and found useful ideas, and while none of them could be applied without alteration, there was a wealth of wisdom that came in handy.[5] Additionally, I had a rare opportunity to talk to the object of Magsaysay and Lansdale's efforts back in the 1970s when the Philippine government released Luis Taruc, the *HUK* leader. He visited the US Command and General Staff College at Fort Leavenworth, Kansas, where I was an instructor and I had a rare opportunity to talk to a live loser. During a one-on-one talk, I asked him to explain the defeat of his movement. He made a point of stressing Magsaysay's reforms as the major cause of his strategic defeat. Land reform undercut the *HUK*'s recruiting base in Luzon, and other reforms, included disbanding the militia, long a source of abuse in the countryside, and their replacement with regular army courts to adjudicate disputes between *campesinos* and landowners, were crucial. Additionally, a system of bounties and rewards further undermined the insurgents. Taruc said many veteran insurgent leaders took advantage of the amnesty program and surrendered, often with weapons, information, and followers, with devastating impact on the morale of those still in the field.

On the tactical level, his comments were particularly revealing, confirming my own experience. Taruc said there was never any real danger from the large and by definition, ponderous multi-battalion-sized sweeps by the Filipino army. The *HUK* intelligence sources always provided enough warning for the guerrillas to avoid being netted. The *HUK*s were able to predict the direction and duration of large-scale operations. Rather, it was the small hunter-killer teams that went into and stayed in the jungle that caused Taruc the most grief. These teams would track the guerrillas, fire into their camps and then melt back into the jungle. In the end, it was these teams that were the deciding factor. Taruc told me the inability of his people really to rest and even to take off their boots took a tremendous toll on insurgent morale. It was this wearing down process that caused the guerrilla military force to deteriorate. Once again, it was smaller is better.

I helped the Salvadorans to relearn some of Taruc's tough lessons. There were some similarities both in their societies and in their insurgent experiences. One key advantage the Salvadorans already enjoyed were the reforms resulting from the Officers' Coup of October 1979. Land, banking, and commodity reform were moving along and had done much to garner popular support. On the military front, however, they were following the bad habits of other US-supported conventional establishments. Like the Filipinos, the ESAF had been conducting multi-battalion operations without much to show for their effort besides blisters and heatstroke. There was a crying need for the ESAF to get out of the big-unit rut and operate at night in small groups. Massive firepower and more troops would only be appropriate once the guerrillas were concentrated. They had to be located first.

One problem was self-confidence. We needed to prove small units could survive and get results. We began training Long Range Reconnaissance Patrols (LRRPs) in Panama and in El Salvador. The LRRPs were loosely modeled on the Special Operations Group (SOG) operations in South Vietnam. Putting small teams deep into "Indian Country" required dedicated communications, standby helicopters, cockpit-ready pilots at forward deployed launch-sites, as well as extensive specialized training on a hundred-odd hand-picked soldiers. There was resistance from the ESAF to allocating scarce resources to a program with little visibility, and there was skepticism about the cost-effectiveness of their training. But when LRRPs started making kills and providing invaluable information, cost ceased being an issue, and there arose demand for even more. I remember one mission in particular where one *Faribundo Marti* Liberation Movement (FMLN) guerrilla column was tracked for days by a LRRP team. Each time the guerrillas stopped, they were hit with either air strikes or artillery. They suffered extensive casualties and were harassed constantly, and the LRRPs were never detected. Echoes of the *HUK* experience and Luis Taruc's lament! Pound for pound, the LRRPs were the most lethal weapon the ESAF put into the field and proved once again that size was not the true measure of effectiveness.

It was at the national/strategic level where real work was needed. As US aid increased, the Salvadoran military was asking for lots of stuff, stuff we questioned. Material assistance requests were being justified by the increase in the number of large-scale operations they wanted to conduct in the countryside. I believed simply doing bigger sweeps, and multi-battalion operations would have little positive effect. They were reacting to the enemy's moves with bigger ones, and an analysis of the guerrillas' strategy was lacking. When we questioned the ESAF as to what were the FMLN's operational goals in the field, we got vague answers. I thought I saw a pattern in the FMLN's operations but needed confirmation. If my suspicions were correct, I would need to be careful in walking the ESAF through the problem and have *them* arrive at the same conclusion. Simply pushing the ESAF was unlikely to get results. A more subtle approach was required.

I asked two of my Special Forces NCOs to troubleshoot the railroads. They did an in-depth survey of the guerrillas' methodical destruction of the Salvadoran rail system which pointed out a disproportional focus on two departments. I then asked for an examination of the FMLN's attacks on the power grid, irrigation system, crop-dusting operations, and other agricultural activities. These reports once again portrayed a disproportionate emphasis on the same two departments. When reports of clandestine resupply operations were added to the mix, it became obvious even to the comatose that the guerrilla campaign was not targeted against the ESAF but against the economy and specifically in two departments. Salvador's economic viability depended upon three export crops, coffee, sugar, and cotton. While there were attacks elsewhere in the country, the attacks in San Vicente and Usulutan departments in eastern El Salvador were more numerous. Attacks on military targets elsewhere served the guerrillas' purpose of distracting the ESAF from their economic warfare objectives in the two key departments.

Now what? I scheduled a briefing to the ESAF high command and demonstrated in successive overlays what we had learned. We offered the information without comment or conclusion and let the Salvadorans draw their own conclusions. The cumulative visuals told the story. The ESAF asked that the same briefing be given to President Alvaro Magaña Borja. That briefing led to the first National Campaign Plan in 1983. This plan focused on the economic, social, political, and military operations in the two targeted departments. In the years that followed, the ESAF became less reactive to attacks on their troops or installations and more likely to ask tough questions about non-military targets and the guerrillas' real agenda. At first, the ESAF tended to see guerrilla attacks as some type of personal affront against their honor or manhood, affronts that must be dealt with in a forceful military manner. A closer look revealed the guerrillas were using military targets as a smokescreen for a war on El Salvador's economy. The analysis led the Salvadoran government to arrive at a more realistic approach and a workable solution. The National Campaign Plan was the result and eventually helped win the "hearts and minds" of the people.

A few words regarding prisoners and Human Rights are in order. During my early visits to the various departments, I asked to talk to some guerrilla prisoners. The responses were usually a 1,500 meter stare, or "they were killed trying to escape." After a year of US-applied pressure, the ESAF began to equate humane treatment with positive results and amassed a large number of prisoners, many of whom had surrendered. On my last pass around the departments I talked to one guerrilla prisoner (they would usually say they "were kidnapped and forced into the guerrilla movement"), who admitted that his role had been an active one. He had turned himself in because his brother had been captured six months earlier and was not only still alive but had been well treated. This does not seem to be that difficult to understand. Lansdale and Magsaysay got it right a quarter century before – there is a correlation between fair treatment and success.

In that regard, when traveling with the Minister of Defense, General Vides Casanova, I made a point of not preaching Human Rights as such. In quiet conversations with the young combat officers and NCOs using my best Socratic method, I had asked them a series of questions about their dealings with the villagers. These questions were designed to lead these junior leaders to conclude that if you treated the *campesinos* with dignity and kindness, you stood a good chance of getting not only timely warning of danger but also good long-term intelligence regarding guerrilla activity. By reducing humane treatment to its practical level, we not only got positive results in battle but materially diminished the abuse quotient across the country. This latter result helped make our case for continued support for the Salvadoran government. The issue of leverage over a client was never quite grasped by those who opposed our Central American policy on Human Rights grounds. If you expect to influence behavior, you have to have dialogue, and to achieve dialogue, you need to have an entree, that is, an attention-getter. SA gave us the entree to push the ESAF in the right direction. America's own record in the Human Rights arena gives us a degree of credibility that permits us to encourage others to do good. In El Salvador, it was obvious that the best way to effect changes in ESAF attitudes was with patiently applied pressure rather than aggressive, obnoxious, and "preachy" oratory – the usual *gringo* approach.

US policy at that time was walking a fine line, trying to help a flawed ally with a lousy Human Rights record while thwarting the Communist insurgents. That peace finally came to El Salvador was not a direct result of SA, but our role in the process at least gave us some leverage to do the right thing and help lead the ESAF down the path toward civilian control within a democracy. US military and economic assistance to the government of El

Salvador were key ingredients in steps toward economic improvement, in achieving political change, and in improved military performance.

North American military professionals performed two functions in the Salvadoran Insurgency. They trained, advised, and equipped as was expected, but it was not just the training and the stuff we provided. Vastly more important was the constant pressure and the example provided by the long line of CINCs, trainers, and advisors. It was in their second role – that of conscience in influencing the ESAF's treatment of El Salvador's population – that they were the critical factor in the war's outcome. Although access via SA did not guarantee influence, it did provide the opportunity for our influence to be applied. Unlike Vietnam, we kept the level of personnel involved in that assistance at an exceptionally low level, and the commitment of US combat forces was never required. So:

- Popular support is the key objective in any insurgency. Our client must win that support to win the war.
- We can win by helping an ally win his war; if we can overcome our own impatience and stay the course.
- If we cannot move our clients to a human rights posture that lets us sleep at night, they probably deserve to lose.
- Smaller is better. In someone else's insurgency, that means a small US footprint.
- Objective analysis is not easy. The toughest part is getting the client to recognize he or she may be part of the problem.
- The integration of US effort is best located in the ambassador's office.
- Aid is leverage up to a point. Support should not be unconditional, and in the last extremity, we must be prepared to walk away.

In 1985, I was selected to command the 7th Special Forces Group. The 7th's missions were by then totally re-focused on Latin America and included working with the Honduran army in its defense against a Nicaraguan invasion. On my first visit, I met with a gathering of Honduran officers. I wanted their views on the threat or threats they faced. When asked to describe their major concerns, seven out of ten saw Nicaraguan Daniel Ortega's Soviet-supplied army poised on the border as their most pressing threat. The remainder, looking both backward to the "Soccer War" of 1969 and beyond the current Nicaraguan threat, viewed the Salvadorans as their chief problem. When asked about an unconventional threat, they unanimously denigrated the idea. The consensus was the Honduran (PRCTH) guerrillas had been destroyed in the Olancho Valley in 1983. I understood how that particular fiasco, in which 95 of 97 guerrillas were killed, captured, or defected, might lead to an opinion of guerrilla incompetence or irrelevancy. I was less than sure that that incident really meant the end of an internal threat.

I had been reading the Honduran traffic and noticed some "blips" on the radar that indicated that something was going on in the north coastal region. It appeared that both our people in Honduras and the Hondurans themselves were not taking those "blips" seriously. The US embassy, including both the CIA station chief and the Military Attaché and the Task Force Bravo Intelligence Officer (J-2) at Palmarola agreed with the Hondurans. Rather than argue the point, it seemed prudent to gather information quietly and, only if the data warranted, then make the case.

Prior to my assuming command, the 7th was in the habit of deploying to Honduras on a battalion or group-sized exercise each year. I was of the opinion these spasmodic and expensive drills were more show than substance, and I directed we change to small-scale detachment-sized deployments on a constant schedule. By this move, individual A detachments could focus on the type of training they needed, it gave junior officers experience in developing training programs, in dealing with the Hondurans as well as their own deployment issues, and it meant we now had "two-legged sensors" deployed throughout the country at all times. Beginning early in 1985, we had in-country at any one time three to five A Detachments (12 men each) commanded by captains, and a B Detachment (five men) element for command and control commanded by a major to provide a little adult supervision. My charge to the teams was to do their training, get closer to the Hondurans, keep their eyes open, stay alert, and record everything. I provided an old Vietnam-era checklist as a rough guide which the teams used to keep track of ten "insurgency indicators."[6]

Over the next several deployments, we began to see a pattern emerge. Propaganda operations in San Pedro Sula, reports of infiltrations by sea near La Ceiba, strange activity in the coastal mountains, lights at night, and the mysterious death of a policeman were some of the more significant indicators. The senior police official in La Ceiba said he had a phase I insurgency on his hands[7] and no assets with which to deal with it. The Honduran army, however, for the most part remained unimpressed.

As each returning team was debriefed, we plugged their information into the intelligence reporting system. It was at this point I was reminded of an ancient lesson about turf. The intelligence people at the US embassy and TF Bravo went ballistic. Where they had been reporting the Honduran equivalent of "All's Quiet on the Western Front," along comes some show-off "Green Berets with an agitation agenda!" Luckily my relations with General John R. Galvin, C-in-C SOUTHCOM, were such that he was willing to listen. When I briefed him regarding our findings, his reaction was extremely positive and that caused the intelligence communities' hatchet men to back off. In the spring of 1987 SOUTHCOM published an in-depth study entitled "The Phase One Insurgency on Honduras' North Coast." It took almost two years, but we finally got the US intelligence community to focus on the subject.

Even if we got our own house in order, the real problem was how to get the Honduran military to look somewhere besides across their borders. If the

Hondurans were to focus on their internal threat, it would only be accomplished via self-assessment as it had in El Salvador and would require subtlety. Back at Ft. Bragg, I had started a series of officers' calls dealing with counter-insurgency operations. The idea of exporting a seminar seemed worth pursuing. The team deployments to Honduras begun in 1985 now had an added twist. I directed them to begin a series of evening seminars to discuss counter-insurgency subjects. This educational effort served two purposes. It was designed to support the Special Forces' ability to assess the ambient conditions in their areas of operation. I felt these seminars would sharpen their analytical skills by discussing the indicators. The seminar participants were to pay particular attention to the analysis of the insurgency and the questions, How do you know there's a problem? What are the indicators of an insurgency? and What responses are indicated? I attached a Psychological Operations (PsyOps) specialist to help orchestrate the seminar discussions for each deploying SF team. Once the team leader and his PsyOps "commissar" were satisfied, with the team's level of understanding, they invited the Hondurans officers, with whom they were training, to sit in.

By the end of 1987, at about the same time, SOUTHCOM's J-2 (Intelligence) was focusing on the insurgency, Honduran officers in growing numbers were participating in the seminars. The final proof that the sensitizing sessions were working came when the Honduran army began to have firefights with the guerrillas in the mountains above La Ceiba. Casualties were inflicted on the insurgents, and their training was disrupted. Eventually, it was the Hondurans that put the guerrillas out of business. Lessons anyone?

- Police often have a better feel for what is happening on the street or in the countryside than does the military.
- As with other bureaucracies, military establishments and intelligence organizations suffer from inertia that may be difficult to overcome.
- Self-assessment is hard but necessary.

So that is about it. I hope these musing of some of my more memorable experiences in advising may be of value. Now that the Marxist–Leninist–Castroite insurgency era is past, these ruminations probably no longer have any direct applicability. However, if my pessimistic view of the human condition is accurate and men continue to try to shoot their way into power, then maybe not. It may very well be that friendly governments will continue to resist, and the United States may again be called upon to provide assistance in the form of advice and training. Should that be, then some of the generic lessons learned, with some serious "situationally specific" tweaking, might be useful to some other soldier–diplomat–advisor. There may be times when a yard full of Labrador retriever puppies seems well organized. But, when your advice is constructive, your support is timely and appropriate and your advisees take the bit and it all clicks, you will understand how Lawrence, Wingate, or Lansdale might have felt.

Notes

1 Under normal conditions, an A Detachment would train and advise a battalion.
2 Company D, 7th SFG deployed to Panama in December 1962, and Colonel Arthur D. "Bull" Simons, Commanding, activated the 8th SAF in April 1963. The SAF included the 8th SFG as well as a Psychological Operations Battalion, a Military Intelligence Company, an Engineer Battalion, a Medical/Hospital Company, a Military Police Company, and a Security Detachment.
3 US troops intervened in the DR from 1916 to 1924, and the US supervised DR finances from 1905 to 1941.
4 Portions of my El Salvador and Honduras experiences were published in "Ruminations of a Pachyderm or What I Learned in the Counter-Insurgency Business," *Small Wars and Insurgencies* 5 (Winter 1994): 360–78, and "Military-to-Military Contacts: Personal Observations – The El Salvador Case," *Low Intensity Conflict and Law Enforcement* (Summer 2003): 1–45.
5 Edward Geary Lansdale, *In the Midst of Wars: An American's Mission to Southeast Asia* (New York, San Francisco, and London: Harper & Row, 1972).
6 The checklist's ten indicators were disposition, activities, intelligence, propaganda, strikes, infiltration, new organizations, clandestine operations, outside assistance, sabotage, assassinations, and guerrilla activity. *Counterinsurgency Planning Guide, ST 31–176* (U.S. Army Special Warfare School, Ft. Bragg, NC, 1964), pp. 238–9.
7 I assumed he was referring to the first or pre-revolutionary of Mao Tse-tung's phases of insurgency in which the guerrillas are preparing or building.

10 "Imperial grunts" revisited

The US advisory mission in Colombia

Douglas Porch and Christopher W. Muller

Despite the technological, operational, and tactical proficiency, combined with the force projection capability, of US forces, American success in the Global War on Terrorism (GWOT) will depend to a great degree on the military capabilities of its allies. While many of Washington's NATO partners possess sophisticated and proficient military organizations, others outside NATO require assistance in modernizing their forces. The traditional mechanism for transferring knowledge of US practices, enhancing capabilities and professionalism, promoting stable civil-military relations, encouraging regional cooperation and integration and advancing military-to-military (mil-to-mil) contact in partner nations is through Security Assistance Organizations (SAOs). SAOs are teams of US military personnel dispatched by the Department of Defense (DOD)to organize and execute a full spectrum of programs, collectively known as Security Cooperation, tailored to the Partner Nation's specific needs.[1]

In the era of the "Long War," the SAO mission might find itself authorized to supply more robust assistance to an ally in perilous circumstances, support that nevertheless stops short of combat operations.[2] This is the case in Colombia, where the mission of the SAO is to provide "indirect support" to the host nation within the context of Foreign Internal Defense (FID), Security Assistance and Security Cooperation.[3] This indirect support offers the United States an important international "force multiplier" in the GWOT – a handful of personnel propagate through knowledge and technology the "revolution in military affairs" to partner nations. Indeed, Andrew Krepinevich has called military advisors "the steel rods around which the newly poured concrete" of allied armies "will harden."[4]

Krepinevich and Kaplan argue that SAOs offer a key component to American success in the GWOT. US forces are directly committed to combat in Iraq and Afghanistan as well as tasked to stand up the security forces of those two countries. Some scholars have also argued that mil-to-mil contacts benefit US National Security objectives through "state socialization."[5] Because military organizations number among the most organized institutions in developing countries, bonds of trust established between US and foreign officers serve to socialize leaders into American, or at the very least Western democratic ideas, beliefs, and values, which in turn can influence institutional development as a whole.[6] The clear expectation is that SAOs – organizations that consist of a handful of US military personnel assisted by local nationals, endowed with diminutive budgets[7] – can have an impact beyond their numbers by building long-lasting relationships, importing technical expertise, encouraging reforms and efficiencies in host nation forces, coaxing them toward actions, attitudes and behaviors that support both US and partner nation policy goals.

The effectiveness of mil-to-mil engagement is clearly linked to the receptiveness of the environment. For instance, Eastern European countries offered especially fertile ground for conversion through mil-to-mil contact, given their European culture, and the allure of NATO and EU membership. Colombia, too, would appear to offer a successful test of the impact of SAOs on host nation practices for several reasons: first, mil-to-mil contact between Colombia and the United States is historic, dating back to World War II. The US military has played a central role in the development and modernization of the Colombian forces at critical periods, beginning in 1943, through the Korean War and during the violence of the early 1960s, and especially since the advent of *Plan Colombia* in 2000.[8] Today, US influence is obvious, from structural similarities such as the replication in Colombia of US doctrine with the formation of Joint commands to cosmetic similarities such as uniforms.

Second, Colombia shares with the United States a tradition of democratic, civilian control of the military, which certainly facilitates the mil-to-mil dialogue. Third, US policy in Colombia is leveraged by significant resources. This has required a robust SAO component that stops short of outright combat but whose size and mission have ballooned beyond the modest six-man, security assistance role. Therefore, the SAO effort in Bogotá offers a test case of the Krepinvich – Kaplan contention that SAO missions can have an important influence on the GWOT. The "optimistic ecumenicism"[9] that Robert Kaplan believes inspires the SAO mission has undoubtedly influenced the development of modern Colombian military (COLMIL) practices and institutions. "This should be a model of how to support a sovereign nation," exudes a lieutenant colonel in the SAO mission that, as in most Latin America countries, travels under the name of US Military Groups, abbreviated to USMILGP–Colombia (MILGP-COL).[10] Indeed, the Colombian forces would look different were MILGP–COL assistance factored out. Furthermore, by transferring organizational concepts developed from US experience to Colombia, enforcing conditions for military aid and helping to create mechanisms for Human Rights education and enforcement, MILGP–COL has added muscle to US policy and reinforced calls by Human Rights Groups and Colombians, including soldiers, for respect for Human Rights and democratic institutions.[11] This contributes to the goal of enhancing the legitimacy of the Government of Colombia.

MILGP–COL maintains an advisory, operational support and technical assistance role and through its influence and command of eye-watering military assistance budgets has assisted improvements in Colombian military efficiency and civil-military relations, to include the formulation of strategy. Nevertheless, the benefits of mil-to-mil relations have been, at times, circumscribed in some areas by differences over strategic priorities, competition and bureaucratic inefficiencies among the various agencies involved in Security Assistance. Above all, MILGP–COL operates in a strategic and political context that is uniquely Colombian. As anywhere, organizational concepts developed from the experience and adapted to the culture of one country seldom transfer unaltered to another national environment, especially one as unique as that of Colombia. Furthermore, while US sponsored Security Cooperation programs have helped to improve the combat effectiveness of the Colombian military, Colombian strategies, military institutions and practices with roots deep in a national political, social and military culture have been able to resist alteration despite MILGP-suggested changes.

A brief history of USMILGP influence in Colombia

A desire to avoid a replication of a Venezuelan-style Caudillo tradition following the fragmentation of Gran Colombia in 1830 meant that Colombians preferred to fight their frequent civil wars between partisans of the Liberal and Conservative parties with private militias. As a consequence, the war that erupted between Colombia and Peru in 1933–1934 showcased an undermanned Colombian army deficient in logistics, planning and training. A US Military Mission became a permanent feature in Bogotá from 1939, with the goal of shoring up the defenses of the Panama Canal.

However, it was Colombia's decision to commit its forces to support UN efforts in Korea that impelled the modernization of the Colombian army. "One can affirm that the modern Colombian Army was born through its participation in Korea," according to Colombian security specialist Andrés Villamizar.[12] US officers in Korea found soldiers in the 1,000-man Colombian battalion to be "well disciplined and the officers well trained and cooperative." Assigned to the US 21st Infantry Regiment, 24th Division, the Colombians received high marks from their US comrades.[13] Veterans from Korea, trained to US standards, returned to infuse the Colombian Army (COLAR) with a new sense of professionalism that included better staff work, more comprehensive training of junior officers and skills at night patrolling. Korean War veterans utilized their contacts with former US comrades to expedite US military equipment and to overcome Embassy restrictions on the use of military assistance in Colombia's internal war, to bring Colombian officers for training in the United States and to form the *Escuela de Lanceros* at Tolemaida modeled on the US Army Ranger School in 1955. During the decade of the 1950s, Colombia, with a battalion and a ship in Korea and wracked by civil war, received more security assistance than any other Latin American country.[14]

The triumph of the Cuban Revolution in 1959 allowed Bogotá to argue plausibly that the formless and only marginally ideological conflicts between Liberal and Conservative militias and assorted bandit gangs that had characterized *la Violencia* (1948–1958) had transmogrified in the 1960s into a communist insurgency orchestrated from Moscow via Havana. US fear that the Cuban Revolution might contaminate Latin America stimulated the Kennedy administration to combine the president's Alliance for Progress (*Alianza para el Progreso*), a new regional development initiative, with counter-insurgency support for the Colombian military. The 1961 Foreign Assistance Act set the parameters on the activities of military missions.[15] The Nixon Doctrine of the 1960s built on this premise and sought to assist countries willing to provide troops to solve their own internal problems, an idea the evolved into Foreign Internal Defense. This accorded well with trends in Colombia, where a handful of forward-thinking Colombian officers had concluded that their country's endemic revolutionary violence had sociological roots and were eager to transform the Colombian military into a modern counter-insurgency force.[16]

Some questioned whether Washington was getting a good return on its security investment in Bogotá. A US assessment team sent to Colombia in early 1962 concluded that lack of coordination and planning, poor utilization of resources, lack of equipment, reliance on static outposts, sporadic collection and untimely dissemination of intelligence, patchy civic and psychological action programs and poor military–police cooperation combined with the country's systemic problems of underdevelopment to put the Colombian military on the defensive. The recipe for improvement included a $1.5 million security package, including vehicles and communications; Military Training Teams (MTTs) to instruct Colombians on all aspects of counter-insurgency; soldiers and police dispatched to Panama to train at the US-run School of the Americas; a revamping of the intelligence structure of both the military and police and the creation of special operations units and self defense groups. These improved military capabilities helped the Colombian army to swell from roughly 6,000 soldiers in the 1940s to 65,000 by the 1960s. Sixty percent of the $40 million that Washington gave to Colombia between 1964 and 1967 went to the military and 40 percent to civic action.[17] These reforms culminated in *Plan Lazo*, a successful July 1962 offensive against the – much depleted – "independent republics" of the upper Magdalena valley, where the most ideological remnants of *la Violencia* had taken refuge.[18] "We had to separate the gangs from the peasants, who saw the government as the enemy, and these bandits as their army," former Army Chief-of-Staff General Alvaro Valencia Tovar remembered of *Lazo*. "We had to go after the leaders. Once these caudillos were killed, they were not replaced." Psychological Operations (PSYOPS), *acción cívico-militar* and intelligence were closely coordinated, while the military built health clinics, schools, water treatment facilities and linked isolated villages by road. The military offensive culminated in May 1964 with OPERATION

MARQUETALIA, aimed at Manuel Marulanda Vélez's "communist republic."[19] By 1966, the insurgents who remained had been driven to remote areas, and Colombia seemed to have acquired an elusive stability.

Nevertheless, US military cooperation with Colombia did not end but rather gained momentum as Colombia's drug problems contributed to a growth in insurgent and paramilitary movements and criminal cartels in the 1980s and 1990s. Special Forces personnel were deployed as advisors to Colombia's police and soldiers in the 1990s, hundreds of Colombian soldiers were trained in the "School of the Americas" and Washington contributed millions to buy equipment for the police. By 1997, US military aid had reached $100 million annually. But concerns in the US Congress about human rights violations by uniformed personnel or their allies in paramilitary organizations led to the passage in 1996 of the Leahy Amendment to the Foreign Operations Act. Sponsored by Vermont Senator Patrick Leahy, this provision prohibited the delivery of assistance to foreign militaries known to have committed human rights violations. The following year, the US State Department required human rights vetting of all military units in receipt of US aide.[20]

The role of the United States since 2000

US–Colombian relations since 2000 have revolved around *Plan Colombia*. By 1999, as the plan was being sketched out, the proceeds gained from drugs and other criminal enterprises had allowed Marulanda's *Fuerzas Armadas Revolucionarios de Colombia Ejército del Pueblo (FARC-EP)* not only to survive and expand but also to seize the momentum in its war against the Colombian state. The Counter-Terrorism Bill passed by the US Congress in 2002 permitted US funds originally earmarked exclusively for the counter-drug fight to be expended and invested in the counter-insurgency (Counter Narco-Terrorism or CNT) war as well.[21] Critics argue that, under Washington's influence, the original economic and social focus of the $5.3 billion support package for *Plan Colombia* was scaled back and the plan heavily militarized. This was due in part to the failure of the European Union to deliver on the non-military support they had promised Colombia. In 2006, for instance, an estimated 80 percent of US aid to Colombia was funneled into the military and the police.[22] The number of US soldiers allowed in Colombia doubled to 800, backed by up to 600 security-sector contractors. US dollars, which amounted to 7 percent of the Colombian defense budget, translated into US assistance in training, intelligence, helicopters, fuel and equipment. However, even though the personnel cap increased, competing personnel demands in the USCENT-COM Area of Responsibility (AOR) has prevented Colombia from receiving its full complement of personnel. The payoff for the Colombian military has been an increase in both the quality and the quantity of trained troops, greater mobility and more firepower, which has broken the FARC's grip on Bogotá and other urban centers and pushed it back to remote jungle redoubts.[23]

"Expanded Authority" has challenged MILGP–COL to evolve a structure to manage this significant plus-up in personnel and funding. Doctrine is lacking to guide an organization that operates in an environment that is neither war nor peace: "Colombia is in the middle, between combat and a peacekeeping operation," a Mission Chief in Bogotá notes, although he concedes that this view is not necessarily shared by all US services represented in MILGP–COL. Before September 11, 2001, MILGP–COL was organized, as other Security Assistance missions in USSOUTHCOM, around a small headquarters section that coordinated the activities of the three service sections (land, air, maritime), assorted "deployed organizations" and a joint logistical mission. The post-9/11 mission re-focused US efforts on improving the military capabilities of the Colombian military to include operational support to missions in the field as well as acting as liaison for DOD activities in Colombia. In the capacity of a "subordinate joint headquarters of USSOUTHCOM," the MILGP is tasked "to advise, provide logistical and other operational support, support institution building, mil to mil engagement, developing operational level intelligence and providing force protection and administrative/logistical support to all DOD organizations involved in the security cooperation effort." The enlarged mission required significant addition of new structures.[24] It also challenged the MILGP commander to coordinate and control a significant plus-up of different subordinate elements and organizations, far exceeding the standard military span of control. This was exacerbated by the fact that several senior officers, who led subordinate MILGP sections, held rank equivalent to that of the MILGP commander and were reluctant to acknowledge his joint authority.[25]

To improve the synergy of the advisory effort, insure unity of command and minimize inter-service tribalism, a significant, internally driven reorganization of MILGP–COL is under way. There are some similarities with the US effort in El Salvador in the 1980s that required a rapid expansion of the MILGP without a doctrine to guide it, to rescue a government on the verge of defeat by a left-wing insurgency. The Planning and Assistance Training Team (PATT) program in Colombia, for instance, is modeled on the Operational Planning and Assistance Training Team (OPATT) program in El Salvador,[26] although force protection requirements mean that "the Colombians own their battle space. We teach how to synchronize operations, communications training, medical training, etc."[27]

Nevertheless, Colombia replicates the Salvadorian experience in several respects, not the least in that the advisory effort was an ad hoc one driven by pragmatism rather than anchored in a body of doctrine developed for such contingencies.[28] The revised MILGP–COL organization includes a Deputy Commander, a PATT that includes an Operational Planning Group to provide up-to-date strategic advice to the Colombian Joint Staff as well as to advise the COLMIL at the operational level. Other MILGP–COL components include material assistance to Colombian units and an Operations Section tasked with collating information from the various MILGP-COL sections to give the MILGP Commander a unified picture of his command's activities. PATT teams were expanded to act as the core of an operational-level Advisory Group to "lead the overall advisory effort in support of COLMIL operational and tactical operations." The PATT is a living organization that changes form regularly to meet the dynamic needs of the COLMIL. Located in eleven locations throughout Colombia at division and brigade level, officers in the PATT group help Colombians with planning and training and help to coordinate logistical support that is provided through the Logistics Mission (LOGMIS). A Mission Chief argues that logistical support is one of the MILGP's most important functions: "Without US contract flights and fuel support, the Colombians couldn't operate."

Intelligence collection and dissemination in support of Colombian military operations has also challenged traditional operating procedures. Historically, intelligence is an attaché (DAO) rather than a security assistance (SAO) mission. To adapt intelligence support to a country in conflict while obeying US protocols has not been easy. An Embassy Intelligence Fusion Center (EIFC) was created to combine the intelligence resources of several organizations. As most of the assets are DOD-supplied, it works better than most interagency enterprises. Interagency personnel in leadership roles of the interfacing organizations act as the primary liaisons to ensure all agreements, policies and guidelines are adhered to when working closely with the COLMIL.[29]

The combined strategy being considered by the COLMIL, the MILGP and the Department of State (DOS) is that of "Nationalization." "'Nationalization' is the developing plan for the Colombian government gradually to take control, to include funding, of some of the US-supported programs," explains a former MILGP–COL executive officer. The goal is to build "Colombian Military capabilities in order to defeat the narco-terrorist threat,"[30] or, in the words of this officer, "shape the military environment" by helping the Colombians to create institutional structures that they can sustain. The focus on long-term institution building offers a break with past strategies, which centered on the creation of tailored units to accomplish specific tasks, like the operational intelligence crafted and resourced to track notorious drug-dealer Pablo Escobar or the subsequent formation of the Counter-Drug Brigade (BRCNA).[31] The short-comings of this strategy eventually became obvious – Colombia's problems are endemic ones that require an integrated, sustained approach beyond quick-fix solutions supplied by specialized units. Furthermore, experience showed that unless units are institutionalized with an appropriate military culture that will maintain focus on a specific mission set, special units tailored for specific tasks rapidly lose their edge as highly trained people rotate out or the mission changes. Developing such a culture in the partner nation military is the most challenging task faced by SAOs. "We don't want to create capacities that only the US can support, so that when we go away we leave nothing behind, no institutional knowledge is created," one MILGP lieutenant colonel argued.

We have several missions: advisory, logistics, administration, intelligence, and training. (Colombian) institutions must be robust enough to assume the burden of funding, training, etc. We are starting with the small pieces first. Then we can work on the big pieces.

MILGP–COL has taken a page out of the El Salvador playbook and added a few of its own plays to implement a two-pronged strategy of plugging the gap with quick-fix solutions while simultaneously implementing a long-term plan to institutionalize capabilities.

In both Washington and Bogotá, doubts are expressed about Colombia's ability or desire to assume the costs of "Nationalization," especially as Washington insists that air assets continue to support fumigation. Bogotá's view is that if Colombia pays the piper, Colombians call the tune.[32] Bogotá's priority is counter-insurgency, not fumigation. They may well decide to employ air assets to increase mobility and effectiveness in operations against the FARC rather than against drugs. In any case, this diplomatic squabble may become irrelevant unless Colombians can solve problems that, with the curtailment of US logistical support, may cause operational readiness rates for air assets to nosedive.[33]

Fog and friction in the MILGP–Colombian relationship

The DOD's MILGP and the DOS's Narcotics Affairs Section (NAS) have undoubtedly helped to shape the way Colombians do business. Emphasis on human rights, jointness, intelligence collection and utilization, and operational planning offer positive examples. And the relationship between the MILGP and COLMIL has been overwhelmingly positive. However, despite the additional personnel and the creation of what might turn out to be a more efficient administrative structure, MILGP–COL's ability to shape the military environment is circumscribed by factors related to US practices and to Colombian nationalism and military culture.[34]

Problems with the US effort in Colombia begin with the uneven quality of MILGP personnel and proceed to the organizational level. Historically, a MILGP assignment in general is not a fast-track career move in services that search out "operators" rather than Foreign Area Officers (FAOs) or advisors to fill their senior ranks.[35] Because Washington's relative lack of interest in Latin America deprives it of political and professional clout accorded to service in the other Geographical Combatant Commands (GCCs), SOUTH-COM is considered the strategic economy of force of the GCCs. While fast trackers may move through SOUTHCOM, or earn their spurs in a difficult assignment like Colombia, most officers do not see service in the SOUTH-COM AOR as career enhancing.[36] Officers volunteer for service in Colombia because they feel that much important and interesting work is to be done there, even if they acknowledge that it may not be a career-enhancing decision.[37]

Recent MILGP–COL Commanders have received excellent reviews largely because the importance and complexity of the position has meant that the incumbents have been personally selected by the SOUTHCOM Commander. The job requires an agile and experienced US Army colonel with a FAO (Foreign Area Officer) or SOF background, fluent in Spanish, with prior SAO and COLMIL experience, able to operate simultaneously on the strategic, operational, and tactical levels of war, with the patience of Saint Thomas and the diplomatic skills of Metternich. Unfortunately, recent changes in the US Army personnel system mean that a person combining these exceptional skills may be even more difficult to come by in future.[38]

Beneath the level of the MILGP Commander, however, the system for officer selection for MILGP assignments functions poorly.[39] Screening for maturity, character or qualifications, not to mention motivation, is rudimentary. The PATT teams, who interface directly with the COLMIL, are most at risk from a system that basically searches out language ability and little else. An unfortunate appointment can jeopardize years of effort to build confidence, cooperation and efficiency.

The increase in numbers of MILGP–COL personnel since 2003 offers testimony to the depth of US involvement in Colombia's conflict. But numbers offer poor indicators of effectiveness: in fact, according to the MILGP, a hefty percentage of the permanent positions remained unfilled, while a majority of MILGP personnel come to Colombia from three to six months on "temporary duty" (TDY). The remaining personnel are stationed in Colombia for 2 years (Permanent Change of Station). "There is a steep learning curve, and when they (TDYers) know what to do, it's time to leave. It takes time to get to know this country." Colombians, too, complain about a churning US personnel system that makes it difficult to establish relationships with their US interlocutors before they are replaced by an entirely new face.

The problems of under-staffing and the high percentage of TDYers increase the requirement for contractors. Contractors bring continuity and expertise with decreased political visibility – indeed, some are former US soldiers with MILGP experience. Contractors are hired to support administrative and logistical rather than operational functions, with the advising reserved for the Special Forces and PATT teams. "I won't use contractors for operations," a lieutenant colonel noted. "They're more like mercenaries. Active duty officers have the responsibility for intelligence and operations." But given the competition for quality active duty officers, contractors have become essential to the mission: "The key is hiring good guys. That's why good contractors are worth their weight in gold. Many are ex-military who know Colombia well. I can run them with little supervision, and they will be here when I'm gone."[40]

Colombians are less enthusiastic, however, because they understand that contractors represent some of the disadvantages, and dilemmas, of US support. Bogotá grumbles that the US reliance on contractors is an expensive jobs program driven by US, rather than Colombian, requirements: "We design what we need," a Colombian flag officer complained, "and the United States turns it over to contractors." Is the purpose of US aide to increase the effectiveness of Colombia's war effort, or to benefit American companies?

A MILGP officer's trump card is that he can speak truth to power, and if he is clever and diplomatic, he can empower a Colombian senior officer by making him successful. On the other hand, an advisor's influence depends on the chemistry he can establish with his local interlocutor. Deployed MILGP officers are sometimes resented as "reporters" for the Americans. Most, however, are welcomed "because the assumption is that, where the gringos are, they have a conduit to the Embassy for equipment or assistance." "MILGP influence is subtle," a mission chief concludes. "The Colombian military likes people who are like them. The US military is accustomed to dealing with civilians. The Colombian military is not. When you are in uniform, for Colombian soldiers, you're a *compañero*." Aggressive or unpopular officers with a "gringos know best" attitude might simply be ignored: "If the Colombians don't like them, they just wait for them to leave," one lieutenant colonel noted. Furthermore, the advice of a US captain or major may safely be disregarded by an old school Colombian colonel or general who has been fighting the insurgency his entire career and is disinclined to take counsel from a junior. Other more progressive Colombian officers turn to the US advisors based on competence not rank. The historic tension between soldiers and civilians in Colombia reinforces MILGP influence. "The Colombian military feels that it has been abandoned by the government," a mission chief noted.

> This was true in the 1990s when the mission was: 'just keep the guerrillas away from the cities, and stay away from Bogotá.' The COLMIL has an emotional dependence on US support. The COLAR says, 'you're the only friends we've got.'[41]

Force Protection (FP) requirements that limit deployment of US personnel to division and brigade headquarters where they might influence planning, but are prevented from accompanying the Colombians into combat, diminish their credibility when they seek improvements in the operational and tactical level of war where counter-insurgencies are won or lost. "We would like US troops to participate in our operations as observers," former Colombian Armed Forces Commander General Carlos Ospina argued, although he understands that "if we lost several US troops, Congressional support would drop."[42] And while some MILGP–COL officers believe these fears overblown, the Embassy position is that combat casualties in the MILGP would cause "support from Congress (to) evaporate, it would destroy it."[43] The ability of the MILGP to effect changes in how the Colombians fight is also diminished when so much of their time is spent in other security assistance activities and when they are forced to take a backseat while the Colombians fight the war their way. "Our role is behind the scenes, not to lead the charge," a senior PATT officer points out. "Because we are not in the field, the Colombians think that they know better than us." But this is all for the best. Quite apart from the "PR nightmare" in Latin America of the spectacle of US forces involved in combat, the Colombians must fight their own battles. "One reason that we are successful is that we are not involved in combat," a senior MILGP officer notes.

Colombian officers acknowledge the contribution made by US assistance to the turnaround in Colombia's military since 2000. Nevertheless, they complain that US agencies do not always appear to coordinate their efforts. In Colombia, the US Embassy supports the counter-drug campaign through NAS. USAID runs a variety of programs that fall under the general rubric of enhanced democratic governance, expanded economic alternative to illicit crops, and support to internally displaced people to include demobilized paramilitary and guerrilla forces.[44] Meanwhile, the MILGP focuses on restructuring and reform of the COLMIL for the counter-insurgency war. "The State Department wants to eradicate coca. We (the military) want to kill bad guys. Which is a better idea?" asked a US soldier assigned to the Colombian base at Tolemaida. In theory, planning for a unified strategic approach begins with SOUTHCOM's Theater Security Cooperation Support Strategy. The Colombian piece of TSC plan becomes the military component of the Embassy's Mission Strategic Plan (MSP), which is written by the Country Team.

What looks like a coordinated strategy breaks down on application. The US Embassy supplies the interagency mechanism for coordination and control of US programs and for their interface with their Colombian hosts. "Joint doctrine that establishes command and control relationships approach it from a theater of war perspective – a perspective that fails adequately to address the unique USG interagency and combined nature of the security cooperation effort," a MILGP reorganization paper concludes.[45] Each component of US policy answers to a different chief, operates on its own with minimal coordination and little reassessment. "NAS is totally focused on police business. They need to think on a higher level," a senior Colombian officer argues. "They need to see what areas are not producing results and base their allocation of resources on that." Of course, competition between the police and the military is a varsity sport in Colombia, and it is difficult for the Embassy to step in without setting off bureaucratic infighting among Colombian services and agencies. Above all, Colombians are baffled and frustrated by some Washington policies and practices. Bureaucratic inflexibility is a major grumble – once priorities and dollars are assigned to a task, they become set in concrete despite altered circumstances. "Once they get an idea in their head, it is hard to change their mind," a Colombian flag officer complains. The thicket of Washington-imposed regulations that Colombians must negotiate to secure some equipment are especially galling to

Colombian military leaders anxious to react to the tactical and operational innovations of an agile foe.

US officials acknowledge the problem but counter that Colombians fail to appreciate the realities of the budget and lobbying process in Washington and that their job is to execute the plan, not question its logic. The requirements of US forces in the Middle East take priority over those in Colombia, while the expansion of MILGP–COL's mission has strained its command and control capacities. "Nationalization" has led to hard, and so far unresolved, negotiations over who is to bear the costs, and determine the missions, of rotary wing assets.

One downside of US cooperation – the confusion of strategic focus

Colombia's *Democratic Security and Defence Policy*, *Plan Colombia* and *Plan Patriota* provide a strategic framework to attack Colombia's *conflicto*. The US-sponsored *Centro de Coordinación de Acción Integral* sets priority areas and coordinates the activities of several agencies to build a civilian infrastructure once the military has secured an area.[46] Nevertheless, insurgencies, especially ones as venerable as those in Colombia, are very difficult to attack because they present a variety of targets – leadership, resources, enemy forces, C4I, popular support, etc. – while also requiring a comprehensive strategy that combines political, economic and social programs with military force. Not surprisingly, different US and Colombian agencies bring their energies and resources to bear on different elements of Colombia's problems. For many associated with the MILGP, this has translated into a lack of strategic focus – "What are we fighting here?" a MILGP officer asks. "A drug war? A civil war? For Colombians, this has become a way of life." Some US officers express frustration that some within the Colombian military do not appear to understand that insurgencies are about legitimacy,[47] although General Ospina fervently propagated this view during his tenure as Armed Forces chief. Under US pressure, human rights training has become mandatory and widespread. "Through US training, the COLAR treats the *campesinos* better," General Ospina believes. "We have to win hearts and minds."[48]

However, despite the plethora of resources provided under *Plan Colombia* and improvements in operations and tactics, US intervention may also have contributed to confusion over the targeting of resources and imperiled a coordinated response to Colombia's multiple security challenges. According to General Ospina, the eagerness of the Colombian political leadership to access US bounty was matched by the historic indifference shown by Colombia's political elite to military matters and their assumption that insurgent violence was a security issue best dealt with through military means. "There was great pressure, especially from the American allies, to focus on narcotics as the center of gravity," Ospina noted of plans put in place to attack the FARC from 1998. "But the real strategic center of gravity was *legitimacy*."[49]

Some in the MILGP agree: "The counter-drug policy was too limiting," one MILGP officer with long experience in Colombia remembered. Everything was tied to drugs, and it hampered strategic thinking. Everyone in the SOUTHCOM and DC said that drugs were the Center of Gravity. One component of the problem blinded people to other things. We needed to talk about control of territory, legitimacy, etc.

The focus on counter-drug strategy meant that much US assistance initially was funneled through the NAS directly to the police, or to build up specific anti-narcotics military units, rather than evolve a coordinated counter-insurgency campaign. "There are different agencies with other priorities – USAID, MILGP, DEA, NAS. These stovepipe their problems. It is the Ambassador's responsibility to bring this together, but he is overwhelmed."[50]

Peru learned the hard way in the 1980s that bending to Washington's desires to stem the flow of cocaine by attacking drugs rather than guerrillas actually benefited the insurgents by alienating the peasants, who depended on drugs for a livelihood, from government. Some argue that the same has happened in Colombia.[51] Only in 2002 did Washington officially permit dollars and intelligence earmarked for crop eradication in Colombia to be applied toward insurgent eradication, when it abolished the distinction between counter-insurgency and counter-narcotics.[52] But even then, *Plan Patriota*, a military component of *Plan Colombia*, tackled Putumayo because it was a major drug-producing area. "This is a difficult area. They picked the hardest target. We were going to fumigate it, and the Colombians find alternative crops. But counter-drug policy drives everything."

Above all, do no harm

The combination of Irregular Warfare (support to counter-insurgency and Foreign Internal Defense) and Peacetime Military Engagement (Security Cooperation) activities in Colombia has allowed the United States to participate more fully in the transformation and modernization of the Colombian military.[53] Part of the conceit of attributing the evolution of Colombian military institutions to the "optimistic ecumenism" of US influence is that it factors out or minimizes the role of Colombian history and practice in shaping military institutions, as well as the incentive for change supplied by internal reformers and conditions. In the modern era, identifying the impetus for Colombian military transformation is a sensitive subject in the proud Andean nation. Former MOD Vice Minister Andres Penate argues the Colombian military transformation has been largely internally generated, the product of constant combat:

> The hostilities have transformed the army. We learn from the enemy. US assistance is critical, but we must not exaggerate US influence.

Certain aspects of what the United States brings cannot be replicated. But the dynamic is internal and a result of the fight.[54]

And indeed, one must not exaggerate US influence, which is concentrated on training, logistics and operational support. The Colombians, for instance, developed mobile brigades in the 1990s, although critics argue that the lack of airlift means that they are "mobile" in name only. In an effort to mitigate the lack of mobility, the MILGP recently has leveraged Security Assistance funds to purchase commercial trucks to support the BRIMs.

Nor is the United States interested in micromanaging Colombia's response. "Most of our relationship goes through the MILGP, USSOUTH-COM, to DOD," Vice Minister Eastman notes.

> The United States never gets involved in operational decisions, SOUTHCOM doesn't want the details. They have a very light touch. They want the big picture. What is the way forward? They need this for Congress. The US military has more accountability to Congress than does the Colombian military. Sure, everyone has their own views. The Colombian military can say, 'Thank you for your help, but we will do it our own way.' What you have to do is to have a good relationship.[55]

The interactive nature of the war in Colombia combines with the fact that Colombia has not lacked for talented military leaders to make this true to a point. A trio of remarkable Colombian generals – Tapias, Mora and Ospina – are credited with guiding a Colombian military renaissance from 1998.[56] The evolution of Colombian military practices and organization did not occur in a political vacuum, however, but is connected with political and defense sector globalization.

Since World War II, the US military has served as an organizational model, a source of doctrine and training, and as a resource base without which the Colombian military would have been hard-pressed to modernize and adapt to the evolving conditions of the conflict. US influence has been instrumental in determining how the Colombian military is used and how it fights. Much of the reorganization of the Colombian military for counter-insurgency operations follows the recommendations of SOUTHCOM. Eastman acknowledged that the United States "brings a rigor of training, focus, organization that we Colombians lacked. It has speeded up what may have been a much slower process. US assistance brings decisiveness, and helps us to make decisions."[57] "We always push them: 'What's your plan?'" a MILGP lieutenant colonel insists.

> SOUTHCOM and the MILGP demands force them to articulate their plan. The Colombians have understood that, in order to get US support, you have to explain the requirements better … Sending troops without a good plan can be a recipe for disaster if ambushed.

MILGP officers note that they have witnessed significant progress in the Colombian forces: better equipment, more professional soldiers, the geographical reorganization of sectors into sixteen versatile mobile brigades and more focus on civil affairs, night training and jointness. Colombians have become more serious about Information Operations and Human Rights. "Colombia has come a long way since 1998," a senior officer in the PATT insists, "when the FARC were everywhere and the roads were non-secure. Before (the COLMIL) just tried to kill guerrillas. Now they realize that they need to develop alternatives," as delineated in Colombia's *Democratic Security and Defence Policy*.

Military culture

Despite the historic relationship between the US and Colombian militaries and Colombian emulation of US military models, Colombians cling to a military culture that works against many MILGP-inspired reforms. This has meant that even as resources have become available and reforms implemented, execution leaves a great deal to be desired. Military culture is

> an amalgam of values, customs, traditions, and their philosophical underpinnings that, over time, has created a shared institutional ethos. From military culture springs a common framework for those in uniform and common expectations regarding standards of behavior, discipline, teamwork, loyalty, selfless duty, and the customs that support those elements.[58]

Most military cultures grow out of an aggregate of values, philosophies and traditions. Certain aspects of the military culture – hierarchical organization, tradition, discipline and self-sacrifice, all of which seek to increase military efficiency on the battlefield – are common to all military organizations defined by hierarchy, and a sense of distinctiveness, if not superiority, vis-à-vis civilians.

> In fact, a military's culture may determine its preferred way of fighting and dealing with other challenges, like incorporating new technologies, more than its doctrine or organizational structure. Officers turn values into action, bring coherence out of confusion, set the example, and articulate the viewpoint of the military institution.[59]

Different services within the military evolve their own subcultures.

Certain US-sponsored reforms, initiatives and assistance have proven disruptive, at least in the short run, because they introduced concepts alien to Colombian military culture and touched off a competition for resources that stoked latent inter-service rivalries. "Jointness" – the idea that all forces should be integrated under a single commander, with a staff made up of officers from all services – has roiled the Colombian military as it did the US military when it was first introduced in the Goldwater/Nichols Act of 1986. US support for *Plan Colombia* has also intensified a smoldering rivalry between the police and the army, two institutions that must cooperate if Colombia has any opportunity to coordinate a coherent counter-insurgency strategy to master its security challenges.

Nothing the MILGP can do will alter historic patterns of civil–military relations in Colombia characterized primarily by the indifference of most Colombians to issues of national security. Nothing more symbolizes the civil–military divide than conscription. Generous exemptions from military service means that the burden of military service in Colombia, no matter what side one fights on, falls on the poorest. "It's the same kid in the Army as in the AUC or the FARC," one US lieutenant colonel noted. "It just depends on who is stronger where he lives, who walks by with a gun." Perhaps the detachment of the population from the conflict and absence of sacrifice demanded through conscription are required to avoid popular demoralization in a conflict that already has stretched over generations. However, given that country's long history of conflict, the detached attitude toward the war exhibited by the upper classes and city dweller has meant that, until the Uribe administration of 2002, the military has operated largely in an atmosphere of political indifference and public apathy. But even Uribe has failed to match his determination to carry the fight to the insurgency with a concerted effort to strengthen civilian interest and over-sight to improve the efficiency. One consequence, however, is that the Colombian military dwells in a largely self-regulating world shielded from serious scrutiny and hence from political pressure to carry out structural changes that would improve performance. MILGP officers complain of an overly-centralized decision-making process, which produces a "group think" among the senior leadership. Mechanisms for internalizing "lessons learned" are lacking, so that operational and tactical mistakes are sometimes repeated. Above all, US officers are struck by the lack of a discussion in the Colombian army about their problems and about ways to deal with them.[60]

"Two stars have probably never maneuvered anything bigger than a bat-talion," a lieutenant colonel argues.

> They just do low level tactics. They never coordinate artillery, air support, or develop a deception plan. They understand counter-guerrilla operations, but not the operational art. Despite more men and materiel, they operate as before. They still think on the small unit level. They never include phase lines, firing lines, coordination points in their plans.

Lack of organization and planning, together with poor cooperation between the army and the police, translates into an inability to operationalize intelligence. Fear that high casualties produced by more aggressive, small unit tactics suggested by SOF advisors may bring a political reprimand, or judicial enquiry, down on the commander's head discourages taking the battle to the enemy. "Colombian commanders are afraid to put a squad of six to nine guys in the bush because they can't extract them. They are reluctant to send out recon squads, because when the guys disappeared, they are fired," a US colonel believes. Besides, when war has become a way of life, why assume extra risks in a conflict that is likely to percolate for some years?

MILGP officers also regret that careerism and "selfishness" in the COLMIL discourage a spirit of self-sacrifice. The rotation between field and staff assignments appears unbalanced: a group of battle-hardened commanders spend years away from their families in Mobile Brigades and Counter-Guerrilla units, while others appear to homestead in the *Centro Administrativo Nacional* (CAN) – the Colombian Pentagon. General Ospina concedes that the equalitarianism and sense of shared burdens and dangers that is the norm in officer-enlisted relations in the American forces offer a good example to Colombians. But the former Colombian commander concedes that, in common with other Latin American armies, the Colombian military does not have a culture of devolving responsibility to Non-Commissioned Officers (NCOs). Instead, the military reflects Colombia's highly stratified, class-conscious society. While the US military is a vehicle for social mobility, the Colombian structure maintains everyone in their station. Officers remain aloof from training, and NCOs lack prestige. Each army division trains its own troops. The USMC has created a DI (Drill Instructor) school for the COLMAR, while SOUTHCOM funded a sergeant major's academy in 2004, whose goal is to improve the professionalism and prestige of senior NCOs.[61] The Colombian Sergeants' Major Academy has been a huge success. The COLMIL now run it on their own and even invite senior NCOs from other Latin American countries to attend. A severe shortage of officers and NCOs means that "professional soldiers" with five or six years' service, who cannot be promoted to NCO, run the units. "Senior soldiers in the squad order people around. Discipline can be a problem. It's not a mob mentality, but the attitude is that officers come and go, but soldiers remain for years," notes a PATT lieutenant colonel.

"Old soldiers" are empowered because, although the Colombian military has progressively expanded and professionalized its ranks, it has steadfastly refused to match this growth with an increase in officers and NCOs. Expansion has compounded leadership and command-and-control problems. While the Army has ballooned to nearly 250,000 men, the Military Academy, which retains a lock on commissions, maintains a four-year curriculum that graduates out about 100 officers a year. This translates into an officer shortage of about 50 percent in the units. The Colombian Marines, soon to become the second largest marine force after the USMC, remain dependant on the Naval Academy and count about 1,200 officer vacancies. Bogotá, however, continues to reject options like ROTC or promotion through the ranks. Higher up, critics contend that the army is hemorrhaging colonels and lieutenant colonels who abandon a low-paying and unrewarding service career to triple or quadruple their salaries in the civilian sector.

"NCOs don't have much education," notes a PATT officer. "Half of the platoons are run by a sergeant or a cabo (corporal). The soldiers are professionals, recruited mostly from the urban poor, but they can't be promoted. Ten year soldiers are the ones making things happen." Training suffers because no unit wants to send their best officers and NCOs for training. Unlike the FARC that trains its soldiers in a specialty and has even devised specialized units like sappers, the Colombian services have no MOS system. So, those trained in one Military Occupational Specialty, like machine gunner or logistician or an infantry officer and a pilot, are considered interchangeable. A strong Ministry of Defense with control over budgets, personnel and training would be in a strong position to rectify this situation.

Personnel problems put a ceiling on operational and tactical efficiency and ultimately damage morale. "There's no motivation for the soldiers to fight, especially as they are fighting their own countrymen." Once with his unit, he is expected to patrol for six months, sleeping in hammocks in the open, with two weeks leave before he plunges back into the jungle. Inadequate logistics caused in part by great distances and rugged terrain, and a lack of field rations, require that he carry most of what he needs on his back. "Units go slow at first because they have too many supplies," a PATT lieutenant colonel notes. "Then they eat their rations and starve." Firefights are dreaded because the lack of heavy fire support weapons means that, rather than send out small patrols to find and fix the enemy, then call in artillery or air strikes, combat is *mano-a-mano* at close range, often on ground selected by the FARC, one well seeded by mines and booby traps. Indications are that quality of life-issues in an Army continually on the offensive has taken a toll on morale and hence retention.[62]

Colombian soldiers also might be more willing to move in smaller units if they were more confident that insurgents, paramilitaries or drug traffickers were not tipped off about their movements. Counter-intelligence works in basic training and fighting units to ferret out infiltrators, while special units are polygraphed. But soldiers constantly chat on cell phones that can be monitored by the enemy. Furthermore, "you can turn some officers in a second with $10,000 or more. A USMC lance corporal makes as much as a Colombian colonel. It's easy to pay someone to look the other way – 'just don't patrol over there tonight'." Soldiers whose families live in areas controlled by insurgents may be pressured to give intelligence. Problems of operational security place a Colombian officer in a dilemma: either he can thoroughly prepare for an operation and take the risk that it will be compromised or he can surprise his unit with an operation and risk that it will collapse from lack of preparation – "small things like the lack of filtered water, the gas tanks of the boats aren't filled, or insufficient ammunition," can short-circuit an operation. Operational readiness rates for equipment like helicopters can plummet without US support: the problem, at least in the mind of one US pilot, is one of culture: "It's not that they are stupid. But this reflects a culture that is hierarchical and class oriented. Colombians don't know how to manage personnel. I attribute this to a lack of initiative due to their rank structure. For instance, they don't assign a crew chief (NCO) to an aircraft. In the States, when I turn up to fly the plane, the crew chief has done the job. All I have to do is a walk around my helicopter. But there is no leadership here. I turn up, and the mechanics haven't even shown up. When they finally appear, no one says anything to them."

Conclusion

In a 1988 study of the impact of Security Assistance on the conflict in El Salvador, four US Army officers concluded that an expanded MILGP backed by millions of dollars dispatched to secure a Latin American country from an insurgent threat is more likely to produce stalemate than "victory." Among the problems that the authors identified were the following: the difficulty of achieving an integrated strategy in counter-insurgency operations; lack of a sustained attention in Washington, in part because of other, more pressing issues but also because policy lacked a domestic consensus because of concerns over Human Rights issues; the requirement for the right "personal chemistry" among US actors to overcome overlapping civil and military authority; "a cumbersome, unresponsive, intensely bureaucratized system of security assistance"; "absence of an overarching strategic vision" for the war; no incentives for the best talent to join the MILGP; attempts to change the ethos of the Salvadorian military and develop an effective NCO corps foundered; finally, US intervention with its emphasis on technology created a dependency that Salvadorians were unable to sustain on their own.[63]

It is perhaps ironic that the FMLN that opposed the Salvadorian government came to the peace table barely three years after this study was completed and so may cast these pessimistic conclusions in doubt. It is also true that President Alvaro Uribe's *Democratic Security and Defence Policy*, *Plan Colombia* and *Plan Patriota* do provide "an overarching strategic vision for the war." But the basic conclusion of the El Salvador study – that Security Assistance to a country in peril is more likely to produce stalemate than victory may apply to Colombia even more than to El Salvador. The FMLN in El Salvador was dependent on support from the USSR, the Sandinistas in Nicaragua and on Cuba and was left vulnerable by the end of the Cold War. By contrast, the FARC is a solitary actor with its own ideology, agenda and resources. There is no doubt that Security Cooperation has allowed the COLMIL to reoccupy ground lost to the FARC in the 1990s. "We have to sustain the effort," a former MILGP executive officer insists.

In the 1990s the FARC was on the one yard line. Now we are at midfield. We call it Security Cooperation. But we are doing counterinsurgency like in the 1960s. The United States has to have the will (to help the Colombians to) finish the job.

In the 1960s, US military assistance helped the Colombians to mop up the remnants of *la Violencia*. Unfortunately, unresponsive political institutions, persistent social and economic inequality, a violent political culture, widespread criminality, government corruption and a revolutionary tradition caused problems to persist that, when joined with drugs, almost brought the Colombian state to its knees. Once again, US intervention has helped to restore a precarious equilibrium. MILGP–COL can boast that Colombia possesses one of the best military forces in Latin America. But this has been at a cost of a significant investment of US – and Colombian – resources. And still the FARC–EP remains undefeated, and the drug culture is barely contained. US resources have their limits, and the challenges remain great. The simple enormity of fighting a vicious counter-insurgency against a determined foe in a country double the size of Iraq with a triple-canopy jungle is a huge task. While much of the MILGP effort has been invested in creating institutions that the Colombians can sustain, "nationalization" may prove a bridge too far for Colombia, which may lack the resources, technical skills, organization or military culture successfully to manage legacy programs. While it is certain that the FARC can claim no significant constituency, it is equally true that much of the country remains beyond the pale of government control. A combination of the interactive nature of the Colombian combat, Colombian innovations and US resources and ideas have certainly helped the Government of Colombia to push back the insurgency. However, the FARC and the coca growers have not been eliminated. Nor is MILGP inability to alter significant aspects of Colombian military culture surprising, given the fact that they are rooted in Colombian society and history. "The feeling is that Colombia is stuck on the twenty yard line," a mission chief argues. "They need institutional change to advance to the goal line. This is a real challenge in Latin America with its antiquated and inefficient institutions." The government has developed a twenty-six point military reform plan to reform training, personnel, medical and acquisitions procedures. However, it remains to be seen if it has the political will to push these through. Above all, the benefit of the military effort can only be realized if the Government of Colombia catches the war's momentum to transform Colombia's disheartening cycle of conflict into one of democratic dialogue and stability. Then, the excellent work of MILGP–COL will have paid handsome dividends, not only for Colombia, but for the United States as well.

Notes

1 Security Cooperation consists of the management of Security Programs (Foreign Military Sales, International Military Education and Training [IMET] and

Excess Defense Articles), joint exercises and training and personnel exchanges to build the capabilities of host national forces. Each partner nation's security cooperation requirements are coordinated and synchronized through the Combatant Command's Theater Security Cooperation Plan. For a description of a SAO mission, see "The United States Military Group (USMILGP)," Embassy of the United States, Tegucigalpa, Honduras. http://honduras.usembassy. gov/english/mission/sections/milgroup.htm

2 Direct support would include assistance with communications, intelligence, logistics, psychological operations and civil–military operations designed to augment host nation shortcomings.

3 Foreign Internal Defense is "the participation by civilian and military agencies of a government in any of the action programs taken by another government or other designated organization, to free and protect its society from subversion, lawlessness and insurgency." Joint Chiefs of Staff. Joint Publication 3–07.1 (Joint TTP for FID). 30 April 2004, p. ix.

4 Andrew F. Krepinevich, "Send in the Advisors," *New York Times*, 11 July 2006.

5 "I define state socialization as the process by which states internalize norms arising elsewhere in the international system." Kai Alderson, "Making Sense of State Socialization," *Review of International Studies* 27 (2001), pp. 415–433.

6 This is part of the benefit of WHINSEC and IMET courses. Carol Atkinson, "Constructivist Implications of Material Power: Military Engagement and the Socialization of States, 1972–2000," *International Studies Quarterly* 50 (2006), pp. 509–11.

7 Any SAO mission that numbers over six uniformed service members requires Congressional approval.

8 Large amounts of US dollars continue to flow into Colombia in 2006 but under the auspices of the Andean Counter-Drug Initiative.

9 Kaplan, *Imperial Grunts*, p. 10.

10 Quotations unless otherwise acknowledged are based on interviews with MILGP officers and senior Colombian officers carried out in Bogotá and Monterey, CA, in 2005, 2006 and 2007. Other types of SAO's found in the SOUTHCOM AOR include US Military Assistance & Advisory Group (USMAAG), US Military Liaison Office (USMLO), Office of Defense Cooperation (ODC) and Office of Defense Representation (ODR).

11 William Aviles, *Globalization, Democracy and Civil–Military Relations in Colombia's Neoliberal State* (PhD diss., University of California Riverside, 2001), pp. 38–9.

12 Andrés Villamizar, *La reforma de la inteligencia. Un imperative demorático* (Bogotá: Seguridad & Democracia, 2004), p. 61.

13 Major William J. Fox, *Inter-Allied Co-Operation during Combat Operations*, Vol. II, Part II, Section B, Military History Section. Headquarters Far East Command, Declassified manuscript, Center for Military History, Washington, DC, pp. 39, 61, 55, 68, 75, 86, 132–3, 145; see also Bradley Lynn Coleman, "The Colombian Army in Korea, 1950–1954," *The Journal of Military History* 69 (2005), pp. 1137–78.

14 Russell W. Ramsey, *Civil-Military Relations in Colombia 1946–1965* (New York: Regent Publishing Co., 1978), p. 8; Bradley Lynn Coleman, "The Alliance Transformed: US-Colombian Security Cooperation 1950–1960," pp. 220–56. Unpublished paper taken from the forthcoming book, *Colombia and the United States: The Making of an Inter-American Alliance, 1939–1960* (Kent, OH: Kent State University Press, 2007).

15 These included: evaluation of partner nation capabilities and requirements; FMS case management; training, program monitoring, rationalization, standardiza-

tion and interoperability; International Armaments Cooperative Program; liaison functions; administrative support.

16 Ramsey, *Civil-Military Relations in Colombia*, pp. 10–11.

17 Dennis M. Rempe, *Counterinsurgency in Colombia: A US National Security Perspective 1958–1966* (PhD diss., University of Miami, 2002), pp. 126, 131–2; Richard Maullin, *Soldiers, Guerrillas and Politics in Colombia* (Lexington, MA: D.C. Heath, 1973), pp. 75, 103.

18 The original name was LASO, for Latin American Security Organization, but became LAZO which means noose or snare. Information provided by Valencia Tovar.

19 Maullin, *Soldiers, Guerrillas and Politics in Colombia*, pp. 73–8; Rempe, *Counterinsurgency in Colombia*, pp. 137–52.

20 William Avilés, *Global Capitalism, Democracy, and Civil–Military Relations in Colombia* (Albany: State University of New York Press, 2006), pp. 101–4; Despite improvements, human rights violations by the military continue to pose problems, according to a March 2007 report by the UN Commissioner of Human Rights. Joshua Goodman, "Colombia's Army Killed Civilians," Associated Press, 16 March 2007.

21 The impact of the CT bill in Colombia is commonly referred to as "Expanded Authority."

22 http://ciponline.org/colombia/aidprop.htm

23 Avilés, *Global Capitalism*, p. 134; *La Semana*, 28 August 2006. Quoted in FIBIS, FEA20060829027033, "Plan Colombia seen as Failure against Drugs, Success against Guerrillas."

24 This brought the total of subordinate MILGP-COL functional sections to 28, to include airlift scheduling, anti-terrorism/force protection, countermine/IED, Information Operations, Intelligence Integration, Medical, Military Justice, Human Rights and Rotary Wing to name just a few. Roughly half of these elements fall under the service missions for command and control, while the remaining half answer directly in one form or fashion to the MILGP.

25 Added were the following: Air Component Coordination Element (ACCE); Planning Assistance Training Team (PATT); SOF Operational Detachment C (ODC); Force Protection Detachment (FPD); Intelligence Integration Teams (IIT); Embassy Intelligence Integration Center (EIFC); SOC C2 Fwd and a number of individual soldiers representing organizations in the United States, "Draft MILGP–COL Reorganization Paper" (unpublished) 1–2.

26 A.J. Bacevich, James D. Hallums, Richard H. White and Thomas F. Young, *American Military Policy in Small Wars: The Case of El Salvador* (Cambridge, MA, and Washington, DC: Institute for Policy Analysis, 1988).

27 There is inherent tension between SOF functions which concentrate on specialized, combat-related missions as opposed to the MILGP focus on support for conventional counter-insurgency, equipment and training. "SOF is perhaps 20 per cent of the effort in Colombia," says a mission chief, who also complains that SOF forces arrive for short deployments, do not understand the operational environment, and seek to apply solutions worked out in Iraq and Afghanistan, Interview, Monterey, CA, 22 February 2007.

28 Robert D. Ramsey III, "Advising Indigenous Forces: American Advisors in Korea, Vietnam, and El Salvador," *Global War on Terrorism Occasional Paper 18* (Fort Leavenworth, KS: Combat Studies Institute, n/d), p. 83.

29 The EIC is a joint interagency intelligence organization comprised of DOD and non-DOD entities. One problem has been that the EIFC officer has been an analyst rather than an operator so that the intelligence provided is not necessarily in an "operational" format, Interview, Monterey, CA, 22 February 2007.

30 Draft, MILGP-COL REORGANIZATION PAPER.

31 Richard Bowden, *Killing Pablo. The Hunt for the World's Greatest Outlaw* (New York: Penguin, 2002).
32 Interview with Luis Lordouny, advisor to the Vice Minister of Defense, Bogotá, 26 September 2006.
33 Among problems cited by US advisors are personnel and logistical practices in the COLMIL that lowers readiness rates.
34 Although significant challenges of adapting specifically tailored Security Cooperation programs exist in the US/Colombian case, far greater challenges loom for US programs in Partner Nations with significantly less cultural compatibility and histories of working relationships.
35 Current systemic changes in the Army's personnel management and promotion system promise to reward service with foreign militaries – but only time will tell if Security Assistance will be accorded the recognition many in the MILGP believe it deserves.
36 General Peter Pace, current Chairman of the Joint Chiefs of Staff, commanded USSOUTHCOM in 2000–2001. Two former senior aides to Secretary of Defense Donald Rumsfeld, General Blantz J. Craddock and Admiral James G. Stavridis moved from the Pentagon to USSOUTHCOM. The last two MILGP-COL commanders at the time of writing have been promoted to general. In the last few years several ideas were floated with regards to USSOUTHCOM. The first was to downgrade USSOUTHCOM from a four to three-star command. The second was to combine USSOUTHCOM with USNORTHCOM. Subsequently, consideration was given to the elimination of US Army South, the Army Service Component of USSOUTHCOM.
37 This may be less important to the many formerly enlisted SOF officers whose career ceiling is probably lieutenant colonel in any case. At least service in Colombia offers the perspective of follow-up employment as a contractor.
38 Officers who must now commit to the FAO career track at their tenth year of service do not return to the dirty boots Army, and so will lack the command experience of a SOF colonel. Realizing the potential problem of dispatching a MILGP Commander (colonel) to advise a foreign military on operations based on troop experience gained when he was a captain, has led the Department of the Army to consider programs to "re-green" FAO officers by giving them the opportunity for Divisional assignments. But for now, the new regulations divorce the FAO and operations career track meaning that operators with SAO experience and vice versa will become as rare as hen's teeth after 2010. OPMS 21 divides officers into FAO functional area between the fifth and seventh year of service, substituting a single track FAO career for a dual track alternation between basic branch (Infantry, Artillery, Engineer, etc.) and FAO. This system produced colonels who would become SAO Chiefs with usually two assignments of four to seven years as a FAO and at least command or executive experience on the battalion level. Soon, FAO colonels will have command experience only at the company level.
39 Andrew F. Krepinevich, "Send in the Advisers," *New York Times*, 11 July 2006. Rather than advertise broadly in the US forces and allow interested and qualified officers to volunteer for MILGP openings, World Wide Augmentation System (WIAS) simply tasks a unit to send someone with the desired MOS and language if required to MILGP-COL. US fighting units may seize the opportunity to off load their least dynamic elements onto a MILGP in response to WIAS requests for temporary duty (TDY) officers, while officers who want to volunteer never learn of the MILGP openings.
40 The Department of State with quality compensation packages has been able to hire two retired O6 former MILGP Commanders, one of which actually commanded MILGP Colombia.
41 Interview, Monterey, CA, 22 February 2007.

42 Interview with General Carlos Ospina, 29 September 2006.
43 Interview with Milton Drucker, Deputy Chief of Mission, US Embassy-Colombia, 24 September 2006; "Democrats to Throw Out Colombia Trade Deal," *Financial Times*, 24 November 2006.
44 "Summary of USAID's Strategy and Program in Colombia for 2006–2008," http://bogota.usembassy.gov/wwwfai01.pdf.
45 "Draft MILGP – COL Reorganization," ibid.
46 www.fuerzasmilitares.mil.co/cgfm.nsf/str/CADAD3B571AAF00E0525722600 53EB82?OpenDocument.
47 Communication with the author, 7 June 2006.
48 General Alberto Ospina, interviewed 29 September 2006, Bogotá.
49 Carlos Alberto Ospina Ovalle, "Insights from Colombia's 'Prolonged War'," *JFQ*, No. 42, 3rd Quarter (2006), pp. 59–60.
50 Defense Attaché's Office (DAO) has the mission of collecting intelligence, and answers to the Defense Intelligence Agency, not SOUTHCOM.
51 Interview August 2006; see also Stephen Dudley, *Walking Ghosts. Murder and Guerrilla Politics in Colombia* (New York: Routledge, 2006), pp. 206–7, 211.
52 Jose E. Gonzales, "Guerrillas and Coca in the Upper Huallaga Valley," in David Scott Palmer, ed., *Shining Path of Peru* (New York: St. Martin's Press, 1994), p. 125; Vanda Felbab-Brown, "The Coca Connection: The Impacts of Illicit Substances on Militarized Conflicts," unpublished paper, Security Studies Program, Department of Political Science, Massachusetts Institute of Technology, April 2004; Thomas Marks, "Sustainability of Colombian Military/Strategic Support for 'Democratic Security'," (Carlisle, PA: Strategic Studies Institute, Army War College, July 2005), p. 3; "Forward Operation Locations in Latin America: Transcending Drug Control," pp. 8–9; Transnational TNIB Briefing, Series no. 2003/6, www.tni.org/reports/drugs/debate8.pdf.
53 One example of this is the *Centro de Coordinación de Acción Integral*, an updated version of *acción cívico-militar*, headquartered in the Casa de Nariño, which seeks to apply a coordinated, inter-agency approach to the reoccupation of territories once controlled by insurgents within the context of the President's "Democratic Security" policy. This was financed by the US embassy. www.presidencia. gov.co/sne/2004/noviembre/20/06202004.htm; http://bogota.usembassy.gov/ wwwsww26.shtml.
54 Interview with Andrés Peñate, 1 July 2005.
55 J.M. Eastman, Vice-Minister in charge of Budgets, Strategic Planning, US – Colombian relations (Plan Colombia). All quotes come from an interview with the author on 28 June 2005, Bogotá.
56 Marks, "Sustainability of Colombian Military/Strategic Support for 'Democratic Security,'" p. 6.
57 Eastman interview.
58 Thomas Marks, "American Military Culture in the Twenty-First Century," CSIS International Security Program (Washington, DC: CSIS, February 2000), www.csis.org/pubs/am21exec.html+military+culture&hl=en&gl=us&ct=clnk&cd=6.
59 Marks, "American Military Culture."
60 Based on several MILGP interviews.
61 Ospina interview.
62 "Voluntary Discharge Rates Reflect Pressure on Colombian Military," FIBIS, 7/14/2006; *El Tiempo*, 2 July 2006. The COLMIL has a medical corps which is slowly increasing its capabilities. A USAF Major (medical service) is assigned to the MILGP to work with the COLMIL.
63 Bacevich *et al.*, *American Military Policy in Small Wars*, pp. v–viii.

11 Training the new Afghan tank force

A multi-national advisory mission, 2 June 2003 to 3 December 2003

Jonathan Byrom[1]

As I watched US Forces on CNN invade Iraq in a *blitzkrieg* of tanks, jets and countless other combat and support vehicles in early 2003, I could not help but feel consternation at the thought of not leading a cavalry troop into high-intensity conflict. Stationed at Fort Irwin as a commander of one of the Opposing Force (OPFOR) Cavalry Troops at the National Training Center, I felt that the talents of arguably the best-trained desert fighting unit, the world-class OPFOR, were being wasted in mock battles involving high-tech laser-tag. The common joke among my peers was that unless the world decided to start World War III, the 11th Armored Cavalry Regiment (ACR) did not have a chance of being deployed to fight. We accepted our role as the trainers for Army Brigades, in which we provided the most highly skilled enemy they could possibly face. We understood that we were the final exam for units before they deployed into harm's way. Little did I know that I would find myself on a C-17 in a few short months as part of a hand-picked team of approximately 28 officers and senior enlisted non-commissioned officers (NCOs) on our way to Afghanistan to embed as advisors with the newly forming Afghanistan National Army (ANA).

The tasking sent to the 11th ACR requested a group of experienced trainers to deploy to Afghanistan as advisors. The mission for the team was to help the leadership of the newly forming 3rd Battalion, 3rd Brigade of the Central Afghan Corps, quickly establish a disciplined and well-organized unit in order to provide security for President Karzai's regime during the upcoming Loya Jirga Constitutional Convention (November 2003) and the national elections in 2004. The dates later changed because of the political situation in Afghanistan, but both the convention and the election were held. The ANA already had two operational brigades of approximately 1,000 soldiers each of light infantry and commando units organized in the same manner as US infantry brigades. The addition of the 3rd Brigade to the 1st Corps would lend legitimacy to Karzai's regime by providing heavy and light armor battalions consisting of T-62 tanks and BMP-1 and BMP-2 troop carriers. The brigade would also possess heavy weapons support in the form of DS-2 artillery pieces. The long-term plan for the ANA consisted of eventually having five corps – one each in the northern, southern, eastern and western provinces, and one in Kabul.

The plan for the 11th ACR to accomplish its advising mission was to assign advisors at all levels of leadership within the brigade. The commander of the US advising team was led by a lieutenant colonel (LTC) and a 1st Sergeant and advised the brigade commander and brigade sergeant major. Teams of nine to twelve US advisors were then assigned to each battalion in the Brigade. The commander and 1st Sergeant of each US Battalion training team advised the Afghan battalion commanders and sergeants-major. A captain and senior NCO worked with each Afghan company commander and 1st Sergeant. Individual US advisors worked with the battalion staffs and were augmented by the US company trainers. Every key leader in the Afghan chain-of-command had a personal advisor assigned to his unit to provide officer and NCO assistance.

The leadership of the US training team believed the Afghan officer corps was already a professional and competent component of the Afghan Army. Thus, a critical mission for the US advisors became the establishment of a professional, competent, and empowered NCO corps. The 11th ACR leadership understood this focus and picked their top senior NCOs for the assignment. These NCO trainers proved invaluable in developing an aggressive training plan to convince the Afghan commanders of the importance of developing their NCOs and convince the Afghan NCOs themselves that they were responsible for the training of their soldiers.

Deploying to Afghanistan

The preparation for deployment of the 11th ACR Blackhorse team was fairly uneventful. With only 28 people from the 11th ACR deploying, along with a team of 12 Marines from the Marine Mountain Warfare School, the logistics were relatively uncomplicated. The team conducted the normal pre-deployment training, including weapons qualification, combat lifesaver courses, physical training tests, medical evaluations and briefings, updating of shot records and numerous other administrative tasks.

The most challenging aspect of the deployment was consolidating equipment from various troops to outfit the members of the team. The property book coordination was especially tricky. The leadership decided to temporarily create a property book for the team consisting of equipment from various troop property books throughout the Regiment. This coordination created tension between the deploying team and the companies donating the equipment. First, the deploying team borrowed the best equipment from the companies, including the newest night vision goggles, laser designators and M4 assault rifles. Second, the company commanders lending the equipment felt that they might never see this hard-to-replace equipment again.

The benefit of assigning the equipment to the team was that it was self-sufficient when it arrived in Afghanistan. The members of the team carried M240 machine guns for heavier weapons support, and each advisor had an M4 and a 9 mm pistol, as well as night-vision and global-positioning equipment. The 11th ACR team did not have to request equipment from the 10th Mountain Division, the unit it would be attached to in Afghanistan. Moreover, this equipment gave the team flexibility, confidence and adequate internal protection because it had trained with it.

The team went by C-17 out of Nellis Air Force Base in Las Vegas, Nevada. The journey to Kabul was long due to a maintenance stop in South Carolina and scheduled stops in England and Germany. The movement to Afghanistan was efficient, though, because the Air Force allowed the team to move all of its equipment onto the plane and not switch between aircraft.

The flight into Kabul was one of the last flights for weeks into the Kabul airport due to the air-to-ground missile threat. Our team flew into Kabul blacked-out during the night of 2 June 2003. A security detachment from the 2nd Brigade, 10th Mountain Division, met us and escorted the team's bus to their headquarters base camp on the eastern side of Kabul. This small base camp became the home of the 11th ACR advisory team for the next four months.

Meeting the Afghans

After settling in at the base camp, our team went to Polycharki to meet the Afghan commanders of the 3rd battalion, 3rd ANA Brigade. I met with Captain (CPT) Mohammed Shafeeq, the A Company Commander. He was a bright, articulate 28-year-old commander who had over 14 years of combat experience. Shafeeq's fascinating personal history explained his competence and coolness under pressure. At the age of 14, he had watched his father killed by a Soviet helicopter gunship. This inspired him to join the fight against the Soviets. He became a Rocket Propelled Grenade (RPG) gunner and worked with elite Afghan teams harassing Soviet base camps. After the defeat of the Soviets, he fought the Afghan communists and then became a company commander with the Northern Alliance in the fight against the Taliban. He participated in numerous campaigns under Ahmed Shah Massoud's leadership, which gave him the experience to join the ANA as an officer.

I then met with the leadership of the Headquarters and Headquarters Company (HHC) for the Afghan armor battalion. The Afghan HHC was organized similarly to a US HHC with a medical platoon, maintenance platoon, support platoon, scout platoon, mortar platoon and the various staffs for the battalion. This Company was much more difficult to advise because they were tasked with a myriad of support missions due to the diversity of platoons. This diversity of missions required me to have an understanding of many different types of potential platoon tasks.

Our first problem arose when the HHC leadership did not clearly designate which platoon each officer was commanding. This confusion resulted in upset platoon leaders as the Company leadership moved platoon leaders between platoons. The Afghan battalion commander solved this problem very quickly by assigning each platoon leader in the HHC to a particular platoon.

During the initial period of contact with the Afghan leadership, the American advising teams primarily worked in pairs, one officer and one senior NCO. SFC Willie Brown, the senior NCO that I was teamed with, stressed to the Afghan leaders with whom we were working that the US advising NCO would focus on NCO leadership and I would focus on the officer leadership. The most productive times with the Afghan leadership at the beginning of our relationship came during meetings in offices over tea and candy. We spent hours getting to know the officers and senior NCOs, while weaving questions and recommendations for the units into these relationship-building times. What would normally take hours of official meetings was solved in much more efficient 'socializing' over Afghan tea.

Next, the American and Afghan leadership met the soldiers that would form the new armored company. All of the men had recently graduated from the Kabul Military Training Center (KMTC) – the Afghan equivalent of basic training. The US Special Forces and the French army ran this school, the Special Forces training the enlisted men, and the French the officers. The recruits came from all over Afghanistan and included both ethnic Dari and Pashtu; most were uneducated. Moreover, the official language of the Afghan Army is Dari, and this created problems because Dari is the language of the minority northern Tajiks, whereas Pashtu is spoken by the majority southeastern Pashtun tribes, which spawned the Taliban regime. Thus, during training, there were soldiers who had no idea what was being taught because they only understood Pashtu, not Dari. Despite this language barrier, the competence level of the boot camp graduates was acceptable, and I did not see many problems between these two ethnic groups in the day-to-day operations.

Initially though, the soldiers did not understand the American advisor role. They tended to think we were in charge and would approach SFC Brown and myself with problems. We redirected them to their Afghan commanders and NCOs.

Training the Afghan tankers

Training began immediately with the initial training focusing on basic military skills and tank maintenance. The basic skills instruction was conducted primarily by the Afghans and consisted of standard tasks: holding formations, collecting accountability reports of soldiers and conducting basic troop movements by marching units between points. The ANA companies were fairly adept at the basic skills since they had recently graduated from basic training. The HHC soldiers, though, required more training to master their basic military skills because of the requirement to master a diversity of support missions.

The initial T-62 tank maintenance training was more challenging for the Afghan units than basic soldier training. A Romanian contingent of eight soldiers, led by two 1st Lieutenants, did the primary instruction on the T-62s and developed a plan to train the Afghans in basic maintenance. They were taught how to enter a tank, how to perform pre-operation, during and post-operation checks. The Romanians taught the Afghans to identify the components, replace fluids and identify problems in the tanks. The Romanians also created a driving program that began with classroom instruction before focusing on driving skills in a stationary tank and then completing a driver's course that earned graduates a T-62 license.

The differences between the two military cultures – the Soviet-style Romanian versus the US – were dramatic and forced us to compromise with the Romanians on the perceived proficiency of a tank crew. For example, the Romanians were very focused on entering and exiting the tanks in a very disciplined and concise manner, whereas the US trainers emphasized practical maintenance and driving skills. By making suggestions versus declarations, we met our training goals for the Afghans without dramatically disrupting the Romanian training plan. Overall, the Romanian/US relationship was mutually beneficial and allowed the US advisors to focus on individual relationships with the commanders, while the Romanians actually conducted the maintenance and driver training.

After we were satisfied that the Afghan soldiers could maintain and drive their tanks, we shifted focus to tactics training, which was provided by two teams, one American and one German. The US trainers were from the Fort Knox Officer Advanced Course and conducted officer instruction, while the Germans trained the NCOs and soldiers. Classroom instruction was followed by practical, real-world training. The tactics training began with basic tasks such as road-marching and assembly area operations, eventually graduating to platoon maneuvering, and then to more realistic field exercises. The training involved exercises where a platoon conducted a tactical road march, reacted to mine strikes, reacted to enemy contact and established a real-world checkpoint. We used platoons not involved in the training to act as the enemy. The Afghan leadership conducted medical evacuations, took enemy prisoners and recovered vehicles following 'training' mine strikes. We also challenged the Afghans to react to Taliban infiltrators. Most importantly, the advisors had the mechanized infantry and armor platoons conducted combined arms operations, which forced them to work together using BMP-1 personnel carriers and T-62 tanks in high-stress training scenarios simulating conditions that they would likely see during patrols in Kabul during the national elections and the Loya Jirga Constitutional convention.

While the Afghan tank battalion was learning to maneuver and conduct basic maintenance of their tanks, the Afghan mechanics (former Mujahadeen mechanics) finished fixing the majority of the firing control systems for the 105 mm main guns. After acquiring tank rounds from local warlords and weapons caches and remote firing the main guns using rope lanyards, the Afghan companies were ready to learn how to shoot. The advisors decided the best method for teaching the Afghans to fire their weapons was to teach them to conduct an organized and safe gunnery in the US manner. Tank gunneries consist of firing at targets at different ranges with different weapon systems – the main gun and machine guns. This training though proved challenging for a number of reasons.

First, the US master gunners had to adapt the US tank firing scenarios to vintage T-62 tanks. These tanks were unfamiliar to the US advisors who had to take precious time to learn the T-62 weapons systems. After learning all the weapon ranges, the US master gunners created reasonable target scenarios for the Afghan tank commanders.

Second, the Afghans did not have a computerized range of 'pop-up' targets. Thus, the US master gunners adapted and used old tank hulls placed at the appropriate ranges as targets. They created an effective gunnery range with four firing positions and numerous targets for the T-62 main gun and 12.7 mm machinegun.

The next challenge was convincing the Afghan leadership of the necessity of conducting an organized and safe gunnery rather than the traditional Afghan practice of tanks firing at targets with minimal order or discipline. Hence, we held numerous classes explaining how the Afghan leadership should control both movement and firing using radios from a central point called the 'tower.' We also convinced them to follow the scenario created by our master gunners and track the number of target hits by each crew to determine crew accuracy. We also focused on ensuring that the Afghan tank commanders understood weapon safety and how to keep their main guns pointed down-range. After classes, we conducted a rehearsal for the crews of the tanks by allowing them to maneuver through the tank range and identify all the targets before firing live ammunition. This rehearsal proved invaluable during the first day of live firing.

The US advisors' training model was designed to teach the Afghan leaders to plan and conduct their own training and was applied to this first Afghan tank gunnery instruction. The US master gunners focused on training the Afghan master gunners to run the tank range and design their own gunnery scenarios rather than have the Americans running the range. The Afghan master gunners for the T-62 tanks underwent in-depth one-on-one training with the US master gunner advisors. After a few days of running the range with close US supervision, the Afghan master gunners could run the range with little US help.

The first tank gunnery exercise of the new ANA Army was a success and generated a number of lessons. First, the Afghan tankers had the same problems in the first few days as American trainees moving their tanks efficiently through the gunnery scenarios. In order to bring the training to an acceptable standard more quickly, the US advisors encouraged the Afghan leadership to expedite the movement of tanks through the training exercise. The Afghan leadership began to understand the sense of urgency when the US advisors personally lined up the tanks, had one ready to move onto the range when another finished firing and colorfully motivated the Afghan crews via radio from the command center. This focus on efficient training by the US advisors and Afghan leadership allowed the Afghan tank crews to move through the training quickly but safely and complete the training in the required time.

Second, they also developed a quantitative system to measure the proficiency of their crews. By tracking the number of hits for each crew, the Afghan leadership discovered that some of the crews had skilled gunners while other crews had less-experienced gunners. The US advisors challenged the Afghan leadership to identify these weaker crews and have designated experienced gunners provide on-site training before allowing them to fire the scenario a second time. The Afghan leadership embraced this advice and qualified over 95% of the crews during this first tank-firing exercise.

Overall, the Afghans conducted an organized and beneficial tank-firing exercise and felt confident that they could hit a target with the weapons on the tanks. This confidence in their weapons systems was pivotal to the soldiers as they prepared to deploy into harm's way in support of President Karzai during the upcoming constitutional convention and national elections.

The first operations: conducting checkpoints

The US advisors also focused on checkpoint training. The logic behind our training plan was to concentrate initially on basic soldier skills such as marching and maintenance, move to basic tactics training to teach the Afghan soldiers to maneuver both dismounted and mounted on their tanks, shift to live-firing their tank weapons on an organized gunnery range, and then learn to conduct effective and efficient checkpoints in preparation for the ANA real-world mission of securing Kabul. All of this training was accelerated because the tank battalion had to be ready for combat operations by November 2003.

The checkpoint training began with classes on organizing and conducting checkpoints. Because of time constraints, we immediately moved to setting checkpoints in training scenarios in the ANA motor pool. This training focused on checkpoint security. We taught the Afghans to place tanks at the entrances of the checkpoint, put Afghan leaders at key locations, search areas for vehicles and personnel, and establish prisoner-holding areas within the checkpoint perimeter. We built real-world scenarios into this training with rehearsals involving obstinate civilians, weapons-carrying Taliban, drug dealers and any other scenario we could envision the Afghan soldiers encountering at a typical checkpoint.

The necessity of deploying the Afghan soldiers for real-world operations soon took precedence. In September and October of 2003, the ANA tank battalion received orders to begin conducting real-world checkpoints throughout Kabul in support of the country's upcoming constitutional convention and national elections. The US advisors deployed with their Afghan companies as the companies began operations to demonstrate to the citizens of Kabul that the ANA was active, professional, competent and capable of keeping the populace safe.

The checkpoint locations initially focused on avenues of approach into Kabul from all cardinal directions. They involved one company of soldiers securing and operating the checkpoint, two to three tanks for security and a show of force, a battalion scout platoon providing long-range reconnaissance and an Afghan company commander providing command and control for the checkpoint. The Afghans used mirrors for searching vehicles, sandbags for speed bumps to control traffic within the checkpoint and designated teams to search people. The leadership stopped random or suspicious vehicles and had them move to the designated search areas within the checkpoint itself. These checkpoints led to numerous interesting events and scenarios that I will discuss in further detail below.

The logistic aspects of setting a checkpoint were always exciting and dynamic, especially on very busy roads at the exit of mountain passes into Kabul. The pass that opened into Kabul near Pol-e-charki provided special challenges. Even though the checkpoint was near their home compound, the ANA would transport their tanks on large trucks to the checkpoint location to prevent unnecessary mileage on the finicky tanks. Unloading the tanks on one of the busiest roads into Kabul always caused quite a traffic jam of civilian vehicles.

One checkpoint caused special challenges for future advisors to note. The troubles began when half the trucks passed the checkpoint location and began to unload their tanks, while the other trucks began to unload at the desired checkpoint location. The Afghan leadership decided to turn the confused trucks around on a two-lane road and bring them back to the original site – a virtual physical impossibility. This circus of vehicles moving in all directions on a busy road helped the US advisors immeasurably in their quest to convince the Afghan leadership of the value of full rehearsals and reconnaissance of checkpoint locations with all of the key players, including the truck drivers.

One of the first checkpoint locations chosen by the Afghan leadership provides an excellent illustration of the importance of carefully choosing checkpoint sites. After the initial reconnaissance, the ANA leadership picked a spot with the blessing of the US advisors. Upon arriving at the site the next day, we found a Beduin encampment – one that was not there the day before. The ANA leadership decided to simply set up the checkpoint right next to the nomad camp. Thus, the checkpoint had numerous nomad children and camels pass through its boundaries along with the hundreds of

Afghan cars and trucks. The Afghan leadership did not see any problem with the breach of its checkpoint security by these animals and children, but their American advisors had quite a different opinion.

One purpose of these checkpoints around Kabul was to introduce the Afghan Army to the Kabul population. One of the attractive byproducts of the checkpoints, though, was the interdiction of the flourishing drug and weapons trade from Pakistan and other regions of Afghanistan to Kabul. We soon discovered that the Afghan soldiers had a gift for detecting potential drug laden vehicles, and the checkpoints began to discover drugs hidden in creative places. Drug seizures were usually raw opium in amounts that stretched from ten pounds to hundreds of pounds.

We learned a valuable lesson about the intelligence of the drug traffickers after a seizure of over 50 pounds of raw opium. The normal Afghan operating procedure at the checkpoints allowed the vehicles of non-governmental organizations (NGOs), as well as Afghan government vehicles, to pass through unhindered. One day the Afghan checkpoint commander stopped an NGO vehicle because the driver attempted to bribe him. The search team discovered drugs and arrested the man. The leaders immediately disseminated this information through the Afghan units, which led to a sister infantry unit discovering over 400 pounds of raw opium in the walls and doors of an ambulance.

The Afghan leadership and American advisors also began to vary the locations and times of their checkpoints. Sometimes, they would set them up late at night or early in the morning. This varying of times and locations produced captures of weapons and drugs. One of the favorite locations of the Afghan leadership was approximately five miles into a mountain pass where vehicles had no chance to see the checkpoint and turn around. This location yielded many seizures of drugs and Afghan criminals.

Taliban hunting

After completing the training of the ANA in basic tactics, maintenance, gunnery and checkpoint operations, the US advisors felt the Afghan leadership had established a foundation that would allow them to successfully provide security during the national elections. The next focus for US advising turned to preparing the armored ANA battalions to deploy to various regions – primarily in the Gardez region and Zormat Valley of Afghanistan. The commando battalion of the ANA was already actively patrolling the Gardez region with two commando companies. The next phase for the ANA consisted of deploying mechanized infantry and armored units to these and other provinces as a demonstration of Karzai's growing ability to project force far from his bastion of strength in Kabul. Our team leader sent a reconnaissance element with the ANA brigade leadership to Gardez and Zormat to observe the deployed commando companies, meet with Mujahadeen commanders and coordinate the logistics necessary to support the troops and tanks. This reconnaissance mission proved successful and allowed the US advisors to meet with the Special Forces A Team whose members knew the region and the key Afghan figures that we would need to work with on logistics, intelligence and security.

During this mission in October 2003, our recon team, along with the two Afghan commando companies, experienced a 107 mm rocket attack the Taliban and other disgruntled insurgents favor, and were able to see the Air Force F-16s do their work, along with the Afghan mortars. I was especially impressed with the speed and precision of the ANA commandos, who launched accurate mortar fire at registered targets in less than two minutes from the time of the surprise rocket attack.

After returning to Kabul from Gardez, the US advisors shifted focus to an undercover mission of capturing a Taliban insurgent leader who was believed to have recently ambushed a team of American advisors returning from a weapons range. This mission involved a company of Afghan mechanized infantry and a company of Afghan tankers that had trained together numerous times in combined checkpoint missions. This mission involved setting a checkpoint at a key location and intercepting the insurgent as he traveled to a meeting with friends. The ANA soldiers rehearsed seizing the individual and transporting him to a secure location. They were excited to have an actual mission against their hated enemy and conducted the mission professionally with little guidance from their American advisors.

After waiting for three to four hours for the guerrilla leader to pass through the checkpoint, we concluded that our intelligence for his movements was inaccurate and scrubbed the operation. The clean preparation and execution of the mission, though, proved to the US advisors that the ANA tank and mechanized infantry battalions were prepared to plan, rehearse and conduct combat operations with little US advisor guidance.

In November 2003, the Muslim month of Ramadan began, which limited our training with the ANA. We also found out that the Loya Jirga Constitutional Convention was moved to a future date. Thus, we shifted our focus to turning over our mission to the 45th National Guard Unit out of Texas. We spent days introducing our replacements to the ANA leadership and briefing them on the intricacies of the state of the ANA's training. We also shared our vision for the future role of advisors with the ANA. They were very professional and took over our mission with no difficulties.

We redeployed to the US at the beginning of December 2003. The team lost no soldiers and returned with all of its equipment. We learned a great deal during our time with the ANA, much of which is useful to future trainers of foreign armies who want to learn from our mistakes, as well as our successes.

Lessons learned

Funding

The most substantial hurdle that the US advisors encountered at the small unit level was funding. Funding from the US government was substantial. By February 2004, Congress had spent $500 million on the ANA and police force training.[2] Using this money, the US forces did an amazing job of helping establish a basic training program for the ANA. This money also built new, modern barracks and facilities for the ANA soldiers. The real issue for the advisors was acquiring funds to deal with the numerous operational matters that arose daily. The most important of these issues brought training to a standstill and are discussed below. Also, many of these funding issues would not have been serious if not for the short amount of time, approximately five to six months, that the ANA had to train its soldiers.

First, maintenance of the T-62 tanks was the most difficult hurdle for the US advisors and the ANA in building a viable national military. The T-62 tanks that the warlords donated were dilapidated when they arrived on trucks at the ANA compound. It was not unusual for the trucks to back-up, then stop abruptly so that the tanks would slide off the back of the trucks.

When the US advisors arrived, four of the 44 tanks in the battalion were operational but none of them were ready to fire their main gun. The warlords had donated equipment, over half of which was missing important components for the fire control systems of the main gun or for the engine. The ANA also lacked the mechanics and parts necessary to fix the maintenance problems. This lack of resources became especially troublesome because there were no funds allocated to the advisors at the small unit level to attack this problem. The US advisor leadership informed its higher command that the mission might fail if they could not get past these barriers, and the US leadership eventually worked out a system to provide money to a designated US advisor for purchasing parts and equipment for daily military operations. The delay of this money cost the ANA precious weeks for mechanics to begin fixing the tanks.

This method of designating a US advisor to handle the funds fixed the problem but exerted extreme stress on this individual because he was forced to handle all the requests for equipment and money for the entire brigade. He did not have a staff, which forced him to monitor all of the transactions and administrative paperwork. I would recommend having a staff for this budget officer so he could focus on managing the various projects needing funding.

The lack of experienced mechanics was the other great obstacle. The ANA had large numbers of soldiers designated as mechanics, but few of them had any experience with tanks. Thus, the ANA tank battalion was dependent upon five Mujahadeen mechanics. These men, though, were not paid by the ANA and thus had no motivation to fix the tanks, let alone work long hours.

The US advisors overcame this problem in a two-fold way. First, they focused on building relationships with the colonel in charge of the Mujahadeen maintenance company. We initially had no resources to pay him but found that by building a friendship with him he was willing to help us fix the tanks. In other words, rather than telling him to help us, we asked him for help.

It always amazed the US advisors how parts would appear and tanks would miraculously be fixed by this Afghan Colonel's men who were not even in the ANA. Once we received funds, we were able to pay the colonel for the parts that he acquired. Because we had no supply chain for parts for T-62 tanks, all parts came through him. Thus, it was important to maintain the personal relationship with him to keep the tanks running.

Our second method for fixing the mechanic problem was to assist the ANA commanders in building a training program. This program allowed the ANA mechanics to shadow the experienced Mujahadeen mechanics and learn more in-depth the maintenance issues of the T-62 engine and fire control system. The ANA mechanics were able to observe depot-level maintenance tasks, begin helping the experienced mechanics and then perform the tasks themselves with supervision from these experienced mechanics. This mechanic training plan began to reap benefits by the time we redeployed to the US. The unseasoned ANA mechanics were beginning to fix the simpler mechanical problems themselves rather than relying totally on the non-ANA mechanics.

Building relationships

As discussed above, relationships played a pivotal role in producing success as an advisor in Afghanistan. I would even assert that building positive relationships with an Afghan counterpart is the most important variable for success as a military advisor. My NCO counterpart came to the same conclusion and demonstrated it to perfection. We would spend countless hours with our Afghan commanders, drinking tea, swapping stories, telling jokes and learning about each other's lives. This time spent in non-business discussions proved invaluable in building rapport.

The Afghan culture is a very relational culture where many of the agreements between people are based upon relationships. As an advisor, I learned over time that the Afghan commanders respected the opinion of the US advisors but would do whatever they thought was best for their unit. We could tell them to do something, and they would nod and agree to do whatever we asked out of politeness and then would still do what they wanted. Thus, we had to *convince* them that what we were asking was in their best interest without any authority to make them do what we asked. After they figured out that we had very little control over the purse strings, we lost the majority of our leverage to force them to do what we asked. This lack of leverage forced us to rely even more heavily on building relationships.

We built these relationships with our commanders primarily by building mutual respect. They did not respond well to yelling. Thus, we did not do a lot of yelling. They responded to strength and competence; so we showed them that we knew what we were talking about in regard to their training and kept ourselves in shape physically. Since they responded extremely well to humor we kept the attitude light and laughed at every opportunity. This fun attitude was not difficult because they were a fun-loving people who were truly a pleasure to be around. Based on my experience with the Afghan people, I recommend that anyone advising them to not take themselves too seriously and schedule time for socializing without talking business. Focusing on building a friendship with the Afghan counterpart paid back ten-fold when an advisor was forced to ask the ANA commanders to do something they did not want to do.

Corruption

As the US advisors worked through funding issues and focused on building relationships, we also learned a great deal about the problem of corruption in Afghanistan. The bulk of the corruption I witnessed was due to the drug trade. Many of the Afghan leaders, whether warlords or government officials, funded their operations through the opium trade. The clash of the new Afghan government with the drug trade proved discouraging for our advising team. It especially became discouraging when we learned the ANA generals were tied to illegal activities.

The biggest drug seizure by the ANA during my deployment came after we determined that NGO and official vehicles such as ambulances were carrying drugs through ANA checkpoints. This seizure by a sister Afghan unit yielded over 400 pounds of raw opium found in the walls of an ambulance. The normal operating procedure following a drug seizure was to invite the Afghan press to report on the success of the new ANA army in improving security for the Afghan people. The ANA leadership would then burn the opium so that it would not have a chance to filter back into society.

After this seizure of 400 pounds of raw opium, the ANA battalion commander discovered a black book with phone numbers among the drugs and began to call each number to collect intelligence on the drug dealer's contacts. One of the calls he placed was answered by what was thought to be a ranking official in the Afghan Ministry of Counternarcotics. This official offered the ANA commander $100,000 to return his drugs. The Afghan commander refused, but the news of this bribe was highly discouraging. The question that crossed my mind was, 'Were we making any difference in this country that has such rampant corruption ingrained in the tribes and new government?' After investing our hearts and souls into helping the ANA become a viable force, at the time we were disheartened to think that all of our work might be for naught.

I am convinced that advisors participating in nation-building missions throughout the world will tend to experience corruption in all levels of the government they are attempting to help. This corruption is not something that should discourage advisors. Nation-building needs to begin at some point and US advisors, military and government civilians, are an effective catalyst of positive change in a nation. This was driven home to me later. During a checkpoint mission in a mountain pass on the outskirts of Kabul in September 2003, Captain Mohammed Shafeeq restored my hope in the mission of helping the ANA become a legitimate force in Afghanistan's nation-building efforts. During this operation, I saw his soldiers direct a United Nations vehicle into the search area of the checkpoint, which caught my attention because we had not been pulling over official vehicles. They immediately began a thorough search of the vehicle and discovered approximately 50 pounds of raw opium in a spare tire.

What I had not seen during this search was the one-on-one exchange a few minutes earlier between Captain Shafeeq and the driver of the car. Apparently, the driver had offered Captain Shafeeq over $2,000 in cash to pass through the checkpoint unsearched. Captain Shafeeq refused and directed the man into the checkpoint, where the soldiers discovered the drugs.

This $2,000 bribe was equivalent to approximately two years wages as an Afghan company commander, and none of his soldiers would have even known about the exchange. Plus, he knew the man would likely be released within the week and continue smuggling drugs. I asked him why he had not taken the money and allowed the man to pass through the checkpoint. Shafeeq's answer stunned me and gave me hope for the mission we were conducting, as well as hope for the recovery of Afghanistan as a nation. He told me that 'our recovery needs to begin somewhere. I am tired of fighting and want our nation to have peace. I am tired. If I don't start the change, then who will?'

Corruption is rampant throughout Afghanistan but not all-encompassing. There are pockets of resistance that want to see change. Captain Shafeeq's reaction to this bribe revived my hopes and reenergized my efforts in advising the ANA.

Culture

One of the valuable experiences of embedding as an advisor in a different country is the chance to learn the culture through immersion. My experiences with the Afghan soldiers taught me numerous cultural lessons. The first and toughest cultural issue was the Afghan interpretation of time, both to general timeliness and time dedicated to mission preparation. The leaders I worked with did not have the same sense of urgency as the US advisors in regard to meetings, formations and mission start times. They did not see the same need for having all the personnel and equipment prepared to execute a mission.

Many times during my initial months of advising, I found myself arriving for a mission minutes before the agreed upon start time and finding no tanks or Afghan soldiers even close to being ready to deploy. This cultural difference created tension between the US advisors and the Afghan leadership because the Americans often coordinated with other multinational units participating in a mission or training event and were responsible for ensuring the Afghans were at the link-up points. Because we did not have command authority, we could not force the Afghans to be on time, which led to professional embarrassment at times. I found myself having numerous talks with my Afghan counterparts, attempting to convince them of the necessity of timeliness. As we built stronger relationships with them, and also became more adamant about abiding by schedules, I saw a marked improvement in the ANA's punctuality. I also discovered that at appropriate times, it worked to be more animated and raise my voice to motivate the Afghan leadership.

Another cultural difference that I experienced was the use of the phrase 'Enshallah,' which means 'god-willing.' This phrase caused consternation and tension among the US advisors numerous times. The Afghan commanders I worked with used this phrase often when planning missions. If I asked probing questions about possible deficiencies in mission planning, I would often hear the phrase 'Enshallah' from the leaders. For example, during preparation for a checkpoint mission, I would ask the Afghan leadership if they were prepared to deal with prisoners or casualties. Sometimes, they would respond with 'Enshallah.' This answer frustrated the US advisors because we did not know if they had a plan or were simply planning to address all of the issues as they encountered them on the mission.

The Afghan leaders also liked to use this phrase when discussing safety precautions. This seeming disregard for safety frustrated the US advisors because we were trained to prevent accidents by identifying safety risks ahead of time, and then designing plans to mitigate the risks. It is very likely that these Afghan leaders were considering this answer humble and pious, but the advisors had to learn how to deal with this attitude when it appeared to discourage proper mission planning.

The Afghan soldiers used the phrase 'Enshallah' on the firing range. It took the advisors a while to understand why numerous Afghan soldiers were having a difficult time hitting targets when attempting to qualify with their AK-47 assault rifles. Some of the experienced US NCOs determined that soldiers were closing their eyes or not aiming their weapons using the sights. When questioned why they were doing this, the soldiers claimed 'Enshallah,' meaning they believed that they would hit the target if God wanted them to hit the target. This mindset frustrated the US NCOs, who had to adapt their training to account for this response.

My recommendation for dealing with the use of this phrase by an Afghan counterpart is to discuss it frankly and with respect. I became openly agitated with my Afghan counterpart after hearing this phrase for a few months and finally told him never to use it around me again when discussing training or missions. This approach fixed the problem but is not recommended. The only reason I felt the liberty to approach this issue aggressively was because I had a very strong relationship with him. We both had earned the other's trust. He knew I was not attacking his faith, and I made sure to highlight my respect for his beliefs and culture. Even so, I do not know if this approach negatively affected our working relationship. The Afghans take their religious beliefs very seriously and do not take kindly to perceived attacks against their faith. Thus, the brusk approach may not be the best approach for an advisor to employ.

Another key aspect of Afghan culture that our US advising team paid particular attention to was the holy month of Ramadan. During this month, the Afghans do not eat, drink or smoke throughout the daylight hours. They also focused more on prayer and their Islamic faith than other times. The Ramadan observances impacted advisors by influencing the Afghan training schedules. The Afghans only worked half a day during this month due to the food and water constraints. It also limited the type of training they could conduct for the same reasons. For the advisors, it turned into a time of catching-up on all the administration and planning that we pushed aside due to the high operational tempo of the previous months.

Based on our team's experience, I would not recommend that advisors plan on conducting valuable training events during this month unless the chain-of-command decides to suspend some of the restrictions with the blessing of a Mullah. Be careful about planning demanding physical work or road marches that require heavy hydration. Also, be careful about the complexity of tasks during training because the soldiers tend to be very tired and have short attention spans due to the change in their diets, their nicotine consumption and sleep habits.

Another important lesson learned was the importance to the Afghan soldiers of tribal connections. The Afghan government did its best to have a representative army consisting of both Tajik and Pashtu soldiers. This attempt to balance ethnicities in the army was successful, and there was a fairly representative ethnic mix in the Afghan armor battalion during my time in the country. Advisors need to understand the importance of these ethnic ties. Tribal ties span hundreds, and even thousands of years, and are far more important than any month and year-long connection to a new national army. I recommend not discounting tribal connections.

As I discovered in the ANA armor battalion, these tribal connections are not always steadfast. Five months into our deployment, I learned that the company commander I was working with had actually fought against one of the other battalion company commanders during the recent war against the Taliban. My Afghan counterpart had led a company of tanks for Massoud's Northern Alliance, while the other commander had commanded a Taliban tank company. These two commanders had fought each other in a pitched battle where both were attempting to kill the other. They had not succeeded and actually laughed about the situation when I asked them about it. It amazed me that they could be in mortal combat against one another in the past and fast friends now.

The lesson I learned from their experience was that there are many events from the past that advisors are not aware of that influence the decisions that each of the Afghan leaders make. I did not spend enough time with the Afghan leaders to know if their memories were short or long, but history suggests that past betrayals do not die easily in Afghan culture. Beware of the past lives of the Afghan leaders you are advising. There will likely be much below the surface that is not apparent. Most likely, though, loyalties will tend to fall to the tribe that the Afghan soldier was part of before joining the ANA.

Nevertheless, the differing ethnic groups in the ANA contributed to a much richer and more competent fighting force. Not only was the Army representative of Afghanistan, but this integration planted seeds of friendship that spanned the tribal lines. I did not see cliques forming among the soldiers along tribal lines. Rather, the soldiers were learning about each other and building lasting relationships with mutual trust. I would encourage all advisors to foster this integration of various ethnic groups by working with the Afghan commanders at setting a healthy command climate for all soldiers within the unit.

Conclusion

There are hundreds of lessons learned from my short six-month deployment with the ANA 3rd Armored Battalion, 3rd Brigade of the Afghan Central Corps. The most important and encompassing lesson I learned in Afghanistan was the role that the US advisors played in the overall nation-building strategy in Afghanistan. The chance to institute positive change is available to any hard-working and open-minded advisor.

Military advising is a necessary tool of nation-building in Afghanistan. By August 2004, Karzai had deployed the ANA to remote parts of Afghanistan to fight Taliban insurgents and maintain peace between warring factions.[3] Rather than the US military having to fight these insurgents by itself, the ANA had begun to take over the mission of defending its own country.

The US advisors were pivotal to the speed of the ANA learning curve and the ANA's success in combat. My personal experience as an advisor in Afghanistan with the ANA was a small part of the overall US strategy of fighting the war on terror. This experience demonstrated to me that a few individuals in advisor roles who are motivated and focused can make a measurable difference in the lives of soldiers in another country and also in the implementation of national strategy.

I have been focused on making a positive difference in this world throughout my career. Embedding in another culture to work with the

ANA has been one of the most challenging and rewarding experiences of my military career because of the chance to participate firsthand in helping a nation on its road to recovery.

Notes

1 The views expressed herein are those of the author and do not purport to reflect the position of the United States Military Academy, the Department of the Army, or the Department of Defense.
2 'By February 2004, US$500 million spent on ANA and police force training,' www.globalsecurity.org/military/world/afghanistan/army.htm, 30 September 2005, p. 3.
3 In July 2003, six ANA companies, approximately 1,000 soldiers, deployed as part of a US-led coalition called Operation Warrior Sweep near the Zormat District. By August 2004, ANA forces were deployed throughout Afghanistan. Three battalions, 1,500 soldiers, were deployed near Herat to 'intervene between warring parties and start policing the region.' These forces contributed to a ceasefire between the warring parties, including Ismail Khan's forces. See www.globalsecurity.org/military/world/afghanistan/army.htm, 30 September 2005, pp. 3–4.

12 The evolution of combined USMC/Iraqi army operations

A company commander's perspective, Fallujah, Iraq, September 2005 to April 2006

William H. Grube[1]

I deployed to Fallujah, Iraq, in early September 2005 as part of the advance party for the Second Battalion (Bn) of the Sixth Marine Regiment (2/6). I was fortunate to have an outstanding Company Gunnery Sergeant, as well as an extremely capable Staff Sergeant whom I designated my company "intel chief." Based on my experience leading a task-organized unit in Afghanistan, I made some changes to the structure of my company in order to facilitate conducting counterinsurgency operations (COIN). Fighting a counterinsurgency requires different capabilities and force structure than is available in the traditional rifle company configuration; all the rifle companies of the Bn changed from a three rifle platoon, one weapons platoon organization, to a four-platoon structure with roughly equal capabilities (now with organic machinegun and assault assets) and manning. This change was essential due to the continuous nature of operations and the necessity of having a general-purpose force to fit the rotation of taskings ranging from security/force protection to raids and combat patrols. The Bn augmented the companies with enough corpsmen to detail two corpsmen to each platoon – this better supported the tempo of operations and was, literally, a lifesaver on a number of occasions. Finally, the headquarters element was augmented with additional personnel.

Considering the situation in Fallujah and the restrictions on the employment of some weapons systems, I decided to make my mortar section into a company intelligence cell. When I first arrived, I planned to keep the mortarmen/Intel Cell Marines under central control to support tasking for fire support in extremis. However, as my understanding of the situation on the ground evolved, I decided that the mortarmen could be better used in the Intel Cell, for which I permanently selected two, while the rest I allotted to the platoons for duty as riflemen. I used the Intel Cell to collate, organize, and analyze intelligence under the supervision of the staff sergeant – within my guidance. They also fulfilled the role of an organic site-exploitation team in the event of the capture of enemy personnel or equipment. Finally, they fulfilled the role of maintaining a chain of custody on equipment and information and liaised with the Bn analysts via normal reporting procedures and "analyst" to analyst meetings. Overall, this system facilitated better intelligence both up and down the chain of command.

Bn also augmented the Company with additional Motor Transport Marines and Engineers, along with the appropriate assets. I maintained these assets under the command of my Company Gunnery Sergeant in general support of the company. These assets were essential due to the broad spectrum of capabilities (mobility, logistics, force protection, cache detection and exploitation, etc.) necessary to conduct operations in support of COIN.

I was also lucky enough to conduct a Relief in Place (RIP) with another Captain whom I had gone to college with and lived with as a Lieutenant when we were both stationed at Camp Lejuene. The advance party's mission was to orient ourselves to the particular situation on the ground, complete the operations order by filling in the remaining gaps in the plan, and facilitate the transition between USMC forces assigned to the Northeast sector of Fallujah. As a subset of this advance party mission, my friend introduced me to the Military Transition Team (MiTT), are also known as a Military Training Team.[2] The MiTTs I interacted with initially were all US army personnel, although there was an active USMC MiTT assigned to an IA Bn in northwest Fallujah, and the IA Bn I was paired with was later augmented with some Marines from our Bn.

From the outset, the situation was unusual. My Bn Commander assigned me as the operational commander of the whole sector. Regiment, in September 2005, divided Fallujah in half – with 2/6 responsible for the Northern half and 2/7 responsible for the Southern. Our Bn further subdivided its area of responsibility roughly in half, with my company responsible for the Northeast quarter of the city and operations with an Iraqi Bn. The sector's IA Bn, as well as the US army forces, fell under my authority (operational control). This created the strange circumstance of a USMC Captain exerting authority over an Army MiTT (with a lieutenant colonel and two majors) and an IA Bn (with a colonel and various other officers). Fortunately, my predecessor and his Bn Commander had set the precedence for the chain of command, so the assumption of this authority was not difficult.

To say that I controlled the IA Bn would overstate my role. I exerted more of an executive authority, where my company's operations center became the higher headquarters for reporting and patrol coordination. The MiTT operations officer, the IA Bn operations officer and I coordinated USMC Company to IA Company/Bn operations. We would follow up the initial planning with a confirmation brief where the commanders would agree to the final plan. While I could wield what was effectively an executive veto on operations or certain aspects of them, I sought to find ways to subtly suggest that some tactics or ideas might be better than others in order to prevent a loss of face for the IA officers. The MiTT operations officer and I developed a congenial relationship, thus avoiding potential conflicts. We also discussed operations prior to planning in order to provide a unified front and avoid niggling tactical debates, while trying to develop the IA officers' operational skills. The MiTT commanding officer concerned himself with MiTT-specific tasks, such as development of the Iraqi staff and the staff planning process, while designating others to develop and train the IA Bn on individual and small-unit tactics, techniques, and procedures.

Before my company arrived, I conducted several combined operations with the IA Bn and my friend's company. I participated in the planning process, made my initial contacts with the key officers (the Commanding Officer, the Executive Officer, the Operations Officer, the Assistant Operations Officer, and the Company Commanders) and began to develop relationships. From this initial experience and conversations with other commanders, I began to develop a more refined view of the enemy situation in Fallujah.

An evaluation of the situation in Fallujah

Any discussion of Iraq should start with an evaluation of the situation in terms of the enemy (who is doing what to whom). There seems to be much confusion amongst the media, pundits, and Washingtonians about the complex situation in Iraq; there seems to be a tendency toward a dangerous simplification of the situation or toward presentation of the circumstances as monolithic or uniform throughout the country. From this confusion come multifarious policies – ranging from scorched earth to withdrawal – some addressing one element of the problem, some two elements, some none. These policies have effects at all levels within Iraq, from the strategic to the tactical, impacting the military's ability to achieve national objectives. Chart 12.1 attempts to define the destabilizing elements operating in Iraq, outlining these different elements in general terms in order to present an accurate but facile representation of the situation. It is not necessarily to scale.

First and foremost, the enemy is not monolithic; the enemy is divided into different, sometimes competing, cells. Second, I have avoided using the term "terrorist" to name any one of the groups as they all employ at least some of the tactics that terrorists typically use. Instead, I grouped them according to their motivations and objectives. The different enemy groupings all use cell structures, but there are potential linkages between the groups. In other words, there are cells that fall purely within one grouping (such as a cell that sees itself as patriotically repelling the Americans), while another cell may be ideologically sympathetic to two of the groups (such as a Sunni cell in Al Anbar province that opposes both the Shia and the Americans but has no design past Iraq), and yet a third cell might meet at the intersection of all three (a Sunni cell that opposes the Shia and Americans but also supports a global jihad – or Al Qaeda, specifically). Obviously, there are a number of permutations for the alignments of various cells.

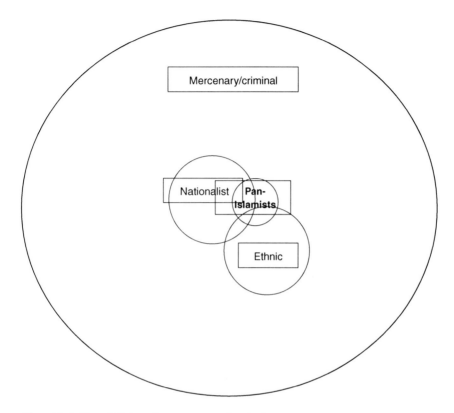

Chart 12.1 Destabilizing elements operating in Iraq.

The Mercenary/Criminal element serves as the substrate of non-ideological Iraqis from which various groups draw support for operations. These Iraqis, who either by circumstance (poverty) or by inclination (criminal predilection), perform tasks for profit as directed by various cells. Examples of some of their activities that support the other enemy elements include burying and/or detonating IEDs, drive by attacks, kidnapping for ransom, assassination/intimidation, and smuggling. The kidnapping of journalists, contractors, and the relatives of rich or influential Iraqis has turned into a warped business venture for this group. Confusing the situation further, they also engage in undirected criminal activity for their own profit, an activity made easier by the absence of proper civil authority in the form of the police.

The Nationalists fight the foreign "occupiers" and the Iraqis who assist the "occupiers" simply because the US forces are there and it is their country. This group is more akin to the classic insurgent/guerilla model. They focus primarily on US forces, although they will also attack the Iraqi army. Examples of some of the activities that this group engages in or sponsors include small-arms attacks (simple or complex), mortar attacks (for those with military training), IED attacks, sniping (for those who are highly trained), and the assassination or intimidation of those they see as collaborators. This group usually strikes military targets while generally eschewing suicide attacks.

The Ethnic grouping is intended to designate the groups involved in internecine violence. While this could be imperfectly described as sectarian violence, there are also relevant ties to the underlying extended family/tribal structures in Iraq, adding an important ethnic element to the conflict.[3] This rivalry generates the internal civil war dynamic within Iraq. These groups hate and fight each other because of historical memory or myth, real or perceived injustices, and a sense of "otherness" (the visceral reasons that bring people into conflict, globally). This group uses most of the tactics of the Nationalists, while adding extermination and execution, but focuses on attacking different Iraqi groups, and not necessarily combatants.

The Pan-Islamists are the Iraqi and foreign terrorists who operate in Iraq in support of Jihad. Their missions are to fight the infidels and those who aid and abet them, establish a Pan-Islamic caliphate, and prosecute the wider Jihad against the United States (thinking globally but acting locally). Al Qaeda, or Iran's Revolutionary Guard, *et al.*, support the two opposing sects, Sunni and Shia, respectively. While these groups bring the "War on Terror" dynamic to Iraq, they also bring an element of proxy war to Iraq, with various external actors, including nation-state proxies, struggling for influence or control. This element uses the most brutal tactics, including all of the tactics of the above groups, but also including suicide attacks. The purpose of their tactics is to break the will of the American decision makers in Washington by creating terror, mayhem, death, and destruction that disrupts US efforts to facilitate the transition of control of Iraq to competent Iraqi civil authorities. Casualties are a means of attacking the will of America to persevere and maintain its support for the effort in Iraq. Of all the groups, this element tends to have the most highly trained personnel and individuals who possess fervent dedication to their mission. They also tend to execute the most sophisticated, well-coordinated, and largest (in terms of casualties) operations.

While this assessment comes from a snapshot in time from my experience in Al Anbar province from September 2005 to September 2006, I believe that this enemy situation can be generalized in order to characterize the situation across Iraq. For instance, while some of the Sunni in Fallujah formed an ethnic cell to operate against the predominantly Shia military (we captured one such cell and attacks against the Shia army units dropped off immediately), the Shia militia in Baghdad formed a parallel group to intimidate and exterminate the Sunni there. Also in Fallujah, my company, along with the Iraqi army, captured several nationalist/terrorist fusion cells. These sorts of cells (with differing alignments) propagated across the country.

Considering this framework, the debate on whether Iraq was in a Civil War or not was, at best, merely academic.[4] It was and it was not, depending on which element one observed, and what level of the conflict was being analyzed. All at the same time, the conflict in Iraq *was* a civil war, *and* an insurgency, *and* the War on Terror, *and* a war on crime and uncivil behavior. All of this occured while the new Iraqi state was attempting to provide stability and establish itself.

This analysis produces both tactical and operational implications. Knowing the prominent cells that operate in one's area of responsibility allows a commander to assess enemy capabilities, tactics, most likely course of action, and most dangerous course of action. This assessment allows a commander to tailor his force protection (always trying to improve it to the highest level), and the tactics one uses to execute patrols and other operations to eliminate cells. Further, a commander then can allocate appropriate intelligence and operational assets to neutralize the cells, depending on its membership and goals.

At the operational and strategic levels, an assessment of the enemy can assist operational planners in allocating resources to identify, locate, and neutralize the enemy. Understanding the civil power structure and the demographic interests of a particular area of operation allows the commander to broker deals and "alliances" through local engagement and, at a higher level, elections. This power sharing can have the effect of splitting off the politically pragmatic wings of the nationalist and ethnic cells (and their supporters), thereby allowing American and Iraqi forces to isolate and neutralize the remaining radical elements, to include the pan-Islamists. From my experience in Fallujah, following the constitutional referendum and the general elections, there was a significant shift in support within the predominantly Sunni population from the insurgents to the Coalition forces. This allowed the coalition to capitalize on the split in order to neutralize the radical elements and the pan-Islamists in Al Anbar province, in a continuing effort.

While the situation in Iraq is arguably the most complex in which the US military has ever been involved, the non-monolithic nature of the situation allows smart operational planners to exploit gaps to divide and stabilize, although this will take time, will, and discipline.

Operations in the field with the Iraqi army

Our first operation was a nighttime raid to capture some high value individuals. The USMC element moved to its positions and waited to link-up with the IA Company. The IA Company moved up the street to the link-up point, with the element's leader not wearing his blouse because it was hot that night (this made an interesting first impression on me). The operation proceeded with what I came to term the usual "whack-a-mole" approach. The "whack-a-mole" approach comes about due to imperfect intelligence or

imperfect orientation (with the Marines, good maps, and GPS largely elimi-
nates the orientation factor). The imperfect intelligence on the exact location
of the target, along with the propensity of targets to move and stay with any
of numerous relatives in the city (due to a quasi-tribal extended family
structure), impels the raiding force to conduct multiple "hits" on various
target houses in one night, following the trail of new intelligence gathered
on site to the next house in an effort to capture the target. As the operation
progresses, the unit tends to lose organization unless it is well trained and
has good command and control procedures. At this juncture in their development, the IA units tended to become disorganized, use poor movement
techniques, and "crowd" into buildings rather than managing sites, or tactically dispersing to secure the area; the IA would improve considerably over
the course of our future operations.

This was all part of the learning process for the Iraqis. The Marines
employed a "train, show, do" variation on the standard "crawl, walk, run"
approach to training. US forces basically trained the Iraqi Bns before entering the battlespace, and then operational American units paired with them
in order to mentor the Iraqis on what "right" looks like. After an evaluation
of Iraqi capabilities by the MiTT and the paired American unit commander,
the Iraqis assumed the main effort's tasks with Marines supporting to
further monitor and mentor. Finally, after another evaluation, the Iraqis
would be cleared for independent operation under their higher headquarters.

The second operation we conducted was a daylight clearing operation
intended to find insurgents or caches. Again, I participated in the planning
and confirmation process as part of my orientation and RIP. The clearing
operation began by putting a USMC cordon on the sub-sector to be cleared.
Once the cordon was set, the USMC and IA clearing elements proceeded to
clear their assigned areas, the movement of the elements being coordinated
with phaselines, a standard military control feature used to by a commander
to monitor, coordinate, and regulate subordinate unit movement and operations. There was some cross-attachment of USMC/IA personnel as the IA
had a significant communications advantage with the local population. The
operation proceeded relatively well as it was more focused on searching than
executing difficult tactics. The IA element found a small weapons cache but,
in their exuberance at the find, failed to maintain the integrity of the site
(we tried to maintain insurgent sites for exploitation for both intelligence
purposes and for crime scene evidence for future Iraqi court prosecutions).
Overall, the operation achieved its basic purposes by clearing the sector,
finding a small cache, and, most importantly, continuing to train the Iraqis
in clearing operations, even though there were challenges in site exploitation
procedures. The IA search element, proud of their performance during the
operation, left the scene after the operation with a bit of pomp, marching in
formation toward the cordon – showing the beginnings of unit *esprit*.

After the rest of my Company arrived, along with the rest of our Bn, the
RIP was completed and I assumed control of the sector. My company occu-

pied a Forward Operating Base (FOB) with a company from the IA Bn, while another IA company and the IA Bn headquarters occupied two separate FOBs. We manned FOB combined security positions, along with three combined Observation Posts (OPs) and a combined Entry Control Point (ECP). This arrangement allowed individual Marines and IA soldiers to work together; in some cases this led to learning and increased proficiency, while in others it led to friction. I was blessed with a capable, professional NCO corps, but over time, they became increasingly displeased with the individual discipline and proficiency of the IA soldiers. Combined disciplinary challenges, instead of being able to be handled at the lowest level (NCO), immediately vaulted to my level. In instances of conflict, I would have to convene a meeting between myself, the MiTTs, and the controlling IA officer in order to address and resolve the issue. At my Bn's level, the Bn Commanding Officer assigned the Bn Gunner the task of providing weapons and tactics training, with a NCO course developed later. This provided a useful augmentation to the MiTT, which lacked the personnel or facilities to do this training while concurrently conducting operations.[5]

My company and the IA Bn operated together for two weeks prior to the October 2005 constitutional referendum. During this time, we conducted at least three clearing operations (taking down one insurgent cell in its entirety) and numerous raids to capture high value individuals. During this short period, the MiTT operations officer and I worked to improve the IA Bn's operational performance and improve the Iraqi officers' ability to plan operations. The Iraqis, at this point, had the ability to plan rudimentary operations but depended on American direction to plan and properly coordinate more complex operations. The MiTT operations officer and I increasingly demanded that more of the plan be completed by the Iraqi officers – with a full confirmation brief on their plan. With my Bn taking the lead on the coordinated planning for election security for the area in and around Fallujah, the IA Bn and my company fleshed out our parts of the operation and executed the plan. The security for elections went extremely well, with the city being essentially free of violence that day.

Between the October constitutional referendum and the December 2005 general election, the improvement of the IA Bn continued. We continued to conduct combined operations and the IA Bn developed more operational experience, more confidence, and a nearly independent planning process. During this period, we switched roles in the raids. For most raids, initially, the USMC element was the assault/support element and the IA was the cordon/security element. We switched roles for most of the raids launched from late October to December; only the most sensitive targets were hit using the old model or USMC personnel, exclusively. This change in roles was essential to the process of developing the operational maturity the IA Bn's needed to become autonomous.

In November 2005, the MiTTs forwarded a key evaluation of the IA Bn up the chain of command. The monthly report, which covered aspects of planning, administration, operations, logistics, and other aspects of military readiness, stated that the IA Bn met the minimum criteria for their being returned to the operational control of their higher headquarters (with oversight from my Bn). I concurred; they were deficient in terms of logistics and administration, but they were operationally capable and met the necessary metrics. IA Bns had been completely under American operational control up to this point. This marked a crucial transition point for the IA in Fallujah.

From the end of November through the beginning of December 2005, the command relationships changed in a complex, phased manner. In some cases, the areas of responsibility and unit relations would change from day to day, or least week to week, as my Bn reassigned areas of responsibility in Fallujah. My FOB changed from the Northeast of the city to the center of the city, the Government Compound, where we conducted a RIP of an adjacent USMC Company from that sector. "My" old IA Bn now became an adjacent unit, rather than a subordinate unit, controlling about two-thirds of our old combined area of responsibility. Meanwhile, I temporarily picked up executive authority (operational control) of another IA Bn and an adjacent unit relationship with a third IA Bn. After two weeks, the IA Bn over which I had newly assumed authority transferred out of Fallujah. During this period, I maintained my relationship with the old IA Bn and developed new working relations with the other IA Bns while conducting combined operations with all three in preparation for the December 2005 general election.

We conducted highly effective surge operations in support of this election. The two adjacent IA Bns both performed well in their own ways during the lead-up to and during the election. Each of the IA Bns had their strengths and weaknesses, with one being better at personal discipline and individual techniques, and the other being better at planning and then synchronizing the broader plan during execution. Both had some shortfalls in administration, logistics, and in some billets, leadership. Again, there was no major violence on the day of the election.

After the December election, we continued to conduct combined operations and maintain very close operational ties although the IA Bns had now assumed adjacent unit status. Both IA Bns maintained the ability to communicate with my Command Operations Center (COC) so that we could provide quick reaction and support if they needed it, and vice versa. Also, the communications facilitated cross unit coordination in the event of an emergency cross-boundary operation. During this time, other elements from my Bn began to operate directly with the IA Bns, notably my Bn's more mobile assets from the Weapons Company. This gave the IA Bns more experience with different tactics, techniques, and capabilities.

From the end of December 2005 until April 2006, the performance and esprit de corps of the IA units continued to develop. The IA Bns faced IED attacks, mortar attacks, small arms ambushes, and episodic snipers. The IA Bns had come far enough with combined operations (after initial training) that they continued to operate effectively without collapsing. Noting their increasing capabilities, my Bn Commander gave the IA Bns more battle-space in accordance with their ability to control it. By the end of my time in Fallujah, the city had changed from an area of operations controlled completely by USMC forces, to a city where IA Bns controlled over 50 percent of the battlespace.

While we continued to work with the IA Bns, by January 2006 we had begun working more closely with the Iraqi Police (IP), attempting to develop them along a similar model to the IA Bns. As of April, this effort was still in the beginning phase with a newly embedded US army Police Transition Team (PiTT, also known as a Police Training Team) who conducted rudimentary combined operations, such as basic patrols and ride-alongs with the IP.

Observations and lessons learned

The combined IA/USMC operations were an essential bridge to enable the IA Bns to become fully functional, mature, combat-ready Bns. Introducing inexperienced, autonomous IA Bns to the battlespace after just their initial formation and training would have been disastrous in the complex environment that exists in Iraq.

The MiTTs, while capable and proficient in terms of skills, do not have sufficient manning to continue large-scale unit training and unit development while simultaneously conducting combat operations and supervision. The assumption of some of the individual and NCO training by my Bn allowed the MiTTs to conduct and supervise operations, while continuing to develop the staff planning process and the leadership in concert with those operations. While my Bn assumed the role of refinement and continuation of training on the troop and NCO level, the MiTT sub-divided itself into an operations/supervision "section" and a staff planning "group." The operational section provided augmented command and control, within their capabilities, and critical liaison with American units. The staff planning group focused on officer development and education on the Military Decision Making Process (MDMP – the Army planning process). Due to manning issues and commitments, my Bn's operations section could not assume this role while continuing to effectively exert command and control over the whole battlespace. This critical division of labor allowed both the MiTTs and my Bn to focus on those roles which each was best able to accomplish. The pairing of IA Bns with American units also provided the additional opportunity for inexperienced IA units to gain operational experience, while preventing IA units from collapsing under pressure. The American units acted as operational role models for the Iraqis and as a key reaction force that provided "stiffening" for IA units under pressure. After the IA Bn gained the ability to act autonomously, the standing relationships and communications between the now adjacent American units provided cement for the gaps between unit boundaries and operations, which are notoriously hard to bridge between multinational task forces.

Culture, as has been noted in many other discourses on counterinsurgency and coalition operations, can be a serious impediment to cross-unit training and operations. Before deployment to Iraq, I sent many of my Marines to language and culture courses at Camp Lejeune. While we had a limited capacity for communications and cultural understanding, there were many misunderstandings associated with small unit combined operations. My NCOs and Marines were frustrated by the "as Allah wills" attitude of many of the IA soldiers. The problem was not with the religion; it was with the fatalism that was instilled by the culture. The IA soldiers manifested this fatalism by not wearing protective equipment or remaining vigilant. Some IA soldiers thought that they would die if they were meant to die, therefore it was unnecessary for them to be overly concerned with onerous force protection measures. In most cases, the IA soldiers would not change their behavior until the IA officers became involved. Over time, the IA officers established norms for equipment and discipline.

Another aspect of the culture was a great reliance on personal relationships. While every culture has this dynamic to a certain extent, this phenomenon was so pervasive that it limited advancement by merit. To an American, it seemed as though the best and most capable junior officers were seen as a threat to senior officers, rather than an asset. Therefore, their commanders either marginalized or transferred these officers and replaced them with sycophants or officers of middling ability. The IA has a very traditional, hierarchical military system that seems to have some residual institutional memory of control (under the Saddam system) rather than command (in the American sense). Over time, and with experience working with US forces, this situation will change as the Iraqi military becomes a professional, modern force.

The IA has no real functional equivalent to American NCOs. IA NCOs currently function as senior troops with limited additional responsibilities and latitude, like in most other militaries in the world. Their lieutenants perform the functions of US NCOs, Staff NCOs, and lieutenants such as detailed inspections, discipline, logistics, planning, and tactical control at all levels, with no concept of micromanagement. With the span of command and control needed in combat, along with the redundancy necessary if the unit takes casualties, NCOs are vital to the success of small units. The MiTTs tried to develop NCOs in conjunction with my Bn's NCO training course, which was intended to develop technical, tactical, and leadership skills. Some of the Iraqi NCOs improved; others could not break from the old model. It may take a generation or more to develop a professional, dynamic NCO corps. This, coupled with the concept of "face," or pride, made it difficult to have the kind of hard-nosed discussions to identify failures and make the appropriate leadership changes to address leadership deficiencies.

Another challenge was continuity of leadership. The IA tends to reassign and move officers frequently between commands for reasons that were not entirely clear to me, with the exception of the marginalization of some officers discussed previously. Also, the IA has a very liberal leave policy with leadership changing at the company level suddenly. The effect was that you did not always plan the combined operation with the same leader who was going to execute it. Obviously, this can lead to coordination problems and disruption of the operation. We overcame this difficulty with confirmation briefs and brief-backs where the "new" commander would explain, in detail, his plan to me to insure that there were no discontinuities in operations or misperceptions as to roles, tasks, and responsibilities. Additionally, the constant shifting of the leadership has a detrimental effect on developing small unit cohesion and Standing Operating Procedures (SOPs).

The administration, manning, and pay of the Iraqi soldiers were substandard. Although the MiTTs engaged this problem at a much higher level than I, the three issues were related. The IA Bns did not properly maintain the lists of their soldiers, half because of poor administration, and half by design. The IA higher headquarters used the lists to show the manning of the Bn for pay, as well as other purposes. The inaccuracies of the lists, along with possible skimming of pay, kept some soldiers from being paid and/or promoted. This chronic lack of pay fed into an already weak manning situation, with some soldiers going on leave and not returning. The result was IA Bns hovering at around 60 percent strength during my tour in Fallujah. The IA Bns had the ability to "surge" manning (by canceling leave) for critical events, such as the elections. The situation did improve marginally toward the end of my tour, but the problem was far from solved.[6]

The MiTTs had a good checklist with measures of effectiveness for their monthly evaluations of the IA Bns. It covered areas like operations, planning, logistics, and so on. This method of evaluation was useful but ultimately had to be weighted by judgment. In other words, it was not necessary for an IA Bn to be fully functional administratively to assume its role in the battlespace as an adjacent unit – those issues could continue to be addressed by the MiTTs after the transition. Getting the IA Bn up and running operationally was my main focus for this portion of my overall counterinsurgency mission.

At the time of my service in Fallujah, the IA Bns had severe shortfalls in equipment and logistics support. The IA had poorly maintained, self-armored Toyota trucks and subjected them to quite a bit of stress from operations. IA Bn maintenance sections lacked sufficient parts and equipment. The IA Bns also had a limited ability to supply and maintain small arms and used captured insurgent caches to supply weapons like AK-47s. By the end of my deployment, the IA seemed to have solved some of its weapons supply problems and was being fielded, through American sources, with High Mobility Multi-Wheeled Vehicles (HMMWVs, also known as Hum-Vs or Hummers).

The IA troops learned to use American tactics but with Iraqi twists. The differences in manning, equipment, and leadership culture generated these differences. For instance, while conducting cache searches, the Iraqis lacked technical equipment, so when operating independently they used different, more rudimentary search techniques until they started getting some technical equipment of their own. Likewise, IA leaders (especially at the lieutenant level) configured operations slightly differently so that they could personally control different aspects of the operation rather than coordinate and command subordinates. The Iraqis became basically proficient in their operations, sometimes doing well, and other times barely clearing the bar. In the final analysis, the IA's role requires them to be marginally better than the insurgents and terrorists. By the time they transitioned to their adjacent roles, they met that criterion. In the future, as combat operations continue, units achieve some cohesion and experience, and junior and mid-level leaders develop, the Iraqi army can be expected to develop into the most capable Middle Eastern military force.

Conclusion

The combined USMC/IA Bn operations greatly enhanced the ability of the MiTTs to accomplish their mission. The combined operations filled an important gap in training and preparation for the IA Bns to assume their own independent areas of operation. The regular forces, supplied by the USMC, and the advisors, supplied by the MiTTs, combined in a synergistic effort, covering one another's capacity shortfalls in order to prepare the whole IA Bn for autonomy. The relationship was not only beneficial, but essential to accomplishing the ultimate transition of Iraq to an Iraqi civil authority with the capacity to insure the rule of law, defend its sovereignty, and deny safe harbor to transnational terrorists.

Notes

1 The views expressed herein are those of the author and do not purport to reflect the position of the United States Marine Corps, the Department of the Navy, or the Department of Defense.
   As with all accounts this close to the actual events, this is my personal assessment of the situation – a snapshot in time, in a particular area – thus, not all of the observations or lessons learned are applicable across the theater, or necessarily applicable for use in other conflicts.
2 For more on USMC MiTTs see Major Jonathan P. Dunne, "Developing Fledgling Iraqi Headquarters: A MiTT Perspective During Operation Iraqi Freedom 5–7," *Marine Corps Gazette*, Vol. 91, No. 3 (2007): 20–1.
3 Sectarian violence is a subset of this group, imperfectly describing the nature of the "civil strife" within Iraq. Viewing the civil dimension of the conflict within Iraq strictly through the lens of religion selectively overlooks violence (or potential violence) between Sunni Kurds and Sunni Arabs or violence perpetrated on or between any of the various other ethnic groups who may share the same religion.

For this reason, I chose family, tribe and ethnicity as being a better predictor of groupings as it relates to civil/disorder and violence.
4 For an evaluation of the issue of whether or not Iraq is in the midst of a civil war see David A. Patten, "Is Iraq in a Civil War?" *Middle East Quarterly* (Summer 2007), www.meforum.org/article/1694.
5 The MiTT was split between two FOBs, both conducting 24/7 operations with no more than 12 individuals each.
6 As an example of this continuing problem, see Pauline Jelenik, "US Officer: Iraqi Police Disappearing," 13 June 2007, http://news.yahoo.com/s/ap/20070613/ap_on_go_ca_st_pe/us_iraq_29.

13 A justified heaping of the blame?

An assessment of privately supplied
security sector training and reform in
Iraq – 2003–2005 and beyond

Christopher Spearin

It is an understatement to say that the rationale for and the effects of the decision made by the administration of President George W. Bush to invade Iraq were controversial. Contentious issues such as the implications of preventative war, the lack of sanctioning provided by the United Nations, the missing weapons of mass destruction, and the justifications for invasion on humanitarian grounds are the focal points for discussion and criticism. One particular issue concerns the unprecedented degree to which private security firms support and backstop the US-led coalition's efforts in Iraq. Because of the estimated tens of thousands of private security personnel in Iraq, and the wide variety of important functions they perform, this substantial private presence has received the label of "the coalition of the billing."[1] In 2003, one of the tasks allotted to private firms such as Vinnell Corporation, DynCorp, and Erinys was the training and reform of Iraq's security sector institutions. This choice received considerable criticism in large part because of the poor showing of privately trained Iraqi security sector personnel as evident in desertion rates and operational performance. While security sector training and reform are very important in the Iraqi context, responsibility for these problems, for the most part, should not rest on the shoulders of private firms. Factors related to the insurgency, a lack of planning by government departments and challenges in terms of funding, supply, and actual capabilities all served to militate against a strong performance of privately trained Iraqi security sector personnel. Nevertheless, longer-term issues pose considerable challenges for firms, the stability of Iraq, the normative development of the security sector institutions, and the array of policy options available to the United States.

Private trainers and their importance in Iraq

The US government gave three private security firms the primary responsibility for executing the regimen for security sector training and reform.

First, in June 2003, the Pentagon awarded Vinnell Corporation, a subsidiary of Northrop Grumman, the US$48 million contract to train the new Iraqi army. This US firm, in business since 1931, has accumulated considerable experience as a defense contractor, from being a supplier of thousands of support personnel during the Vietnam War to training the Saudi Arabian National Guard (a contractual relationship held with the kingdom since the 1970s). With respect to Iraq, Vinnell Corporation was to prepare the new Iraqi army for traditional military tasks, a point emphasized by the one-time US advisor for defense and security in Iraq, Walter Slocombe: "This will be a military, not a security or police force."[2] Under the terms of the contract, Vinnell Corporation was, from 1 July 2003 to 30 June 2004, to train nine 900-troop battalions. As we shall see below, though it was not exercised, the contract contained the option for Vinnell Corporation and its participating subcontractors to be responsible for training all of the new army's projected 27 battalions.[3]

Second, on the internal front, DynCorp, a subsidiary of Computer Sciences Corporation, won the April 2003 State Department contract to train the new Iraqi police force. Though this US-based firm's origins as California Eastern Airways date back to 1946, more recently DynCorp has added policing capabilities to its roster of services. Since the end of the Cold War, DynCorp has received US government contracts to provide police trainers to Afghanistan, the Balkans, East Timor, and Haiti. In the Iraqi case, 1,000 DynCorp personnel are charged with the training, advising, and mentoring of Iraqi police, both on the beat and in academies, in regard to forensics, investigatory techniques, firearms, and human rights. Additionally, a subcontract granted to Science Applications International Corporation involves the training of police recruits at the Jordanian International Police Training Centre, located outside of Amman. The State Department renewed DynCorp's initial one-year contract valued at US$50 million, and given the need to train upward of 135,000 cadets, the total value of the contract may reach into the hundreds of millions of dollars over several years.[4]

Third, unlike the previous two firms, Erinys Iraq, an affiliate of British and South African staffed Erinys International, was a relatively unknown firm when it won the contract to train and manage the guard force that would protect Iraq's oil infrastructure. In the words of Patrick Grayson, because Erinys International itself dates from only 2001, "These are the hero-from zero guys .... They won a huge contract from under the big boys' noses."[5] Erinys' activities fulfilled a considerable part of the mandate of Task Force Shield, the program overseen by the Multi National Force-Iraq on the behalf of Iraq's Oil Ministry to protect 140 oil wells, in addition to refineries and 7,000 kilometers of pipelines.[6] The initial one-year US$40 million contract, launched in August 2003, called for the training and management of 6,500 Iraqis. However, the Coalition Provisional Authority (CPA) modified and extended the contract in order to compensate for insurgent attacks and the sheer enormity of the task. In the end, 15,000 Iraqis and 350 foreign staff were in the field. In addition, to facilitate its expanded presence, in December 2003, Erinys signed a US$10 million lease with the US firm AirScan Incorporated to provide aerial surveillance for upward of two years. By the start of 2005, Erinys' presence declined as the Oil Ministry assumed responsibility for the protection of oil infrastructure and the management of the force.

Even though these three contracts together account for only a fraction of the tens of billions of dollars allotted for the stability and reconstruction of Iraq, their importance should not be underplayed. As asserted by Frederick Barton and Bathsheba Crocker, "[t]he greatest contribution the United States can make to stabilizing Iraq will come in the form of training, supplying, and mentoring Iraq security institutions."[7] One reason for this importance is that the rise of an effective post-Saddam security sector links to the lessening of the US military presence. As simply put by President Bush, "[o]ur strategy can be summed up this way: as the Iraqis stand up, we will stand down".[8] US troop reductions allow the Bush Administration to maintain the credibility of its preventative war posture, made plain in its September 2002 National Security Strategy. By not becoming bogged down in any single country, it allows the United States to deter and threaten other rogue states that might be sympathetic to terrorist causes. Equally, the departure of US troops has domestic political salience, not only in terms of economic costs, but also in light of concerns regarding overstretch and the heavy reliance upon National Guard and Reserve units. Additionally, the significant reduction of the US military presence would lessen the sentiment, held by many within Iraq and elsewhere, that the US military is an occupying force.

As for the Iraqi security sector institutions themselves, much work is required to insure their sufficient operation and sensitivity to human rights norms and good governance. This is important work for the three firms given the linkages between security sector reform, nation-building, and the promotion of democracy, the latter being one of the Bush Administration's goals for Iraq and the Middle East writ-large. In this way, an appropriately functioning security sector not only lessens political intervention, it also helps to forge the links of legitimacy between the state and the citizenry by protecting the citizens from each other and from external threats. In short, the security sector is to "be a force for good."[9] Therefore, in the case of Iraq, the objective is to develop a security sector that eschews the use of secret police in the maintenance of public order and that is more reliable than the regular police and armed forces during Saddam's time. If security is not provided in this way, it potentially leads to instability and the possibility that an authoritarian leader might rise up by promising security, both detriments to democratic structures taking root.[10]

Finally, and in a related way, the importance of the private presence is underscored by the many other goals internal to Iraq that are linked to the effective and appropriate operation of the country's security sector. There are numerous linkages between security and the provision of health care, education, and the sufficient operation of power, water, and communication systems.[11] Similarly, the protection of the oil infrastructure is linked to the employment of thousands of Iraqis, the functioning of the economy, and the filling of government coffers. Hence, it is not surprising that in polls taken of ordinary Iraqis, the provision of security is their number one priority, in terms of both their personal safety and the return to normalcy in their country.[12] In total, as expressed by Larry Diamond, security trumps all:

> Without legitimate, rule-based, and effective government, economic and physical reconstruction will lag and investors will refuse to risk their capital to produce jobs and new wealth. Without demonstrable progress on the economic front, a new government cannot develop or sustain legitimacy, and its effectiveness will quickly wane. Without the development of social capital – in the form of horizontal bonds of trust and cooperation in a (re)emerging civil society – economic development will not proceed with sufficient vigor or variety, and the new system of government will not be properly scrutinized or supported. And without security, everything else grinds to a halt.[13]

This multivariate importance, therefore, makes plain not only the degree to which private firms are a key tool in the US nation-building toolbox, but also the degree to which the future of Iraq seemingly rests upon the successful execution of the contracts held by Vinnell Corporation, DynCorp, and Erinys.

Operational criticism and assessment

Unfortunately, privately trained army and police personnel, for the period under study, had poor showings in their encounters with insurgents. Over half of the first privately trained army battalion deserted. Later, depending upon the locale and the security situation, desertion rates amongst army and police units have sometimes been as high as 80 percent. By August 2004, a great number of "ghosts" populated Iraqi security sector institutions; approximately 30,000 more names were on rosters than could be accounted for.[14] Similarly, because of insurgent-led intimidation campaigns and operational attrition, estimates in late 2004 indicated that Iraqi security sector personnel were dying at a rate greater than that of US military personnel.[15] Because of these problems, commentators and US military officials alike have criticized the decision to outsource the training and reform of Iraq's security sector institutions to private firms. Some note that over the course of one year, almost no progress was recorded, while for others such as John Pike, "[i]t's not that the contractors failed to train the Iraqis. It's that they haven't even attempted it seriously …. Whatever training has been done has been pretty perfunctory."[16]

In particular, the Vinnell Corporation, at least vis-à-vis Erinys and DynCorp, has received the most criticism regarding the lack of operational effectiveness of their charges. Of the three firms, Vinnell Corporation was the only one to not have its contract extended, and the US military largely took over its training program.[17] Many analysts, for instance, noted that the exercise of discipline at army training institutions was deficient; this negatively affected operations. Others asserted that too much emphasis was placed on strategy and tactics rather than on combat skills. Another concern held by critics was that Iraqi army personnel, upon the completion of their training, still lacked basic abilities regarding drill and communications.[18] In contrast, for Erinys, criticism was not as blunt, even though attacks against Iraqi oil infrastructure continued throughout its tenure, because the objectives of Task Force Shield were defensive and the desertion rate of its Iraqi personnel was much lower. For DynCorp, one can argue that criticism has not been as severe regarding the results of its training because there is no other avenue the United States can follow. US military police are too few in number, there is not a national police force or a gendarmerie in the United States upon which to draw, and many traditional US allies possessing such organizations were opposed to Washington's policies toward Iraq.

However, criticism of the private presence, regardless of the firm, is often without a sense of context. Put differently, many factors impacted negatively upon the operational effectiveness of privately trained forces. Vinnell Corporation specifically, and all the firms generally, confronted externally imposed limitations and pressures that severely challenged the optimal implementation of training and reform regimens. First, with respect to Vinnell Corporation, it did make changes to its training program to respond to its critics. It reduced the amount of classroom instruction and increased the number of practical exercises, it brought in more US military personnel, and it utilized Iraqis from the 1st Battalion who had not deserted to impose discipline upon and mentor the recruits in subsequent battalions. But more fundamentally, in light of the growing insurgency, Vinnell Corporation had to respond to the US decision to refocus the army from external defense toward internal duties. Indeed, as was initially requested by the Pentagon, Vinnell Corporation was developing Iraqi forces for one scenario, but they were being applied to a totally different conflict environment almost immediately upon their graduation. This impacted negatively upon operational success, let alone upon consistency in training and reform endeavors.[19] For Don Winter, a vice president of Northrop Grumman, the changing US goals regarding the Iraqi army's role made the training program a "real wild card."[20]

However, this is not to contend that, in principle, the concept of an externally oriented army was ipso facto bad. For instance, Julian Schofield and Micah Zenko assert that in light of Iraq's traditional threats, an adequately equipped and trained Iraqi military would lessen the possibility that it would enter politics and thus hamper the evolution of democratic practices. If external dangers are reduced or deterred, then, so the argument goes, a military is more likely to be content and follow its civilian masters.[21]

But in practice, because the United States did not anticipate or prepare for the possibility of considerable internal upheaval, one that dwarfed external security threats, this speaks to the point that all the private training programs were going to face a steep learning curve and perhaps unreasonable expectations in the short to medium term. Compounding this, the CPA's May 2003 decision to dissolve the Iraqi army and all of the Saddam-era security institutions created a gap for anarchy, criminality, and insurgency that newly trained forces would immediately confront. This disbanding of old forces relates well to pre-invasion assessments made by the likes of the Center for Strategic and International Studies that Washington's rosy expectation was for there to be a quick military victory and a positive political outcome:

> [S]igns of military buildup and humanitarian contingency planning have not been matched by visibly concrete action by the United States … to position civilian and military resources to handle the myriad reconstruction challenges that will be faced in a post-conflict Iraq.[22]

This point was similarly expressed by retired US General Wesley Clark: "When planning finally began that autumn, it was based on the assumption that a US invasion would be welcomed as liberation by most Iraqis."[23] This wishful thinking and the resulting lack of preparedness/anticipation were accentuated by the fact that despite the importance of security sector training and reform outlined above, the three major contracts were signed well after the launching of hostilities in March 2003. As a consequence of this, Lieutenant General Tome Walters, the director of the Defense Security Cooperation Agency, acknowledged that the Defense Department "set a new world speed record at awarding a contract to train and equip a new Iraqi army."[24]

When seen through the lens of security sector training and reform, it is also evident that the conversion of military victory into political accomplishments on the ground was blocked not by the firms, but by under-funding, constricted government resources, or red tape. From one standpoint, army recruits were initially paid a monthly salary of only US$70, an amount described by Walter Slocombe as "a perfectly decent salary for an entry-level job."[25] Though, in the Saddam era, a private would receive only US$2 monthly, high rates of desertion should not have been a surprise given that a monthly wage of at least US$200 equated to "a comfortable middle-class lifestyle" in post-invasion Iraq.[26] In a similar vein, Iraqi police officers at first received only US$129 per month, still well below the line of acceptability. From another standpoint, Defense Department reports released in July 2004 found that of the almost US$3 billion allotted to the Iraqi security sector, only US$220 million had actually been spent. The practical impact of this was that the sector's institutions possessed only 40 percent of their required weapons, less than 33 percent of their required vehicles, and approximately 25 percent of their required communications equipment and body armor.[27] The newly trained forces, therefore, were pressed into immediate action without the necessary weaponry and gear needed to battle well-supplied criminals and insurgents. Overall, they were simply underpaid, poorly resourced, and outgunned.

Finally, the failures of the privately trained forces themselves were inadvertently exaggerated by the reporting done by the CPA, the Pentagon, and others that undervalued the number of Iraqi insurgents and overvalued the numbers of the privately trained security sector personnel. Some US estimates in 2004 suggested that the insurgents numbered as low as 2,000–5,000. Though other estimates placed the insurgency at 50,000, or perhaps even 100,000 strong, the low-balling of insurgent levels conveyed the image that the new Iraqi forces were weak in the face of inferior numbers.[28] Additionally, while stressing the number of security sector personnel trained was perhaps a useful way to suggest progress during a presidential election year, this approach failed to acknowledge that in order to get more Iraqi personnel on the ground faster, the training programs were reduced in time and content. The mandated army training fell to only six weeks, compared to nine weeks of basic training for US recruits, *before* US recruits go on for specialization. The classroom training portion for police recruits was to be 24 weeks, a figure comparable to developed world countries. However, not only was this shortened to eight weeks, an additional 24-week long field training portion was cancelled altogether. As a result, giving emphasis to the quantitative manpower aspects, at the expense of the qualitative components set by US authorities, put the private trainers in a poor light when their trainees did not perform optimally against an underestimated adversary.

Longer-term implications

While considerable attention and criticism have been directed at the operational effects of quickly pressing newly trained Iraqis into service, there are other issues stemming from the private presence that may have challenging consequences, well beyond 2005, for the three firms specifically, private training generally, as well as for Iraq and the United States.

Battling the insurgency and security sector reform

The reputation of these three firms, and of private trainers generally, may suffer as the political and security environment in Iraq continues to unfold. In particular, the speeding up and the cutting of corners may impact negatively upon instilling in the security sector important normative qualities pertaining to human rights, democracy, and the rule of law. Ken Eyre, Jean-

Jacques Blais, and Anthony Anderson contend that maintaining the right balance is a difficult task in a country affected by strife:

> The requirement for states to integrate more fully the broad panoply of intelligence, police, military and other functions in order to combat terrorism will pose problems for burgeoning democracies. There will be serious implications for the world if these states fail to meet the challenge effectively and within the rule of law. Failure could also allow these states to revert to authoritarianism or renewed conflict with serious consequences for regional stability and international security.[29]

Thus, in Iraq, the urgency of immediately combating the insurgency may see the normative aspects ignored in the field and not instilled in the longer term. As one DynCorp employee who advises on human rights commented, "[i]f you infuse them with concepts here, there has to be something ... to sustain it."[30] The current situation in Iraq, however, poses challenges to this sort of sustainment. Because of the lack of context that has accompanied earlier criticisms pertaining to the private presence, if the Iraqi security sector evolves in ways that are harmful to human rights or democracy, it is likely that future disapproval will be leveled at the firms that trained them.

Normative model set by firms

Though firms may be at the mercy of their employers and the shifting security situation on the ground such that normative development is dissipated, it is important to recognize that the individual trainers themselves may not serve as the ideal template. This is a critical point because, as asserted by Alexandre Faite of the International Committee of the Red Cross, "[t]he armed forces of countries like Iraq or Afghanistan that emerge from years of civil war or a bloody dictatorship need to re-learn the basics of a modern, reliable army, and this includes human rights and international humanitarian law."[31] Yet, there is a considerable literature that asserts that more needs to be done to monitor not only the operations of firms, but also their qualifications, manpower, and appreciation of international legal norms.[32] At present, diligence on these latter points rests mostly with the firms. In this regard, after a bombing on 28 January 2004 killed one Erinys trainer and injured another, it was learned that they were previously members of the Koevoet, a South African counterinsurgency organization, notorious for its abuse of human rights, which operated in Namibia during the Apartheid era. One of the trainers, Deon Gouws, had received amnesty from the Truth and Reconciliation Commission for petrol bombing the houses of political activists. While the effects of training conducted by individuals such as these will only become apparent over time, many do argue that it portrays a poor image for the firm and employer alike. In reference to the hiring of apartheid-era operatives, Richard Goldstone, a one-time justice of the

Constitutional Court of South Africa and a United Nations war crimes prosecutor, offers that:

> [t]he mercenaries we're talking about worked for security forces that were synonymous with murder and torture .... My reaction was one of horror that that sort of person is employed in a situation where what should be encouraged is the introduction of democracy. These are not the people who should be employed in this sort of endeavor.[33]

Nevertheless, if more rigorous international or state-level regulation is not forthcoming in the near future, then only firms can heighten their diligence in order to preserve their reputation and that of their employer. Here, DynCorp might offer a template, developed for its Iraq contract, which other firms might follow. The initial decision to hire DynCorp for the Iraqi police contract was met with some concern because of problems encountered in an earlier contract.[34] The State Department hired DynCorp to provide the US personnel for the United Nations administered International Police Task Force in Bosnia. While criticisms existed as to the quality of some of the private personnel, more troublesome were the alleged criminal pursuits in 2000–2001 of a handful of these individuals in activities such as rape and the sex trafficking of women, including minors. In light of these problems, Madeleine Rees, the chief United Nations human rights officer in Sarajevo, simply contends, "DynCorp should never have been awarded the Iraqi police contract."[35]

But in order to dispel concerns regarding the Iraq contract, DynCorp instituted a policy that its employees acknowledge, in writing, the illegality and immorality of prohibited activities such as involvement in prostitution and human trafficking. Furthermore, DynCorp has added to its background checking process improved psychological testing. A DynCorp representative reflected upon the nature of these changes: "If there is any blemish in their work histories, any internal affairs investigations that indicate a problem or any other indication of a problem, the applicants are rejected from the program."[36] Though one has to take DynCorp at its word that appropriate and effective changes have in fact been made to its recruiting process, such an approach, if positively implemented, offers one way for firms to insure directly the quality of their personnel and to instill indirectly the normative content of their training regimens.

Continued training "resiliency"

Since the end of the Cold War, security sector training provided by several US government departments has formed a cornerstone of US engagement abroad. This is manifest in developing relations with former communist states in Eastern Europe and Central Asia, in spreading peacekeeping skills, and in fighting the war on terrorism, let alone in serving as an incentive to cooperate with the United States on other matters.[37] Security sector training has considerable resonance for US policymakers with respect to spreading democracy, promoting good civil–military relations, and enhancing US strategic interests.[38] Moreover, relying upon the private sector to perform this service not only relieves US military personnel of this task so that they can concentrate on other endeavors, it also grants policymakers an added degree of flexibility. This is because outsourcing makes the acceptance of casualties more feasible because the lack of an US uniformed presence usually entails less public exposure and media attention.[39] One can contend that this increased freedom of action contributed to US private security firms training the security sectors of 42 states in the 1990s.

But, in the context of Iraq, the role that contractors play in both backstopping the uniformed presence and representing the US overseas has been publicly highlighted. Personnel from either the three main firms or their subcontractors highlighted here have died in the course of carrying out their duties in Iraq. Contrary to earlier expectations, media from a slain employee's place of origin, and sometimes national media, have covered the deaths. Similarly, US politicians have attended the funerals of these individuals.

Therefore, if the deaths and activities of private security employees now garner media attention and have political salience, then this raises the question of the continued reliance on this form of outsourcing. While they may still spell uniformed personnel, placing firms into dangerous situations may no longer be as easy. One answer might be to rely less upon US civilians and more upon foreigners or firms based in other countries. Already, non-US firms such as Erinys are involved, and the staffs of other firms are not entirely from the United States. A continuation of this trend, however, will potentially negate the development of mutually beneficial public–private relationships between US firms and the US government. For instance, while DynCorp does have some high-profile contracts with foreign clients, state and private alike, approximately 95 percent of its contracts are with US governmental departments and agencies. In light of the shift that has occurred in Iraq, it will be interesting to see how, and to what degree, security sector training is carried out by private firms in the future and how the effects of the possible tradeoffs, now apparent, are mitigated.

The private message

A unique aspect of the Iraq case is that the firms are a key component in the development of new security sector institutions. By contrast, in earlier security sector training and reform operations, the trainers, military and private alike, have generally dealt with forces in being. Because post-conflict, post-dictatorship states are likely to be wracked by tensions and cleavages across ethnic, religious, and political lines, the creation of a state's security sector institutions is going to be a very sensitive undertaking. While the goals are seemingly to insure central control and the delivery of the public good of security, one that is non-excludable, different actors will wish to have a say in the development of these institutions to insure that their interests are protected, if not favored.

Erinys' work in Iraq became the subject of controversy stemming from these sorts of tensions. Analysts and members of the Iraqi National Accord, headed by Ayad Allawi, charged that Erinys had been awarded the contract because several of its key directing and advising personnel were linked to Ahmad Chalabi, leader of the Iraqi National Congress. Another powerful accusation was that Erinys recruited its employees largely from the ranks of the Iraqi Free Forces linked to Mr Chalabi. This raised the specter of a personal force, one that is now responsible for the protection of Iraq's critical oil infrastructure as an Oil Ministry force. Erinys' officials, for their part, offered a spirited defense, and the degree to which any of these accusations is borne out in truth will only be revealed over time.[40] Nevertheless, challenges such as these reveal how firms, unwittingly or not, may become caught in strong intrastate rivalries that may hamper the cause of security sector cohesion and unified direction. If the United States in the future follows the path of preventative war such that regime change and a considerable gutting of the old security sector institutions result, then dissipating the fears and tensions that lead to the politicization and atomization of security sector institutions will come from transparency and an eye toward staffing and elite linkages.

In a different direction, one oriented toward the individual rather than particular groups or actors, US officials will have to be sensitive to the image of a commercially private firm helping to create a public institution. As warned in an editorial in the *International Herald Tribune*, privately supplied training "risks sending the message that loyalty is owed not to one's country, but to whoever gets the contract."[41] Though Erinys' personnel for Task Force Shield eventually became public sector employees, there is the strong possibility that the flow could go in the opposite direction. Already, foreign private security firms, and now many Iraqi firms, are relying upon tens of thousands of Iraqis to perform duties such as site protection. While these forces provide local security that contributes to reconstruction, they are not designed to serve the public good directly and they draw individuals away from public sector employment. Also, security sector personnel, their loyalties not yet solidified, could easily be lured by the possibly better working conditions, opportunities, and money available in the private sector. While, as analysts such as Janice Thomson note, there has always been a shifting of the balance between public and private regarding the management of violence, the situation in Iraq could lend itself to a severe slide toward the private.[42] Therefore, US officials will have to watch how the public/private balance evolves in Iraq and adjust future training regimens accordingly.

Closing remarks

As recognized by James Burk, any number of variables may interfere to inhibit the United States from successfully drawing a state and its citizenry out of violence and fear: "We do not know how to build strong states and a just peace the way we know how to build cars or computers to do brain surgery, or conduct rocket science."[43] Nevertheless, pragmatic, strategic, and moral arguments suggest that there should at least be an attempt to bring about positive change. Moreover, for security expert Robert Mandel, the particular urgency of countering terrorism and the spread of weapons of mass destruction requires a reasoned and open assessment of Washington relying upon non-traditional mechanisms, including non-state actors: "The American government is committed to use every means at its disposal to combat terrorism and so it would be motivated to consider utilizing private help when it felt the benefits deriving from this assistance would outweigh the costs."[44]

In light of thinking such as this, Iraq has served as the laboratory for the unprecedented use, in modern times, of private actors in a conflict environment since the invasion of the country by the US-led coalition. In an effort to draw out the lessons found in the use of firms to train and reform the Iraqi security sector, the focus and criticism have centered on the poor showing and desertion rates of privately trained personnel. This stance, however, ignores the other factors and conditions that contributed to the immediate situation. In other words, there was not a reasoned assessment of the benefits and the costs of relying upon private firms in the then existing context.

But equally so, it is important not to ignore the potential longer-term implications, for firms and states alike, that stem from this case of privately supplied security sector training and reform. Battling an insurgency in the midst of security sector reform mitigates the successful implementation of the latter, perhaps to the detriment of the firms involved. The personnel of firms may not necessarily set the appropriate normative example in the execution of their training and reform responsibilities. Firms may no longer offer the United States, as a primary employer of private training expertise, the same flexibility regarding casualty tolerance. The message sent by utilizing private firms to develop public institutions in the context of societal cleavages and a shifting public/private balance may be problematic at best. In total, this case offers lessons to learn or factors to consider in future endeavors.

What is more, the Iraqi case reveals complexities and controversies that future analysis will have to contend with, both in the context of Iraq and elsewhere. For instance, by ignoring factors of context, criticizing a private firm shifts the spotlight and the onus of responsibility from the employer – the state – to a non-state actor. In other words, this offers substantial political utility. Yet, if firms are increasingly part of the public discourse to the degree that politicians mourn the loss of contracted personnel, then this highlights a shift such that the divide between public and private becomes more blurred. If firms are the face of US policy abroad in their execution of very important foreign and defense policy initiatives, is the relationship now integral, rather than that of the employer and the employed? If so, what responsibilities does this entail for the state to insure the readiness and effectiveness of private actors? This is an important question because, if one follows the words of President Bush, it is likely that future cases will evolve that may emphasize this blurriness and these challenges: "America encourages and expects governments everywhere to help remove the terrorist parasites that threaten their own countries and the peace of the world. If governments need training or resources to meet this commitment, America will help."[45] In light of the many rationales for privatization outlined in this book, "America's help" will increasingly be privatized in the future, but the implications stemming from this decision will continue to evolve.

Notes

1 P.W. Singer, "Outsourcing War," *Foreign Affairs*, Vol. 84, no. 2 (2005): 122.
2 Cited in T. Capaccio, "Pentagon Set to Award Contract to Train New, Smaller Iraq Army," *Bloomberg.com*, 24 June 2003, available at www.bloomberg.com.
3 Vinnell Corporation's subcontractors included Military Professional Resources Incorporated, Science Applications International Corporation, Eagle Group International Incorporated, Omega Training Group, and Worldwide Language Resources Incorporated.
4 "Buildup of Iraqi Security Forces Slowed," *Associated Press*, 31 January 2005, available at www.military.com/NewsContent/0,13319,FL_iraq_013105,00.html?ESRC=eb.nl.
5 Cited in T. Catan and S. Fidler, "The Military Can't Provide Security," *Financial Times*, 29 September 2003, available at http://news.ft.com/s01/servlet/ContentServer?pagename=FT.com/StoryFT/FullStory&c=StoryFT&cid=105948020 2976&p=1012571727126.
6 Under Task Force Shield, some responsibility for the protection of Iraqi oil infrastructure rested with local tribal leaders.
7 F. Barton and B. Crocker, "Progress or Peril? Measuring Iraq's Reconstruction," Post-Conflict Reconstruction Project, Center for Strategic and International Studies, September 2004, p. 79.
8 Cited in A.F. Krepinevich Jr., "How to Win in Iraq," *Foreign Affairs*, Vol. 84, no. 5 (2005): 87.
9 United Kingdom, Department for International Development, "Security Sector Reform and the Management of Defence Expenditure: A Conceptual Framework," Discussion Paper No. 1, Security Sector Reform and Military Expenditure Symposium, London, 15–17 February 2000, p. 3.
10 K. von Hippel, "Back-pedalling in Iraq: Lessons Unlearned," *Conflict, Security & Development*, Vol. 4, no. 1 (2004): 86.
11 F. Barton and B. Crocker, "Progress or Peril? Measuring Iraq's Reconstruction – Iraq Update August-October 2004," Post-Conflict Reconstruction Project, Center for Strategic and International Studies, November 2004.
12 See A.H. Cordesman, "US Policy in Iraq: A 'Realist' Approach to its Challenges

and Opportunities," Center for Strategic and International Studies, 6 August 2004.

13 L. Diamond, "What Went Wrong in Iraq," *Foreign Affairs*, Vol. 83, no. 5 (2004): 37.

14 Cordesman, "US Policy in Iraq," p. 11.

15 "Buildup of Iraqi Security Forces Slowed."

16 Cited in D. Calbreath, "Iraqi Army, Police Force Fall Short on Training," *San Diego Union-Tribune*, 4 July 2004, available at www.signonsandiego.com/union-trib/20040704/news_mz1b4iraqi.html; other examples include the following: M. Boot, "The Iraq War's Outsourcing Snafu," *Los Angeles Times*, 31 March 2005, available at www.latimes.com/news/opinion/commentary/la-oe-boot31mar31,0,4194633.column?coll=la-news-comment-opinions; S. Rosenfeld, "Forget Halliburton", *TomPaine.com*, 17 January 2004, available at www.tompaine.com/feature2.cfm/ID/9781/view/print; J. Krane, "US General: Iraq Police Training a Flop," *Associated Press*, 9 June 2004, available at http://newsmax.com/archives/articles/2004/6/9/213503.shtml.

17 At the time of writing, Vinnell Corporation and many of its subcontractors continued to support the training program, albeit in a less significant way.

18 These criticisms are noted in Calbreath, "Iraqi Army"; A.E. Cha, "Recruits Abandon Iraqi Army," *Washington Post*, 13 December 2003, A1.

19 For instance, Major General Paul Eaton, initially responsible for training and reform, noted that many Iraqi army personnel balked at internal duties given their understanding that the army was to be for external defense. This contributed to the high desertion rate. See Krane, "U.S. General."

20 Cited in G.S. Fein, "Training Iraqi Army Is a 'Wild Card'," *National Defense Magazine*, December 2003, available at www.nationaldefensemagazine.org/issues/2003/Dec/Washington_Pulse.htm.

21 J. Schofield and M. Zenko, "Designing a Secure Iraq: A US Policy Prescription," *Third World Quarterly*, Vol. 25, no. 4 (2004): 677–87.

22 Noted in D. Isenberg, "Apres Saddam, le deluge," *Asia Times*, 28 January 2003, available at http://atimes.com/atimes/Middle_East/EA28Ak02.html.

23 Cited in von Hippel, "Back-pedalling in Iraq," p. 84.

24 Cited in Capaccio, "Pentagon Set to Award Contract."

25 Cited in Catan and Fidler, "The Military Can't Provide Security."

26 Calbreath, "Iraqi Army"; T. Shanker, "US Is Speeding Up Plan for Creating a New Iraqi Army," *New York Times*, 18 September 2003, available at www.nytimes.com/2003/09/18/international/middleeast/18MILI.html?ex10644 62400&en7d335e3ccfc0ff8a&ei5062.

27 Cordesman, "US Policy in Iraq," pp. 13, 17.

28 The estimates are taken from D.C. Hendrickson and R.W. Tucker, "Revisions in Need of Revising: What Went Wrong in the Iraq War," *Survival*, Vol. 47, no. 2 (2005): 19.

29 K. Eyre, J.J. Blais, and A. Anderson, "Expanding the Concept of Security Sector Reform," *Peacekeeping and International Relations* Vol. 30 (2001): 6.

30 Cited in B. Sullivan, "Daily Life in Iraq with a Police Trainer," 1 June 2005, available at www.knoxstudio.com/shns/story.cfm?pk=IRAQ-MISSION-06–01–05.

31 A. Faite, "Involvement of Private Contractors in Armed Conflict: Implications Under International Humanitarian Law," *Defence Studies*, Vol. 4, no. 2 (2004): 180.

32 For examples, see E. Krahmann, "Regulating Private Military Companies: What Role for the EU?" *Contemporary Security Policy*, Vol. 26, no. 1 (2005): 103–25; C. Spearin, "International Private Security Companies and Canadian Policy:

Possibilities and Pitfalls on the Road to Regulation," *Canadian Foreign Policy*, Vol. 11, no. 2 (2004): 1–15.

33 Cited in B. Yeoman, "Dirty Warriors," *Mother Jones*, November/December 2004, available at www.motherjones.com/commentary/notebook/2004/11//index.html.

34 See C. Spearin, "American Hegemony Incorporated: The Importance and Implications of Military Contractors in Iraq," *Contemporary Security Policy*, Vol. 24, no. 3 (2003): 26–47.

35 Cited in I. Traynor, "The Privatisation of War," *Guardian*, 10 December 2003, available at www.guardian.co.uk/international/story/0,3604,1103566,00.html.

36 Cited in J. Crewdson, "Contractor Tries to Avert Repeat of Bosnia Woes," *Chicago Tribune*, 19 April 2003, available at www.corpwatch.org/article.php?id=11117.

37 For an in-depth examination, see L. Lumpe, "US Foreign Military Training: Global Reach, Global Power, and Oversight Issues," *Foreign Policy in Focus*, Special Edition (May 2002): 3.

38 D. Avant, "Privatizing Military Training," *Foreign Policy in Focus*, Vol. 7, no. 6 (2002): 1.

39 Arguments of this type are made, for instance, in David Shearer, *Private Armies and Military Intervention*, Adelphi Paper 316 (London: International Institute for Strategic Studies, 1998). See also Lumpe, "US Foreign Military Training," p. 12.

40 See D. Isenberg, "Protecting Iraq's Precarious Pipelines," *Asia Times*, 23 September 2004, available at http://atimes.com/atimes/Middle_East/FI24Ak01.html. See also the subsequent letter responses.

41 "Privatizing War," *International Herald Tribune*, 21 April 2004, available at www.iht.com/articles/516206.html.

42 J.E. Thomson, *Mercenaries, Pirates, and Sovereigns: State-Building and Extraterritorial Violence in Early Modern Europe* (Princeton, NJ: Princeton University Press, 1994).

43 J. Burk, "Introduction, 1998: Ten Years of New Times," in J. Burk (ed.) *The Adaptive Military: Armed Forces in a Turbulent World*, 2nd ed. (New Brunswick: Transaction Publishers, 1998), p. 16.

44 R. Mandel, "Fighting Fire with Fire: Privatizing Counterterrorism," in R.D. Howard and R.L Sawyer (eds) *Defeating Terrorism: Shaping the New Security Environment* (Guilford: McGraw-Hill/Dushkin, 2004), p. 68.

45 Cited in Lumpe, "U.S. Foreign Military Training," p. 5.

14 The transformation of private military training

Patrick Cullen

While as recently as ten years ago any discussion of a market for private military training would have been premature, today, an increasingly consolidated and professionalised sector of the private security industry is changing the way states train their armed forces. The last decade has witnessed private security companies (PSCs) transform themselves from a small-scale and ad hoc domestic training asset or discreet tool of foreign military assistance into an important global supplier of military training. This fact has been most dramatically and visibly underscored by the prominent transnational training role played by PSCs in Afghanistan and Iraq, where private firms have been awarded a spectrum of large-scale training contracts for the new Iraqi military, police and paramilitary forces.[1] Less spectacular yet equally transformative has been the privatisation of the training of Western armed forces themselves. Offering courses ranging from sniper marksmanship and advanced urban combat tactics to more technologically sophisticated flight simulations centres, the private security industry is now offering alternatives to government owned and operated military training facilities around the world.

In a number of previous studies, this new market in military training has been viewed as either a net loss or net gain for the state, often measured in terms of the cost-effectiveness of outsourced training or various contract compliance issues.[2] While this approach is useful, its focus on the relative efficiencies or inefficiencies of public versus private military training obscures and leaves unaddressed other, broader implications related to the privatisation of military training. Specifically, it obscures the fact that PSCs are both the agent and the effect of a de-linking of military training from the state's armed forces that requires an analytical shift in the way we view the institution of military training itself. This is happening in a number of ways. First, the providers of military training are being pluralised. As military training becomes a market commodity and is reconceptualised as a service, governments and defence bureaucracies are increasingly acting as 'customers' that no longer assume the military has a monopoly on military expertise and instead look to both the public and the private sector to fulfil their training requirements. Second, the consumers of military training are becoming pluralised. As Western governments adapt their societies to the pressures of globalisation and to post-9/11 security threats that blur the military/police divide, a host of governmental agencies below, above, and within the state (yet outside of the armed forces) have turned to PSCs to fulfil new requirements for security training typically considered military in nature. Third, as Western states and the private security industry work together to fulfil various aspects of these new homeland security services, both states and PSCs are reflexively involved in creating a new, public–private hybrid 'security training' market that is reinterpreting and transcending the traditional police/military functional divide. In both discourse and practice, PSCs are simultaneously adopting and creating a new vision of professional security expertise that is providing military and police training (and more) to a variety of state, non-state and public–private actors on a global scale.

The origins of modern private military training

While it is accurate to characterise the contemporary market for private military training as increasingly global – in terms of the multinational characteristics of the firms providing this training as well as their international clientele – the modern origins of this training industry are decidedly Anglo-American in nature. One influential first-cut narrative of the origins of contemporary private military training refers to the small firms composed of retired British and European soldiers that specialised in providing small unit tactical military training to post-colonial and pro-Western states during the 1960s and 1970s.[3] British firms in particular have a long and rich history of this type of overseas military training. Often credited with creating the template for the modern 'private military company', David Stirling, founder of the British Special Air Service (SAS), created the Watchguard Organisation in 1967 to provide military training and other services to governments friendly to the United Kingdom in the Middle East and Africa, 'from Abu Dhabi to Zambia'.[4] During the 1980s, dozens of small British firms sought to emulate this business model and met with varying degrees of success. Often working out of converted London living rooms and equipped with little more than a short list of personal connections to potential government clients, a significant proportion of these British companies were built around one or two training contracts and disappeared shortly after their completion. Falconstar's 1982 contract with the Ugandan government to train and organise the Ugandan Police Special Force, a paramilitary force used to operate against domestic insurgents, was typical of many of these contracts.[5] At the other end of the spectrum successful firms such as Defence Systems Ltd (later to become ArmorGroup International) built reputations for professionalism and discretion that allowed them to turn overseas military training into a steady and lucrative business. While these firms would occasionally work as proxies for the British government, providing training to foreign governments that had originally approached the Foreign Office for military assistance – these British firms did not provide training for British armed forces.

By contrast, America's post-Second World War experience with private military training differs from this British model in two important respects. First, since the 1970s, the United States armed forces have used a wide array of small domestic private companies for training in a variety of tactical skills ranging from martial arts, skydiving and advanced driving skills to explosives handling and marksmanship. Unlike their British counterparts, in many instances these private companies did not originally conceive of a 'military training market' per se and instead had intended to sell their services in the civilian sector. Gunsite provides us with an early example. Originally established in 1976 by a retired US lieutenant colonel as one of the first professional shooting schools for civilian marksmanship in the United States, it immediately began receiving telephone enquiries from various military and police units interested in firearms training.[6] Companies such as Gunsite, whose armouries allowed them to offer courses familiarising US soldiers with Soviet and other foreign weapons, became popular with elite military units deploying to regions where these weapons would be commonplace on the battlefield. Similarly, high-end professional driving schools that offered specialised driving courses to the public also began receiving requests to train State Department foreign officers and elite forces personnel. As these training relationships matured, a number of civilian driving schools began incorporating shooting ranges into their driving course properties and offering shooting instruction at the behest of their government clients.[7] During the 1980s, small companies offering tactical fighting courses proliferated throughout the United States, and as the personal reputations of individual instructors or the quality of a company's training facilities spread through the elite forces community via word of mouth, a number of these firms transitioned their core business from the civilian to the military sector. CQD, a firm founded in 1981, exemplifies this kind of transition. Combining martial arts methods with practical experience gained from working with local and federal police agencies to create a training program in 'integrated armed/unarmed fighting techniques', CQD was eventually contacted by the Naval Special Warfare Center to train US Navy SEALS in shooting techniques, prisoner control and dynamic room entry.[8] This trend shifted somewhat during the 1990s, with small start-up firms headed by retired military personnel looking to market their services directly to the military as opposed to civilian marketplace. Tactical Explosive Entry School (TEES) and Direct Action Resource Center (DARC), founded in 1991 and 1996, respectively, were both set up to exploit this niche elite forces training market, with the former focusing on explosive door breaching and hostage rescue and the latter on urban combat training.[9] While these US firms increasingly began looking like the British PSC insofar that they were composed of a small number of retired military personnel, they remained distinguished from them by focusing their training business on their own state's armed forces. As late as the mid-1990s, however, the size of the market for training US armed forces personnel in tactical firearms and small unit combat skills remained very limited in absolute terms. Through the 1990s, there were probably less than a dozen US tactical training firms that could claim to train 1,000–3,000 students per year.

The post-Second World War American experience with foreign private military training provides a second major difference from the British model. In the same way that the US military's use of private military training came from firms not designed to specifically meet these needs, so too does this model correspond to the origins of the American private sector's training of foreign armed forces. During the Vietnam War, the Pentagon funded universities to provide military and police training to South Vietnamese forces and also hired contractors to provide electronics training and develop a South Vietnamese officer corps training program.[10] In 1975, Vinnell, a firm originally specialising in construction and logistics, was awarded a $77 million contact to manage and implement the complete training and force modernisation of the Saudi Arabian National Guard.[11] Whereas British PSCs engaged in relatively small-scale military training contracts for foreign governments with an often tacit approval of the British government, the Vinnell contract illustrates how the US government was willing to use the private sector as a tool to provide foreign militaries with large-scale training packages. This contract – unique at the time – would later be viewed as precedent-setting and a precursor to future large-scale American train and equip contracts in the former Yugoslavia, Afghanistan and Iraq.

Industry structure: growth, transformation and consolidation

Defining the size and structure of the private military training industry has proven to be conceptually problematic due to a number of different factors. First, there is a lack of consensus regarding what precisely constitutes *military* training. For decades, modern militaries have used the private sector to train their armed forces personnel in skills such as foreign languages or computer programming deemed integral to the maintenance of the modern military, yet which have not traditionally been considered skills intrinsically military in nature. The US military's use of the advanced civilian driving and martial arts schools described above, for example, complicates the question of what to include and exclude in any definition of private military training. Second, an added layer of complexity is encountered when one contemplates the possibility of 'military' training being transplanted to various non-military institutions. This is demonstrated by the fact that (as discussed later in this chapter) certain 'military' skill-sets typically seen as functionally specific to the armed forces, such as sniper and close quarter combat training, are increasingly being taught to various government agencies outside of the military. Third, the most commonly cited difficulty with determining the size or structure of this industry is its vast scope and diversity. For example, both SAIC and Gunsite provide armed forces training to personnel from a number of militaries around the world. However, whereas SAIC is a multinational, Fortune 500 company specialising in technology-intensive training simulations and has 44,000 employees with an annual revenue $7.8 billion, Gunsite, in comparison, operates a professional shooting facility based in Arizona employing a few dozen instructors who are sporadically contracted to teach small elite forces units in tactical shooting techniques.[12]

In analytical terms, the notion that these two firms represent different sectors in the same military training 'industry' is a relatively new concept for military professionals, defence bureaucrats and academics alike. This fact, combined with the lack of readily available comparative government data on private training contracts, has rendered statistics on the 'size' of the industry problematic at best. For example, while Peter Singer of the Brookings Institution and Doug Brooks of the security firm trade group International Peace Operations Association (IPOA) are ostensibly discussing the same industry, Singer has estimated its annual global revenue at $100 billion, while Brooks places the figure at $20 billion.[13]

Nevertheless, there is a broad consensus that the private security industry is experiencing a rate of tremendous growth. Throughout the 1990s, the value of PSCs with publicly traded stocks grew at twice the rate of the Dow Jones average, while corporate estimates have increased the value of the private security industry from $55.6 billion in 1990 to $202 billion by 2010.[14] This growth has occurred in tandem with a growing consolidation between the defence armaments and military training sectors as major defence manufacturers such as Boeing have entered the training market to take advantage of its expanding revenues.[15] The acquisitions of the PSCs MPRI and Vinnell by the defence contractors L-3 Communications and Northrop Grumman exemplify this trend towards consolidation. As the military training industry has evolved and matured, so has its ability to project itself as a professional and legitimate member of the defence industry. The Washington, DC, based IPOA and the British Association of Private Security Companies (BAPSC), founded in 2001 and 2006, respectively, represent the new and formalised advocacy efforts being made by these security firms.

Changes within defence bureaucracies and defence associations have also contributed to this transformation. In 1998, the Pentagon's acquisition process was radically revamped by establishing online electronic 'shopping malls' that brought potential government 'customers' together with private security firms selling, among other things, military training services. These government websites created a massive virtual market in training services that have exponentially increased the visibility of government training contracts, thereby allowing a myriad of small PSCs to bid on contracts previously hidden by a complex and paper-intensive DoD procurement process.[16] This, in turn, has exposed government contracting agents to a much larger pool of PSCs, creating a feedback effect that has increased the government's solicitation of private training contracts. While the United States has taken the lead in this revolution, it is far from a unique case. For example, the Israeli defence export organisation, Sibat, has created an online Defense Sales Catalog that advertises the military training services of a series of Israeli PSCs. Similarly, organisations such as the United Kingdom's Defense Manufacturers Association (DMA) traditionally geared towards promoting the country's defence industry *products* have also turned to the Internet to facilitate a growing demand in the international market for defence-related *services*. Describing itself as a 'one-stop consultancy shop' for all aspects of defence and security related needs, the DMA actively seeks to create online networks between British firms offering training services to foreign militaries and other overseas customers looking for military training.[17]

These structural changes, along with the billions of dollars in revenue generated from the wars in Afghanistan and Iraq, are causally linked to three features of the current private military training industry. First, firms such as MPRI and Vinnell that specialise in large-scale train-and-equip programs for foreign militaries and technology and classroom-based training are continuing to grow their scale of operations. Second, as a new generation of PSCs reinvest their earnings from providing armed security services in Afghanistan and Iraq into large-scale tactical combat training centres, they are transforming a once niche tactical training market focused on small elite forces units into a large-scale business increasingly being used to train large numbers of regular enlisted soldiers in tactical combat techniques. Lastly, these PSCs are increasingly looking for opportunities to expand their companies into truly global providers of military and security training. These characteristics can be seen in the PSCs highlighted below.

Global PSCs

Founded in 1987, MPRI has developed into one of the largest premier suppliers of doctrine-based military training both within the United States and abroad. Over the past decade the company has seen rapid and steady growth. Between 1997 and 2005, MPRI grew from 400 employees and a business volume of $48 million, to over 3,000 employees worldwide and reported revenues exceeding two billion dollars. Headquartered near the Pentagon in Alexandria, Virginia, MPRI draws on an online database of over 15,000 individuals, composed primarily of retired military personnel, to undertake a wide array of training functions, including pre-deployment training, new equipment training and force on force training.[18] Within the United States, MPRI has provided instructors to various military schools such as the US Army Force Management School, and the US Army Sergeants Major Academy, and has also designed the doctrine and curriculum used by the US army to train and educate its soldiers. In this capacity, MPRI has written numerous field manuals, authored future war-fighting concepts and has written strategic opposition forces doctrine for the US military. Internationally, MPRI has operated in more than 40 countries worldwide and opened subsidiary offices in Europe and the Middle East.[19] In Africa alone, MPRI has supported the US State Department's African Contingency Operations and Assistance (ACOTA) program, conducted armed forces re-professionalising programs in Nigeria, operated a sophisticated maritime simulations centre in Egypt, trained the armed forces of Equatorial Guinea and worked in a wide range of training programs in support of the South African Department of Defence. Most recently, MPRI won a $15 million contract to provide instructors for a Baghdad Counterinsurgency Center for Excellence through the year 2010.[20]

While MPRI has been at the forefront of doctrine-based classroom and technology-intensive training, Blackwater USA has positioned itself at the leader of the private security industry's rapid expansion into tactical military training. Between 2002 and 2005, its annual revenue increased an estimated 600 per cent, winning over $500 million in contracts since 2000.[21] With 100 trainers on staff, the Blackwater Training Center – a massive 6,000 acre facility including 40 computerised shooting ranges, sophisticated shoot-houses, parachute drop zones, a mock village, two mock ships and miles of driving track – exemplifies the new, infrastructure-intensive penetration of the private security industry into the tactical military training market. This large facility, based in Moyock, North Carolina, has allowed Blackwater to conduct thousands of short-term contracts training soldiers at the unit or infantry company level in advanced driving, marksmanship and urban warfare courses.[22] Success with these contracts has led to an unprecedented expansion in privately sourced tactical military training. In its single largest contract to date, Blackwater was hired to train 50,000 US navy personnel in weapons handling and force protection.[23] As a result of this volume of work, Blackwater has expanded their training facilities nationwide, purchasing and refurbishing a firearms training centre in Illinois while currently negotiating the construction of another 800 acre canyon facility in Southern California near the Mexican border.[24]

Internationally, Blackwater has completed numerous training contracts for the military and security forces of governments around the world. As with MPRI, some of this training is done on behalf of the US government, with Blackwater acting as an auxiliary foreign military assistance tool, replacing overstretched US Special Forces personnel normally tasked with these training missions. Operating in this capacity, Blackwater has trained foreign forces both at their US training facilities (such as the Greek and Colombian government forces trained in high-threat executive protection) and in the client's country (as in the case of a 2005 maritime commando enhancement program conducted in Azerbaijan). Chris Taylor, Blackwater's vice-president, anticipates significant growth in this aspect of their business, stating that they receive 'more than a few calls every week' from various foreign government agencies enquiring about their training services.[25] This increasing demand for security training from foreign military and security forces has led Blackwater to look into creating overseas training facilities, with one such project leading them into negotiations with the Subic Bay Metropolitan Authority for a training site in the Philippines.[26]

The security firm Olive Group is displaying similar international expansionist tendencies. Founded in 2001 by a small group of retired British SAS soldiers operating out of a small London office, Olive has grown and diversified rapidly into a self-described 'global company in terms of our presence, perspective, and people'.[27] In a testament to this, the firm has moved its headquarters to Internet City, Dubai, and operates from 30 locations in five continents employing over 500 personnel with annual returns of $90 million, while maintaining offices in the United States, Britain, Kuwait, India, Singapore, Jordan, Afghanistan and Iraq. Though the vast majority of its revenue comes from providing armed security details, Olive Group has invested heavily in expanding its business in the military and security training sector. Within the United Kingdom, Olive Group is actively marketing itself as a professional military training provider to the Ministry of Defence, and an expedient way to relieve the country's overstretched armed forces.[28] Within the United States, Olive has opened offices in Washington, DC, to lobby the Pentagon for lucrative defence training contracts for its new US-based training centre. Based in Nesbit, Mississippi, Olive Group is using their 780 acre Olive Security Training Center to build a 'mock combat village – a nine block city replica complete with residential areas, government buildings, schools, retail stores and roundabouts designed in Middle Eastern architecture' in an effort to win 'military operations in urban environment' contracts from the US Department of Defense.[29] More generally, Olive Group's North American subsidiary has won a number of contracts within the broader US security establishment by both assisting in the design of US government training facilities and conducting training courses at established government training centres. Through these training contracts – which include the training of US military elite forces personnel as well as border guard units – Olive Group has exhibited the ability to successfully market itself as a professional provider of security training that is capable of delivering a security training product across the military/police spectrum.

Operating for over 25 years and currently listed on the London Stock Exchange, ArmorGroup International's evolution as a provider of security training offers an insight into the changing dynamics of the military training industry. Founded in 1981 by a retired British SAS officer, ArmorGroup International (originally Defense Systems Ltd) was a quintessential exemplification of the British model PSC described in section one; the firm provided high-end armed security services to various diplomatic corps and resource extraction firms operating in unstable regions of the world while simultaneously offering low-profile military training to foreign governments. As the firm developed over the years, it moved away from its emphasis on military training and diversified its training services to include a wide array of hostile environment training programs aimed at corporate and other non-military markets. More recently, however, the company has returned to its roots as a provider of military training. Seeking to take advantage of the post–9/11 paramilitary homeland security market in the United States (and to a lesser extent in the United Kingdom), and the ballooning military training market in Iraq and Afghanistan, ArmorGroup International has opened a series of training centres in these four countries. As part of this business strategy, they opened the first commercial training centre in Afghanistan, a two-million dollar facility built to house and train 300 students with a close quarter battle house and weapons systems simulation. In Iraq, they created a training compound south of Baghdad equipped with North Atlantic Treaty Organisation (NATO) standard shooting ranges used to train Iraqi security personnel. Together, these Middle Eastern training facilities have trained thousands of local national security personnel.[30] At the same time, the firm's US branch, ArmorGroup International Training, has expanded its firearms training capabilities with a variety of specialised shooting ranges for pistols, shotguns and carbines. These training centres, based in Texas and Virginia, have provided counterterrorism and force protection training to a wide spectrum Department of Defense and Department of State personnel.[31]

This trend of replacing or supplementing 'mobile training teams' – a featured component of all the PSCs mentioned thus far – with permanent or long-term 'brick and mortar' training facilities has been a crucial component of the growth in private tactical military training. As a result, some smaller multinational PSCs, such as the Israeli firm International Security and Defence Systems (ISDS), have formed partnerships with civilian firearms training centres to compete for military training contracts that require such infrastructure without incurring the associated construction costs. In 2003, ISDS created such a partnership with the arms manufacturer Smith & Wesson to offer counterterrorism training to military and police personnel at its shooting academy in Springfield, Massachusetts.

With the kind of growth exemplified by the PSC Triple Canopy, which in its first year of operation in 2003 grew to over 800 employees and had revenues exceeding $100 million, the private security industry has gained the capital necessary to create multimillion-dollar military training facilities. This sheer magnitude of growth, combined with the evolution towards permanent, private military training centres, is enough to substantiate Triple Canopy's claim that it and firms like it are 'reshaping the entire security industry'. However important these changes are, the most significant aspect of the private security industry's expansion into military training has been its role in constituting a new, hybrid *security training* market where PSCs such as Triple Canopy *are increasingly providing training in military skill-sets outside of the state's armed forces.* It is to this blurring of the boundaries of private military training that we turn next.

The pluralization and hybridization of private military training

A crucial aspect of the transformation of private military training has been the private security industry's central role in the dispersal of military training above, below and outside of the institution of the state's armed forces. At the supra-state level, numerous organisations have looked to PSCs for a broad array of military and specialised security training. NATO, for example, has solicited international bids from PSCs to train the NATO International Security Assistance Force (ISAF) operating in Afghanistan in the identification and avoidance of roadside improvised explosive devices.[32] Other supra-state organisations whose civilian personnel are increasingly posted in regions suffering from low-intensity conflict, and who are being targeted for kidnapping and other terrorist violence, have also turned to PSCs for new forms of robust security training. In July 2006, for example, the European Union sent 26 members of its diplomatic mission to Israel and the occupied territories on a course conducted by the PSC Hart Security designed to teach the diplomats skills in, among other things, defensive and off-road armoured car-driving techniques.[33]

At the local or sub-state level, PSCs conduct a variety of specialised counterterrorism training programs for law enforcement agencies. The London Metropolitan Police Department has conducted a survey of the training services available from PSCs to help assist them in their role as a 'first responder' to terrorist incidents, and in the United States it has become a common practice for PSCs to provide Homeland Security training to police forces. Within this new post-9/11 security context, PSCs are transferring military techniques in advanced marksmanship, close quarter combat, explosive door breaching, and other military skill sets to police forces across the United States and around the world. Many of these small paramilitary training contracts illustrate the increasing degree of local–global networks that pervade this industry, with local police clients receiving their training transnationally from foreign security firms. For instance, Task International, a PSC headquartered in London, has trained a number of special police units for Caribbean and Asian governments, while the firm Britam Defence provides anti-terrorism training to police personnel worldwide at a number of overseas facilities.

At the same time, requirements for military training are increasingly being dispersed horizontally to a plethora of state-level non-military agencies. Absent an indigenous capacity to provide such training – and with overstretched militaries being unable to provide it – many of these agencies have turned to the private sector. This 'horizontal' diversification of state agencies requiring military training can be seen most vividly within the United States government, where non-military state organs have acted as customers of PSC training for both internal US and foreign security forces. Domestically, the Department of Energy (DoE) has relied upon PSCs to train its own security force designated to protect the nation's nuclear facilities up 'to paramilitary standards'. This training has included, among other things, the operation of M60 machinegun mounted on armoured vehicles, sniper training and M16 automatic rifle marksmanship.[34] Internationally, the US Drug Enforcement Agency (DEA) has relied upon PSCs to train foreign security personnel as part of its international drug interdiction effort. In one such contract, Blackwater USA was hired by the DEA to train units from Afghanistan's Ministry of the Interior, combining basic law enforcement skills – such as crime scene investigation – with military training due to the rough terrain and hostile security environment this paramilitary force was required to operate in.[35]

In another salient example of the complexity of this diversification of US Federal Government consumption of private military training, an analysis of the US State Department (DoS) reveals a number of its various sub-agencies contracting with PSCs for a broad array of training requirements. One sub-department, the DoS Bureau of International Narcotics and Law Enforcement Affairs, has solicited positions for retired US soldiers to conduct field training of foreign troops in support of US efforts at drug eradication programs in South America. One online State Department solicitation advertising a year long $61,081 position in Lima, Peru stated the following:

> Train U.S. government employees and Peruvian Counterparts in the following subjects (but not limited to): paramedic, pathfinder, air mobile operations, helicopter external load operations, fast rope, rappelling, STABO, emergency extraction, water safety/survival, rescue swimmer, small boat handling, helicopter gunnery, and survival-evasion-resistance-escape (SERE) ... set up and run range qualification courses for the M-4 carbine, 9 mm pistol and 357 revolvers.[36]

Another DoS sub-department, the Bureau of Diplomatic Security, has turned to the private sector for its training needs. Unable to draw on an overstretched military to either provide the guard manpower or provide the DoS with security trainers – and absent a sufficient in-house capacity of its own – the massive, one-billion dollar Worldwide Personal Protective Services (WPPS) contract was awarded to three PSCs to provide a cadre of diplomatic security personnel with 'counter assault team' and 'long range designated marksman' training.[37] This security force – administered and controlled by the Department of State, yet staffed and trained by a myriad of PSCs – exemplifies not only the expanded post-9/11 paramilitary security market being penetrated by PSCs but also the new public/private security hybrids that these partnerships create.

While these examples of the dispersal of paramilitary training to various governmental agencies outside of the military illustrate the changing nature of the military training market, perhaps the most dramatic example of the fragmented nature of contemporary military training can be seen in the provision of paramilitary training conducted by PSCs *beyond the state* to a variety of private sector clientele. Between 1990 and 1993, for example, the British multinational agricultural conglomerate Lonrho hired the British security firm GSG to train its security forces to repel attacks conducted by Renamo rebels against its Mozambique tomato plantations. During the course of its contract, GSG trained hundreds of Lonrho security personnel in counterassault combat tactics with the use of government supplied tanks, AK-47 automatic rifles and RPG-7 grenade launchers.[38] More recently, the United States Merchant Marine Academy has partnered with Blackwater USA to provide 'world class tactical maritime security training' in counter-piracy and counterterrorism to government, military and *private sector* clients.[39]

Conclusion

At the beginning of the twenty-first century, transnational private security firms are fast becoming important actors in an expanding global military training market. At the same time, these PSCs are challenging and upsetting a number of our implicit understandings – and often tautological assumptions – regarding the modern state's relationship to military training. First and foremost, the massive growth of this industry suggests that we may be witnessing a long-term pluralization of the providers of military training, with PSCs joining state militaries as providers of professional military training. However, this phenomenon cannot be interpreted merely in terms of the state's outsourcing the training of its armed forces to the private sector. Instead, the privatisation of military training needs to be understood as part of a complex shift in the nature of military training itself – a process that increasingly includes the provision of hybrid paramilitary training to a variety of public and private actors external to the state's armed forces.

This new *security training* market – itself the combined product of material changes associated with globalisation and new understandings of the private sector's role and responsibility in shaping global security – is perfectly suited to both the rhetoric and the global strategic vision of this new breed of transnational PSC. Partly as a result of this, Triple Canopy's claim to be 'a security solutions company [that] delivers comprehensive training programs customised to meet the demanding requirements of law enforcement, military, government and corporate clients worldwide' has become standard within the private security industry. Crucially, this language of 'security training' should not be interpreted merely as a cynical (or logical) attempt by the security industry to expand the scope of its market but rather as part of a new security discourse that is shared with governments themselves. The Pentagon's transformation of the National Defense University – its premier educational institution – into the National Security University as a result of it 'acknowledging the complexity of the 21st century security environment' and recognising the need to 'support the educational needs *of the broader US national security profession*' is a case in point.[40]

Ultimately, the cumulative effects of these changes in government and PSC rhetoric, as well as the changing realities on the ground, suggest that we can no longer regard either the provision or the consumption of 'military training' as a functional field of expertise monopolised by the state's armed forces. Furthermore, as PSCs continue to evolve into established, multinational firms that operate training facilities in multiple countries around the world, they will also unsettle our understandings of what, precisely, constitutes 'foreign' military training.

Notes

1 For instance, Dyncorp was awarded a contract reportedly worth $1.7 billion to train over a quarter of a million Iraqi and Afghan police officers. See Renae Merle, 'Coming Under Fire: DynCorp Defends Its Work in Training Foreign Police Forces', *Washington Post*, 19 March 2007, D01. The Northrop Grumman subsidiary Vinnell was awarded a $48 million contract to train the first nine battalions of the new Iraqi Army. See 'Northrop Grumman Awarded $48 million Contract to Train New Iraqi Army', *PR Newswire Association, Inc.*, 2 July 2003. The South African firm Erinys was awarded a $39.5 million contract in August 2003 to train a 6,500 member paramilitary Iraqi Oil Protection Force. See 'Iraqi Efforts to Secure Oil Facilities a Boon to Security Firms', *The Oil Daily*, Vol. 53, No. 163 (2003).

2 For illuminating comparative case studies of the pros and cons in private military training, see Avant, *The Market for Force*.

3 See Kevin O'Brien, 'Private Military Companies and African Security 1990–1998', in Abel-Fatau Musah and J. Kayode Fayemi (eds), *Mercenaries: An African Security Dilemma* (London: Pluto Press, 2000), pp. 43–75.

4 Tony Geraghty, *Who Dares Wins: The Story of the Special Air Service 1950–1980* (London: Arms and Armour Press, 1980).

5 Peter Tickler, *The Modern Mercenary: Dog of War or Soldier of Honour?* (Wellingborough: Patrick Stephens Ltd, 1987).

6 Interview with Ed Head, Gunsite Director of Operations, 12 August 2006.

7 Confidential interview with the CEO of US private military training facility. See also www.bsr-inc.com/SDT.HTM, accessed 25 October 2006.

8 Interview with CQD founder Duane Dieter, 8 September 2006. See also Bob Pilgrim, 'To Fight Is to Risk Death: Training SEALS to be Complete Warriors', *SWAT Magazine: Weapons, Tactics, and Training for the Real World* (April 2003): 44–8.

9 Interview with Alan Brosnan, founder of Tactical Explosive Entry School, 16 May 2006; interview with Richard Mason, CEO of Direct Action Resource Center, 5 May 2006.

10 Avant, *The Market for Force*, p. 114.

11 William Hartung, 'Mercenaries Inc.: How a US Company Props Up the House of Saud', *The Progressive*, April 1996.

12 Head interview, 12 August 2006. See also www.saic.com/news/pdf/corporate-factsheet.pdf.

13 Peter Singer, 'Peacekeepers Inc', *Policy Review* (June/July 2003), www.hoover.org/publications/policyreview/3448831.html; interview with Doug Brooks, Director of International Peace Operations Association, 10 February 2007.

14 Deborah Avant, 'Privatizing Military Training', *Foreign Policy in Focus*, Vol. 5, No. 17 (2000): 1.

15 For example, Aviation Training International, Ltd, a joint venture between Boeing and Westland Helicopters, Ltd, was selected in 1998 to provide training

for the British army for their Apache attack helicopters for up to 30 years. It has four training centres with state-of-the-art flight simulators and computer training. See www.atil.co.uk.

16 Confidential interview with PSC CEO 9 May 2006. See www.fedbizopps.com for a prominent example of one US Federal Government website soliciting military training services.

17 See www.the-dma.org.uk/Products/main.asp.

18 This tactical battlefield training has included training exercises to sustain crew proficiency in tank, armoured personnel carriers, artillery and mortar gunnery.

19 See www.mpri.com.

20 See www.defenselink.mil/contracts/contract.aspx?contractid=3485.

21 See www.fastcompany.com/magazine/103/open_11-jackson.html; see also Bill Sizemore and Joanne Kimberlin, 'Blackwater: On the Front Lines', *The Virginia Pilot*, 26 July 2006.

22 These contracts last on average one to two weeks and generate roughly $35,000, interview with Chris Taylor, vice-president of Blackwater USA, 28 Apr. 2006.

23 Ibid.; see also: www.defenselink.mil/Contracts/Contract.aspx?ContractID=2350.

24 See www.msnbc.msn.com/id/17308917/.

25 Taylor interview, 28 April 2006.

26 Ibid.; see also Chris Taylor, Congressional Testimony, *Subcommittee: National Security, Emerging Threats, and International Relations*, 13 June 2006.

27 See www.olivesecurity.com.

28 Speech given by Lieutenant General Sir Cedric Delves, Director of Olive Group. RUSI-BAPSC first annual conference 30 October 1996.

29 Interview with Alan Brosnan, director of Olive Security Training Center (formerly TEES), 16 May 2006; see also Mark Minton, 'Battlescape Shoots for Profit: State Sees Security Pros Bring War Home', *Arkansas Democratic-Gazette*, 19 February 2006.

30 See www.armorgroup.com/services/securityservices/locations/.

31 See armorgroupiti.com/db4/00335/armorgroupiti.com/_download/Conceptof TrainingandOpsBrochureRev-02–06A.pdf.

32 See *U – NATO Notification of Intent to Issue Invitation for International Bidding – Provision of C-Improvised Explosive Device (C-IED) Training to International Security Assistance Force (ISAF) – Afghanistan* at www.fbo.gov/spg/DOC/BIS/DPD/IFIB-ISAF-C-IED/listing.html.

33 See www.hartsecurity.com/news.asp?rel=1083.

34 The Department of Energy has also hired PSCs to provide 'mobile security detail training' at the Department of Energy's National Training Center.

35 Taylor interview, 28 April 2006.

36 See www.fbo.gov/spg/State/INL/INL-RM-MS/PSC%2D06%2D019/SynopsisR. html.

37 Greg Starr, deputy assistant secretary, Bureau of Diplomatic Security, Department of State, Committee on House Government Reform; Subcommittee on National Security, Emerging Threats, and International Relations, 13 June 2006. See also See Rene Merle, 'Embassy Security Firms Chosen', *Washington Post*, 17 June 2005.

38 Alex Vines, 'Gurkhas and the Private Security Business in Africa', in Jakkie Cilliers and Peggy Mason (eds), *Peace, Profit, or Plunder: The Privatisation of Security in War-Torn African Societies* (South Africa: ISS 1999), p. 127.

39 See gmats.usmma.edu/info/gmats/partners.aspx. See also www.blackwaterusa. com/maritime/.

40 Emphasis added. See the *2006 Quadrennial Defense Review*, p. 79, at www.defenselink.mil/qdr/.

Select bibliography

Additional sources can be found in the notes to the various chapters.

Primary sources

Aaron, Dwayne and Cherilyn A. Walley. 'ODA 542: Working with the Free Iraqi Fighters,' *Veritas: Journal of Army Special Operations History*, Vol. 31 (Winter 2005), 86–8.

Becena, Melchor. 'Advising Host-Nation Forces: A Critical Art,' *Special Warfare* (May 1993), 26–8.

Cherepanov, Alexander Ivanovich. *Notes of a Military Advisor in China*. Alexandra O. Smith (trans.), Harry H. Collier and Thomas M. Williamsen (eds). Taipei, Taiwan: Office of Military History, 1970.

Fahrmbacher, Wilhelm. 'Seiben Jahre Berater bei der ägyptischen Armee,' *Wehrekunde*, Vol. 8, No. 1 (1959), 1–9.

Hall, John E. *My Experiences as an Advisor in El Salvador*. Carlisle Barracks, PA: US Army War College, 1999.

Hoare, Mike. *Mercenary*. New York: Bantam Books, 1979.

Lawrence, T.E. '27 Articles,' *The Arab Bulletin* (20 August 1917). Online, available at: www.lib.byu.edu/~rdh/wwi/1917/27arts.html.

———. *Seven Pillars of Wisdom: A Triumph*. New York: Anchor Books, Doubleday, 1991.

Lynch, Rick and Phillip D. Janzen. 'NATO Training Mission – Iraq: Looking to the Future,' *Joint Forces Quarterly*, No. 40, 1st Quarter (2006), 29–34.

Mendez, Marcos R. 'The Role of an MI Advisor in El Salvador,' *Military Intelligence Professional Bulletin*, Vol. 19, No. 4 (1993), 28–31.

Newell, Peter. 'Building Iraqi Security Forces from the Bottom Up: Task Force 2–2 and the 205th Iraqi Army Battalion in Muqdadiyah, Iraq,' in Kendall D. Gott and Michael G. Brooks (eds) *Security Assistance: US and International Historical Perspectives: The Proceedings of the Combat Studies Institute 2006 Military History Symposium*. Fort Leavenworth, KS: Combat Studies Institute Press, 2006, 599–645.

Secondary sources

Anderson, Robert S. 'Patrick Blackett in India: Military Consultant and Scientific Intervenor, 1947–72, Part 1,' *Notes and Records of the Royal Society*, Vol. 53, No. 2 (1999), 253–73.

——. 'Patrick Blackett in India: Military Consultant and Scientific Intervenor, 1947–72, Part 2,' *Notes and Records of the Royal Society*, Vol. 53, No. 3 (1999), 345–59.

Atkins, George Pope and Larry V. Thompson. 'German Military Influence in Argentina, 1921–1940,' *Journal of Latin American Studies*, Vol. 4, No. 2 (1972), 257–74.

Avant, Deborah D. *The Market for Force: The Consequences of Privatizing Security*. Cambridge: Cambridge University Press, 2005.

Badolato, E.V. 'A Clash of Cultures: The Expulsion of Soviet Military Advisors from Egypt,' *Naval War College Review* (March–April 1984), 69–81.

Benis, Adam Georges. *Une mission militaire Polonaise en Egypte*. Le Caire: Institut Français, 1938.

Bolger, Daniel P. 'So You Want to Be an Adviser,' *Military Review* (March–April 2006), 2–8.

Bran, Roberto. 'An Encouraging Outcome. Why the South African Historical Experience with Executive Outcomes Suggests that Using Private Afghan Military Forces in Iraq Could Benefit Global Security and Afghanistan Society,' CDAI-CDFAI 7th Annual Graduate Student Symposium, RMC, 29–30 October 2004.

Butler, Clifford. 'Recollections of Patrick Blackett, 1945–70,' *Notes and Records of the Royal Society*, Vol. 53, No. 1 (1999), 143–56.

Busch, Peter. 'Killing the "Vietcong": The British Advisory Mission and the Strategic Hamlet Programme,' *The Journal of Strategic Studies*, Vol. 25, No. 1 (2002), 135–62.

Carr, Caleb. *The Devil Soldier: The American Soldier of Fortune Who Became a God in China*. New York: Random House, 1992.

Champonnois, Suzanne. 'Colonel Emmanuel du Parquet's Mission in Latvia, 1919–1920,' *The Journal of Baltic Studies*, Vol. XXIII, No. 4 (Winter 1992), 325–40.

Chau, Donovan. 'East to East: PRC Security Assistance to the Republic of Tanzania, 1964–1976,' in Kendall D. Gott and Michael G. Brooks (eds) *Security Assistance: US and International Historical Perspectives: The Proceedings of the Combat Studies Institute 2006 Military History Symposium*. Fort Leavenworth, KS: Combat Studies Institute Press, 2006, 271–89.

Clarke, Jeffrey J. *Advice and Support: The Final Years, 1965–1973. The United States Army in Vietnam*, Center of Military History Publication No. 91–3, Washington, DC: USGPO, 1998.

Clemens, Peter. 'Captain James Hausman, US Military Advisor to Korea, 1946–48: The Intelligent Man on the Spot,' *The Journal of Strategic Studies*, Vol. 25, No. 1 (2002), 163–98.

Cordesman, Anthony H., with Patrick Baetjer. *Iraqi Security Forces: A Strategy for Success*. Westport, CT: Praeger, 2005.

Corum, James. 'Building the Malayan Army and Police – Britain's Experience During the Malayan Emergency 1948–1960,' in Kendall D. Gott and Michael G. Brooks (eds) *Security Assistance: US and International Historical Perspectives: The Proceedings of the Combat Studies Institute 2006 Military History Symposium*. Fort Leavenworth, KS: Combat Studies Institute Press, 2006, 291–313.

Cox, Frederick J. 'Colonel John Lay's Naval Mission in Egypt,' *Cahier d'histoire egyptienne*, Vol. 5 (1953), 36–46.

——. 'The American Naval Mission in Egypt,' *The Journal of Modern History*, Vol. 26, No. 2 (1954), 173–8.

Curtin, Edwin P. 'American Advisory Group Aids Greece in War on Guerrillas,' *Armored Cavalry Journal*, Vol. 58, No. 1 (1949), 8–11, 34–5.

Daley, John. 'Soviet and German Advisors Put Doctrine to the Test: Tanks in the Siege of Madrid,' *Armor* (May–June 1999), 33–7.

Douin, George (ed.). *La mission du Baron de Boislecomte, L'Egypte et la Syrie en 1833*. Le Caire: Société Royale de Géographie d'Egypte, 1927.

——. *Une mission militaire Française auprès de Mohamed Aly*. Le Caire: Société Royale de Géographie d'Egypte, 1927.

Dunn, John P. 'Americans in the Nineteenth Century Egyptian Army: A Selected Bibliography,' *The Journal of Military History*, Vol. 70 (2006), 123–36.

——. *Khedive Ismail's Army*. London: Routledge, 2005.

Fahmy, Khalid. *All the Pasha's Men. Mehmed Ali, His Army, and the Making of Modern Egypt*. Cambridge: Cambridge University Press, 1997.

Fallows, James. 'Why Iraq Has No Army,' *The Atlantic*, Vol. 296, No. 4 (2005), 60–88.

Forsén, Björn and Annette Forsén. 'German Secret Submarine Exports, 1919–35,' in Donald J. Stoker and Jonathan A. Grant (eds) *Girding for Battle: The Arms Trade in a Global Perspective, 1815–1940*. Westport, CT: Praeger, 2003, 113–34.

Fox, John. P. 'Max Bauer: Chiang Kai-Shek's First German Military Adviser,' *Journal of Contemporary History*, Vol. 5, No. 4 (1970), 21–44.

Froehlich, Dean K. 'The Military Advisor as Defined by Counterparts,' Human Resources Research Organization, March 1970.

Futrell, Robert F. *The Advisory Years to 1965, the United States Air Force in Southeast Asia*. Washington, DC: Office of Air Force History, 1981.

Gedda, George. 'China Increases Foreign Military Training,' *Huron Daily Tribune*, 14 March 2006, <http://customwire.ap.org/dynamic/stories.U/US_CHINA_ LATIN_AMERICA?SITE=MIB>.

Gibby, Bryan. 'Fighting in a Korean War: The American Military Missions to South Korea, 1946–53,' PhD Dissertation, Ohio State University, 1995.

Guthrie, George M. 'Conflicts of Culture and the Military Advisor,' Institute for Defense Analyses, November 1966.

Hausrath, Alfred. *The KMAG Advisor (U): Role and Problems of the Military Advisor in Developing an Indigenous Army for Combat Operations in Korea*. Chevy Chase, MD: Operations Research Office, Johns Hopkins University, 1957.

Hermes, Walter G. *Surveys of the Development of the Role of the US Army Military Advisor*. Washington, DC: Department of the Army, OCMH Study, 1966.

Hickey, G.C. and W.P. Davison. *The American Military Advisor and His Foreign Counterpart: The Case of Vietnam*. Santa Monica, CA: Rand Corporation, 1965.

Kaplan, Robert D. *Imperial Grunts: The American Military on the Ground Today*. New York: Random House, 2005.

Kerst, Georg. *Jacob Mieckel: sein Leben, sein Wirken in Deutschland und Japan*. Götingen: Musterschmidt, 1971.

Kipp, Jacob. 'Soviet Military Assistance to the Democratic Republic of Afghanistan After the Withdrawal of Soviet Forces, 1889–1991,' in Kendall D. Gott and Michael G. Brooks (eds) *Security Assistance: US and International Historical Perspectives: The Proceedings of the Combat Studies Institute 2006 Military History Symposium*. Fort Leavenworth, KS: Combat Studies Institute Press, 2006, 105–21.

Kuznetsov, Ilya I. 'The Soviet Military Advisors in Mongolia, 1921–39,' *The Journal of Slavic Military Studies*, Vol. 12, No. 4 (1990), 118–37.

Ladwig, Walter C., III. 'Security Assistance and Counterinsurgency: The British Experience in Oman, 1964–1975,' in Kendall D. Gott and Michael G. Brooks (eds) *Security Assistance: US and International Historical Perspectives: The Proceedings of the Combat Studies Institute 2006 Military History Symposium*. Fort Leavenworth, KS: Combat Studies Institute Press, 2006, 473–503.

Litten, Frederick S. 'Otto Braun's Curriculum Vitae – Translation and Commentary,' *Twentieth-Century China*, Vol. 23, No. 1 (1991), 31–62.

Marks, Paul. 'Advisers and Advising in the 21st Century,' *Special Warfare* (Spring 2001), 28–37.

——. 'Joint Publication 3–07.15: *Tactics, Techniques, and Procedures for Advising Foreign Forces* and the American Mission,' *Small Wars and Insurgencies*, Vol. 12, No. 1 (Spring 2001), 31–59.

Marolda, Edward J. and Oscar P. Fitzgerald. *From Military Assistance to Combat, 1959–1965: The United States Navy and the Vietnam Conflict*. Washington, DC: Naval Historical Center, 1986.

May, Ernest R. *The Truman Administration and China, 1945–1949*. Philadelphia, New York and Toronto: J.B. Lippincott Company, 1975.

Millett, Allan R. 'Captain James H. Hausman and the Formation of the Korean Army, 1945–1950,' *Armed Forces and Society*, Vol. 23, No. 4 (Summer 1997), 503–39.

Mott, William H., IV. *Military Assistance: An Operational Perspective*. Contributions in Military Studies, No. 170. Westport, CT: Greenwood Press, 1999.

——. *Soviet Military Assistance: An Empirical Perspective*. Contributions in Military Studies, No. 207. Westport, CT: Greenwood Press, 2001.

Preisseisen, Ernst L. *Before Aggression: Europeans Prepare the Japanese Army*. The Association for Asian Studies: Monographs and Papers, No. XXI. Tucson: The University of Arizona Press, 1965.

Ralston, David B. *Importing the European Army: The Introduction of Military Techniques and Institutions into the Extra-European World, 1600–1914*. Chicago and London: University of Chicago Press, 1990.

Riley, William H., Jr. 'Challenges of a Military Advisor,' *Military Review* (November 1988), 34–42.

Rooney, Chris B. 'The International Significance of British Naval Missions to the Ottoman Empire, 1908–1914,' *Middle Eastern Studies*, Vol. 34, No. 1 (1998), 1–29.

Rostek, Horst. 'Zur Rolle der Deutschen Militärberater bei der chinesischen Nationalregierung 1928 bis 1938,' *Bulletin Faschismus/Zweiter Weltkrieg* (1989), 112–27.

Sater, William and Holger Herwig. *The Grand Illusion: The Prussianization of the Chilean Army*. Lincoln: University of Nebraska Press, 1999.

Sharp, Jeremy M. and Christopher M. Blanchard. 'Post-War Iraq: Foreign Contributions to Training, Peacekeeping, and Reconstruction,' Congressional Research Service (CRS) Report for Congress, 22 January 2007.

Shearer, David. 'Outsourcing War,' *Foreign Policy*, No. 112 (Autumn 1998), 68–81.

Sheehan, Neil. *John Paul Vann and America in Vietnam*. New York: Random House, 1988.

Simons, Anna. 'The Military Advisor as Warrior-King and Other "Going Native"

Temptations,' in Pamela R. Freese and Margaret C. Harrell (eds) *Anthropology of the United States Military: Coming of Age in the Twenty-First Century*. New York: Palgrave Macmillan, 2003, 113–33.

Singer, P.W. *Corporate Warriors: The Rise of the Privatized Military Industry*. Ithaca and London: Cornell University Press, 2003.

Spector, Ronald H. *Advice and Support: The Early Years, 1941–1960, United States Army in Vietnam*. Washington, DC: Center of Military History, 1983.

Stoker, Donald. *Britain, France, and the Naval Arms Trade in the Baltic, 1919–1939: Grand Strategy and Failure*. London: Frank Cass, 2003.

Walsh, Billie K. 'The German Military Mission in China, 1928–38,' *The Journal of Modern History*, Vol. 46, No. 3 (1974), 502–13.

Weinert, Richard P. 'The Original KMAG,' *Military Review* (June 1965), 93–9.

Woff, Richard. 'The Soviet-Cuban Military Alliance: The Role of the Soviet Military Adviser, 1961–1986,' in *Soviet Command Changes and Policy Implications*. Rapid Report No. 30, College Station, TX: Defense Studies/Center for Strategic Technology, October 1986, 1–19.

Young, Thomas-Durell. 'Approaching the Need for Defense Reform: Early Lessons Learned in Estonia,' *The DISAM Journal* (Winter 2003–4), 71–5.

Index

Lightning Source UK Ltd.
Milton Keynes UK
01 July 2010

156399UK00001B/47/P